THE FRINGES OF REASON

A WHOLE EARTH CATALOG

Edited by Ted Schultz
Foreword by Stewart Brand

HARMONY BOOKS/NEW YORK

Ted Schultz: Editor
Rebecca Wilson: Designer
Alex Grey: Cover Painting
Susan Erkel Ryan: Production Manager
Don Ryan, Spencer Ewert: Photography
Bill Ryan, Dixon Wragg, Jeff Brody, Hank Roberts: Proofreaders
Elaine Karsevar: Typist
James Donnelly, Joan Gill: Typesetting
Elaine Olson, Jay Kinney, Giovanni Bacigalupi: Electronic Pasteup
Jay Cornell, Gail Miller: Mechanical Pasteup
David Burnor: Index
Kevin Kelly: Inspirational Adviser
John Brockman Associates: Literary Agent
Michael Pietsch: Senior Editor, Harmony Books

Point Foundation Staff: Jeanne Carstensen, Paul Davis, Richard Ditzler,
Cindy Fugett, Dick Fugett, Corinne Cullen Hawkins, Keith Jordan, Richard Nilsen,
Kathleen O'Neill, Susan Rosberg, Richard Schauffler, Lori Woolpert
Point Foundation Board: Stewart Brand, Doug Carlston, Robert Fuller,
Huey Johnson, Kevin Kelly

Special thanks to Wendell Debele, Deborah Nudelman, Paula Romich,
Janet Butcher, Lesley Davis, Valentine Typesetting, Gary Moring, Al Seckel,
and the ant entities from Beta Galactose.

This book was produced on Macintosh II and Macintosh SE computers and an
Apple Laserwriter IINTX, using Microsoft Word 3.01, Aldus Pagemaker 3.0, and
Adobe Illustrator 88 software. The final copy was generated on a Linotronic 100
Imagesetter at Desktop Composition in Petaluma, California. Camera-ready
pages were delivered by Whole Earth to Harmony Books.

Portions of this book were previously published in *Whole Earth Review*.

Published by Harmony Books, a division of Crown Publishers, Inc.,
225 Park Avenue South, New York, New York 10003

Harmony and Colophon are trademarks of Crown Publishers, Inc.

Manufactured in the United States of America

Library of Congress Cataloging-in-Publication Data:

The Fringes of Reason.

Includes index.
1. Occultism—Miscellanea. 2. Psychical research—Miscellanea. 3. New Age movement—Miscellanea.
I. Schultz, Ted.
BF1999.F75 1989   133   88-24505
ISBN 0-517-57165-X
10 9 8 7 6 5 4 3 2 1

First Edition

FOREWORD
by Stewart Brand

Oh God, how did I get into this room with all these *weird people*?

On the other hand, it beats being in your average movie theater, and even your average science conference. The believers of strange, strong beliefs are living a particularly ripe form of myth, tapping directly into hidden cultural structures that probably shape the rest of us as well, though indirectly. But how does one look with them without, you know, succumbing?

The answer is provided by Ted Schultz and cohorts. You look into the strange beliefs with all the tools and skepticism of science, and you look into the strange believers with the tools of science and the sympathy of a good anthropologist or psychologist, seeking not the insult of cure but the compliment of understanding.

The urgent hand points and says "LOOK!" (Aliens! My past life! The spoon is bending!) An infant looks at the pointing hand and the excited face. The adult looks where the hand is pointing. Some adults look again at the pointing hand and the excited face.

The glory is in the details. Psychologist Carl Jung had a grand theory of the psychological function of flying saucers—something about a riven civilization seeking psychic deliverance in flying mandalas from Outside. I confess to preferring the detailed account (p.138) of the 1940s invention of saucers for *Amazing Stories* by Ray Palmer. Usually I feel nothing but dismay at the channeling fad (which seems to be winding down), but one look at the photographs on p. 56 of Jamie Sams when she is and isn't channeling "Leah, a sixth density entity from the planet Venus six hundred years in the future," and I feel better. Jamie Sams is clearly happier and probably is more interesting company as Leah. Long live the invisible friend.

Every now and then the Truth! baldly reveals . . . the truth, small "t". My favorite in the book is the Airplane Game players (p. 41) passionately chanting:

One love! One love! One love! One love!
Love one! Love one! Love one! Love one!
God is money in action!

Reminds me of Peter Warshall's great insight about nature and human endeavor: "Water flows uphill toward money." (He was referring to Los Angeles.)

Do we care which of our urban legends are legendary? I used to tell the one about the wet miniature poodle exploding in the microwave oven, assuming it was true. Now I tell the story about telling the story. In this book the much-loved Parable of the Hundredth Monkey ("scientists can't understand how all the monkeys learned to wash potatoes at once, even on distant islands") is punctured once and for all, and the original perpetrator, Lyall Watson, is given space to comment on the puncturing (pp. 174-86). Now it's become the Parable-of-the-Parable of the Hundredth Monkey, a far more useful tale.

When I started hanging out with scientists in the last few years I was at first startled and then warmed to discover how comfortable they are with science fiction. Most read it, and many write it. The scientific process really is two-minded; it has to be to get anywhere. One mind gleefully speculates, the other ruthlessly slaughters speculation. Such minds will welcome this book of fiction science.

Listen! It's the theme music from "The Twilight Zone" backward. (*Eed eed eed eed, eed eed eed eed . . .*)

YOU
 ARE
  ENTERING
   THE
    DAWN
     ZONE...

CONTENTS

WEIRD SCIENCE

NOT OF THIS EARTH

WHAT IS REALITY?

"You've got to explore the edges to see where the middle is going."

—Stewart Brand, 1986

This is not a book about Orthodoxy.

Instead, this is a book about tinkerers who spend their lives in basements perfecting perpetual motion machines, contactees who converse on a first-name basis with entities from outer space, and reincarnationists who remember past lives as royalty on the lost continent of Atlantis. This is, in fact, a book about people so fed up with Orthodoxy and the mundane bit part it handed them that they did something about it. Something imaginative. Something colorful. Something . . . *different*.

This book is above all a celebration of the strange beliefs and eccentric theories that these people have created. Their unconventional world-views constitute a highly entertaining, subterranean art form that has for the most part been ignored by the mainstream media. Whether or not these peculiar notions are literally true, tales of flying saucer abductions, spontaneous human combustion, astral travel, inner-earth civilizations, and pyramids on Mars possess a haunting surreality and an arcane aesthetic that communicate directly to the unconscious mind.

But *are* they literally true? In addition to appreciating these modern mythologies for their own sakes, in the pages that follow we attempt to answer this question. Whenever possible we include a diversity of opinion, ranging from the extravagant enthusiasms of true believers to the earthbound pronouncements of hard-nosed skeptics. Experts on these neglected subjects (eccentric scholars themselves) present the elusive histories and backgrounds of oddball ideas. And, in true *Whole Earth Catalog* tradition, we've gone to considerable trouble to supply complete access information—names, addresses, titles and sources of books and periodicals—so that you can get directly in touch with outré organizations that you won't find listed in the yellow pages. Write away and experience the unparalleled thrill of a potential secret of the universe arriving in the mail!

So step right up, dear reader, and enter the carnival sideshow of Unorthodoxy, where page after page of peculiarity makes clear that despite our cocksure age of science, rationalism, and homogeneous mass media, mutant ideas continue to spawn, fission, and multiply. Perhaps the reason for this unexpected fact was provided most succinctly by novelist and Merry Prankster Ken Kesey at a "Summer of Love Twentieth Anniversary Celebration" held in San Francisco in 1987, where he proclaimed, "Facts are dull. Stories are interesting. We're up to our noses in facts. We want Story . . . we need Story."

As you'll soon see, fringe theorists may not always provide us with a lot of facts to substantiate their claims, but they sure as hell deliver Story.

—Ted Schultz, *Editor*

The New, Improved Age

Mark Fisher

The End

Th-that's all, folks!

TIME'S UP

H.R.

Harry S. Robins

What better place to begin than with The End? If there are times when the signs of imminent apocalypse seem to loom all around, perhaps you can take heart from the fact, clearly demonstrated in this section, that people of all cultural persuasions have felt the same way throughout recorded history.

And who better to tell the story of humanity's long-term flirtation with doomsday than a writer who chooses to live on the wrong side of the San Andreas fault? Stanley Young, who resides in Venice, California, with his wife Janice, is a former Commonwealth scholar and modern dancer who now works full-time as a freelance writer. He contributes regularly to an eclectic assortment of publications, from People Magazine *to* Whole Earth Review, *and also writes teleplays and books. Stanley believes that the end of the world will take place "in four years or forty thousand miles, whichever comes first."* —T.S.

PEOPLE HAVE ALWAYS PONDERED THE END, SINCE the very beginning. Throughout history prophets arise to preach doom and gloom, mass movements form proclaiming the imminent demise of the planet, groups of believers go up to mountaintops to wait out the earthquake/flood/fire/celestial collision/whatever. So far, their batting average is zero, and whatever differences these prophets display in culture, speech, and dress, they certainly share a common and recurring attribute: bad timing.

Yet these doom-sayers continue to arise and we continue to bend an ear to listen to them. Perhaps it is a sublimated death wish, the need to extend our own inevitable demise onto the cosmos that contains us. More likely, it is simply the need to know the end of the tale, as if history were a detective novel and through these prophecies we are given a chance to peek at the last page.

GOOD TIMES, BAD TIMES, END TIMES

In the Western tradition, born of the Judaeo-Christian heritage, the End has always come first. At least one Christian theologian, Ernst Kaseman, has argued that apocalypticism "was the mother of all Christian theology." Judging by the phenomenal success of au-

Countdown to the Millenium

by Stanley Young

thors such as Hal Lindsey, whose book *The Late Great Planet Earth* shot to the top of the best seller list and is a standard recounting of the Christian conception of the the End Times, Kaseman's remark may still be true, at least for many fundamentalist Christians in America today.

The Christian scenario for Armageddon is set forth most forcefully in The Book of Revelation. Revelation doesn't really add anything new to the basic End Times blueprint that the other Biblical books and Apocrypha have laid out, but what it does say it spouts in Technicolor. For those of you who need a "sense of an ending," this tome will give you a surfeit; this is the book that *defined* Armageddon. It is definitely worth a read even if most of it is obscure beyond the lyrics of Dylan.

The Book of Revelation is the American International Pictures version of the End: *See* the book with seven seals, each one betokening a new set of disasters! *Experience* angels and devils battling amidst flashes of lightning and earthquakes! *Fear* the monster with seven heads and ten horns, carrying a woman drunk with the blood of saints! *Cower* as a beast with horns like a lamb speaks like a dragon! The Book of Revelation is a veritable celestial sideshow, the summa of apocalyptic writing, full of symbolism, allusion, hope, and redemption. Above all, Revelation is an anthem of redemption: Christ is coming soon; He is coming quickly. "Do not seal up the words of the prophecy of this book for the time is near."

The time is near; the End is at hand. This is the message that all millennial movements feed upon. Frank Kermode, in his classic study *The Sense of an Ending*, puts it clearly: "The great majority of interpretations of Apocalypse assume that the end is pretty near. Consequently the historical allegory is always having to be revised: time discredits it. And this is important. The apocalypse can be disconfirmed without being discredited. This is part of its extraordinary resilience."

Early Christians felt they were living at the end of time. As time wore on and Christ failed to reappear, however, this belief was not discredited. Instead, the date of His coming was repeatedly shifted, until the certainty of imminent salvation became a vague "sometime in the future." This vagueness became more specific, however, as the year 1000 A.D. rolled around. Surely the start of the new millennium was to be the great date of His Second Coming at last. Signs and portents were eagerly sought by Christians everywhere, and there was even a brief entente between Emperor Otto III and Pope Sylvester II. In fact, the Emperor's coronation robe had scenes from the Book of Revelation embroidered onto it. All of Christendom threw a party—but Christ never showed up.

No problem. Some quick refiguring indicated that His Coming should have been dated from the Ascension, not the Nativity. The year 1033 was also a bust, however; but the habit of predicting the Second Coming had entered into the fabric of Western Culture, and it's been with us ever since.

Joachim of Flore, a Cistercian monk of the twelfth century, was a major figure in apocalypticism. He developed a scheme of distinctive "ages" *(saeclora)* in history that lead, in linear fashion, to a cosmic conclusion. Being a good Christian, he divided history into three ages (after the Trinity), with the last epoch beginning, by way of some fancy arithmetic, in 1260 A.D. with the arrival of the Antichrist. Once again, Christ missed his appointment, but the concept of "ages" in human (that is, "secular") history, moving toward some sort of recognizable conclusion, entered forever into Western thought. People began to think of themselves as participants in an "age."

Certainly this was true of the newly formed United States of America. The fledgling nation even chose words saying as much on its Great Seal: *"Novus Ordo Seclorum,"* lifted from Vergil, means "A New Order of the Ages." (Check your one-dollar bills for its location.) Even the most current buzzword, "New Age," meant to indicate the thoroughly modern approach to living, is itself a direct descendant of thirteenth-century Joachite historicism, and is simply the latest expression of a long line of generations who felt themselves to be at the end of one era and on the verge of another.

Every few decades after Joachim someone would rise up and claim to have perceived the signs of the impending apocalypse. It happened like sporadic clockwork, and spotting the Antichrist—the being whose appearance heralded the beginning of the End—became a Western preoccupation and sort of a historical parlor game. Candidates for the Antichrist ranged from Frederick II in the thirteenth century to Napoleon Bonaparte in the eighteenth, with a few scattered Popes as suspects in between. Sometimes natural events seemed to betoken the onset of the End Times, as happened in England in the late sixteenth century when the British witnessed several novas, including a spectacular example in Cassiopeia in 1572. When these portents were followed a few years later by a full solar eclipse, many were convinced that they were living "in the dregs of time" and that Judgment Day was at hand. At other times, when no celestial portents were seen and Antichrist-candidates hard to locate, scholars (including Newton) undertook exotic mathematical calculations to try to make the figures in the prophecies jibe with current events.

Occasionally prophets of doom gained considerable followings and engendered mass movements. Five hundred years after the 1033 End-of-the-World, debacle another such movement was afoot: Anabaptists in Holland declared that "the great fulfillment" was at hand. Wealthy members sold off all their goods, forgave their debtors, and renounced worldly pleasures. When 1534 arrived with still no End in sight, the movement did not disintegrate. On the contrary, new adherents invested it with added enthusiasm, and began intensive and successful proselytizing. The End of the World may not have come, but the prophecies were still relevant.

The Majority of theologians and most believing Christians take the symbolism of apocalyptic prophecies in the New Testament as just that: obscure references that are not meant to be taken as tact. The original Church Fathers were wary of including Revelation in the Biblical canon at all, fearing that its mystical signs and portents might be taken too literally. (Revelation was, in fact, the last book to be accepted before the canon was finalized in 367 A.D., and remains to this day outside the accepted testament of the Greek Orthodox Church.) The fears of the Church Fathers have been continuously borne out ever since, and perhaps never more strongly than in the last half of the twentieth century in the United States.

ARMAGEDDON: THE SEQUEL

There are large groups of Americans who believe that certain recent historical events—most notably the founding of the State of Israel and the rise of Khomeini—presage the Second Coming as foretold in the New Testament. Pop eschatologist Hal Lindsey is their spokesman. "All the predicted signs that set up the final fateful period immediately preceding the second coming of Christ are now before us," he states in the introduction to his 1983 volume *The Rapture*. "Few people today doubt that history is moving toward some sort of climactic catastrophe."

Several million people do in fact agree with Lindsey's outlook, or are at least quite interested in it. His book *The Late Great Planet Earth* was the non-fiction best seller of 1980, selling some fifteen million copies, and its sequel, *Countdown to Armageddon*, was the best-selling religious book the following year, making the *New York Times* "Top 15 Bestsellers" list. His other works, including such titles as *Satan Is Alive and Well On Planet Earth*, have also done very well. Lindsey continues to be stocked by most bookstores and has settled down as a steady item. Apparently there is no lack of people willing to read the minute-by-minute agenda of the imminent destruction of the world. At Crown Bookstores you can find his books under "Inspirational."

With Lindsey, it's a numbers game. In the classical Christian tradition of poetic/apocalyptic arithmetic, he claims that God predicted through his prophet Daniel that 70 weeks of years (7 times 70 equals 490 years) were allotted to the people of Israel, beginning with the decree to restore the city of Jerusalem. "Imagine that God had a great stopwatch with 490 years on it," Lindsey explains. In 444 B.C. the decree to restore Jerusalem was signed in Persia by Artaxerxes Longimanus and the celestial stopwatch started ticking. The countdown to Armageddon was off and running.

According to Lindsey's version of the prophecies,

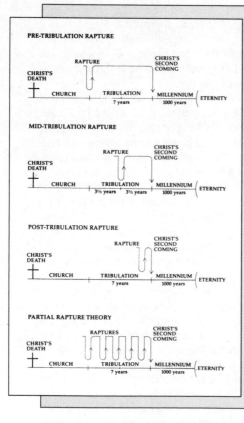

PRE-TRIBULATION RAPTURE

CHRIST'S DEATH — CHURCH — TRIBULATION (7 years) — RAPTURE — CHRIST'S SECOND COMING — MILLENNIUM (1000 years) / ETERNITY

MID-TRIBULATION RAPTURE

CHRIST'S DEATH — CHURCH — TRIBULATION (3½ years — 3½ years) — RAPTURE — CHRIST'S SECOND COMING — MILLENNIUM (1000 years) / ETERNITY

POST-TRIBULATION RAPTURE

CHRIST'S DEATH — CHURCH — TRIBULATION (7 years) — RAPTURE — CHRIST'S SECOND COMING — MILLENNIUM (1000 years) / ETERNITY

PARTIAL RAPTURE THEORY

CHRIST'S DEATH — CHURCH — TRIBULATION (7 years) — RAPTURES — CHRIST'S SECOND COMING — MILLENNIUM (1000 years) / ETERNITY

TRIBULATIONS TRIVIA

"Few people today doubt that history is moving toward some sort of climactic catastrophe," says Hal Lindsey in his book *The Rapture*. "Many secular scientists, statesmen, and military experts believe that the world is heading for a global holocaust involving all-out nuclear war. The only variable with most of these experts is *when*."

Believers in Armageddon are so numerous as to be divided into separate End-Time camps. Indeed, for those Americans who are predisposed to peer over the edge of time, the question "when" is the distinguishing criterion of their belief system. The more literal of the fundamentalists—like the author Lindsey and prominent Christian politicos such as Jerry Falwell and Pat Robertson—are "dispensationalists," a term referring to God's seven-fold eras or "dispensations" of history. Within the dispensationalist school there exist three further subdivisions (pre-, mid- and post-Tribulationists) who quibble and argue about the exact time that Christ will choose to inter-

vene within the extended series of disasters described in the Book of Revelation.

Apparently pre-Tribulationists believe that Christ will come to save living beings and snatch them away to heaven before the plagues, earthquakes, and other sundry disasters scourge and purge the planet. Pre-Tribulationists are considered soft on the End compared to the post-Tribulationists, a more determined, cowboy style, hang-tough-through-the-disasters lot, who believe there will be lots of suffering before Christ arrives with the cavalry. Backbiting between the two camps can get a trifle *ad hominem*. As Lindsey, a staunch pre-Tribulationist, puts it, "I have become a bit bored with those *nouveau* post-Tribulationists who give the impression that if you were truly an intellectual and *macho* Christian, you would charge headlong with them into the Tribulation."

—*Stanley Young*

fully 69 weeks of years (483 Biblical years) were to pass before the Messiah appeared. (This works out to exactly 173,880 days—483 years times 360 days per Biblical year.) And lo! "experts" have figured that this is *exactly* the duration of time that elapsed between the signing of the Persian decree in 444 B.C. and the day when Jesus of Nazareth publicly proclaimed himself to be the Messiah and heir to the throne of David.

Christ was crucified five days later, an event foreseen by the prophets. What the prophets *didn't* foresee, however, was that the destruction of Jerusalem, supposed to follow hard on the heels of the Messiah's being "cut off," did not occur until 70 A.D.—over thirty years out of sync. What happened? Were the prophecies wrong? God forbid. *Humanity* was wrong. Israel had failed to accept Christ as the Messiah, so "God had stopped the prophetic stopwatch at the crucifixion seven years short of completion." With the stopwatch on hold, God turned to other pastimes during this intervening Cosmic Time-Out, for instance the formation of the Church.

In recent years, the stopwatch is on the verge of ticking again. Certain historical events, such as the foundation of the state of Israel, the unification of Jerusalem, and the founding of the European Economic Community, presage the imminent beginning of the final seven-year period left on the clock. We are heading to the final countdown to Armageddon with its beasts, disasters, angels—and salvation.

Lindsey must have caught a mood in the country as he tied prophecies in the Bible to events in the modern world. Nor are his sensational sales exactly a fluke in the publishing business. George Vandeman, associated with the Seventh-Day Adventist Church, has sold seven million copies of his own books, including such titles as *Showdown in the Middle East* and *The Cry of the Lonely Planet*, which contain such chapters as "The Breath of Armageddon" and "Toying with the Nick of Time."

Among the tens of millions of Americans preoccupied with the countdown to Armageddon are Ronald and Nancy Reagan. During his 1980 campaign Reagan, influenced by Hal Lindsey's *The Late Great Planet Earth*, mentioned several times that "this may be the last generation." And in response to NBC's Marvin Kalb's question during the final 1984 presidential debate "Do you feel that we are now heading perhaps for some kind of nuclear Armageddon?" Reagan replied that he had indeed spoken with people about "the Biblical prophecies of what would portend the coming of Armageddon and so forth and the fact that a number of theologians for the last decade or more have believed that this was true—that the prophecies are coming together that portend that."

In April 1988 Nancy Reagan was reported to have changed the street number of the couple's Bel Air gift-mansion from 666—the sign of the Beast in the Book of Revelation—to the far more innocuous 668. (Interestingly, Hal Lindsey never changed his publisher, Bantam, even though that publisher's address is 666 Fifth Avenue in New York.)

Reagan is a good example of this obsession for Armageddon not only because he held his finger over the but-

The Four Horsemen of the Apocalypse, as envisioned by the German artist Albrecht Dürer (1471-1528).

ton that could have brought it about, but because he demonstrates how truly pervasive and deep-rooted this belief is in America today. It is clear that for the Reagans the book of Revelation is not an example of interesting literature but a collection of facts—realities—to be realized. For several tens of millions of Americans, the End is indeed nigh.

MILLERITES AND MESSIAHS

The current American interest in the End Times is nothing new. There have always been home-grown prophets of doom, the forerunners of Hal Lindsey and his ilk. After a two-year study of the Bible in 1818 and some fancy arithmetic, a New York farmer named William Miller came to the disturbing conclusion that the End of the World would occur in 1843. He kept the facts to himself for five years, but at last disclosed the bad news to a few of his friends. For the next eight years he continued his public campaign and built up a small group of followers. In 1839 Miller met Joshua V. Himes and convinced him of the veracity of his claims. Himes started a newspaper called *Signs of the Times* in Boston. As 1843 approached, the Millerite following grew in an eschatological feeding frenzy. They began publishing *The Midnight Cry* in New York, followed soon after by *Philadelphia Alarm*.

Opposition from other religious groups had little ef-

David Attenborough / Man, Myth & Magic

Myths of cosmic cataclysms are extremely widespread among primitives. They tell how the world was destroyed and mankind annihilated except for a single couple or a few survivors. These myths—implying, as they do in clearer or darker fashion, the re-creation of a new universe—express the archaic and universal idea of the progressive degradation of a cosmos, necessitating its periodical destruction and re-creation.

The myth of the end of the world was also popular in ancient India, Mesopotamia, Persia and Greece. In Judaeo-Christian theory, the end of the world will occur only once, just as the cosmogony occurred only once. The cosmos that will reappear after the catastrophe will be the same cosmos that God created at the beginning of time, but purified, regenerated, restored to its original glory. This earthly paradise will not be destroyed again but will have no end.

Now it is especially this type of myth that admirably illustrates the relevance and significance of mythology to people today. For the myth of the end of the world is at the center of countless prophetic movements, of which the best known are the Oceanian Cargo Cults. These movements announce that the world is about to be destroyed and that the tribe will regain a kind of paradise: the dead will rise again and there will be neither death nor sickness. But this new creation—or recovery of paradise—will be preceded by a series of cosmic catastrophes. The earth will shake, there will be rains of fire, the mountains will crumble and fill the valleys, the whites and the natives who have not joined the cult will be annihilated. Thus, in 1923 the prophet Ronovuro, of the island of Espiritu Santo (New Hebrides), predicted a flood to be followed by the return of the dead in cargo ships loaded with rice and other provisions. In 1933, in the valley of Markham in New Guinea, a man named Marafi declared that the return of the dead would be preceded by a cosmic cataclysm; but the next day it would be found that the dead had already arrived, loaded with gifts and there would be no need for the people ever again to work.

Similar phenomena occurred in the Congo when the country became independent in 1960. In some villages the inhabitants tore the roofs off their huts to give passage to the gold that their ancestors were to rain down. Elsewhere everything was allowed to go to rack and ruin, except the roads to the cemetery, by which the ancestors would make their way to the village. Even the orgiastic excesses had a meaning, for according to the myth, from the dawn of the New Age all women would be held in common by all men. —Mircea Eliade

From *Man, Myth, and Magic* (edited by Richard Cavendish; 1970; New York: Marshall Cavendish).

fect on the rapid expansion of Miller's following. A crowd of 3,500 people dedicated a Millerite tabernacle in Boston in 1843. Then the Millerites waited for March 21 and the End of the World, but the day came and went like any other. Miller claimed that he had made a slight miscalculation: he had foolishly used the Jewish calendar. The *real* date was to be March 21, 1844.

There was a moment of doubt, but the movement rallied toward this new date with destiny. The fervor reached a renewed crescendo as March 21, 1844, approached. Proselytizing activity increased as believers made a final effort to indoctrinate others into the Millerite Church. When this second date passed uneventfully, the movement—amazingly—remained largely unaffected, and by the middle of July Miller was again traveling about the East Coast lecturing to packed halls.

A third date was proposed—October 22, 1844—and Miller's expanded following was adamant: The Messiah would come before the passing of another winter. Throughout New England, farmers either failed to plow their fields or left their crops to rot unharvested. Once again the appointed hour approached and again activity in the Millerite organization increased to a fever pitch. Camp meetings were packed with ordinary folk desperate to renounce their sins. The Millerite Church exhorted followers to leave their everyday activities. "Let your actions preach in the clearest tones," wrote the editors of *The Midnight Cry*, "The Lord is coming, the time is short. Prepare to meet thy God."

October 22 came and went, and with it, a large part of the Millerite movement. Surprisingly, it had taken three separate disconfirmations over a period of a year and a half before any appreciable doubt arose among Miller's followers. Millennial movements die hard, if they truly die at all. The direct descendants of Miller's church are still with us today: the Jehovah's Witnesses and the Seventh-Day Adventists.[1]

The Millerite movement arose during the early stages of industrialization on the Eastern seaboard. Perhaps its popularity relates in some way to the anxiety and apprehension people felt about the changes they saw taking place around them. Certainly things could have been worse. Conditions were not as bad, say, as they were for the Jews in the second century B.C. when their religious infrastructure was under severe and constant attack. Their response was the Book of Daniel (one of the earliest examples of apocalyptic literature) and guerrilla warfare.

In the case of the Millerites, there was mass hysteria of a mild sort: some people sold their worldly goods and a few farmers lost their crops to neglect. No massive dislocation was involved. The extent to which millennialists actually change their lives in accordance with their belief in the imminent end seems to be directly linked to the general level of desperation. Miller, like Lindsey in modern times, claimed only to be a "seer," a prophet. There have also been occasions in history when a man has arisen who claimed to be the messiah himself.

---

[1] The Jehovah's Witnesses continue to forecast the exact date of the End, and have struck out thrice more, in 1874, 1914, and 1975, with no appreciable loss of church membership.

Shabtai Zvi is just such an example. A Jew raised in the city of Smyrna in Turkey, in 1648 Zvi privately declared himself the messiah to a small group of disciples. His rise to power was to be heralded, as usual, with miracles, portents, and so on. When these did not occur, his messiahhood was not discredited. On the contrary, when he disclosed his identity to the community at large, he was expelled from Smyrna but his following swelled. The date of his miraculous messianic revelation was pushed off to 1666, and by 1665 his following among the Jewish communities in Eastern Europe had grown astronomically. The following year Zvi set out to Constantinople to depose the Sultan of Turkey, thereby fulfilling one of his own prophecies. Before he could carry out this plan of action the would-be messiah was captured by understandably concerned Turkish authorities and jailed.

Now his followers grew ecstatic. Jews from as far away as Hungary sold their possessions, abandoned their houses, and prepared to see Zvi where he was holding court in the Turkish jail. The Sultan, fearing that Zvi's execution would make him an instant martyr, chose a different route, and somehow convinced the messiah to forsake Judaism to become a Muslim. It was only after his conversion to Islam that Zvi's following dwindled, although many followed his example and converted themselves. To this day a small number of Jews believe that Shabtai Zvi was the true messiah.

THE GHOST DANCE

Native Americans have had their own messianic movement, a short-lived phenomenon culminating in the Ghost Dance religion of the early 1890s. The central tenets of this religion concerned beliefs in a messiah and a return to an idyllic existence where the land would be restored to its aboriginal state, without the presence of the white man.

Fearing that this doctrine might secretly encourage renewed hostilities, the U.S. Government sent one of its finest ethnographers, James Mooney, to study it. His monograph, "The Ghost-Dance Religion and the Sioux Outbreak of 1890," is a rare and detailed insight into this classic messianic movement.

According to Mooney, the Ghost Dance movement began in 1870 when a medicine man called Tavibo appeared among the Paiute. He claimed that within a few moons there would be a great upheaval: whites would be swallowed up, but their artifacts (houses, tools, etc.) would remain untouched. His gospel claimed few adherents, so Tavibo undertook a second vision quest. The prophecy was altered. *Both* whites and Indians would be swallowed up, but three days later only Indians would rise up to enjoy the bounty of a renewed world. (The influences of a Christian doctrine are obvious here.) While this second message made somewhat more sense, it still lacked sufficient appeal to create a following among the tribe, so Tavibo made a third and final visit to the mountain.

A captain in the U.S. Infantry described Tavibo's third vision as follows: "The divine spirit had become so much incensed at the lack of faith in the prophecies that it was revealed to his chosen one that those Indians who be-

Waiting for the Apocalypse

We humans are an egocentric lot. Once we were sure we occupied the center of the universe—then astronomy proved otherwise. Well, certainly we were the pinnacle of creation—but then Darwin came along. Today we console ourselves that, though we may not occupy a central position in interstellar space or in organic nature, at least we occupy a pivotal point in time: the final days before the End of the World. But Daniel Cohen's **Waiting for the Apocalypse** *pops this last bubble of morbid egocentrism by demonstrating that, no matter how convincing this viewpoint may seem at this time in history, people have felt this way since the beginning of civilization and—up until now at least—they've always been wrong. Cohen's book includes selected histories of doomsday beliefs, including Norse mythology, medieval astrologers, and the nineteenth-century Millerites. It also discusses catastrophist scenarios and modern visions of the End, including nuclear war, meteoric and cometary collisions, extinctions, and the inevitable death of the sun.*

There's plenty of large-scale grist for the compulsive worrier's mill here, but remember: of the many choices presented, only one will ultimately do the deed. Don't place your bets till you've read the program. —T.S.

• Why are catastrophists eternally popular with the general public? There are several reasons. As we have already pointed out the idea that the world has undergone and will continue to undergo enormous catastrophes is an ancient and deeply ingrained one. Catastrophes simply make sense to a lot of people, whereas slow processes like erosion and evolution do not. It is hard to think in terms of millions of years.

The catastrophist can write broadly and dramatically about grand themes like universal floods and world-shaking earthquakes. The arguments of geologists and paleontologists are dull by comparison. Often the scientific arguments are technical or even mathematical and thus not easily understood by the general public.

Finally the catastrophist usually roundly denounces the scientific "establishment" as being blind, pigheaded, and prejudiced against anyone who is not a member of that establishment. The catastrophist thus presents himself as sort of a martyr, or at least an underdog, being either persecuted or ignored by this vast and closed scientific establishment.

Falling stars, eclipses, earthquakes, and other signs of the Last Days, as depicted in a Millerite publication.

Prophecy: A History of the Future

Old Testament prophets, space brothers, American Indian shamans, medieval soothsayers, and other assorted sybils, doomsayers, and apocalyptists—they're all here, all given equal time in what is perhaps the most egalitarian of all prophecy books. Included are chapters on Biblical prophecies, European prophets, Nostradamus, American prophets, and even "earth changes" and far-out theories of fringe physics.

Möbius Rex, who has done his homework well, is an uncritical believer in prophecy, writing in his introduction: "Prophecy is clairvoyance—clear vision—across time and space, and it is a proven talent of the human mind." His stated intent in assembling this book is to help humanity "to know the signs of the times and to recognize the shadows that great events cast before them." But mostly he doesn't burden the reader with a lot of interpretation or commentary. Instead, you get the raw text of the prophecies themselves, with just enough history thrown in to put the predictions in context. —*T.S.*

• The Gaelic Coinneach Odhar Fiosaiche, or Kenneth MacKenzie, the Brahan Seer or "Warlock of the Glen," was the most highly respected of the Scottish prophets. The one-eyed magician foresaw the future through a hole in a smooth pebble that he always carried with him. Most of his predictions concerned seventeenth-century Scotland, but he also foretold of the Industrial Revolution and developments such as gas and water mains: "Fire and water shall run in streams through all the streets and lanes of Inverness" and locomotives: "long strings of carriages without horses shall run between Dingwall and Inverness."

• Hopi prophecy states that World War III will be started by the people who first received the Light—China, Palestine, India, and Africa. When the war comes, the United States will be destroyed by "gourds of ashes" which will fall to the ground, boiling the rivers and burning the earth, where no grass will grow for many years, and causing disease that no medicine can cure. This can only mean atomic bombs; no other weapon causes such effects.

• In 1956 Father Ernetti began to investigate the possibility of reviewing the past with a television-like device. In 1957 he contacted the Portuguese Professor de Matos, who was researching the same problem. His theoretical approach was based on Aristotle's concept of the disintegration of sound, according to which light and sound waves do not disappear after being produced, but are transformed in some way and remain present indefinitely.

He has revealed "photographs" of events long past, including Christ's crucifixion and recorded voices of ancient conversations. He has succeeded in reconstructing Quintus Ennius's tragedy "Thyestes" in Latin, the language in which it was written and originally performed in 169 B.C. Father Ernetti also claims to have recovered the original text of the Ten Commandments given to Moses. However, he has refused to reveal details of his invention, and the machine has been suppressed by the Italian government. The Padre warns, "The machine can produce universal tragedy."

Prophecy
A History of the Future
Möbius Rex
1986; 340 pp.
$20
postpaid from:
Rex Research
P.O. Box 1258
Berkeley, CA 94701

lieved in the prophecy would be resurrected and be happy, but those who did not believe in it would stay in the ground and be damned forever with the whites." This vision apparently became widely known but still prompted no activity on the part of the Indians.

Over the next two decades, the situation of the Native Americans deteriorated. Since the first messiah had preached his visions, the traditional lives of the Indians had been all but eradicated. Nation by nation the indigenous people who lived on this continent had been moved off their ancestral lands, seen their buffalo disappear, and been forced to suffer the degradation and deprecation of an invading culture. Indians were everywhere under the threat of cultural genocide and ripe for salvation from the white juggernaut of Manifest Destiny. The irony is that the same culture that had all but destroyed the Indians' way of life was also to provide the beliefs that were to give them a few fleeting years of hope.

The new messiah/prophet, also a Paiute, was called Wovoka and rumored to be the son of Tavibo. He preached a new doctrine that spread like prairie fire among Indians from Oklahoma to California. Newspapers and settlers grossly misunderstood the new religion, and alarmists claimed that it entailed the preaching of a bloody campaign against all whites. The truth was otherwise: Wovoka had spent some time with the family of David Wilson, a Mormon rancher in Mason Valley, and much of the doctrine that he later espoused was profoundly influenced by his unique understanding of Christian theology.

"The great underlying principle of the Ghost Dance doctrine is that the time will come when the whole Indian race, living and dead, will be reunited upon a regenerated earth, to live a life of aboriginal happiness, forever free from death, disease, and misery," wrote Mooney.

The doctrine, for all its simplicity and apparent innocuousness, was a radical departure for those tribes who espoused it. Wovoka was asking them to forego traditions that had always been a part of their heritage. Most important was his proscription against violence: "You must not hurt anybody or do harm to anyone. You must not fight." There were other proscriptions: "Grandfather [God] says, when your friends die you must not cry," meaning that Indians were to forego their age-old tradition of grieving for their loved ones by rending the hair and inflicting wounds on the body.

According to Wovoka, there was no need for mourning. No matter how oppressed the tribes may have felt, salvation was at hand. They would all shortly be rejoined with their loved ones. Their freedom from white domination was not to be found through battle but through spiritual means, by dancing, chanting, and visions.

"Jesus is now upon the earth. He appears like a cloud. The dead are all alive again. I do not know when they will be here; maybe this fall or in the spring. When the time comes there will be no more sickness and everyone will be young again." The reference to next spring was taken literally, and tribes from Oklahoma to California entered into a frenzy of activity in preparation.

"When you get home you must make a dance to con-

An illustration from James Mooney's first-hand monograph, "The Ghost-Dance Religion and the Sioux Outbreak of 1890." For days on end, men, women, and children danced a shuffling step to the steady beat of drums, preparing for the end of the world.

tinue five days. Dance four successive nights, and the last night keep up the dance until the morning of the fifth day when all must bathe in the river and then disperse to their homes." The Ghost Dance itself was the heart of the movement. Men, women, and children chanted and danced a shuffling step to the steady beat of drums. Hand in hand they moved for five consecutive days, breaking only for food and sleep. During this dance-time some members of the tribe fell into trances or dropped from exhaustion. Many had visions connected to the messianic prophecy, and each tribe used these revelations to embellish Wovoka's basic teachings.

Wovoka had asked that the Ghost Dance be performed once every six weeks, and so it was done, in combination with sweat lodge ceremonies and fasting. Despite the pacifist message, there was a definite anti-white tenor to the movement. "Do not refuse to work for the whites and do not make any trouble with them until you leave them. When the earth shakes do not be afraid. It will not hurt you." In most tribes all vestiges of the white man were removed from clothing during the Ghost Dance. All metal, for instance, was removed, even the fine German silver ornaments so prized by some Native Americans of the time. The Sioux, the only tribe where the Ghost Dance happened to coincide with a violent uprising, even went so far as to develop special garb for the Ghost Dance: a shapeless fringed cotton shirt and pants, which Mooney believes were modeled after Mormon religious garb.

The Sioux Ghost Dance shirts were soon after thought to have magical powers to repel bullets—a belief that was dispelled in the tragic uprising of Wounded Knee. The outrage of Wounded Knee shattered illusions for many of the tribes, and by 1893, a few short years after the zenith of the movement, it was almost totally extinct. "The Shoshoni," writes Mooney, "lost faith in it after the failure of the first predictions." The Paiutes and many tribes from the Oklahoma area incorporated the Dance into their tribal life and continued to believe in the coming of the

Great Disaster. But the original frenzy, the cultural delirium fueled by the expectation of imminent salvation, devolved into a more diffused, almost Christian hope in "a reunion with departed friends in a happier world at some time in the unknown future." Wovoka himself appeared as an exhibition at the Midwinter Fair in San Francisco, and then disappeared, like his movement, into obscurity. He died in 1932.[2]

SAUCER SAVIORS FROM OUTER SPACE

Between the Ghost Dance of the 1890s and the Eisenhower era of the 1950s lies a historical chasm. Where once there were the chants and the beats of the drum, now there was the Jet Age, and kitchens in chrome and formica. America seemed firmly established on an assembly line of progress. The fifties was also the decade that discovered the term "anomie," and even among apparently comfortable suburbanites End of the World movements sprang up like mushrooms on a well-manicured lawn.

On August 27, 1952, a middle-class medical doctor sent fifty copies of a seven-page mimeographed letter to newspapers around the country. It outlined important information concerning the fate of the world: "The great tilting of the land of the U.S. to the East will throw up mountains along the Central States. . . . a great wave rushes into the Rocky Mountains. The slopes of the side to the east will be the beginning of a new civilization upon which will be the new order, in the light." These prophecies had been received through an entity called Sananda who communicated with the human race via the automatic writing of a fairly ordinary housewife in her fifties. "All things must first be likened unto the housecleaning in which the chaos reigns first, second the ORDER," were the words of Sananda via the housewife. "It

[2] The Ghost Dance religion has recently been revived by Wallace Black Elk, a Sioux Indian shaman who believes that the details of the prophecy describe the events leading up to global nuclear war, which will occur within the next five years.

15

When Prophecy Fails

Using students as "participant-observers" (that is, academic spies), the authors of this fascinating book—three sociologists from a midwestern university—followed the individual members of a middle-class cabal of end-of-the-worlders from the earliest phases of their belief to the appointed day when a UFO mother ship was supposed to come and rapture them away.

Although the events depicted are over thirty-five years old, the book describes an amalgam of beliefs that is surprisingly popular today: twentieth-century science fiction blended with nineteenth-century occultism, information received from entities via automatic writing and channeling, and spacemen/saviors in flying saucers. The only thing missing to bring it up to date are those ubiquitous contemporary talismans: crystals.

The characters in this tale are delightfully limned, and their self-supporting delusions build to an inevitable disappointment that is both pathetic and touching. What is most troubling about them is not their strange beliefs, but their otherwise apple-pie conventionality. These odd folks are clearly normal enough to be your neighbors (and if you live in California, they probably are). —Stanley Young

• Sananda informed Mrs. Keech on July 8 that "The Guardians are beings of the UN [intelligence of the Creator; mind of the High Self] who have risen to the density seven or eight, who are UN as the Oneness with the Creator, who can and do create by the UN the casement or vehicle they chose to use in the seen." Another Guardian, on May 14, speaking from "the Seventh Sector Density of Creton" (presumably a planet in the "constellation of Cerus") explained: "We are in the avagada [space ship] of light force propulsion. We are like the human beings of Earth and have much in common; though there are millions of years difference in our cultures, we are still brothers. What we enjoy as natural everyday enjoyments, you of the world cannot yet imagine." Sananda briefly commented on the planet Clarion, "It is a beautiful place to live. We have weather—snow and rain. We adjust our bodies to the temperature." He described the diet of the Guardians as "the bread of increase, which is like a snowflake."

• About two hours after the formal meeting had started, it broke up, for refreshments, into small groups of two or three. Some discussed spiritual transmigration, others college football. Some of the girls served the tea and cake—a handsome monument covered with pink and blue frosting in the design of a "mother ship" and three small flying saucers, bearing the words "Up in the Air." One or two of the members seemed to be of an experimental turn of mind, for they had brought a ouija board which they attempted to use. Dr. Armstrong warned them that it wouldn't work because the "charges" around the house were "positive" whereas the ouija board was "negatively charged," in addition to being of "low vibration," again unlike the atmosphere of the house. Later, a few of the young people attempted levitation of one another, though this venture also failed.

When Prophecy Fails
Leon Festinger, Henry W. Riecken, & Stanley Schachter
1964; 253 pp.
$7.50
($9.00 postpaid) from:
J.B. Lippincott
Route 3, Box 20-B
Hagerstown, MD 21740
800/638-3030

will be the beginning of a new civilization." The date of evacuation was slated for December 20, one day before the cataclysm.

Few editors took notice of this eccentric press release, although it did appear in the newspaper of a small university town. Three sociologists caught sight of it and jumped at the chance to investigate firsthand this group of people proclaiming the End of the World. The professors used students who posed as interested parties ("participant-observers") to record the inner workings of these eccentric believers.

The book that was born of this effort, *When Prophecy Fails*, is a wonderful insight into how this group came to believe their peculiar gospel, and how they went about spreading the word of disaster. The book also examines how the believers came to terms with the fact that, as the title indicates, their prophecies failed.

The eschatology this group espoused was thoroughly modern. In fact, their scenario of the cataclysm most closely resembled a bad 1950s science fiction movie. According to Sananda, the entity/spokesman for a higher race of beings who were to appear as spacemen, flying saucers would come on the appointed day to take away the true believers to the safety of their own planet. (Perhaps the fact that the central members of the group had dabbled in Scientology and Theosophy explains certain science-fiction aspects of their belief system.)

The group's original idea of going to a mountaintop on the eve of the cataclysm was eventually abandoned in favor of being picked up at the house by flying saucers, "pea-pod ships" sent down from a great "Mother Ship." Theirs was a truly suburban apocalypse. Dr. Armstrong (all the names in the book were changed), the central theoretician of the group, was on good terms with these spacemen, calling his future saviors "the boys upstairs."

The authors of *When Prophecy Fails* describe the exacting preparations that the group of a dozen believers made for the arrival of the flying saucers. They'd been told through the housewife/channel that metal would produce severe burns in the flying saucers. (Could this be some subconscious throwback to the rejection of metal in the Ghost Dance?) "Dr. Armstrong was busy ripping the zipper out of the fly of his trousers, while Mark Post energetically removed the eyelets from a pair of his shoes. Frank Novik was wearing a piece of rope in place of the belt that usually encircled his waist, as was Clyde Wilton."

On December 17th the group assembled outside the suburban meeting house to wait, shivering in the cold, for "the boys upstairs to come." They never came, but this setback caused no disappointment: it was only a drill, they were subsequently informed. In fact, disconfirmation only fueled their efforts to proselytize and spread the word. The group stepped up their efforts to inform the press of the imminent demise of the world, and their house became a media circus.

At last, on the evening of December 21, the small group of believers assembled to await their deliverance. A horde of newsmen covered the event while a crowd of some two hundred taunted the group, who stood singing Christmas carols in the freezing drizzle. Huddled to-

PROPHECIES THAT FAILED

In the late '60s, Aquarian Agers fully expected Atlantis to rise somewhere in the Carribean. The trance visions of Edgar Cayce (pronounced Kay-sec), the "sleeping prophet" of 1920s-1940s America, had included a revelation that "Poseidia will be among the first portions of Atlantis to rise again. Expect it in '68 or '69. Not so far away!" Strike one. In 1941, Cayce predicted that "in the next few years, land will appear in the Atlantic as well as in the Pacific. . . . New York City itself will in the main disappear . . . [within] another generation." Strike two. But even "much sooner" than this, "the southern portions of Carolina, Georgia, these will disappear." Strike three: Mighty Cayce has struck out.

Modern America's Seer of State Jeanne Dixon has gained fame as "the psychic who foresaw President Kennedy's assassination." Popular folklore (promoted by Dixon herself) has it that she predicted that Kennedy would be shot and killed if he went to Dallas, and even specified the location of the bullet wounds and other details. Actually, her prophecy, reported in the May 13, 1956 issue of *Parade* magazine, was much simpler: that a Democrat would be elected in 1960, and that he would be assassinated or die in office, "though not necessarily in his first term." Kennedy, a Democrat, was elected in 1960 and assassinated on November 22, 1963.

At first glance, Dixon's prediction seems uncannily accurate—even without the details usually attributed to it. But consider that Dixon undoubtedly knew that whoever was to be elected in 1960 was heir to the "twenty-year curse" that had claimed the lives (by illness or assassination) of six presidents elected at twenty-year intervals, from Harrison in 1840 to Roosevelt in 1940. (This helps to explain Dixon's forecast, but of course the "curse" itself remains a curious phenomenon.) Further, she had at least a fifty percent chance of getting the party affiliation right. Whether Dixon's prediction was luck or prophecy is perhaps best revealed by the fact that, when Kennedy was a contender in the Democratic primaries, she predicted that he *wouldn't* be the man elected!

Like most psychic forecasters, Dixon uses the "scattergun" approach, issuing literally thousands of prophecies every year. Virtually all of them never come to pass, but in hindsight it is sometimes possible to pick one out—like the Kennedy prediction—that vaguely resembles an actual event. For example, in the December 25, 1979, issue of *The Star*, a tabloid to

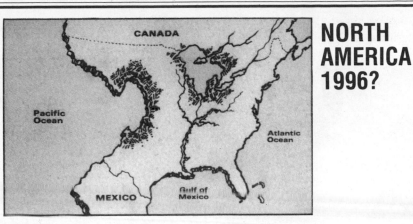

NORTH AMERICA 1996?

If you live in Nebraska, buy a surfboard. As depicted in this map from Jeffrey Goodman's 1978 crackpot classic, *We Are the Earthquake Generation* (New York: Seaview), by 1996 the North American continent is due for some remodeling (or "earth changes," as they are called in the New Age). Goodman correlated the prognostications of "psychics with remarkable records of prediction"—including the ubiquitous Edgar Cayce and Nostradamus, as well as a team of modern clairvoyants—and came up with a timetable for earth changes. Some sense of just how "remarkable" the predictive powers of Goodman's psychics are can be determined now, over ten years since his book was written, by examining what is already *supposed* to have happened on the way to the new "underwater America":

Between 1980 and 1985:

The Imperial Valley in Southern California starts to fill with water.
Palm Springs is submerged.
San Diego, Los Angeles, and San Francisco are destroyed.
The California coastline is pushed back to Bakersfield, Fresno, and Sacramento.
A seaway is opened up through central Oregon (from west to east) reaching to the Idaho border.
Land rises in the Bering Strait, creating a land bridge between Siberia and Alaska.
The Aleutian Islands begin to disappear as a result of volcanic eruption and earthquakes.
The Great Lakes and St. Lawrence Seaway grow larger.
A major earthquake destroys a large part of New York City.
Land rises off the southeast coast of the United States, near Bimini in the Bahamas.

Between 1985 and 1990:

Major tidal waves and earthquakes severely damage India.
Tidal waves and earthquakes severely damage Japan.
A major eruption of Vesuvius in Italy is initiated by a violent earthquake that causes damage as far off as France and Scandinavia.
New York City is now completely broken up.
Land rises in the Atlantic ocean west of England.
Land rises near Gibraltar, creating a land bridge between Europe and Africa.
The Black Sea grows larger as a result of shoreline subsidence and earthquakes.
The earth's axis of rotation tips a few degrees.

Think you'll lose any sleep over these predictions for 1990-2000?:

Major sections of the western U.S. fall into the sea as the coastline moves eastward in a series of violent surges. Final coastline established in Nebraska and Kansas.
Major submergence in the Great Lakes area, with portions of Wisconsin, Michigan, and Illinois going under watrer.
Eastern coastal states such as South Carolina and New Jersey are inundated by ocean.
Large quakes and coastal inundations in Connecticut and Massachusetts.
Major submergence in Florida, Louisiana, and Texas.
Major quakes in China. Lake forms west of Peking.
USSR experiences minor coastal inundation and earthquakes.
The return of Jesus Christ, with many helpers.
Space people visit planet to observe.

—T.S.

which Ms. Dixon regularly contributes, she made her "Predictions for the '80s," hundreds of forecasts about world events and famous personalities like Dolly Parton and Marie Osmond. It's hard to find even one that came true! For instance: In 1983, "income taxes will be slashed to a fraction of their present levels, and across the land Americans will stop paying property taxes." In 1985, "first commercial use will be made of icebergs, snagged in Arctic or Antarctic waters and sailed to seaports for water or cooling," and "the era of Fidel will finally come to an end when a new government takes over in Havana." In 1987, "startling signals will be received from outer space between

April and May indicating the existence of some form of alien life." In 1988, "lasting peace will come to Northern Ireland." In her book, *My Life and Prophecies*, published in 1969, she says "I have seen a comet strike our Earth around the middle of the 1980s."

Dixon likes to claim that she met Reagan at a movie-star party in the '50s and "I predicted then and there to him that one day, he would be sitting behind the big desk in the Oval Office," and even Reagan likes to tell it that way. In truth, when he was running for governor she told him "I don't see you as President. I see you here at an official desk in California."

—T.S.

Jim Berenholtz, one of the coordinators of the Harmonic Convergence, celebrates the transformational event at the Great Pyramid in Egypt.

gether in a tight knot, suffering the jeers of the nonbelievers, they waited and stamped their feet, each member clutching a blank envelope with a three-cent stamp: their ticket to the flying saucer and salvation.

When Prophecy Fails reveals the suburban White Bread version of the apocalypse. Gone are the beasts and flaming pools of blood, the two-horned lambs that speak like dragons. Yet we see clearly here the formation of entirely new elements in the age-old apocalyptic paradigm. While there is certainly a necessary cataclysm, there is no mention of God, retribution, or Tribulation. This is a purely secular affair with no real religious (Christian) dimension. For the first time, perhaps, we witness an example of salvation by Mother Ship.

THE HARMONIC CONVERGENCE: ESCHATOLOGY, '80S STYLE

Over the next two decades other End of the World movements continued to appear regularly in the media, a staple offering in newspapers, like stories of brave dogs and heroic children. In the late sixties, for instance, a group of four hundred "hippies" converged on a mountaintop near Boulder, Colorado, to await the imminent collision of the asteroid Icarus with the planet Earth. The *Chicago Tribune* headline shouted: "We're Safe! Icarus Misses Earth, but Hippies Stay Put." The gathering was probably a pleasant affair and everyone no doubt breathed a sigh of relief when tomorrow turned out to be just another day. What is important is the fact that the "hippies"

felt that the End Time was the result of something absolutely external. The imminent End of the World was an independent and random event, a cataclysmic fist smashing into history over which they had no power. They came to the mountaintop to survive, nothing more.

By the eighties, however, much of so-called "New Age" thinking had been absorbed into popular consciousness. Foremost among these tenets was the belief that "we create our reality," and that our "thought-forms" can alter our world. The next time that an End of the World movement was to capture the popular imagination, we frail humans would at last have a say in the future of the planet. In the newest eschatology, we could take responsibility for our future. At last, humans could "make a difference" when it came time for the age of the apocalypse.

The Harmonic Convergence (August 16/17, 1987) was just such an event. Unlike the linear Christian eschatology, the Harmonic Convergence was based on a *cyclical* conception of time, the Mayan calendar. The Harmonic Convergence marked the beginning of the last cycle of Mayan ages, and involved pilgrimages to sacred sites, as well as the other accoutrements of the New Age: crystals, meditation, chanting, hugging, and ceremonies.

The precursors of the Harmonic Convergence were global activities such as Earth Day and Band-Aid, but the philosophy behind it was more difficult to fathom than the ideals and issues around which those other globe-spanning demonstrations revolved. Like the name of the New Age publication that was among the first to publish some of the far-out theories behind the Harmonic Convergence, the belief system was a "Magical Blend": the eschatology of geomancy.

The theoretician behind the Harmonic Convergence was Jose Arguelles, a forty-eight-year-old artist and historian from Boulder, Colorado. The idea hit him in 1983 when he had a vision while driving along Wilshire Boulevard in Los Angeles. "I had this, like, sudden vision of a type of Earth Surrender ritual taking place all over the world," he reported. Arguelles had been studying the configurations of the Mayan Calendar, and had computed that August 16/17 was a moment of cosmic importance. His ideas were set down in a book called *The Mayan Factor*.

For one thing it was the first time in 23,142 years that seven of the nine planets were in grand trine configuration. According to Arguelles, the Aztec Calendar, with its 13 cycles of Heaven and nine cycles of Hell, was coming to an end on August 16, 1987. Hopi legends, he added, claimed that this same date was the time when 144,000 Sun Dance-enlightened teachers would help awaken the rest of humanity. And finally he cited predictions based on the Mayan calendrics.

Numbers and an exact sense of time played an important part in Mayan cosmology. Hunab Ku, the Mayan name for god, for instance, can be translated as "he who gives measurements," and Arguelles, as a student (or creator) of neo-Mayan science, depended upon dates and measurements no less than the civilization he was studying. The Mayan great cycle runs from 3113 B.C. to 2012 A.D., a total of 5,125 years, itself only one-fifth of the greater cycle of 25,625 years. August 16th marked the inception of the last phase, the last 25-year period before all the cycles converge and begin their ineluctable revolutions once again. "August 15th and 16th is like a vortex reaching its apex, or point, and then it opens out again. . . as the vortex opens out, it starts another cycle where we enter a condition where we'll be experiencing a mental repolarization."

Although Arguelles gave voice to the theoretical background of the Harmonic Convergence, the date itself had been bandied about by other independent sources. Jim Berenholtz, a New Yorker who had been interested in Native American prophecies since his early teens and who later coordinated the ceremonies at the sacred sites, had come across the importance of the date August 16/17 on his own, long before hearing of Arguelles' arcane calendrics. He had noticed that it coincided with Krishna's birthday and that August 17th marked the rising of Sirius as the Morning Star (and thus the flooding of the Nile). One friend had told him "he got the word" about the auspicious date while sitting in the bathtub. And he had heard of a woman, who, while in the throes of an ecstatic orgasm, heard a voice yell in her ear "August 16th." (She didn't understand the significance of this information until some time later, when she happened to hear a lecture about the Harmonic Convergence.)

Arguelles described the phase entered after that date as a reversal of the "resonant field paradigm" (in Mayan terms the 13th "baktun"), which began in 1618 with Descartes' publication of *The Meditations*. The new resonant field paradigm will be less rational, more in tune with the needs of the planet. The Harmonic Convergence marked the inception of a new era of history; it was Childhood's End.

In an interview in *Magical Blend*, Arguelles had this to say about the coming years: "By the summer of 1992 the resistance of the collapsing old mental house will pretty much come to an end. At this point, we enter another twenty-year phase . . . the very last twenty years of the entire Mayan Great Cycle, which began in 3113 B.C. In this last twenty-year cycle, once we've got the old machine stopped, we'll witness the final full flowering of the species we call *Homo Sapiens*. We're just about done . . . we're going to be given the opportunity to relax and let a final flowering occur. By 2102 A.D. when the cycle closes out, that's when we shift to evolutionary patterns and that's when we get completely interfaced with what I call the galactic federation."

It is not clear that all those who participated in the Harmonic Convergence understood that the fate of the planet hung in the balance. Some did. Several hard-core groups of believers made pilgrimages to the sacred sites. Jim Berenholtz, the self-appointed head of the coordination of the sacred sites, had visited many of them in preparation for the important date. The task of those who journeyed to the sacred sites was specific: they were "laying the circuitry." "The result is that we are acting collectively as 'cosmic electricians', charging up power points and ley lines, Weaving the Great Web, so that when our ceremonies 'flick the switch' on Harmonic Convergence, the lights will go on!"

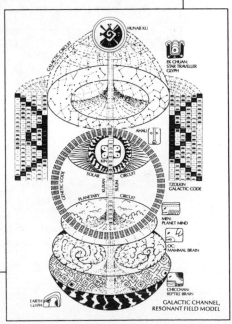

GALACTIC CHANNEL, RESONANT FIELD MODEL

Berenholtz printed literature that many people followed for ceremonies at the sacred sites to align the energies of the planet and make the transition beneficial. As in the Talmud, minutiae of conduct became important: ". . . sleep in spirals or concentric circles with your heads to the center and Dream as One. If possible, have a large drum in the center of your dream circle to align with the heartbeat of the Earth. Let nine people keep the beat at any given time . . . in this way will our consciousness be patterned through the dream state to the planetary rhythm we are all simultaneously experiencing."

Berenholtz himself spent the Harmonic Convergence inside the King's Room of the Great Pyramid. "I felt a convergence in my being of all time and space," he related. "I felt as if an initiation was taking place, a planetary initiation. I felt like my genetic code was being changed." Berenholtz claims that during the Harmonic Convergence a "critical threshold was achieved, an implantation, a seeding of the new genetic information for the entire earth."

Not everyone who participated in the Harmonic Convergence traveled to exotic locations. A few thousand went to domestic sites such as Mt. Shasta in California, or Central Park in New York, where they engaged in less rigorous activities such as humming, chanting, and dancing. Others spontaneously climbed onto hilltops to observe the sunrise. In the Topanga and Malibu areas of Los Angeles, for instance, it was not uncommon to find knots of people —groups up to fifty strong—who happened to choose the same summits for their harmonizing. Then there were those who did their bit toward saving the planet by sitting in meditation wherever they were at noon (Greenwich Mean Time) on August 17th.

All these participants were crucial to the success of the mission. The number of people needed to align the energies of the planet—144,000—was mentioned both in Mayan prophecies and the Book of Revelation. "I didn't feel it was incumbent upon me as an individual to save the earth," explained Berenholtz, "but it was critical that this threshold number [144,000] be reached. I never feared. It was merely a matter of doing the work to facilitate the fulfillment of the prophecy."

No one disputes that more than 144,000 people took part, so we can breathe easier knowing that the planet was switched onto the right track. And they took part all over the globe, from Australian aborigines who travelled to

Nostradamus

Nostradamus (Michel de Nostredame), born in France in 1503, has been remembered by occultists as the author of about 950 enigmatic, four-lined verses (called "quatrains") through which he is supposed to have predicted future world events like the rise and fall of Napoleon, World Wars I, II, and beyond, the death of Kennedy, air travel, submarines, AIDS, and more.

In the last few years, Nostradamus has become more popular than ever. A book on Nostradamus by Jean Charles de Fontbrune, published in France in 1980, caused a sensation by predicting that World War III would break out in the 1980s and that both Paris and Istanbul would be annihilated. Meanwhile, in the U.S., Californians held their breaths in May of 1988 when the "New City" (interpreted as either San Francisco or Los Angeles) was supposed to be destroyed in an earthquake, a notion that originated with a popularly distributed videotape of a 1982 television special about Nostradamus, **The Man Who Saw Tomorrow**, narrated by Orson Welles.

A woodcut from Nostradamus' day depicting large-scale disaster, from LeVert's The Prophecies and Enigmas of Nostradamus.

What such failed prophecies demonstrate is that Nostradamus' deliberately vague quatrains are eminently adaptable to interpretation, and twisting the verses to fit historical events ex post facto has been a favorite occult parlor game since Nostradamus was alive. For instance, in a famous quatrain (Century I, Quatrain 35), Nostradamus is thought to have predicted the death of his benefactor Henry II, when in fact the quatrain has been modified by later writers to duplicate history. (The original refers to "two knells, then one," which overzealous students of prophecy have rewritten as "two wounds made one" to match Henry's death by a lance injury to the head.) Actually, Nostradamus could not have been referring to Henry in this quatrain, because he had written another verse (VI:70) predicting fame and fortune for Henry, and, furthermore, he had dedicated a letter to Henry (June 27, 1558), referring to him as "invincible"!

The search for historical "matches" for the quatrains continues with modern interpreters who believe, for instance, that Nostradamus used the word "Hister" to refer to Hitler, when "Hister" is actually Latin for "Danube." Nostradamus enthusiasts can hardly be blamed, however, since very little objective writing exists about his work. Perhaps the only such book in the English language is **The Prophecies and Enigmas of Nostradamus** by Liberté E. LeVert. LeVert, an authority on sixteenth-century French language and history, at last puts the quatrains into context. He returns to the original sources to avoid the modifications that have been inserted by later "interpreters," translates with special attention to the formalized tradition of the quatrain style of verse, and points out the allusions to contemporary life that were more likely the intent of Nostradamus' poetry, purposely couched in double meanings. LeVert's conclusion: "[Nostradamus] did not take himself seriously as a prophet. . . . He filled his books not with prophecies (which were only occasionally present), but with verse about current events, past history, generalities, social criticism, economics, court scandal, plus a fair amount of shudder-verse built on fears of war and religious persecution."

Aside from LeVert's book, a refreshing viewpoint on Nostradamus is presented in three separate articles in the Fall 1982 issue of the **Skeptical Inquirer**, available as a back issue.

—T.S.

Ayer's Rock to Tibetans who journeyed to the sacred Himalayan Mt. Kailash. Europeans turned out in large numbers to celebrate the event, and, according to reports, many indigenous peoples from South America and Mexico took the date seriously. Berenholtz claims that the entire population of Easter Island, some 2,500 souls, gathered to mark the day. "Never before do we know of people from so many different cultures and religious persuasions gathering to pray for peace," Berenholtz emphasizes. "It was the largest pan-spiritual event in history." Eschatology had gone global.

2000 A.D.: SHAKE AND BAKE

As far as millennial movements are concerned, the Harmonic Convergence was more pleasant than most. Humming and hugging on Mt. Shasta certainly beats standing out on a cold night with no zipper waiting for the flying saucers and the "boys upstairs" to arrive. Unlike many of the other millennial movements throughout history, the Harmonic Convergence was born not out of a sense of desperation, but a growing sense of malaise. It did not focus, as do most others, on a cataclysm.

Perhaps its appeal lay in the vagueness of its prophecies. As we head into the nineties, however, there is no lack of doom-sayers to assuage our need for an ending with exact and dire predictions. In May of 1988 there was a mini-crisis and heightened anxiety as many, especially those on the West Coast, felt that some sort of major disaster was about to occur. This consternation was caused by the prophecies of Nostradamus, a man who had lived in the south of France over 450 years before. Nostradamus is credited by some with having correctly prophesied the French Revolution, Napoleon, Hitler, Hiroshima, and the Kennedy assassinations—and now Khomeini and Abu Nidal—among other important events.

What does Nostradamus have to say about our future? In two words: "Ruin approaches." According to some interpretations, by 1993 half the world will be infected by AIDS. Shortly afterwards, sometime in the mid-1990s, a series of "superquakes" will hit the earth. New York and Florida will be flooded; California will break away from the mainland. In 1996 an Arab attack on Europe will begin with an invasion through Italy, and a year later New York will be under nuclear attack. July 1999—the end of the millennium—signals the End of the World as we know it. "In the year 1999 and seven months / The great King of Terror will come from the sky / He will resurrect Ghengis Khan / Before and after war rules happily." The seventh and final millennium will be ushered in by the year 2026.

Others follow in Nostradamus' footsteps. Take Elizabeth Clare Prophet, president of the Church Universal and Triumphant. She is a woman who is a Messenger for the Ascended Masters, and as her name humbly suggests, is someone who can see into the future. "I think that earthquakes are geological events on the planet whose time has come," she explained to an interviewer from the *Whole Life Times*. "The probability is there, the prophecies are there, the scientific statements are there." Her church organization, which she had developed at its Malibu headquarters since 1961, was recently relocated to Montana. "Our important mission in Montana is to hold the balance in terms of earth changes, earthquakes, and so forth. We've done that with our mantras and our Violet Flame decrees," she explained.

Be prepared for more interviews with prophets of dire events such as these appearing with increasing frequency in the near future. Whether you believe there is a divinity which shapes our ends, rough-hewn though they may be, or if you hold to a more participatory eschatology, such as the Harmonic Convergence, where your very actions make a difference to the planet's future, the fact is: The year 2000 approaches. With all those zeroes jostling each other, our thoughts—as a culture—are bound to turn both backward and forward. The end of a millennium tends to do that kind of thing to people. Book your mountaintop today. They're bound to be in short supply in the coming decade.

THE END?

APOCALYPSE NOW! ...AND ALWAYS

Despite the many real concerns modern technology offers us for the destruction of our world, most doomsday cosmologies foretell an ending through natural or supernatural disasters. Is this because we find comfort in the idea of a greater power interceding to save us from our folly, or does it suggest that apocalypse is a symbol which addresses a deeper psychological need?

Anthropologists have noticed basic similarities in apocalypse belief systems throughout history and in most of the world's cultures. They are usually based in a sense of paradise lost, and have to do with the resurrection of some golden age past, usually at the hands of some hero endowed with superhuman powers who will vanquish evils against which we are helpless, as in the Second Coming of Christ or the return of King Arthur. Usually the believers are to be spared from the disaster, and will inherit the freshly purged earth. In most cases the restored order is seen as a permanent happy ending, though in some cultures it is perceived as part of the ongoing cycle of decay and resurrection observable in nature.

These belief systems are especially prevalent in cultures which have been colonized by more powerful civilizations, as in the cargo cults of Melanesia or the Ghost Dances of Native American tribes. This seems a fairly natural reaction to the loss of land and freedom; but what about those cultures which have never experienced this type of deprivation? Do Christian fundamentalists perceive themselves as living in the vestiges of a culture colonized by Satan and characterized by sin and moral decay, or New Agers in a world colonized by technoscience and characterized by greed and inhumanity?

Are our 'memories' of a more idyllic past based on our infant experiences of being nurtured and protected by a seemingly omnipotent parent? Are apocalypse belief systems the adult equivalent of childhood revenge fantasies about the playground bully? Are they an attempt to grapple with, glorify, or possibly transcend our mortality? Whatever the reason, the archetype seems to exist within most of us, and it has often been manipulated politically to mollify people with dreams of better days ahead in order to keep them from taking control of the problems of their lives. —*Rebecca Wilson*

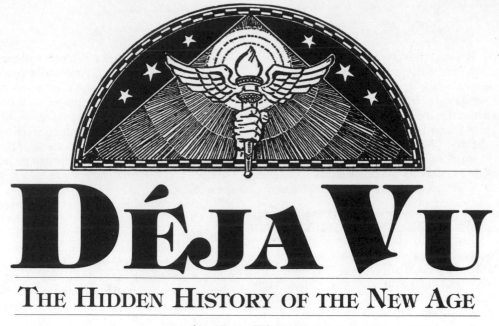

DÉJA VU

THE HIDDEN HISTORY OF THE NEW AGE

by Jay Kinney

FROM CHANNELERS TO CRYSTALS TO Shirley MacLaine, the "New Age" is the latest fad to sweep America. Yet, although marketing categories such as "New Age music" and "New Age books" may be recent arrivals on the scene, the New Age itself is hardly new. Nearly every spiritual or cultural phenomenon associated with the term dates back at least several generations and, as we'll see shortly, a striking number of them—including the occult concepts of "karma," "auras," "chakras," and "astral projection"— were first introduced to the public by a single little-known nineteenth-century organization and its offshoots.

The highest profile New Age phenomenon, channeling, dates back well over a hundred years to 1848, when the Fox family of Hydesville, New York, reportedly communicated with disembodied spirits that responded to questions with ghostly rapping and knocking noises. The Fox daughters ultimately went on tours demonstrating this "ability," and a spirit-rapping craze swept the U.S. In short order, mediums acquired the ability to receive far more sophisticated communiques from the dead, including spiritual teachings and materialized objects. Spiritualism as an organized movement had its ups and downs in the ensuing years as scandals over fraudulent mediums erupted and popular curiosity was satiated. Still, it persisted as a mass phenomenon into the 1920s, and a dedicated core of proponents remains to this day. The only things really distinguishing modern channeling from this earlier form of trance mediumship are the sophistication in marketing techniques that mediums such as J. Z. Knight (channeler of "Ramtha") have brought to the field, and the ability of all the '80s spirit guides to speak the lingo of the moment.

The phenomenon of Eastern gurus arriving on our shores to teach Americans the virtues of yoga, Hinduism, and Buddhism isn't new either. It can be traced back to the World Parliament of Religions, held in Chicago in 1893 at the Columbian Exposition. Along with Confucians, Shinto priests, and Buddhist monks, Swami Vivekananda, a devotee of the Indian saint Sri Ramakrishna, came to that groundbreaking ecumenical conference and found the U.S. to be surprisingly hospitable to "new" religious teachings from other shores. The Parliament was the hit of the Exposition, and turnaway crowds attended the public lectures. The Vedanta Society of America, founded by Vivekananda the next year, continues to this day, the granddaddy of Eastern spiritual groups transplanted to the U.S. And in the early 1930s, the Indian teacher Paramahansa Yogananda, author of the bestselling *Autobiography of a Yogi*, set up the Self Realization Fellowship in the Los Angeles area and ministered to the seekers of Southern California for decades, giving Americans one of their first practical tastes of yoga.

Even the term "New Age" begins to show its age with a little digging. The late Corinne Heline, a long-time mainstay of metaphysical bookshelves, founded her quarterly magazine, the *New Age Interpreter,* in 1940, well before most present New Agers were born. Even older, *The New Age Magazine*, the monthly magazine of the "Supreme Council, 33°, Ancient & Accepted Scottish Rite of Freemasonry of the Southern Jurisdiction," won its second-class mailing privileges in 1914, and has been publishing since the turn of the century! Clearly, the hope that we are entering or have already entered a new era of spiritual enlightenment and progress has been with us as we've gotten into and out of both world wars, seen the proliferation of nuclear weaponry, and experienced the onset of the "greenhouse effect." But then, perhaps the

---

Just how new is the New Age? Not very, according to Jay Kinney, who here delineates the New Age's origins in the antics of the nineteenth-century Theosophical Society. On matters of esoteric spirituality, Kinney knows whereof he speaks: He's editor of Gnosis: A Journal of the Western Inner Traditions *(see p. 30). He's also a past editor of* Whole Earth Review *(when it was known as CoEvolution Quarterly) where, among other things, he organized special issues on "Politics and Religion" and "Islam."* —T.S.

(Left) The term "New Age" has been used in the titles of a number of occult publications since the 1800s, including *The New Age Magazine,* founded at the turn of the century, and the *New Age Interpreter,* which began publication in 1940. (Center) Madame Helena Petrovna Blavatsky (1831-1891), co-founder of the Theosophical Society. (Right) The Theosophical Society's other co-founder, Colonel Henry Steel Olcott (1832-1907), along with Annie Wood Besant (1847-1933) and Charles Webster Leadbeater (1854-1934), who assumed the leadership from Blavatsky and Olcott.

ability to sustain the expectation of a new beginning just around the corner is akin to the fundamentalist Christians' inextinguishable faith in an imminent Armageddon.

Influences and forerunners for the New Age abound, ranging from the Zen preoccupations of the '50s "beat" movement to the revival of witchcraft in England following World War II. However, when all is said and done, the single group with the most influence on today's New Age terrain is the little-known Theosophical Society.

MEET THE THEOSOPHICAL SOCIETY

Most people have never heard of the Theosophical Society (T.S.), while those few who *have* rubbed elbows with it tend to regard the T.S. as an aging holdover from an earlier era. Certainly anyone who has happened to stop by at the stately T.S. headquarters in Wheaton, Illinois, during the last twenty years will have been impressed with the quiet atmosphere in the grand brick headquarters building, where a seemingly endless supply of devoted octogenarians tiptoe around and whisper to each other in numerous offices. I know I was impressed when I paid a visit to the venerable San Francisco T.S. Lodge in the early '70s, stuck off in a corner several floors up in the downtown Native Sons of the Golden West building. Stepping out of the elevator and walking through the deserted and dimly lit anteroom into the ancient meeting hall, I happened upon three or four elderly ladies gathered around an old untuned piano, singing unidentifiable hymns of an inspirational nature. This may be as close as I've ever gotten to actual time travel, and the sensation was rather unnerving, believe me.

Such appearances can be deceiving, however, for over the years the T.S. has played a pivotal role in fostering the openness to alternative spirituality, Eastern religions, and psychic powers that are associated with the present New Age movement. It has also seen more than its share of grandstanding, schisms, sex scandals, and just plain eccentricity. For the uninitiated, what follows is a short his-

tory of the T.S. and its considerable influence on the rise of modern occultism.

THE MADAME AND THE COLONEL

The Theosophical Society was founded in New York in the fall of 1875 by a group of solid middle-class citizens whose mutual interest in the occult had brought them to the evening salons held by the mysterious Russian emigré, Helena Petrovna Blavatsky. Madame Blavatsky (or H.P.B., as she was often referred to) was a portly woman with a commanding presence and a larger-than-life reputation. Her earlier exploits were said to have included a stint as a circus equestrian in Constantinople, piano teacher in Paris, factory manager in Tiflis, and traveler to India, Tibet, and Egypt. Upon her arrival in the U.S. in 1873, she immersed herself in spiritualist circles where she met Col. Henry Olcott, who was to become her primary collaborator in matters esoteric over the next two decades.

From almost the start of her sojourn on the East Coast, H.P.B. claimed to be in touch with distant adepts and secret societies. First there was a mysterious spirit named "John King," whom she contacted through her mediumistic talents. King was shortly followed by the Brotherhood of Luxor, supposedly "an Egyptian group of the Universal Mystic Brotherhood," as H.P.B. explained to Olcott. However, this group was soon succeeded by the two Tibetan adepts (usually referred to as the "Masters" or the "Mahatmas") known as Koot Hoomi and Morya. These Masters were to become the special guides of the T.S., communicating telepathically through Blavatsky and via mysterious letters sent to various T.S. members. The Masters would also psychically dictate H.P.B.'s two enormous books, *Isis Unveiled* and *The Secret Doctrine.*

In 1878 Col. Olcott made contact with a recently formed Hindu reform group in India, the Arya Samaj. Their attention turned to the East by this contact and by the Masters, who supposedly lived in Tibet, Olcott and H.P.B. set sail for India at the end of the year. For the

The Occult Underground and The Occult Establishment

Most histories of the occult are hopelessly partisan and untrustworthy. James Webb's two volumes come the closest to objective history that the subject has ever seen. In **The Occult Underground**, Webb takes on the occult explosion of the nineteenth century when, by his interpretation, a backlash occurred against the rationalist paradigm of the Enlightenment. This reaction radiated out from the Hydesville, New York, cottage of the Fox sisters, founders of Spiritualism, through the Parliament of Religions at the 1893 Columbian Exposition in Chicago, the founding of Theosophy, the rise of Mormonism and Christian Science, the influences of the Rosicrucians and Utopians, and on into the twentieth century.

The Occult Establishment takes up where its predecessor leaves off, outlining the progress of twentieth-century occultism. It covers the further adventures of Theosophists, Anthroposophists, health cults, and Westernized Eastern doctrines. Webb reveals how diverse elements of occultism, including a tendency toward political conspiracy theories, found their way into the "establishment" doctrines of Nazi Germany. He brings his account right up into the 1960s and the psychedelic revolution. Both books are examples of excellent scholarship, crammed with meticulously researched facts. You won't find this fascinating story told so thoroughly anywhere else.
— T.S.

• Anna Kingsford herself was sufficiently convinced of the justice of her cause [anti-vivisection] to commit murder for its sake. By a simple curse she was convinced that she had killed Professor Claude Bernard, who was conducting experiments on the heat tolerance of animals which included baking them to death. This was not enough. In the summer of 1886 she agreed to a proposal to study what Maitland refers to as "occultism," but is obviously practical magic. Her tutor was "a notable expert, well-versed in Hermetic and Kabalistic science." This was almost certainly MacGregor Mathers of the Golden Dawn. Anna Kingsford proposed to use the power to kill more vivisectors.

Her first attempt was directed against Louis Pasteur. It exhausted her, but she was soon restored to spirits by hearing that Pasteur had been struck by a dangerous illness, and that the mortality rate among his patients had greatly increased. Whilst visiting H.P.B. [Madame Helena P. Blavatsky] at Ostend, she took chloroform, and was enabled to see that

The Occult Underground
James Webb
1974; 387 pp.
$18.95
($20.70 postpaid)

The Occult Establishment
James Webb
1976; 535 pp.
$9.95
($11.70 postpaid)

Both from:
Open Court
Attn: Order Dept.
P.O. Box 599
Peru, IL
61354

her "projections" were not only successful, but perfectly justified. H.P.B. and other Theosophists demonstrated with her, but to no avail. Anna Kingsford tried again, choosing as her target a professor Paul Bert. Paul Bert died. The following diary entry is frighteningly indicative of its writer's state of mind:

"Yesterday, November 11th at eleven at night, I knew that my will had smitten another vivisector! Ah, but this man has cost me more toil than his master, the fiend Claude Bernard . . . The will can and *does* kill, but not always with the same rapidity . . . I have killed Paul Bert, as I killed Claude Bernard; as I will kill Louis Pasteur and after him the whole tribe of vivisectors, if I live long enough. Courage: it is a magnificent power to have, and one that transcends all vulgar methods of dealing out justice to tyrants." — *The Occult Underground*

• The chief uses [Rudolf] Steiner made of his [clairvoyant] faculty were enunciating moral doctrine, describing the structure of the universe, and elucidating the history of man. Human history could be surveyed as far distantly as the seer might wish—because of its impress on the "Akashic Record." This mysterious and convenient chronicle is a legacy from Madame Blavatsky; and like her, Steiner made great play with the doings of man on the lost continents of Atlantis and Lemuria. In Atlantis, for example, the inhabitants had thought in pictures, possessed extraordinary memories, and used the energy latent in plants to drive airships. The most evolved among them were gathered together by a great leader in Central Asia and subjected to a refining process with the object of making them understand the divine powers. From this group were descended the early priest-kings of the Aryans.
— *The Occult Establishment*

---

next seven years, H.P.B. spent most of her time in India, establishing and then presiding at the T.S. world headquarters in Adyar. While there, H.P.B.'s contacts with the Masters continued, as did a variety of psychic phenomena including the sounds of astral bells and materialized letters and flowers. These manifestations culminated in an investigation by the British Society for Psychical Research, which concluded that at least some of the phenomena were produced fraudulently. The S.P.R.'s star witnesses were Mr. & Mrs. Coulomb, the former handyman and housekeeper of the Adyar estate, who alleged that they had connived with H.P.B. to produce various psychic marvels. An enormous stink was raised in India, much to the T.S.'s embarrassment. Shortly thereafter, in 1885, H.P.B. and Olcott departed India for good and regrouped their forces in England, though Adyar would remain the official headquarters of the T.S.

Another scandal accompanied the publication of H.P.B.'s two masterworks. These gargantuan volumes, which were said to have been dictated by the Masters,

succumbed to textual analysis by a spiritualist critic, William E. Coleman. His study of *Isis Unveiled* (1877) revealed that over two thousand passages were lifted intact from other books without credit. Similar charges were leveled against *The Secret Doctrine* (1888), which was said to derive primarily from just three other books.[1]

The final years of H.P.B.'s life were marred by her poor health and power struggles with Col. Olcott for control of the T.S. While Madame Blavatsky had the charisma, the good Colonel had the administrative abilities,

---

[1] Coleman recorded his painstaking analyses in "The Unveiling of 'Isis Unveiled': A Literary Revelation" in *Golden Way* 1:2-8; *Blavatsky Unveiled* (London, 1891?); and *Plagiarism in Theosophical Teachings* (Bombay, no date). According to Coleman, Blavatsky plagiarized extensively from about a hundred books to write *Isis Unveiled*, chief among them Ennemoser's *History of Magic*, Dunlap's *Sod: Son of Man*, and *Demonologia*. The primary sources for *The Secret Doctrine* were H.H. Wilson's translation of the *Vishnu Purana*, Alexander Winchell's *World Life or, Comparative Geology*, and Dowson's *Hindu Classical Dictionary*. Ignatius Donnelly's *Atlantis* also served as a source.

"MICRO-PSI" OF ATOMS

Did two Theosophists use psychic powers to accurately describe subatomic particles unknown to the scientists of their day? According to an article by British physicist Stephen Phillips in the December 1986 *Theosophical Research Journal*, modern physics has recently confirmed that Theosophical Society leaders Annie Besant (1847-1933) and Charles Leadbeater (1847-1934) performed such a paranormal feat in the early 1900s.

Through intensive study, Besant and Leadbeater supposedly acquired the "knowledge of the small, the hidden, or the distant by directing the light of a superphysical faculty," as described by the Indian scholar Patanjali in his book *Yoga Sutras* (400 B.C.). The two Theosophists applied this power to the study of the elements, perceiving small units common to all substances, which they identified as "atoms." They found that these "atoms" came in seven shapes, corresponding to the seven rows of the periodic table of elements. But the atom of hydrogen (the most basic element) was different, and was "seen to consist of six small bodies, contained in an egg-like form . . . It rotated with great rapidity on its own axis, vibrating at the same time, the internal bodies performing similar gyration. The whole atom spins and quivers and has to be steadied before exact observation is possible. The six little bodies are arranged in two sets of three, forming two triangles that are not interchangeable."

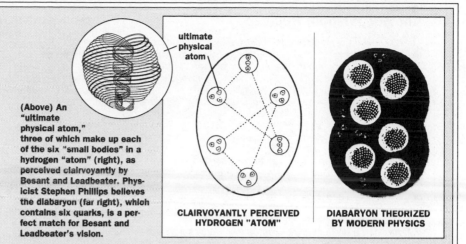

(Above) An "ultimate physical atom," three of which make up each of the six "small bodies" in a hydrogen "atom" (right), as perceived clairvoyantly by Besant and Leadbeater. Physicist Stephen Phillips believes the diabaryon (far right), which contains six quarks, is a perfect match for Besant and Leadbeater's vision.

ultimate physical atom

CLAIRVOYANTLY PERCEIVED HYDROGEN "ATOM"

DIABARYON THEORIZED BY MODERN PHYSICS

The "little bodies" within the atoms in turn contained three "points of light," which were named by Besant and Leadbeater "ultimate physical atoms" (see diagrams).

The clairvoyant duo's picture of the hydrogen "atom" matched nothing known to the science of their time. Phillips believes that what the two psychics identified as a hydrogen "atom" was neither an atom nor a molecule (H_2) of hydrogen, but instead was something modern physicists call a *diabaryon*. According to Phillips, the six little bodies within this diabaryon were *quarks*, subatomic particles first described in 1963. And the "ultimate physical atoms" that Besant and Leadbeater said occurred in triplets within each of the six bodies were *subquarks*, controversial particles thought to exist by some physicists (including Phillips).

What can we make of these claims? Phillips is not without bias; he is obviously predisposed toward the idea of micro-psi and even authored a book on the subject, *Extrasensory Perception of Quarks*, published by the Theosophical Publishing House in 1980. Furthermore, Besant and Leadbeater made many predictions about molecular and atomic structure (recorded in their 1908 volume *Occult Chemistry*) for which there are no correspondences in past or present scientific theory—perhaps Phillips's examples are just lucky matches. And the existence of subquarks, which Phillips identifies with Besant and Leadbeater's "ultimate physical atoms," is by no means certain. It would be extremely interesting to hear from a neutral physicist who has taken the time to look into Phillips's claims.

—*T.S.*

---

and like a pair of battling siamese twins, neither seemed quite comfortable with sharing the power. H.P.B. died from influenza in May 1891.

Olcott, though getting on in age, maintained leadership of the T.S. for the next few years as a new power struggle erupted. Predictably, a battle for successorship to the founders' mantle was taking shape. On one side stood Annie Besant, a birth-control advocate, free-thinker, and former Fabian socialist who had joined the Society in 1889 and risen quickly to leadership of the Esoteric Section founded by H.P.B. On the other side was William Q. Judge, a lawyer who had been in on the T.S.'s founding in New York and who had become leader of the American Section and T.S. vice president after Blavatsky and entourage left for India. With H.P.B. now dead, contact with the Masters was hard to come by, so when Judge claimed to possess new letters from the distant sages, he acquired considerable influence. Besant was initially impressed by Judge's communiques, but a trip to India and a confrontation with some critical evidence convinced Besant that Judge's Mahatma letters were a fraud. A fracas ensued. The T.S. at large shilly-shallied back and forth for a

couple of years until public exposure of the controversy compelled action. Judge was asked to resign as vice president and stand for re-election in 1894. Shortly thereafter, in April 1895, the American Section, six thousand members strong, voted to secede, and an independent "Theosophical Society in America" was formed with Judge as its head. Ironically, Judge died within a year of the schism, leaving the new group to thread its own way into the twentieth century. (In later years, the majority of American Theosophists found their way back into lodges affiliated with Adyar, and the Judge schism became a minority within the movement as a whole.)

CLAIRVOYANCE AND YOUNG BOYS

With Judge out of the picture, Besant's star continued to rise without hindrance, and she shared leadership of the surviving T.S. with Olcott until the Colonel's death in 1907 at the age of 75. About the time of Judge's departure, another unique individual who was to wield great influence on the T.S.'s future returned to London after a 12-year stay in India and Ceylon. This was the clairvoyant

Ancient Wisdom Revived

It's taken a century for this book to be written, but here, finally, is an objective history of Theosophy. Given the colorful eccentrics that populate its pages, this story can't help but be entertaining, and it doesn't shy away from Theosophy's many scandals either, including Blavatsky's plagiarisms, Leadbeater's penchant for young boys, and the faking of messages from the enlightened "Masters" who supposedly communicated Theosophy's seminal teachings. But at the same time, **Ancient Wisdom Revived** *treats Theosophy's founders and their beliefs with a healthy dose of sympathy, reflecting perhaps author Campbell's own former membership in a Theosophy-related group called the Nature of the Soul.*

Campbell, a professor of religious studies at the University of California in Santa Barbara, has done an admirable job of providing an historical perspective on the origins, controversies, and factionalisms of a nineteenth-century "New Age" movement that has had a profound influence on twentieth-century spirituality, including the New Age explosion that's happening right now.
—T.S.

• Most Theosophists believe that the real founders of the Theosophical Society were not Helena Blavatsky and Henry Olcott but, on the contrary, mysterious personages called the Mahatmas. Referred to also as Adepts, Masters of Wisdom, Masters of Compassion, and Elder Brothers, the Mahatmas are thought to be not spirits but rather highly evolved living men. Their chief residence is said to be in Tibet. Madame Blavatsky claimed that they were the source of her major writings and that she had known them for many years prior to the founding of the Society. . . . Two Masters have been associated prominently with Theosophy: Koot Hoomi (also spelled Kuthumi) and Morya.

The Masters came to public attention principally through a series of letters received by the Anglo-Indian journalist and Theosphical Society member A.P. Sinnett. . . . Sinnett received more than 100 "Mahatma" letters, most of which were signed by "K.H." Many of them were delivered to Sinnett by Madame Blavatsky. Some came through the mails or appeared mysteriously within another letter, fell suddenly from the ceiling, or arrived in other marvelous ways. Sinnett used the material in the letters to write *The Occult World* and *Esoteric Buddhism.* The books and the phenomena associated with the letters gave Theosophy wide publicity both in India and the West, and were important to the development of the movement. . . .

Ancient Wisdom Revived
A History of the Theosophical Movement
Bruce F. Campbell
1980; 259 pp.
$25
($26.50 postpaid) from:
University of California Press
Attn: Order Dept.
2120 Berkeley Way
Berkeley, CA 94720
800/822-6657

The most thorough investigations by non-Theosophists of the Mahatmas and the letters attributed to them have produced the conclusions that the letters were fraudulent, that Madame Blavatsky wrote most of them and confederates the rest, and that the Mahatmas were invented by her. . . .

Just as Madame Blavatsky's acknowledged writings have not escaped the charge of plagiarism, so, too, the Mahatma letters contain some evidence of unattributed borrowing. . . . The most embarrassing example of plagiarism . . . was a passage from a speech by Henry Kiddle. Kiddle, former superintendent of schools in New York City and a spiritualist lecturer, identified a long passage in [Sinnett's] *The Occult World* as taken verbatim from one of his own speeches. Though attributed by Sinnett to Koot Hoomi, the words had been printed nearly a year before publication of Sinnett's work in the prominent spiritualist weekly *Banner of Light.* . . .

Blavatsky at first tried to make light of the affair by ridiculing the *Banner of Light.* She wrote to Sinnett: "Plagiarize from *Banner of Light!!* That sweet spirits' slop-basin—the asses!" Then Koot Hoomi himself wrote to Sinnett to declare that "I have a habit of often quoting, *minus* quotation marks—from the maze of what I get in the countless folios of our Akasic libraries. . . ." Later Sinnett received a second letter from K.H. on the subject. This missive declared that the problem had arisen because he had been tired and had been inattentive to the work of an inexperienced chela to whom the letter had been dictated. He included what he claimed was the full passage as originally dictated. The new version reversed the intention of the original passage. Sinnett incorporated these explanations in several subsequent editions of *The Occult World,* but later they, and the offending passage, were dropped entirely.

Charles W. Leadbeater, formerly an Anglican priest, later converted to Buddhism, and later still a leading light in the peculiar strains of Theosophical Catholicism, Freemasonry, and messianism that swept through the T.S. Leadbeater and Besant collaborated on a number of celebrated clairvoyant investigations of the past lives of T.S. members, molecular chemistry, and the inner planes of consciousness.

Alas, it seems that Leadbeater also had a penchant for investigating the drawers of young boys left in his spiritual charge by trusting Theosophical parents, and he was eased out of the picture in 1906 after charges were leveled that he was schooling his lads in the mystical arts of masturbation. Leadbeater's eclipse was not to last for long, however, and within a year or two of Annie Besant's ascension to T.S. leadership, her clairvoyant collaborator was back. His official return precipitated mass resignations, including some of the T.S.'s most influential members, such as occult scholars G.R.S. Mead and A.P. Sinnett; but in due time Society membership was to rebound with a vengeance.

In a manner akin to that of today's most celebrated channelers, Besant and Leadbeater enthralled their public with clairvoyant revelations that have never been beat for colorfulness. When Leadbeater attended Mass, for example, he professed to see with his inner eye the influx of grace from heaven, flowing down the arms and body of the priest's vestments in orderly fashion. Such marvels were chronicled in his book, *Science of the Sacraments* (1920). Another book, *Thought-Forms: A Record of Clairvoyant Investigations* (1901), co-authored by Leadbeater and Besant, included garish color prints of the vivid pinks and greens engendered by their colleagues' mental processes.

In due time, Leadbeater's nascent interest in the clerical profession returned, and he became a founding Archbishop of the Liberal Catholic Church, an independent Catholic denomination whose membership overlapped almost entirely with the T.S. Leadbeater and Besant also beat the drums for Co-Masonry, an irregular Masonic formation that admitted women for initiation, much to the chagrin of the staid Grand Lodge of England.

But the *tour de force* of the Besant-Leadbeater regime was their proclamation of the imminent return of "the World Teacher" (also known as Christ, but not to be confused with Jesus, you understand). In 1909, Leadbeater's penetrating clairvoyance revealed that this returning Great Being was due to take over the vehicle of Jiddu Krishnamurti, the young Brahmin son of a T.S. employee at the Adyar headquarters in India. Leadbeater and Besant proceeded to claim Jiddu and his brother as their special charges, much to the annoyance of the boys' father. Long drawn-out court battles ensued, and though Besant was otherwise a champion of Indian independence, in this case English paternalism won out, and on the third appeal Krishnamurti was allowed to continue with the special training that Leadbeater and Besant could best provide.

Throughout the 1920s, suspense built in T.S. ranks as Krishnamurti's vehicle became ever more polished in preparation for the Second Coming. The Order of the Star in the East, an independent organization formed around Krishnamurti's messiahship, grew to 30,000 members at its peak. Probably in spite of, rather than because of, his acclaimed tutelage, Krishnamurti apparently had a profound mystical experience in 1922, and began to provide a spiritual guidance of sorts to his followers. This culminated in 1929 at an Order summer camp attended by thousands, when he delivered a shocking speech dissolving the Order, disowning religious organizations altogether, and indicating his primary interest in setting men "absolutely, unconditionally free." This came as a rude surprise to Besant, Leadbeater, and many in the T.S. who had hung all their hopes on the Theosophical messiah. The T.S. went into a period of deflation and the clairvoyant duo were both dead by the spring of 1934.

It would be fair to say that the Theosophical Society has never been quite the same since, and perhaps this is all for the better. The Society presidents who succeeded Annie Besant shared little of her verve or *chutzpah*, and the organization settled down to a low-profile role of "preserving and realizing the ageless wisdom," and promoting "understanding and brotherhood among people of all races, nationalities, philosophies, and religions." This it continues to do to this day, through a program of publishing, public lectures, and summer conferences and camps.

THE MASTERS LIVE ON

The deaths of Besant and Leadbeater also marked the end of direct T.S. communication with the Masters. The void this created in spiritual affairs was rapidly filled by a multitude of other claims of contact with the Masters. Undoubtedly the most flamboyant of these was promulgated by the "I Am" movement, led by Guy and Edna Ballard. Founded in 1934, the movement centered around the Ballards' contact with the "Ascended Masters," most prominent among whom was the Master Saint-Germain; but the Theosophical Masters were also included to round things out. The Ballards went stumping around the country holding meetings full of florid "decrees" in packed

The enlightened "Masters" of the Theosophical Society, as reinterpreted by Guy and Edna Ballard's "I Am" movement: Morya (left), and Koot Hoomi (right).

auditoriums. Donations poured in and the Ballards lived a luxurious lifestyle that foreshadowed a whole generation of TV evangelists to come. The bubble burst in late 1939 with Guy's death—an unexpected event, since this blessed messenger of the Masters was expected to "ascend" himself, not die like a mere human. An indictment for numerous counts of mail fraud hit widow Edna and son Donald the next year and the mighty "I Am" movement soon became "I Was," except for a few die-hard supporters hidden away in the hills of California.

Curiously enough, the 1950s saw a new married couple, Mark and Elizabeth Clare Prophet, alleging contact with the same Ascended Masters, using the same dated paintings of Saint-Germain, Koot Hoomi, and company that graced earlier "I Am" publications, and delivering similar purple-hued "decrees" to new throngs of seekers. Their organization, the Summit Lighthouse (now mainly known as the Church Universal and Triumphant), weathered Mark's death and "ascension" in 1973 far better than the "I Am" movement had weathered Guy Ballard's, and is today an active and prolific presence on the New Age scene.

Another independent contact with the Masters was maintained by Alice Bailey, who produced at least two dozen blue-bound books psychically dictated to her by "The Tibetan," a Master also known as Djwhal Khul (or D.K. for short). Alice and her husband, Foster Bailey, had been high officials in the American Section of the T.S., but left in 1920 after losing a mini-power struggle with the T.S. hierarchy led by Annie Besant. Bailey's trance-channeled volumes went into copious detail on the inner workings of the universe, and predicted their own "Return of the Christ" (not to be confused with Krishnamurti, of course). The Baileys founded the Arcane School, a correspondence course and esoteric lending library, and inspired the creation of an amorphous network of "New World Servers" who continue to publicize a non-sectarian prayer called "the Great Invocation," and to encourage meditation. Alice Bailey died in 1949. ☞

Lost Continents

*Atlantis played a key role in the cosmologies of Blavatsky, Steiner, and others influenced by Theosophy. And in the New Age, I've met many people who are as sure of the existence of Atlantis as they are of the Roman Empire. Most of them even recall "past lives" lived there (as kings and princesses rather than as serfs and slaves, of course). Since the nineteenth century, the lost continent of the Atlantic has provided occultists with a blank screen onto which to project their wildest mythic fantasies, unfettered by consideration for historical accuracy. But where did the Atlantis legend come from? Is there any truth to it? What book to read for an accurate history? L. Sprague de Camp's **Lost Continents** provides reliable answers, exploring the origin of the story (a dialogue by Plato from 355 B.C.), its embellishments over time, and even its use as a setting in fantasy novels. Also discussed is the lost continent of Mu, a.k.a. Lemuria (which now lies beneath the Pacific, according to various occult writers). De Camp even outlines the relevant research in geology, geography, and archaeology and, in a useful appendix, he reprints all of the major references to Atlantis from classical texts. —T.S.*

• The late Guy Warren Ballard, alias Godfré Ray King, founder of the I AM cult, claimed to have met his personal Master, Saint Germain, on Mount Shasta. Saint Germain seems to be a Mahatma remotely derived from the Comte de Saint-Germain, a slippery eighteenth-century European occultist and industrial promoter. Ballard, who graduated from selling stock in imaginary gold mines to old ladies, into occultism, picked elements of his grotesque mythology from Oliver's book, from Theosophy, from Christian Science, from Rosicrucianism, and from the Swamis, and reduced the resulting mishmash to the mental level of those comic-books whose covers show a muscular hero in a ballet-suit tearing a battleship asunder with his bare hands.

Ballard told how his Master showed him . . . magical movies of his former lives. He was delighted to learn thus that he was a reincarnation of George Washington and his wife of Joan of Arc. And of course he learned about Atlantis, Lemuria, and other vanished civilizations.

• From some unnamed source [English Theosophist W. Scott-Elliot] quotes a description of a Lemurian: He was between twelve and fifteen feet tall with a brown skin, a flat face with a protruding muzzle, and small eyes set so wide apart that he could see sideways as well as forward. He had no forehead, but was furnished with a third eye in back, which among us is still represented by the pineal gland in the brain. His long limbs could not be completely straightened, and he had huge hands and feet, the heels of which stuck out so far to the rear that he could walk equally well backward and forward. He wore a loose robe of reptile skin, carried a wooden spear, and led a pet plesiosaur on a leash.

Map of Atlantis from Athanasius Kircher's *Mundus Subterraneus* (1644). Note that, in contrast to modern maps, north is down and south up.

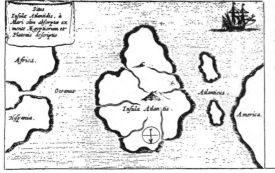

Lost Continents
The Atlantis Theme in History, Science, and Literature
L. Sprague de Camp
1954, 1970; 348pp.
$6.50
($7.75 postpaid)
from:
Dover Publications
Attn: CRX
31 East Second St.
Mineola, NY 11501
800/223-3130

Mark Prophet (1918-1973) and his wife Elizabeth Clare Prophet (1940-present), who founded the Summit Lighthouse (a.k.a. the Church Universal and Triumphant) in 1958. Mark died in 1973, but under Elizabeth (the "Messenger of the Masters"), the Church has continued to grow, currently sponsoring three different cable television shows, a publishing house, and an educational institution.

In the 1970s, Benjamin Creme, an English follower of the Bailey teachings, established his own psychic contacts with the returning Christ (also referred to as "The Maitreya"), and began to release channeled messages and announcements, many of which promised the Christ's unveiling as an Asian immigrant in East London. Every few years, Creme would set off on a new lecture tour and run newspaper ads announcing that the Christ was about to go public, only to have the imminent date pass uneventfully. Perhaps this indicates uncommon wisdom on the Christ's part, since an actual public appearance would likely result in His disembowelment by fundamentalist Christians convinced that he was the Antichrist!

This is not the place to determine whether the Masters might be considered an enduring hoax or represent an actual force for good at work behind the scenes. In a recent study, Steve Richards (see bibliography) has dug up some intriguing circumstantial evidence suggesting that the original Masters behind the T.S. were actual members of the Tibetan Kargyu sect, supporting the early Theosophists' assertions that the Masters existed in flesh and blood, commonly writing letters with normal pen and ink. At what point the Masters became "ascended" and accessible only by channelers is unclear, though Richards notes that a scheduled visit in 1917 by the Master Morya to H. Spencer Lewis, founder of a Rosicrucian group (The Ancient and Mystical Order of the Rosae Crucis, or AMORC), was cancelled because "it turned out he [Morya] had died the very day he was supposed to arrive in New York"!

OTHER THEOSOPHICAL SPROUTS

Movements as diverse as biodynamic farming and the Waldorf Schools owe their existence to the teachings of Rudolf Steiner, who began his esoteric career by joining the T.S. in Berlin in 1902. He shortly became general secretary of the German Section and remained so for the next decade. Steiner's own views were much more aligned

(Left) Rudolf Steiner (1861-1925), who broke away from the Theosophical Society in 1909 to form his own Anthroposophical Society. Steiner wrote prolifically, applying his occult theories to every facet of life. Anthroposophy remains a large movement, especially in Europe. (Right) Benjamin Creme (1923-present) claims to have been in telepathic contact since 1975 with the new messiah, "Maitreya the Christ," who has been reborn as an Asian immigrant in East London.

with Christianity and Western esotericism than were those of the T.S. elsewhere, and he ended up splitting from the T.S. over the issue of Krishnamurti, taking 55 of the 69 German Theosophical lodges with him. This was the genesis of Steiner's Anthroposophical Society, which remains active in Europe and the U.S. today.

Though the T.S. was never an advocate of magic (either black or white) itself, its atmosphere of inquiry into the occult gave various proponents of ceremonial magic their first taste of the arcane. The group most responsible for reviving the modern interest in magic, the Hermetic Order of the Golden Dawn, was founded by Masons operating in the Theosophical milieu, and the Order briefly considered affiliating with the T.S. W.B. Yeats, one of the Golden Dawn's most famous members, was a member of the Dublin lodge of the T.S. prior to joining the Order. Similarly, Dion Fortune, author of many popular books on magic and the occult, was a member of both the T.S. and a later offshoot of the Golden Dawn. Her own magical group, the Fraternity of the Inner Light, was originally fashioned as a special-interest lodge within the T.S., though that affiliation was short-lived.

Theosophy even left its stamp on modern art, playing a significant role in the formation of the aesthetics of Wassily Kandinsky, Piet Mondrian (who joined the T.S. in 1909), and numerous others. The major art exhibit organized by the Los Angeles County Museum of Art in 1986, "The Spiritual in Art: Abstract Painting 1890-1985," documented parallels between the color representations of Besant and Leadbeater's "thought forms" and early abstract art, and noted the influence of Theosophical, alchemical, and mystical ideas on everyone from Hugo Ball and Jean Arp to Marcel Duchamp, Edvard Munch, and Hilma af Klint.

THE EAST IS YEAST

I would be remiss if the reader was left with the impression that the sometimes-humorous antics of various

The Aquarian Conspiracy

It was big news in 1980—the counterculture had grown up and joined the work force. Thousands of people across the nation with a common vision were quietly working for change in their respective fields. It's still news now, although "New Age" is a tarnished term, co-opted by consciousness con-artists selling get-enlightened-quick schemes. Marilyn Ferguson recounts what it did mean, should mean, could mean: not a perfect world, but a world with a healthier set of assumptions. The universe as an organism, not a mechanism (handle with care); body/mind as an unbroken connection; the oneness of all people as crew of spaceship Earth—these concepts are part of the mental stew of a growing number of people. That's the Aquarian Conspiracy. —Corinne Cullen Hawkins

• With its periodic Great Awakenings, the United States has always attracted mystics and evangelists. Long before the spiritual revolution we see now, Eastern and Western mystics influenced mainstream American thought. Their ideas were daily bread to the American Transcendentalists and the "beat generation." Yet, as Oriental religions scholar Robert Ellwood pointed out, all these exports are filtered through the American psyche and experience. Zen, Swedenborgianism, Theosophy, or Vedanta in the United States are not what they were in Japan, eighteenth-century England, or nineteenth-century India. American adherents may sometimes use Eastern symbols, but their essential spiritual life is better understood through the American lineage of Emerson, Thoreau, Whitman, the Shakers, and others. "Down-home Zen" is the term Rick Fields used to describe the Zen center in the heart of the Wilshire business district of Los Angeles.

• A Gallup poll released in February 1978 reported that ten million Americans were engaged in some aspect of Eastern religion, nine million in spiritual healing. Those involved in Eastern religions tended to be younger adults, college-educated, living on either of the two coasts, about equally men and women, Catholic and Protestant. "Although [they] are not as likely to be church-goers . . . they are just as likely to say that their religious beliefs are 'very important' in their lives."

Spiritual experience moved beyond the borders of the establishment so quietly that only the poll takers have measured the change. Addressing fellow scholars and historians in the field of religion, Jacob Needleman remarked ironically in 1977 that these ideas and practices are now—"without our prior permission, so to speak—entering the real lives of real people, causing trouble, having real effects on marriages, careers, politics, goals, friendships."

• In one sense, Zukav [Gary Zukav, author of *The Dancing Wu Li Masters*] said, we may be approaching "the end of science." Even as we continue to seek understanding, we are learning to accept the limits of our reductionist methods. Only direct experience can give a sense of this nonlocal universe, this realm of connectedness. Enlarged awareness—as in meditation—may carry us past limits of our logic to more complete knowledge. The end of conventional science may mean "the coming of Western civilization, in its own time and in its own way, into the higher dimensions of human experience."

The Aquarian Conspiracy
Personal and Social Transformation
in Our Time
Marilyn Ferguson
1980, 1970; 468pp.
$10.95
($12.20 postpaid) from:
St. Martin's Press
Attn: Cash Sales
175 5th Ave.
New York, NY 10010
800/221-7945

Illustrations like this one from Besant and Leadbeater's *Thought Forms* (1901) had a strong influence on the rise of modern art. Depicted here is the "thought form" generated by an organist's rendition of a Gounod chorus. "The organist has evidently finished some minutes ago, and the perfected shape floats high in the air, clearly defined and roughly spherical . . ."

past T.S. leaders negates the positive influences of the T.S. on the rise of twentieth-century spirituality. The T.S. was instrumental in introducing many Eastern religious concepts to the West that we now take for granted, including reincarnation and karma. It also brought to the surface more esoteric metaphysical teachings such as those of the chakra system, the bodily aura, and the division of consciousness into several subtle planes—all concepts that have been embraced by New Age groups. In many cases, books published by Theosophical publishers on these subjects were the first of their kind, and many remain in print to this day.

Moreover, while the present T.S. may seem superficially less exciting than its predecessors, it is also a stabler and more reliable source of information about the esoteric streams of spirituality than in days past. The Olcott Library at the T.S. headquarters in Wheaton, which loans books by mail to the public, has arguably the best circulating collection of books on all aspects of metaphysics and the occult in the U.S. The monthly introductory letters that new T.S. members receive for their first two years in the organization are a uniquely succinct introduction to the basics of esotericism. New Age fads come and go; organizations and gurus rise and fall; and still the T.S. remains, calmly offering information and assistance.

I have no idea whether a planetary New Age is really in the offing (and frankly, I doubt it), but if it does arrive I'm sure that the Theosophical Society will deserve a good share of the credit. ∎

BIBLIOGRAPHY

I am indebted to the following sources for much of the material that appears in this article. However, they should in no way be saddled with responsibility for my judgments or interpretations.

Anonymous. (The United Lodge of Theosophists.) 1925. *The Theosophical Movement 1875-1950.* New York: Dutton.

Bruce F. Campbell. 1980. *Ancient Wisdom Revived: A History of the Theosophical Movement.* Berkeley: University of California Press.

Michael Gomes. 1987. *The Dawning of the Theosophical Movement.* Wheaton, Illinois: Quest Books.

Los Angeles County Museum of Art. 1986. *The Spiritual in Art: Abstract Painting 1890-1985.* New York: Abbeville Press.

Steve Richards. 1988. "The Mystery of the Great White Brotherhood," Parts 1 & 2. *The American Theosophist,* March & April, 1988.

Gregory Tillett. 1982. *The Elder Brother: A Biography of Charles Webster Leadbeater.* Boston: Routledge & Kegan Paul.

James Webb. 1974. *The Occult Underground.* La Salle, Illinois: Open Court Press.

The Theosophical Society keeps many classics of occultism in print, and publishes new works as well. It also issues the *Theosophical Research Journal* and *The Quest,* a general-interest magazine. For information contact: Theosophical Society, 1926 N. Main Street, P.O. Box 270, Wheaton, IL 60189; 800/654-9429.

Gnosis

The author of the accompanying brief history of Theosophy and its relatives is editor of his own magazine. It's called ***Gnosis: A Journal of the Western Inner Traditions***, and, so far at least, each issue has been devoted to a different esoteric topic, including "Secret Societies," "Oracles and Channeling," "Heresies and Heretics," and "The Kabbalah." Largely due to editor Kinney's refreshing perspective on the subject, ***Gnosis*** possesses a combination of characters rare in the contemporary literature of spirituality: a high level of scholarship, a "hands on" approach to inner exploration, and a healthy sense of humor and fun. Thus you might find an article about the mystical revelations of science-fiction writer Philip K. Dick side-by-side with an erudite history of Freemasonry, or a tongue-in-cheek look at the Priory of Zion by Robert Anton Wilson juxtaposed with a Jungian interpretation of alchemical symbolism. If you'd like to delve deeper into esoteric Western mystical traditions, tap into the ongoing dialogue in ***Gnosis***. —T.S.

Gnosis
A Journal of the Western Inner Traditions
Jay Kinney, Editor
$15/year
(4 issues) from:
Gnosis
P.O. Box 14217
San Francisco, CA 94114

• Much remains mysterious about the oracular procedure at Delphi, but a few details are known. Before delivering an oracle, the priestess of Apollo, known as the Pythia, underwent a period of fasting and purification, bathing in the Castalian Spring. After rituals of purification, she would enter the inner sanctum of the temple where she chewed laurel leaves from the grove of Apollo. A small fire of laurel leaves and barley was ignited on the altar and the priestess drank from the spring Cassotis, a streamlet of which flowed into the temple. The Pythia then sat upon the sacred Tripod and delivered the oracles which were recorded by priests. Certain statements of ancient writers have been interpreted as indicating that there was a chasm beneath the Tripod from which oracular vapors issued from the Earth, but archaeological evidence has not been found to support this.

CRYSTAL POWER

Welcome to the Stone Age

by Lawrence Jerome

ARE CRYSTALS ALIVE? Can crystals capture your thoughts, your desires, your feelings? Can crystals heal, increase your ESP powers, purify water, and improve the taste of wine? Many people believe that crystals—especially quartz crystals—can do all these things and more, including: facilitate astral projection, improve gas mileage, enhance channeling (communicating with dead or disembodied spirits), energize people and machines, control the earth's electromagnetic field, and serve as the energy sources for the legendary civilizations of Atlantis and Lemuria.

In the last few years, dozens of books have been written about crystals and crystal power, and more are coming out almost daily. Crystals have been featured in many movies and TV shows (most notably in Shirley MacLaine's television movie *Out on a Limb*), and almost every magazine and newspaper—even *Time* magazine—has run articles on crystals. As a result of all this publicity, crystal prices have quadrupled in the last few years, making millionaires of dealers who jumped on the bandwagon early.

Proponents of "crystal power" call attention to its long history, pointing out that crystals were prized by prehistoric shamans (medicine men and women) for their healing powers, and that the Egyptians used crystals in their religious rituals. Some writers even go so far as to state that the pyramids were once faced with or capped by crystals. Unfortunately, so much that is dubious has been written about the history of crystal power that it's now difficult to separate fact from fantasy. Certainly, shamans did use crystals in their healing ceremonies thousands of years ago—given the beauty and symmetry of crystals, it would be surprising if they hadn't—but it's doubtful if shamanistic crystal power was as universally widespread as many modern writers proclaim.

Egyptians, too, probably used crystals in some of their rituals, but if the pyramids once were covered or capped with crystals it seems strange that no writer of the time mentions that fact. Herodotus, for instance, who visited the pyramids around 460 B.C., makes no mention of crystals on or atop the pyramids in his famous book *The History*, although he does describe the "crystal coffins" used by the Ethiopians to display their dead. Museums and books on Egyptian art are strangely devoid of any samples of ceremonial crystals, so it's unlikely that crystals played much of a role in Egyptian society.

Crystal pendants, probably worn as necklaces, have been unearthed from neolithic archaeological sites dating back 80,000 years, and an inscription on a 4,000-year-old Babylonian cylinder seal reads: "A seal of Du-Shi-A (quartz crystal) will extend the possessions of a man and its name is auspicious."[1] While similar evidence of the use of crystals in primitive societies is scarce, the fact that shamans around the world—in Australia, Siberia, Africa, and both South and North America—still use crystals today gives credence to

Even though an incredible amount has been written on crystals in the last couple of years, it's difficult to find anything even remotely objective on the subject. Enter Lawrence Jerome. There's no doubt that Mr. Jerome has a handle on crystals from a physical-science viewpoint: he holds an advanced degree in Materials Science, and has worked for many years as a technical writer and consultant in the field. But he's also qualified to comment on the less scientific side of the coin — the current "crystal power" craze — because he's spent over a year researching the subject for a book. In fact, in the past months Jerome has slept with crystals under his pillow, attached a crystal to his car's carburetor (to see if it improved gas mileage), and interviewed crystal-power proponents from all over the country. If you're intrigued by what he's written here, you might want to check out his book from Prometheus Press (see page 200).
—T.S.

the idea that crystal power is indeed an ancient esoteric art, providing a "bridge to the heavens." Shamans consider crystals to be "living rocks" thrown down by the gods from the firmament, thus linking the human and spirit worlds.

Most shamans use crystals in much the same manner as witches and mystics use crystal balls, literally "seeing" the patient's illness inside the crystal with the aid of spirit helpers believed to live within the stone.[2] One American Indian tribe, the Southwestern Pomos, employs quartz crystals in a very unique healing ceremony: the Pomo "sucking doctor" sucks the pain from her stricken patient, then produces a quartz crystal from her mouth as "proof" the pain has been removed.[3]

Other North American Indian tribes are said to have used crystals as an aid to "spirit dreaming" (astral projection and communicating with the spirits) by placing quartz crystals on their eyelids before they went to sleep (presumably on their backs). And, of course, wizards and magicians were wont to use crystals on their magic wands, while the many jewels adorning the crowns of kings and queens were supposed to increase their "cosmic energy," turning the king "into a living battery of power for the nation."[4]

The idea that crystals are "living" things has gained even more credence today than in the past, now that we know crystals actually "grow" from source chemicals, given the right geological conditions of heat and pressure, or from water seepage and evaporation. Somehow, people have the idea that only "living" things can grow but, of course, storms can "grow," deserts can "grow"—even ideas can "grow." Crystals are no more "alive" than storms, deserts, or ideas—at least in the biological sense of "alive." Today, artificial man-made crystals can be grown in the laboratory under conditions simulating the natural conditions deep within the earth (natural crystals are brought to the surface by the processes of mountain building, uplifting, and erosion). The silicon and germanium crystals that form the substrate for the integrated circuits in our computers, TVs, and microwave ovens are grown by dipping a tiny "seed" crystal in molten silicon or germanium, then slowly drawing up the rotating seed and its growing cylindrical crystal; lengths of 18 inches have been achieved by these methods. But growing such a crystal hardly qualifies as creating a living thing! In fact crystals "grow" simply because their symmetrical molecular arrangement is more "energetically favorable" than the non-crystalline liquid or gaseous state the chemical begins in.

One biochemist, Alexander Cairns-Smith, has even suggested that tiny quartz crystals in clay at the bottom of river beds were the original source of life on the planet (by growing and duplicating, along with attached amino acid molecules).[5] Oddly, the "crystals are alive" proponents fail to point out that diatoms (primitive algae that make up most of the plankton in the world's oceans) grow crystal-like cell walls of silicon dioxide, the same chemical in quartz crystals and glass.

Proponents of crystal power point to the fact that quartz and silicon crystals are used in all of our electronic gadgetry, from radios to digital watches to computers. Quartz crystals are used as "clocks" because they vibrate (resonate) at precise electronic frequencies, and crystal power advocates believe that these crystal resonant frequencies prove crystals can indeed be energized by one's thoughts. However, quartz crystals electronically resonate at extremely fast frequencies (millions of cycles per second), while brain wave patterns have frequencies of only eight to several hundred cycles per second. In addition, the brain generates very tiny electrical pulses, only 50 millivolts at synapses deep within the brain. Away from the scalp, brain waves are undetectable by even

"Crystal Power" Claims versus Scientific Properties of Crystals

	CLAIMS	SCIENCE
Crystal "Energy"	Crystals have an "energy" field extending several feet around the crystal.	Piezoelectricity: mechanical strain (pressure) produces a small electric field within quartz and other asymmetrical crystals.
	Crystals held in the hand produce an "energy" that can be felt as a tingling sensation.	Pyroelectricity: heated quartz and tourmaline crystals produce a small electric field; however, the heat of one's hand is far too low for this. (Tourmaline heated in a fire will attract ashes.)
Vibrations	Crystals can pick up "vibrations" from thought patterns which are then "locked in" the crystal.	Crystal oscillation: thin slices of quartz are used as oscillators in the thousand- and million-cycles-per-second range; brain waves are in the eight-to-several-hundred-cycles-per-second range.
	Prayers, thoughts, and feelings can be transmitted to a crystal several feet away.	Brain wave electrical patterns are barely detectable on the surface of the skull, much less several feet away.
Healing Powers	Crystals, especially quartz, act as "healing centers"; wishes and thoughts of good health are "locked in" the crystal which is then worn by the patient.	Placebos (fake drugs, fake therapy, and even fake surgery) can cause 30% to 50% of patients to improve, feel less pain (placebo effect).
Crystals are "Alive"	Because crystals grow & reproduce themselves, they are alive, perhaps even the source of life itself.	Crystals "grow and reproduce" via chemical energy, not because they are "alive." Diatoms, a type of algae, come closest to "living crystals," but their cell walls are more like glass, not crystal.

the most sensitive instruments so, scientifically speaking, it would be impossible for brain waves (thoughts) to "energize" a crystal.

Crystal power proponents, of course, dismiss this brain wave argument by stating that the crystal energies they use *can't* be measured because they are "bioplasmic" or "orgone" energies, the same energies used in pyramid power, Orgone Energy Accumulators, and Kirlian photography. "And," believers say, "what type of energy we use isn't important: what counts are the positive effects, the many people healed, and the thousands of people who feel better about themselves."

In a sense, they're right; what difference does it make *how* results are achieved, so long as people are freed of pain and disease, so long as they live better, more productive lives? Medical doctors do much the same thing when they give patients and test subjects placebos (fake drugs), knowing that thirty to fifty percent will show improvement and/or feel less pain (the well-known "placebo effect").

The difference between crystal power and the placebo effect is, of course, that medical doctors ascribe the very real benefits to the mind of the patient and not to the placebo itself. Many crystal power proponents, on the other hand, seem to attribute an ever-increasing reality to the crystal lore. For them, the legends of Atlantis and Mu (Lemuria) are not legends, but real historical places where 25-foot-long crystals provided unlimited energy, guiding the future of all mankind, and guided visualizations are actual excursions in which participants bodily enter their favorite crystals to write down their desires on a magic blackboard (for example, "a new Porsche" or "to win the lottery"). Most crystal power practices are undeniably harmless or even helpful, such as using crystals as focal points for meditation and relaxation (much as Zen students use a candle flame), or as placebos in minor healing sessions. A few have proven dangerous, such as the case of the crystal-wielding "mummy cult" that convinced two diabetic brothers in Chicago to give up their insulin, resulting in their deaths.[6]

Perhaps it is the coolness and clarity of crystals that has made them such perfect projection screens for our own externalized imaginings since time immemorial. And perhaps today, in the age of polystyrene and formica, it is especially soothing to meditate upon an object of such undeniable natural beauty. Whatever the reason, the current crystal fever—which shows no sign of abating— is only the latest and perhaps most widespread manifestation of our continuing fascination for these mysterious shards of "frozen light."

[1] Cornelius Hurlbut. 1968. *Minerals and Man.* New York: Random House, p. 228.

[2] Mircea Eliade. 1964. *Shamanism: Archaic Techniques of Ecstasy.* Princeton, New Jersey: Princeton University Press, p.4.

[3] *Pomo Shaman* (a film). 1964. Berkeley, California: University of California Extension Media Center.

[4] Mellie Uyldert. 1981. *The Magic of Precious Stones.* Wellingborough, England: Turnstone Press, p. 53.

[5] Randall & Vicki Baer. 1984. *Window of Light.* San Francisco: Harper & Row, p. xiv.

[6] "Mummy-Health Cult." February 14, 1988. Associated Press.

The Curious Lore of Precious Stones

George Frederick Kunz, who as a consultant to Tiffany's assembled many of the greatest museum collections of precious stones, was probably the all-time world expert on the traditions and folklore surrounding gems. His book, first published in 1913, provides an excellent overview of the subject free of the distortions that have been added by the current crop of New Age "crystal power" books. Lore from every culture is covered, from ancient times to modern. The subtitle says it all: "being a description of their sentiments and folk lore, superstitions, symbolism, mysticism, use in medicine, protection, prevention, religion, and divination. Crystal gazing, birthstones, lucky stones and talismans, astral, zodiacal, and planetary."

— *T.S.*

• The visions seen in crystal gazing were often supposed to be the work of evil spirits, seeking to seduce the souls of men by offering the promise of riches or by according them an unlawful glimpse into the future. Here, as in other magical operations, there was both white and black magic, recourse being had in some cases to good, and in others to evil spirits. As an illustration of the latter practice, a sixteenth century writer relates that in the city of Nuremberg, some time during the year 1530, a "demon" showed to a priest, in a crystal, the vision of a buried treasure. Believing in the truth of this vision, the priest went to the spot indicated, where he found an excavation in the form of a cavern, in the depths of which he could see a chest and a black dog lying alongside it. Eagerly the priest entered the cavern, hoping to possess himself of the treasure, but the top of the excavation caved in and he was crushed to death.

• Rock-crystal is included among the various objects used as fetiches by the Cherokee Indians. This stone is believed to have great power to give aid in hunting and also in divining. One owner of such a crystal kept his magic stone wrapped up in buckskin and hid it in a sacred cave; at stated intervals he would take it out of its repository and "feed" it by rubbing over it the blood of a deer. This goes to prove that the stone, as a fetich, was considered to be a living entity and as such to require nourishment.

Crystal ball, supported by bronze dragon. Japanese.

The Curious Lore of Precious Stones
George F. Kunz
1913, 1971; 420 pp.
$7.95
($9.20 postpaid)
from:
Dover Publications
31 East Second St.
Mineola, NY 11501

What Is a Crystal?

Crystalline solids: There are two types of solids: crystalline and amorphous (glasses). Crystalline solids have regular, repetitive, three-dimensional molecular structures. All minerals and metals are crystalline, composed of thousands of tiny crystals wedged together at "grain boundaries"; only a few minerals form the familiar large "single crystals" such as quartz (silicon dioxide in hexagonal crystals) and diamonds (carbon in tetrahedral crystals). Amorphous or non-crystalline solids are sometimes referred to as "solid liquids" because their molecules are so tangled in the liquid state that they cannot "untangle" and form crystalline solids. Common examples are plastics and glass.

Crystal symmetry: Because crystals grow in regular, repeated, three-dimensional patterns, they can be symmetrical about a point, a line, or a plane.

Crystal systems: All crystals can be classified into one of seven *crystal systems* (see illustrations below).

Crystal growth: Crystals grow at the rate of 16 trillion atoms per hour. Those that we find or buy grow in one of five ways:

Crystallization from molten material: as volcanic magma cools, metals and gem crystals crystallize from the melt.
Sublimation from gas: hot volcanic gases pass over cool surfaces and deposit crystals of sulphur, fluorite, halite, etc.
Evaporation of water solution: in arid, desert regions, water containing dissolved minerals evaporates and leaves crystals known as evaporites; can also occur in underground caves and openings.
Metamorphism: earth shifts and volcanic pressures can change the crystalline structure of existing rocks and minerals.
Weathering: acidic water chemically attacks and changes minerals.

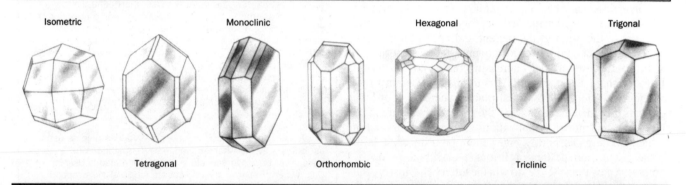

Isometric   Monoclinic   Hexagonal   Trigonal

Tetragonal   Orthorhombic   Triclinic

Modern Uses of Crystals

Many "crystal power" proponents point to the use of crystals in modern technology as proof of their claims. What exactly are the roles of crystals in electronic devices?

Radios, TVs: Thin slices of quartz crystals are used as frequency tuning devices because they oscillate at precise electronic frequencies, ranging from thousands of cycles per second (AM frequencies) to millions of cycles per second (FM and TV frequencies). This crystal oscillation occurs in asymmetric crystals because they are *piezoelectric*: electrical fields cause mechanical strains and deformations; placed in an oscillating circuit, these tuning crystals precisely select the desired frequency, which is then amplified so we can see or hear the broadcast.

Integrated circuits: Specially grown single crystals of silicon or germanium six inches in diameter are sliced into thin wafers; the microscopic circuitry is then etched and deposited on this wafer using photolithography techniques. The fact that the wafers are crystals has little to do with the operation of integrated circuits; the wafer substrates must be single crystals to provide uniform semiconducting properties so that the thousands of tiny transistors manufactured through photolithography will behave in a predictable, uniform manner.

Sonar devices: Piezoelectric crystals not only produce an electrical field when mechanically deformed, but the reverse process also takes place: when an electrical field is applied to such crystals, they contract or expand accordingly — *converse piezoelectricity*. Thus, plates of quartz crystals can be used to detect and transmit underwater sound waves.

Strain gauges: Piezoelectric crystals such as quartz can also be used as strain gauges to detect minute strains and deformations in metals; as the metal deforms, the strain gauge (again, a thin slice of quartz crystal) produces a corresponding electrical current that tells the researcher how much strain and deformation has taken place.

Pressure gauges: Using the same principle as in strain gauges, piezoelectric crystals can also be used as pressure gauges.

Temperature sensors: Some piezoelectric crystals are also *pyroelectric*: changes in temperature produce an electrical field across the crystal, which in turn produces a current which can be used to measure the temperature change. Quartz is somewhat pyroelectric, but tourmaline has the strongest pyroelectrical properties.

Non-electrical uses: Quartz and related minerals are also used in enormous tonnages in the construction and manufacturing industries: as building stone, as aggregate in concrete, as sand in mortar and cement, as a flux in metallurgy, in the manufacture of glass and ceramics, as an abrasive, and as an inert filler.

Inside a New Age Pyramid Scheme

by Jeff Greenwald

The man called Icarus had had a rough week. In February of 1987, eight days before our first conversation, he had attended a strange and secret meeting in a home in Berkeley, California. The house was full of bright-eyed men and women drawn from the East Bay's vast New Age community. These people had come together to play a game—a prosperity game that would "revitalize their relationship to money," exposing all their doubts and aspirations connected with it. The cost of joining in the fun was $1,500; but, if all went as expected, everyone would be able to walk away with a bulging purse of $12,000.

The day after the meeting, Icarus went to the bank, withdrew fifteen $100 bills, placed the money in an unmarked envelope and handed it over to a complete stranger. This sum would have been enough to buy a round-the-world ticket from any discount travel agency; but what Icarus had purchased was a passenger seat in the Airplane Game.

He had no delusions about what he had done. It was a calculated risk, for the Airplane Game was nothing more than a classic, and illegal, pyramid scheme. It worked like this: Icarus and seven other "passengers" formed the bottom level, four "crew" members formed the next, and above them were two "copilots." At the apex of this pyramid sat the "pilot." Once all the passengers were aboard, the pilot would collect the eight $1,500 fares and "pilot out"—$10,500 the richer.

With the pilot gone, the pyramid would split. Each copilot would become the pilot of a separate plane. The crew members would become copilots, while the passengers—like Icarus—would move up one notch, to the level of crew. Each of these two new planes would have to bring aboard eight new passengers so that another split could take place. By the fourth split, Icarus would be a pilot himself.

The mathematics of all this may seem confusing—in

Jeff Greenwald is a San Francisco Bay Area writer who frequently contributes to Image, *the Sunday supplement magazine of the* San Francisco Examiner. *Early in 1987, the* Examiner *gave him $1,500 to buy into the surreptitious "Airplane Game," a technically illegal New Age pyramid scheme that at that time had reached a frenzy of activity in the Bay Area. Using the code name "Right Livelihood," Greenwald entered a milieu that was at once unique to late 1980s San Francisco and as old as the human traits of folly, greed, and eternal optimism. He would like to acknowledge the considerable help of* Image *editor Peggy Northrop in the writing of this story.*
—T.S.

fact, they're damning—but the potential payoff is deliciously seductive. All one has to do is bring in a couple of friends, who bring in a couple of *their* friends, and before you know it there's $12,000 piled up on your futon—and, providing the chain doesn't break, on theirs. No doubt about it—when games like this begin, they move very fast indeed. At the time Icarus was introduced to the game, players were piloting out in a single, giddy evening.

Icarus was a gambling man, and the chances seemed pretty damned good that he'd score handsomely on this eight-to-one bet. So he handed over his money and began what promised to be a no-sweat campaign to draw friends and associates into this lucrative game. After one week he reached the level of pilot and waited, adrenalin pumping, for the moment when he could bail.

And waited . . . and waited. For just at that critical point, as Icarus stood poised to leap into the wild winds of wealth, two major Bay Area newspapers—the *San Francisco Chronicle* and the *Oakland Tribune*— published scathing reports about the Airplane Game and its dog-eat-dog mathematics. Consider: When Icarus and his seven fellow passengers rose to the level of pilot, eight new airplanes were created—each requiring eight new passengers to keep flying. For those 64 passengers to pilot out, 512 more would have to join in. For all *those* new recruits ever to complete the game, another 4,096 people would have to come aboard. Even if this were possible, in order for them to win, 32,768 *more* people would need to invest a total of $49,152,000. Yikes!

Overnight, the game's momentum faltered. "It's been one of the most intense weeks of my life," Icarus confessed when I first spoke to him. He was spending five to six hours a day on the phone, reassuring the fearful passengers on his airplane and bantering the odds with potential players. It had been hard enough when he only had to worry about himself; now he felt responsible for the friends he had brought in as well. The process of filling up the empty seats on his plane was no longer a game; it was a Sisyphean obsession.

After four days of such profound stress that he could neither eat nor sleep, Icarus experienced a breakthrough. He realized that, come what may, there would be no winning for him. If the airplane crashed, he'd go down with his passengers; and even if he piloted out, he would feel obliged to put that money in reserve for the people he had recruited—assuming, of course, that he was interested in keeping his friends.

When I handed him my envelope (stuffed with cash from the *San Francisco Examiner*'s expense kitty), Icarus still felt certain there was enough residual momentum to allow him and the other pilots to recoup their investment. And even though he made no guarantees about potential windfalls, he continued his attempts to bring new players in—standing by the belief that the "process" itself could be genuinely valuable for some people—"people who are just treading water in their lives," he explained. "To play this game, you have to close your eyes and plunge straight ahead.

"You can play the game like a good sportsman," Icarus insisted, "or you can play it in a scheming, predatory way. There's no doubt that, on one level, there's a bunch of intensely greedy people playing a pyramid game. But don't sell it short; this is a moral arena of tremendous force and scope. It's sort of like a war," he reflected with a wry grimace. "It brings out the best and worst in people."

The "war" that Icarus described was fought on two fronts. There were the endless hours on the phone, cajoling and counseling; and there were the group meetings, the sustenance of the game, redolent with its richest ingredients: a pinch of sales seminar, a dash of football huddle, and a heapin' helpin' of New Age encounter group, served atop a bed of word salad. They were a place to show off the lively pace of the game to newcomers, and an opportunity for veteran players to reaffirm to each other—and themselves—their pristine motives.

The first meeting I attended took place one Sunday night in Emeryville, at the home of a pilot code-named Blue Pearl. A tall man with a squarish jaw and melodious Swedish accent, Blue Pearl had joined the game early. He had already piloted out twice, and he was currently pilot on two or three separate planes.

The house filled up rapidly; soon there was barely room to stand. Blue Pearl called for a period of silence, during which I studied the surroundings. Images of Swami Muktananda and the Hindu deities hung on the walls, along with pictures of dolphins and rainbows. The eighty or ninety guests breathed easily, eyes closed.

If I had hoped to see any stigmata of greed or gullibility upon this crowd, I was disappointed. The gathering was largely young, white, and composed mostly of women, the sort of people you might find at a therapists' convention. I spied several blacks, including a Jamaican with dreadlocks and a couple of men in their 60s.

Once the meditation ended, it became clear that there was a very pedestrian kind of tension in the room—a direct result of the newspaper articles that had appeared that weekend. Pyramid games, the stories had pointed out, were illegal, immoral, and just plain stupid, since simple mathematics proved that this merry romp would have to end with hefty losses for the pawns at the bottom.

The math could wait. Were the players breaking the law or not? The answer seemed to be yes. According to the State Penal Code (section 327), promoting any pyramid or "endless chain" game—including chain letters—is a misdemeanor. In fact, the very same Airplane Game had already been busted—with numerous arrests made—in Denver, Dallas, and sunny Santa Barbara.

But the prevailing attitude that evening was that this game fell into a gray area of the law. This was not, after all, a typical pyramid scheme—it was a *growth experience*. Everyone was here voluntarily. The code names? They were part of the mystery, part of the fun. Sure, all new players had to be brought in by friends. How else could it be assured that the game would be played "in integrity"?

To underline this attitude, and to attempt to circumvent what the players felt was an unjust law, Blue Pearl (who, perhaps because of his relative seniority, seemed to have gratuitously adopted the mantle of "first among equals") mandated that a dramatic step be taken. The game would no longer be called the Airplane Game. It was now the Abundance Workshop, undertaken for a "tuition" of $1,500. There

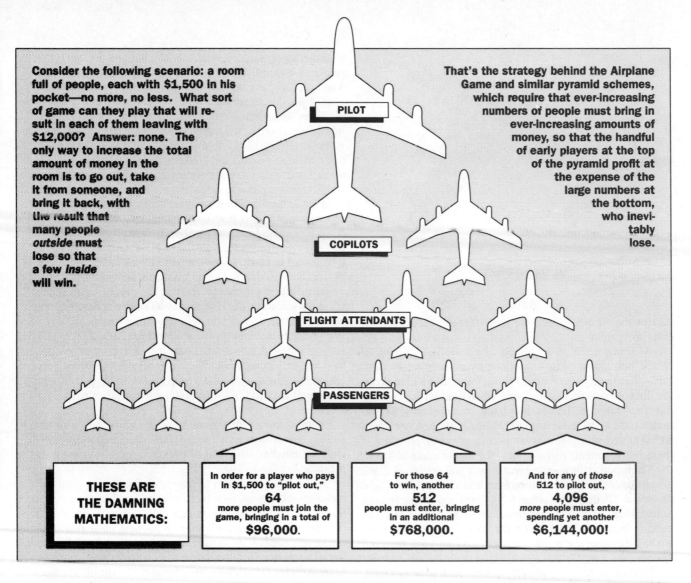

Consider the following scenario: a room full of people, each with $1,500 in his pocket—no more, no less. What sort of game can they play that will result in each of them leaving with $12,000? Answer: none. The only way to increase the total amount of money in the room is to go out, take it from someone, and bring it back, with the result that many people *outside* must lose so that a few *inside* will win.

PILOT

COPILOTS

FLIGHT ATTENDANTS

PASSENGERS

That's the strategy behind the Airplane Game and similar pyramid schemes, which require that ever-increasing numbers of people must bring in ever-increasing amounts of money, so that the handful of early players at the top of the pyramid profit at the expense of the large numbers at the bottom, who inevitably lose.

THESE ARE THE DAMNING MATHEMATICS:

In order for a player who pays in $1,500 to "pilot out," **64** more people must join the game, bringing in a total of **$96,000**.

For those 64 to win, another **512** people must enter, bringing in an additional **$768,000**.

And for any of *those* 512 to pilot out, **4,096** *more* people must enter, spending yet another **$6,144,000!**

---

were no more pilots or copilots, only facilitators and cofacilitators. The crew were now staff; the passengers, students.

"We're talking about prosperity here," Blue Pearl pronounced every syllable. "*Abundance*. This is an Abundance Workshop. If you take a violin workshop, you learn how to play the violin; if you take an Abundance Workshop, you generate abundance." His words had an insidious effect, simultaneously calming and intimidating.

To further affirm the game's enlightened focus, a volunteer began reading aloud from a sheet titled: "The Infinity Process: Abundance and Support Workshop Guidelines." The eleven rules it contained were based on a book called *Finite and Infinite Games*, by James P. Carse,[1] which has become a virtual Bible for the game players. (The book had long ago sold out at the dozen stores I checked. Carse even canceled a lecture tour to the San Francisco Bay Area, concerned that he might be viewed as a promoter of the pyramid scheme itself.)

"The purpose of the infinity process is growth, expansion, and looking at what comes up in you in the process," the

guidelines began. "The workshop is not just about making money." There followed a series of by-laws, read in the gently emphatic style of a self-hypnosis tape. They emphasized the need for "integrity" and the requirement to "receive at least one friend into the process before becoming a facilitator." The final rule was where the infinity process diverged dramatically from lesser pyramids, ensuring that everyone in the room understood that this was a gamble: "This workshop does not guarantee that you will receive money for your participation," intoned the facilitator, "and there are no refunds."

"Why do people freak out when they hear about these things?" demanded a woman called Carousel. "People think nothing of spending thousands of dollars on a courtship that doesn't lead anywhere, or on a fancy car that some advertisement has convinced them they wanted. Why are they so intent on trying to stop us from doing what we want with our money?"

Several days later I attended a second meeting at the North Berkeley home of a woman called Flame. Flame had already reached the top of the pyramid and collected once, but she recycled the money back into the pyramid in the form of "sponsorships"—putting up all or

---

[1]James P. Carse. 1986. *Finite and Infinite Games: A Vision of Life as Play and Possibility*. $4.45 from Ballantine Mail Sales, Dept. TA, 201 E. 50th St., New York, NY 10022.

part of the $1,500 tuition for a new passenger-student to enter the game.

At first glance, this seemed like a selfless sharing of spoils, but sponsorship—practiced by many pilot-facilitators—was hardly a free ride. The recipient still had to do all the dirty work—recruiting—and when (and if) they finally did "facilitate out," half of their booty plus the initial $1,500 loan would go to the sponsor. If Flame had taken her initial $12,000 and sponsored seven people plus herself—and if these reinvestments panned out—she would make $54,000.

The mood at the meeting was upbeat and optimistic. "We always have the choice to come from love or fear," Star Child observed. "People who come from fear keep saying it's not gonna work, or the cops are gonna get us. But some of us are coming from love," she continued, "and the knowledge that we're all connected at the spirit level. What I ask the god/goddess for, I get!"

"Purity of intention is everything," said Soaring Heart. "Where your attention goes," cried Earth and Wind, "your energy flows!"

A warm tide of New Age panegyrics washed through the room, and everyone felt very good about themselves. The hubbub was joined by a bearded, beaming man called Godspeed. "I read another article in the *Oakland Tribune* two days ago," he announced. "It says they're not going to go after us!"

"That's true," Icarus declared. "The police won't get involved unless there are complaints." His words set off a new round of debate, as speculations about this information began to circulate, like wind devils, around the room.

Blue Pearl picked this moment to enter. He surveyed the scene with alarm. "What is this?" he boomed, in the pitiless tone of a Nordic schoolmaster confronted with an unruly kindergarten. The chatter abruptly ceased. After a moment, a woman named Laughing Buddha called out, "Take it easy—everything's fine!"

Blue Pearl pressed his lips tightly together. He stared menacingly at Laughing Buddha and spoke very slowly. "Did I say it wasn't beautiful?" There was dead silence. "*Did I say it wasn't beautiful?*"

"No," she whispered. Someone began to laugh, then another. Blue Pearl smiled thinly, and the meeting slowly resumed its previous joviality. It was a wonderful lesson in primate posturing. Despite a few million years of evolution, a roomful of New Age therapists differs very little from a clan of jungle monkeys.

After the meeting broke up into the smaller workshops, it became clear that the media storm really had damaged the game's "energy flow." It was confusing. On the one hand, there was the go-get-'em spirit of the big meetings; on the other hand were the curt rejections, even ridicule, from friends and neighbors.

People who dwelled upon the math were about as welcome as vegetarians at a moose hunt. It was far too early, the general wisdom held, for numbers to be a problem. It had to be the fault of the press—and the fact that people just weren't trying hard enough, or long enough, with the right people. Worse, the fear that the game was faltering would surely be a self-fulfilling prophecy. You couldn't recruit a friend in good conscience unless the game was working, but the game wouldn't work unless you kept recruiting friends.

Trying to sort out this head-splitting Catch-22 was provoking states of something close to panic in some people. One haggard-looking woman, code-named Artemesia, confessed that, in spite of the group's goal to keep the game "light and playful," she had taken a tranquilizer before the meeting.

"I do think about the money," she admitted. "I'm not sitting here with a smile on my face. The responsibility is endless, and that's fine, but I'm not enjoying it. My integrity is on the line."

Icarus sympathized. The days of cashing in in one or two meetings were over; new recruits were looking at a week at least and maybe much longer. Still, nobody dared say "never."

Jewel, another woman in my group, was more reassuring. The reason for the present slowdown was obvious. Mercury, she explained—the planet that controls transactional encounters, communication, and money—was in retrograde. On March 14 that astronomical cycle would end, and the game would surely pick up. "Until then," Jewel advised Artemesia, "think about technique."

John Porter, supervising deputy attorney general for consumer fraud in San Francisco, eyed the infinity process guidelines and leaned back in his chair. "Based on that sheet of paper," he said, "I can't tell that it's a pyramid. The question is, do you make money by bringing new people into the workshop?"

That, I admitted, was the general idea. "Then it's a pyramid," he said. "The money is delayed through a few levels, but the *inducement* is for you to become a facilitator."

Porter, a sixteen-year veteran of consumer fraud, has a file drawer full of the pyramid schemes that found fertile ground on his beat—from Holiday Magic to Dare to Be Great, Koscot Interplanetary to the Circle of Gold. All of these scams were similar, once you stripped away the veneer, to the Abundance Workshop. All played up a pipe dream of easy, dramatic gain on a small investment; all pretended to serve noble goals; all required an ever-expanding base of new investors. And all had been busted. I asked whether the Abundance Workshop could be far behind.

"Look," Porter sighed, thumbing midnight blue suspenders. "We have two people working here—two. This is not the major thing we're worried about. Right now I'm trying to stop foreclosures on peoples' homes. I won't put that aside to play this intellectual game.

"I think that if people lose money on this, they get what's coming to 'em. What people who play these games are really saying is, 'I don't care if I steal from my neighbor, as long as my neighbor steals from someone else.' Maybe the ultimate guy who suffers the loss will be two or three neighbors away. It's a very self-centered greed. Most people who participate in this," he concluded disgustedly, "have a little larceny in their hearts."

Porter's attitude was echoed by law enforcement agents in Marin, San Francisco, and the East Bay. The game was illegal, no doubt about it. Officers could indeed go into meetings and make arrests. But unless complaints were filed, it would be very difficult to get any convictions. So, at least for the time being, no action would be taken; and it was quite possible that none would be necessary.

For about a month, Rich Michaels, assistant district attorney for consumer fraud in Alameda County, had been receiving calls from people who wanted to know if the Airplane Game was legal or not. He informed them it was not, "which didn't seem to be, in most cases, what they wanted to hear," he said. "But there's been a substantial drop-off in inquiries during the past week and a half," he told me in mid-March. "It could be because the games are slowly dying. They'll fade and die, there's absolutely no question about that—and the people at the bottom will lose their investment. The question is, how far can prosecutors go to protect people who should be in a position to protect themselves? It seems to me that these people are victims only of their own greed."

I did speak with one officer, Detective Patrick Fahy with the fraud division of the San Rafael Police Department, who had actually infiltrated a meeting of the Airplane Game in Marin County. Fahy and Detective Michael Miller had gotten in right in the thick of things but, as reported in the *Oakland Tribune*, they had not made any arrests. I wondered about this.

"They had about 200 people," Fahy explained. "We weren't prepared for it." Fahy compared the level of energy and enthusiasm to something you might encounter at a European soccer game. "If we had attempted to make an arrest," he said, "I think it could have turned out to be a riot, to be perfectly honest."

Regardless of the press, the police, or even common sense, the Abundance Workshop obviously had an uncanny appeal that cut clean through questions of legality. As this story was first going to print in 1987, I heard that the game was beginning to take hold among the professional staff at San Francisco's city jail.

The Airplane Game reportedly surfaced in San Rafael as early as January 1986. A woman who attended one of the first meetings recalled that a Houston yoga instructor named Morning Star emceed the session. "We've spent years dealing with issues of fitness and enlightenment," she crooned. "Now we need to focus on *money* in order to survive." Morning Star then shared a touching story

Extraordinary Popular Delusions and the Madness of Crowds

Most of us are cursed by the tunnel vision of our own brief lives and times. We imagine that the enthusiasms that sweep through popular consciousness have been discovered de novo by our contemporaries. A rare book like Charles Mackay's venerable classic, first published in 1841, can provide a larger, wiser perspective on human nature. Mackay gives spirited histories of mass delusions and popular fads that were bygone in his day—alchemy, the Crusades, witch-hunts—and others that had both historical and current manifestations: "get-rich-quick" schemes, magnetic healing, fortune-telling, haunted houses, personality cults, changing fashions of the hair and beard, and short-lived but popular slang expressions. His subject is inherently fascinating, and his message echoes across the space of nearly a century and a half, all the clearer for the distance: human nature doesn't change. Understand this and see your world anew.   —T.S.

• The tulip-jobbers speculated in the rise and fall of the tulip stocks, and made large profits by buying when prices fell, and selling out when they rose. Many individuals grew suddenly rich. A golden bait hung temptingly out before the people, and one after the other, they rushed to the tulip-marts, like flies around a honey-pot. Every one imagined that the passion for tulips would last for ever, and that the wealthy from every part of the world would send to Holland, and pay whatever prices were asked for them. The riches of Europe would be concentrated on the shores of the Zuyder Zee, and poverty banished from the favoured clime of Holland. Nobles, citizens, farmers, mechanics, seamen, footmen, maid-servants, even chimney sweeps and old-clothes-women, dabbled in tulips. People of all grades converted their property into cash, and invested it in flowers.

• London is peculiarly fertile in this sort of phrases, which spring up suddenly, no one knows in exactly what spot, and pervade the whole population in a few hours, no one knows how. Many years ago the favourite phrase (for, though but a monosyllable, it was a phrase in itself) was Quoz. This odd word took the fancy of the multitude in an extraordinary degree, and very soon acquired an almost boundless meaning. When vulgar wit wished to mark its incredulity, and raise a laugh at the same time, there was no resource so sure as this popular piece of slang. When a man was asked a favour which he did not choose to grant, he marked his sense of the suitor's unparalleled presumption by exclaiming Quoz! When a mischievous urchin wished to annoy a passenger, and create mirth for his comrades, he looked him in the face, and cried out Quoz! and the exclamation never failed in its object. When a disputant was desirous of throwing a doubt upon the veracity of his opponent, and getting summarily rid of an argument which he could not overturn, he uttered the word Quoz, with a contemptuous curl of his lip and an impatient shrug of his shoulders. The universal monosyllable conveyed all his meaning, and not only told his opponent that he lied, but that he erred egregiously if he thought that any one was such a nincompoop as to believe him. Every alehouse resounded with Quoz; every street-corner was noisy with it, and every wall for miles around was chalked with it.

about how she had been struggling to make ends meet since her husband's oil wells went bust.

"Everything that you ever needed to explore about your personal growth in relationship to money will come up in this process," Morning Star reportedly explained. "And don't you *deserve* to have money—just for *being*?"

"Morning Star seemed frantic—almost desperate," the woman remembered. "She kept saying it was the energy, but she was rubbing her hands together like she was playing craps."

According to some, the game came to Marin from Houston, while the East Bay promoters hailed from Denver. I wasn't able to trace that connection. It hardly matters; pyramid games are like bacteria—they can catch on and proliferate anywhere. When the pool of available investors no longer satisfies the pyramid's appetite, someone moves the game on.

Had we already reached that point in the East Bay? After only six weeks—I'd been along for two of them—the game was beginning to wither. Perhaps the East Bay, I suggested to Icarus, was not a very efficient place to run a pyramid game.

"No, it's not!" he laughed. "The commitment to community is too powerful. In the end, the money's going to get redistributed. There are already people reinvesting every dime they've got, because they couldn't live with it if their friends lost money."

"That's nuts—it really *will* go on forever that way," I said.

"But it's true—people who have been in it from the start are still in it. And they're exhausted. I'll bet there are people who would gladly give back all the money and just say, 'Listen, could you redistribute all this properly so I can go home and get some rest?'"

Icarus was too charitable. During one of the later meetings, when it seemed clear that the game was trucking along about as speedily as a salted snail, I asked several groups of people if they would consent to Icarus's plan of shaking hands, redistributing the money, and getting on with their lives.

They looked at me as if I were a Morton Thiokol engineer suggesting that an O-ring might freeze. "Oh, no, no!" they exclaimed impatiently. "We want to *play*!"

I have looked inside myself," Blue Pearl said at the next meeting, "and realized that money represents everything in my being. I have come to see the money as energy. The more I grow with this process, the more I feel comfortable accepting the money."

Several workshops down the line, as more and more students hovered on the brink of dropping out, he expanded this philosophy to include a new definition of greed: "The real greed," he expostulated, "comes when we back out of a process that's helping us expand." Blue Pearl then shared an aspect of his own growth. Previously, he had felt the need to give part of his bounty to charity "as a means to feel good about myself." But by the last meeting I attended, Blue Pearl had evolved so dramatically that he could now unhesitatingly keep all the cash for himself.

Blue Pearl's insipid satori notwithstanding, I could not deny that people were gaining legitimate insights from the often frustrating—but always dynamic—"process." Carousel reflected that the game made her realize that cash was not a "lump" that sat in a bank, but "a liquid thing." "Another aspect," Pennies from Heaven pointed out, "is *time*. It's interesting how I've made time for this, even though I was already overcommitted. I've learned that I *can* free up my time for processes that are important to me."

Even the agonizing process of combing through Rolodexes in the hopes of enrolling friends and acquaintances had lessons to offer. Three women, for example, claimed that the task had increased their self-confidence and taught them how to hold their ground in the face of adversity.

And there were indeed examples of relatively pure altruism. In Marin, where the game was flying at a steady throttle through the lesbian and feminist communities, groups were reshuffled so that women with critical financial needs could cash in almost immediately. In San Francisco, a woman submitted a proposal to start a foundation that would "maximize our intent and capability of truly redistributing money and power in society."

Finally, players at every stage of the pyramid were learning difficult but useful lessons about risk taking, greed, and—most painful of all—the strength of their friendships. "A few people who I thought were my friends," Icarus told me, "look at my involvement in this and say, 'Well, the very fact that you're doing this means you must be a scumbag.' Conversely, I'm discovering who my real friends are—who will stand by me and trust me, even when they choose to disagree with me.

"I haven't piloted out yet," he said, reverting to the less bombastic jargon of the initial game, "and even if I don't make anything I will still say, in absolute good faith, that this was totally worth it. That's why I'm resentful of the media. I read moralistic accounts that leave no room for what I'm going through. You're either a manipulator or a dupe. It's just too simplistic."

It was an article about the pyramid game in the *Oakland Tribune* that first encouraged me to look at the phenomenon and its players in a more equitable light. While lying in bed reading that particular Sunday edition—February 22, 1987—I discovered that I could see right through the page to the Lotto numbers printed on the other side.

Gambling is gambling, and it was clear that those who

had bought into this silly infinity game had done so knowing that there were no guarantees of making money. Okay, so it's a scam, a con game, and a lot of otherwise clever people swallowed it whole. But was it really that much worse than betting on the horses? Or a late-night game of five-card stud? In a vitriolic column in the *San Francisco Chronicle* on February 20, columnist Jon Carroll argued that the latter kind of gambling is all right, since one man's gain doesn't rely on another man's loss. So who pays the winners? Mother Theresa? At least the people at the Abundance Workshop were getting three parties a week for their investment. What does a low-income family, cajoled by flashy advertisements into spending hundreds of dollars a year on Lottery and Lotto tickets, get for theirs?

Granted, the basic premise of the infinity process—that it would generate limitless abundance—is such cloying nonsense that it's tempting to dismiss participants' "growth" as mere self-deception. But then again . . .

One morning, way back in junior high, all the eighth graders were marched into the auditorium to watch a film about the evils of marijuana. I well recall that particular sequence, in which a common myth—that food tastes better when you're high—was firmly debunked: An experimental group of ten adults—five clinically stoned and five completely straight—were given identical hamburgers to eat. The control group ate their burgers laconically, without any special enthusiasm. The pot-heads, on the other hand, raved about how tasty theirs were and complimented the chefs at Jack in the Box.

"So you see," the narrator sneered, "food doesn't really taste better if you're stoned; you just *think* it does."

Twenty years have gone by, and uncounted hamburgers. But I am no closer to deciphering the riddles of subjectivity posed by that narrator's claim. Did those participants in the infinity process *really* get their money's worth, or did they just *think* they did?

By the third meeting in March, it was evident that the recruitment process had, in the words of one facilitator, "ground to a halt."

"Receiving a friend into the process" had become a catch-as-catch-can affair, relying on distant acquaintances or random encounters. Jewel brought a physicist she had met somewhere who resembled Sigmund Freud. He listened through one meeting with apparent interest; at the next he exploded in a frenzy, leaping around the room and handing out numbers tables. "Your heads are buried in the sand!" he cried, beating a hasty retreat.

For most players, the energy of the game had changed: Instead of sitting atop a big fat snowball of abundance, they were being chased downhill by snowballing mathematics. A surprising number of people, however, didn't see things this way. Yes, some inexplicable and malignant force had somehow sabotaged the infinity process, but the forces of good would prevail. Extreme measures were taken. No Strings Attached passed around a couple of baseball caps filled with "prosperity quarters," hypothesizing that a conditioned prejudice against easy money was at the root of the trouble.

A tougher tactic was adopted by one of the Gelt Sisters, who made an impassioned speech about how pedantic and artificial the workshop theme had become. "Back when this was the Airplane, it was *fun!*" she cried. "I don't want to be part of a psychotherapy process! I want money, and I want to play the game!"

"Will you listen to what's happening here?" The Swedish accent was more than familiar. All eyes turned toward a red-faced Blue Pearl. "I mean, *really listen!* Now I've been in this game for a month, and I am *really annoyed*. Did you come here to discuss if this was an airplane or a workshop?"

There was a delightful conflict of interests here. While these confrontations with doubt, greed, and angst actually made the infinity process a workshop of sorts, they did little to encourage first-timers to join up. Several new recruits watched uneasily from behind a sofa, as the student who brought them grinned sheepishly.

Throughout these exchanges, a ruddy-cheeked woman in a red muumuu sat calmly at the rear of the large living room, cradling an enormous drum. Returning to the theme of increasing the positive energy flow, a facilitator reverently introduced this woman as a feminist shaman, who would now offer the group a powerful prosperity chant.

Everyone closed their eyes. The strong beats of the drum pounded through the crowded room, and the medicine woman began to sing:

"One! One! One! One! One! One! One! One!
Love! Love! Love! Love! Love! Love! Love! Love!
One love! One love! One love! One love!
Love one! Love one! Love one! Love one!
God is money in action!"

Kachina chuckled obliquely, holding the telephone out of the reach of her thirteen-month-old daughter. "I don't see any goddess work in this at all," she said. "At every meeting there are new rationalizations; a new level of deception for what is a wounding situation."

Kachina had gotten into the Berkeley game a month ago,

seeing it as an opportunity to pay off her debts. As an artist and teacher, she had persuaded a number of her students to board various airplanes. None of them made any money, nor did any particularly need to experience the so-called process. When I interviewed her, Kachina had been out of the game for weeks—but recriminations were still wreaking havoc on her business and relationships.

"There's this general philosophy among the winners," she said, "that 'the universe handed me this money.' But no: *I* handed it to you." She claimed to have spoken to women who had lost their money and asked friends who had piloted out for help, only to be turned down flat.

Kachina made the point that those people with the most influence—i.e., those with substantial and closely knit communities—were the ones who had risen to the tops of their pyramids the most rapidly. Although some of them had experienced short-term gain, they had risked that entire community to do so. Now that she was out, she realized how easily thinly-disguised greed had subverted the local New Age, meditation, and therapy movements.

"I envy the people who just lost $1,500," she said tersely. "We who have communities suffered from something much greater."

Kachina is an unusually resilient woman. After her airplane crashed, she doggedly pursued the goal that had

made the game seem attractive in the first place: freeing herself financially in order to open up an art gallery. This time, she did it without the infinity process pretense. She visited her contacts, spelled out her goals, and within a week had the capital she was after.

"I found out that I could raise $6,000 for something I really believed in," she said, "just by asking for it directly.

"I think those big group workshops are a lot like revivalist meetings," Kachina reflected. "Lots of forced good feeling and lots of contact. They're good for people who don't have a lot of engagement in their lives. What would be perfect," she concluded dryly, "would be to run them as a singles group."

By the ides of March, nearly all the East Bay games seemed to be stalled at about the same level: with three to seven open spots (out of eight) at the student level. A meeting at Icarus's house one rainy Thursday night drew only a handful of people. It was agreed that Sunday would tell. "By then," a stately black woman named Sapphire reminded us, "Mercury will be out of retrograde." Icarus regarded her with a wan smile. "You wouldn't believe how many people are depending on that," he said.

The last meeting I attended, held in Richmond, was the most energetic and positive of all. An air of almost manic enthusiasm pervaded the room. Groups from Marin and San Francisco were represented, as well as Berkeley and the East Bay. Faerie Dust read the ubiquitous guidelines, and introductions were made. There were a few peppy testimonies, followed by some words of wisdom from our self-appointed guru, Blue Pearl.

"In an infinite play," he postulated, "the word *need* doesn't exist. It's a continuous play, where *needs* have no place." Few seemed to understand what he was talking about, but those who did applauded loudly.

By now, the buzzword "infinity" had all the appeal of a life sentence. I could see it everywhere: the *need* to get things going, to fly or die. The whole scene seemed more and more like a meeting of the Flat Earth Society, where everyone elects to spend an evening defending an amusing lie.

As soon as we broke up into workshops, Icarus moved our little group outside into the cold night air. There he made an announcement: He had decided to quit the game, tally his losses, and hand his facilitatorship over to whomever was next in line. Although nobody actually yelled "Quitter!" a few pairs of eyes flashed with surprise and irritation.

"I got into the game to make money," Icarus stated. "I stayed in the game to learn how to lose money. I'm no longer going to learn anything new about this process, or how it works as a metaphor. What I want to find out now is this: If I can manage to get a lot of people to rally around the most ridiculous notion in the world, what might happen if I put that same effort and belief into my poetry?"

It took the rest of the evening to work out the splits and new positions on paper. As a happy consequence of Icarus's resignation, I moved up one level—from student to staff. The new Abundance Workshop I now belonged to had eight empty seats to fill. There were no likely prospects.

The night sky was full of old, old stars. Millions of miles away, little Mercury winked against the roaring sun. ∎

ARMCHAIR SHAMANISM
A YANKEE WAY OF KNOWLEDGE

by Chas Clifton
Illustrated by Mark Fisher

> "*Each of the twelve women turned and transformed into her animal spirit counterpart. Standing before me were the luminous forms of many creatures: A polar bear, erect on her hind legs, a deer, an antelope, a horse, an eagle, a wolf, a human-size badger, a red squirrel, a coyote, a mink, and a huge lynx tracking my eyes with hers.*
>
> "*In the center of these glowing forms was the largest creature of all, less luminous, but there was more light around her if possible. She was a jaguar form of human proportions, and her face looked half jaguar and half monkey. Her eyes were large and round, her huge brows arched, and her nostrils flared. The ears were enlarged and jutting out like a monkey's. A coiled serpent held a tuft of Quetzalcoatl plumes atop her head. I thought she might be the jaguar-monkey goddess.*"
>
> "*This is a true story. Some of the names and places in this book have been changed to protect the privacy of those involved.*"
>
> —Lynn Andrews, *Star Woman*

The shamanic model of spiritual experience had virtually vanished from the Western religious world by the beginning of this century. But once again "shamans" have returned to guide late-twentieth century spiritual seekers—and to trick them. Unlike those of times past, today's shamans offer a peculiarly vicarious experience in the form of books and weekend workshops.

This new trend began for many thousands of people when they picked up their first book by Carlos Castaneda in the early 1970s. Castaneda was a graduate student of anthropology at the University of California, Los Angeles, in the 1960s. He started out studying hallucinogenic plants, but Castaneda claims that due to an encounter with Yaqui Indian sorcerer "don Juan," he became heir to a magical tradition that stretches back five hundred years to pre-conquest Mexico. In the process of writing his doctoral dissertation, Castaneda created—or revived—a literary genre, the "magical autobiography," which is the only

While writing this piece, Chas Clifton simultaneously put the finishing touches on his Master's dissertation in Religious Studies at the University of Colorado, where he specialized in new religious movements and native American religions. Clifton first explored the subject of shamanic fiction in Iron Mountain, *a journal of magical religious traditions of which he is a former editor, and further developed the theme in an article in* Gnosis #2 (see p. 30). *Aside from his interest in religion, Clifton leads a double life as an outdoor expert, working as the outdoor editor of the* Cañon City (Colorado) Daily Record, *and contributing to magazines like* Western Outdoors, Outdoor Journal, *and* High Country News.
—T.S.

contact most modern-day seekers have with the shaman's world. Unexpectedly, the book version of Castaneda's dissertation, *The Teachings of Don Juan: A Yaqui Way of Knowledge,* became an overnight best seller. As of this writing, there have been seven sequels.

Castaneda is a reclusive figure who has granted few interviews and rarely appeared in public. (I attended one of his only lectures in January 1970 at Reed College in Portland, Oregon, where I was a freshman. Like my classmates, I was struck by Castaneda's "ordinariness"— in his conservative blue suit, he looked like one of my high school Spanish teachers. We took this as proof of his validity, since we had expected a shaman dressed in beads and feathers.) Unlike Castaneda, however, other "magical autobiographers" have made extensive use of the New Age lecture circuit. Today, "shamanism" is in danger of becoming another New Age buzzword, and, like "channeling" and "crystal healing," it has become the subject of weekend workshops in Boulder, Santa Barbara, and other concentrated locales for esoteric experience.

The book-shamans of modern North America are like traditional shamans in one respect: they provide entertainment. From the old-time Eskimo audience watching the shaman's trance performance, his stage-magic tricks, and his report of doings in the Otherworld to the people who attend Afro-Caribbean or Brazilian ceremonies (Voudou, Candomble, Santeria, Umbanda da naçao) for the drumming, singing, and the dances of the god-ridden mediums, direct human contact with the Otherworld has entertainment value. The difference is this: a traditional shaman is a healer, a specialist in the origins of disease within a given society. Among today's literary shamans of the hotel ballroom lecture circuit, the therapeutic function is mostly missing. "Shamanism" becomes just another self-improvement course, little more than psychic aerobics. This narcissistic "neoshamanism" is, as Lynn *"Medicine Woman"* Andrews describes it, "an act of power, not in the sense of controlling or manipulating, but in the sense of realizing your dreams." You might hear much the same language at a Mary Kaye Cosmetics sales rally. (Do real shamans drive pink Cadillacs?)

The invention of the "magical autobiography" in the Western world can be credited to Lucius Apuleius, author of *The Golden Ass, or The Transformation of Lucius.* Lucius, a happy-go-lucky young Roman traveling in second-century Greece, gets mixed up in wine, women, and sorcery. He is transformed into a donkey and in that form has more adventures, such as being captured by a band of outlaws and being forced to haul their loot. The book's middle portion consists of tales the donkey hears told by the bandits and other persons, including the well-known legend of Cupid and Psyche. After various changes of both owner and fortune, Lucius the ass invokes the goddess Isis by the ocean's edge and is rewarded with an opportunity to reverse the spell. A human once again, he becomes a priest in Isis' temple.

Unlike modern magical autobiographers, Lucius frankly admits his story is just that—a story. But *The Golden*

CARLOS CASTANEDA AND LYNN ANDREWS
A BIBLIOGRAPHY

Carlos Castaneda. 1968. *The Teachings of Don Juan: A Yaqui Way of Knowledge.* New York: Simon and Schuster. $4.95.

—. 1971. *A Separate Reality: Further Conversations with Don Juan.* New York: Simon and Schuster. $4.95.

—. 1972. *Journey to Ixtlan: The Lessons of Don Juan.* New York: Simon and Schuster. $4.95.

—. 1974. *Tales of Power.* New York: Simon and Schuster. $4.95.

—. 1977. *The Second Ring of Power.* New York: Simon and Schuster. $4.95.

—. 1981. *The Eagle's Gift.* New York: Simon and Schuster. $4.95.

—. 1984. *The Fire from Within.* New York: Simon and Schuster. $4.95.

—. 1987. *The Power of Silence: Further Lessons of Don Juan.* New York: Simon and Schuster. $17.95.

All books above are available from Simon and

Schuster, Attn: Mail Order Sales, 200 Old Tappan Rd., Old Tappan, NJ 07675; 800/ 223-2336. Add $2 for shipping.

Lynn V. Andrews. 1981. *Medicine Woman.* New York: Harper and Row. $7.95.

—. 1984. *Flight of the Seventh Moon: The Teaching of the Shields.* New York: Harper and Row. $7.95.

—. 1985. *Jaguar Woman: And the Wisdom of the Butterfly Tree.* New York: Harper and Row. $7.95.

—. 1986. *Star Woman.* New York: Warner. $9.95.

—. 1987. *Crystal Woman: The Sisters of the Dreamtime.* New York: Warner. $16.95.

The first three Lynn Andrews titles may be ordered from J.P. Lippincott, Rt. 3, Box 20B, Hagerstown, MD 21740; 800/638-3030. Add $1.50 for shipping. The last two are available from Warner Books, P.O. Box 690, New York, NY 10019; 212/ 484-2900. Add $1 for shipping.

Ass is also a religious novel, and the conversion experience at the end is told with a sincerity that contrasts with the bawdy and farcical episodes preceding it. Lucius was indeed an initiated priest of Isis as well as a student of Platonic philosophy, during a time when "exotic" Near Eastern religions like those of Isis, Mithras, Dionysius, and Jesus of Nazareth were spreading into the Roman Empire. Some translators of his work, such as Robert Graves, think he wove incidents of his own youth together with traditional stories to create *The Golden Ass*.

To be changed into an animal is one kind of "out-of-body" experience, although it might be that Lucius was also saying that the "donkey" symbolized the prisoner of material needs and desires. In his out-of-body state, Lucius has a true ecstatic experience: his conversion to the goddess, who tells him, "Under my protection you will be happy and famous, and when at the destined end of your life you descend to the land of ghosts, there too in the subterrene hemisphere you shall have frequent occasion to adore me."[1]

The magical autobiography, with its message of transformation, was never quite the same after Lucius Apuleius, thanks to eighteen centuries of Christian orthodoxy. In the hands of writers like Castaneda and Lynn Andrews (author of *Medicine Woman, Star Woman, Crystal Woman*, etc.), however, it is enjoying a surge in popularity. Some things are still the same: readers enjoy adventure, humor, sex, and psychic powers. Other things are different: thanks to five centuries of print-based culture, our standards about what is "fact" and what is "fiction" are actually less sophisticated than those of the reading audience of 1,800 years ago.

Like Lucius Apuleius, Castaneda presents himself as an innocent seeker making an ass of himself while pursuing esoteric wisdom. He revived the tradition of *The Golden Ass*: a spiritual journey with exotic places, mystic initiations, and—like Lucius' vision of Isis—a great deal that the reader must take on faith. Castaneda's readers, however, had a decidedly different set of expectations. Castaneda was an anthropologist; the books were presented as scientific fact. Editors of anthropology texts for undergraduates published excerpts to show the students just how exciting a career in anthropology could be! His first book was hailed as "a sacred text" preparing the reader "to witness, to accept without really understanding."[2]

Unlike the Romans, who didn't mind mixing religious teaching with a tall tale, we are overwhelmed with printed information. We expect our advertising to be labeled as such and our newspaper to keep its editorials on the editorial page. And so we can be suckers for authors (and publishers) who disguise one thing as another. The argument that it is acceptable to mix "true teaching" with fiction is heretical in the Information Age, especially when it comes packaged as "nonfiction" accompanied by the

---

[1]Lucius Apuleius. 1951. *The Golden Ass*, translated by Robert Graves. New York: Farrar, Straus & Giroux, p. 266.

[2]Professor Stan Wilk, writing in the official journal of the American Anthropological Association, as quoted in de Mille's *The Don Juan Papers*, p.20.

Castaneda's Journey and The Don Juan Papers

Richard de Mille is obviously an admirer of Carlos Castaneda's don Juan books—in some ways, the ultimate fan. But his meticulous study of Castaneda's work has led de Mille to an inescapable conclusion: the don Juan books are works of fiction, not fact.

Many anthropologists have reached the same conclusion, based on the inconsistencies of don Juan's brand of shamanism and known Yaqui Indian practices. But de Mille has gone farther, showing that the books in the series contradict one another in details of time, location, sequence, and description of events. He has also located the apparent literary sources of many of the ideas and episodes that Castaneda describes, and, in true don Juan "warrior" fashion, he has "stalked" the mysterious and publicity-shy author, locating and interviewing Castaneda's ex-wife, professors, and fellow students, and filling in the missing biography we readers have always wondered about.

Castaneda's Journey *is written solely by de Mille, while **The Don Juan Papers** is an anthology containing the investigations and expert opinions of over twenty authors. It all adds up to an entertaining unmasking of another side of the multifaceted literary shaman: Carlos the Trickster.* — *T.S.*

• In spending many hours with Castaneda over a matter of weeks, *Time* correspondent Sandra Burton found him attractive, helpful and convincing—up to a point . . . As the talks continued, Castaneda offered several versions of his life, which kept changing as Burton presented him with the fact that much of his information did not check out . . .
—The Don Juan Papers

• A friend of mine asked, "Why are you writing a book about somebody you think is a liar?" That stopped me. Why was I? Shouldn't I simply dismiss Castaneda as Weston La Barre had dismissed him? My friend supplied the answer. Castaneda wasn't a common con man, he lied to bring us the truth. His stories are packed with truth, though they are not true stories, which he says they are. This is not your familiar literary allegorist painlessly instructing his readers in philosophy. Nor is it your fearless trustworthy ethnographer returned full of anecdotes from the forests of Ecuador. This is a sham-man bearing gifts, an ambiguous spellbinder dealing simultaneously in contrary commodities—wisdom and deception. That's unusual. It may be important. And it needs straightening out.
—Castaneda's Journey

Castaneda's Journey
The Power and the Allegory
Richard de Mille
1976, 1978; 205 pp.
OUT OF PRINT
Capra Press
Santa Barbara, CA

The Don Juan Papers
Further Castaneda Controversies
Richard de Mille, Editor
1980; 520 pp.
$19.95
($21.22 postpaid) from:
Ross-Erikson
223 Via Sevilla
Santa Barbara, CA 93109
805/966-2060

Andrews writes novels that bear the same relationship to traditional shamanism that Harlequin Romances bear to a solid, enduring marriage.

The late 1970s and early 1980s saw increased attention paid by American women to the idea that there might be a particularly feminine form of spirituality. Women's groups formed in the more liberal Christian denominations; Catholic nuns denounced the male-dominated church hierarchy and many left their former orders. Female academics produced the *Journal of Feminist Studies in Religion* and denounced the male-dominated initiatory experience of graduate school. Joan McIntyre's observation is typical: "When women come together there is . . . a strong sense of an ancient knowledge that we have done all this before; that we have sat together over aeons of time midwifing each other into greater spiritual awareness."[4]

To meet this hunger came the "shaman of Beverly Hills," Lynn Andrews. More accessible than Castaneda, ready to leap into lecturing and producing tape cassettes, Andrews writes novels that bear the same relationship to traditional shamanism that Harlequin Romances bear to a solid, enduring marriage. Instead of the poor but honorable working girl who marries the moody lord or rising businessman, they feature Lynn the butterfly shaman and her magic carpet of credit cards. She books flights to one exotic locale after another—northern Canada, the Guatemalan jungle, the Australian outback. No sooner does she arrive than she discovers women possessing ancient secrets who scarcely meet the blonde stranger before they fall all over themselves offering her one dizzying initiation after another.

Not stopping to synthesize and apply these dazzling spiritual pyrotechnics, Andrews bats out another book and—we are told—dials her travel agent for another trip to Fantasy Island. She often presents herself as baffled by what she hears. One of her supposed teachers, Zoila the Mayan, rattles off the confusing cosmology of her personal altar, leaving Andrews to say, "Her words had not all made sense to me and had not all followed one another coherently."[5]

This is only a pseudoproblem, however, since Andrews' devoted readers are people who have decided that intellectual structures are not to be trusted. They want to be dazzled, to be told they are special, and if they themselves cannot flit from one shaman to another and be the first white woman to receive the (fill in the blank) tribe's secret teachings, they can relax knowing that she is doing it. And if they can afford to travel to exotic Beverly Hills, they can even book a counseling session : $150 per hour.[6]

One of the most interesting essays on Castaneda in *The Don Juan Papers* is an ecology-based critique by Hans Sebald, a professor of sociology at Arizona State University in Tempe. Titled "Roasting Rabbits in Tularemia or The Lion, the Witch and the Horned Toad," it uses a naturalist's arguments to prove how unlikely it is that Castaneda could have been in the Mexican desert where and when he says. Even as Carlos never gets thirsty in the Sonoran desert during long summer days, so Lynn Andrews is never bitten by a mosquito or blackfly in the Manitoba bush country.

Like Castaneda, Andrews' home base is Los Angeles —not the UCLA anthropology department, but a glittery

appropriate Library of Congress cataloging data, as occurs with both Castaneda's and Andrews' books. (Librarians' journals reveal the surprising extent to which book cataloging is determined by editorial gatekeeping and politics.)

Academia is a jealous place; suspicion that Castaneda was a novelist led to a reaction against him, notably the publication of two books detailing inconsistencies and impossibilities in his works: Richard de Mille's *Castaneda's Journey* and an anthology edited by de Mille, *The Don Juan Papers* (see review, previous page). De Mille accuses Castaneda of changing the tone of his adventures to fit the perceived desires of his readers. As psychedelic drugs became less trendy, he suggests, Castaneda "suddenly discovered a wealth of neglected drugless techniques in some piles of old field notes . . . *Tales of Power* and *The Second Ring of Power* reflected later popular trends toward occultism and feminism."[3]

L.A. of designer clothes and celebrity name-dropping. She presents herself as an art dealer, which leads the astute reader to some curious conclusions. Art dealers—good ones, at least—normally are obsessively concerned with the origins and dating of what they sell: "provenance," they call it. Andrews, who has the annoying habit in *Medicine Woman*, her first book, of constantly dropping the names of just which trendy restaurant or gallery she visited last, is started on the quest for *her* Indian shaman-teacher by a seemingly paranormal vision of an Indian wedding basket. This is a southwestern American artifact; she goes looking for it in Manitoba, but what the heck, this is only the beginning.

Her teacher will turn out to be a Cree woman named Agnes Whistling Elk, who lives on an unspecified Indian reserve. She doesn't travel much, but she sprinkles her conversation with terms like the Hopi-language "katchina." Maybe just Pan-Indianism at work. She has a "thick accent," but speaks like an educated person. That is no marvel; what is marvelous is her ability in later books to turn up on other continents—just when Lynn is arriving there herself.

That initial vision of the basket shakes Andrews up considerably, but she recovers after visiting the nearest Elizabeth Arden salon. Later, at a Bel Air dinner party amid rich oilmen and bankers, she is encouraged on her quest by the controversial Cheyenne author Hyemeyohsts Storm.

"He was definitely Dakota or Montana," Andrews writes offhandedly. No wonder her Crees speak Hopi: "provenance" is not this dealer's strong point. (Later, she will visit modern Mayans who teach her about Aztec deities—only a few hundred miles, three centuries, and a different culture away.)

Storm sends her off to that Manitoba reserve, where she asks herself the question all seekers ask: "I wondered if I had the right clothing. I was wearing Sasson jeans, boots, and a khaki jacket from Kerr's."[7]

Of course, during her apprenticeship with Agnes (and with Ruby Plenty Chiefs, who neatly parallels Castaneda's Don Genaro as the more enigmatic of a pair of teachers), she runs afoul of a rival sorcerer. He is Red Dog, a white man living on the reserve, and he has two Indian apprentices. One night they attack her.

Do they battle on the astral plane? Do they slip funny herbs into her soup? No, they are far craftier. Lynn returns to the cabin from a bugless outing and finds: "My Gucci bag lay open on the floor with the lining ripped out. Credit cards and money were strewn everywhere. Even my makeup case was missing."

Eventually Red Dog is defeated. And defeated. And defeated. In every book Red Dog comes back and is de-feated. I think he must be hopelessly in love; there can be no other explanation. Unless, of course, the whole thing is made up.

Discussing Castaneda, Richard de Mille distinguishes between two types of truth, "validity" and "authenticity." Validity is good enough for the true believers and for broad-spectrum "spiritual" magazines like *New Age,* where a reviewer wrote of Castaneda, "He may be lying, but what he says is true." The true believer who has bought all the books, listened to the tapes, and forked out more money for a lecture from the Great White Shaman might ponder de Mille's thought that "An observer who cannot be trusted to tell us where and how he got his information cannot be trusted to preserve the integrity of that information either."

After I reviewed some of Andrews' and Castaneda's newest works in *Gnosis* magazine and discussed their fictional elements, in came a predictable letter from a reader who asked, "Wouldn't it be wiser to examine the specific effects a particular piece of literature has on the reader's consciousness than whether it is fantasy or reality? . . . Whatever anyone can imagine is considered to be as real as rain. Therefore, even if Castaneda and Andrews produced 'obvious fantasies,' they are still in keeping with shamanic realities." And so on. ☞

Lynn Andrews uses Tibetan bells to administer "spiritual counseling" in her Beverly Hills home. Cost: $150 per hour.

[3] De Mille, *The Don Juan Papers*, p. 17.

[4] Joan McIntyre. "Women Remembering." *Gnosis,* Spring 1988, pp. 21-22. (See review, p. 30.)

[5] *Jaguar Woman*, p. 120.

[6] Beth Ann Krier. "The Shaman of Beverly Hills." *Los Angeles Times*, January 6, 1988.

[7] *Medicine Woman*, p. 21.

T. LOBSANG RAMPA
THE "LAMA" FROM LONDON

In 1956 the book *The Third Eye* appeared, purporting to be the autobiography of a Tibetan Lama named Tuesday Lobsang Rampa. Its pages describe many wonders, including the opening of Rampa's "third eye" in a Tibetan monastery on his eighth birthday. Using a steel instrument with pointed teeth at one end, one of the lamas bored a hole through the flesh and bone of the young boy's forehead. A "very hard, very clean sliver of wood" was inserted into the hole, and "there was a blinding flash." Immediately, Rampa had the power to see auras. "You are now one of us, Lobsang," one of the lamas told him. "For the rest of your life you will see people as they are and not as they pretend to be."

The Third Eye describes Rampa's many psychic powers (astral projection, clairvoyance, levitation, invisibility, past-life recall) and adventures, including encounters with abominable snowmen. Later volumes recount a stint as a medical officer in the Chinese army during World War II, and imprisonment in Japanese and Russian prison camps. *The Third Eye* did remarkably well, selling 300,000 copies in a little over a year. Since then, it has gone through numerous editions, including sixteen printings in the Ballantine paperback version alone. At least eighteen sequels have appeared, including *Doctor from Lhasa, The Cave of the Ancients,* and *My Visit to Venus.* Even his "wife" has gotten into the act, and in recent years books have appeared written by "Mama San Ra'ab Rampa."

There's only one problem: T. Lobsang Rampa never existed. In 1957, a number of experts on Tibet who suspected a hoax hired a private investigator to track down the mysterious lama. Sure enough, it turned out that the author was not a Tibetan at all, but an Englishman, Cyril Henry Hoskin, the son of a Devon plumber. Hoskin, a writer who had never visited the Orient, had brought two manuscripts to British literary agent Cyrus Brooks: one was a history of women's corsets, the other a fanciful story of a Tibetan lama. Brooks encouraged him to work on the latter, and *The Third Eye* was born. The hoax's exposure caused a scandal in both Europe and the U.S. *Time* magazine ran the full story in its February 16, 1958 issue. Hoskin, about to publish a sequel (*Doctor from Lhasa*) and worried about the negative publicity, maintained that his story was true. According to him, Rampa's spirit had "possessed" the body of Hoskin, permanently displacing the former personality.

Readers of the series of books Hoskin wrote, which read more like occult adventure stories than metaphysical teachings, do not seem overly concerned by their questionable authenticity, if indeed they are aware of it. Hoskin died in 1981, but Rampa will no doubt be around for years to come.   —*T.S.*

SHIRLEY MACLAINE
OUT ON A LIMB OR OFF ON A WHIM?

In the tradition of T. Lobsang Rampa, Carlos Castaneda, and Lynn Andrews, Shirley MacLaine has become the most popular "magical autobiographer" of all, selling over eight million copies of her books. Shirley employs a bestselling formula that takes the reader on a vicarious trip into a world of past lives, channeled entities, and aliens from UFOs coupled with jet-set romances, movie stardom, and adventure in exotic places.

In *Out on a Limb,* Shirley learns of her true mission while in the Andes with David, her occult tutor. David's girlfriend Mayan, an alien being from the Pleiades, has told him that Shirley must use her fame to spread the word about spiritual enlightenment to the world. In the TV-movie version of the book, we witness David performing the miracle that convinces Shirley of his authenticity: he drives his truck on a lonely Peruvian mountain road at night with his eyes closed, while Shirley, in the passenger's seat, looks on in amazed horror. (Shirley says she omitted this scene from the book because her readers weren't ready for it.)

Dancing in the Light includes a grocery-list genealogy of Shirley's past lives, remembered with the help of acupuncture, including the obligatory priestess of Atlantis, a Tibetan Buddhist monk, an Indian elephant herder, and a voodoo practitioner. In a scene reminiscent of T. Lobsang Rampa's *The Third Eye,* Shirley describes her life as a young Incan boy initiated into the priesthood by having a hole chiseled into his forehead. She also tells of her tearful reunion with channel J.Z. Knight's "Ramtha," a 35,000-year-old entity who was Shirley's beloved brother in an Atlantean incarnation. (But these days, according to Craig Lee in the *L.A. Weekly,* MacLaine has denounced Ramtha.)

Like other magical autobiographies, Shirley's books cannot be trusted as factual accounts. She freely admits that, for example, "David" is not a real person, but a composite of "four spiritual men" who all had extraterrestrial friends. (One of these, Charles Hurtado Silva, who claims to have been Shirley's guide in Peru, pleaded guilty to fourth-degree sexual misconduct in 1987 when two female devotees charged he forced them to sleep with him. He's now in the process of suing MacLaine for using his writing in her book.) "Gerry," her surreptitious "British" politician lover in *Out on a Limb,* also turns out to be a composite of two men (thought to be the Australian Andrew Peacock and the assassinated Swedish prime minister, Olof Palme). In *It's All in the Playing,* Gerry "dies" in a car crash, leading writer Martin Gardner to wonder how a composite character can die "except in fiction." And as screenwriter Ring Lardner, Jr., wrote in the Fall 1986 *Free Inquiry,* Shirley's earlier, premystical books contain improbable events that, when considered cumulatively, suggest that she is not above "editing the facts a bit to improve the story."

Like other armchair shamans, Shirley has hit the ballroom lecture circuit, charging $300 a head for an afternoon of cosmic advice. She is at least as entertaining a storyteller as other modern magical autobiographers, but shares their common flaw: her books are long on "story" and short on "fact."   —*T.S.*

This attitude may be all right as long as we restrict shamanism to weekend consciousness workshops. It may be all right as regards the entertainment function of shamanism. The "neoshamanism" of Castaneda, Andrews, and their imitators has an important failing, however: it is rarely practiced for the benefit of a community except at second-hand through books. Even if we avoid the academic reductionists who claim that shamanism is the artistic outlet of recovering psychotics, we must remember that traditional shamans are very involved with their communities. I will never forget a remark made to my wife and me in 1978 by Janet Farrar, a well-known English witch who had lived in Ireland the past decade or more. As we strolled down a road near her home in County Wexford, she discussed the local people's reaction to her and her husband Stewart's arrival. Once they are over the initial shock, she said, they accept you. And then, she continued, they expect results: "If they come to you with piles, you had better know where the 'hemorrhoid-wort' grows!" It is a considerable step from entertaining a reader to being a trustworthy guide to the magical healer's world.

Consumers of magical autobiography and weekend workshops often come expecting "easy access" to ancient wisdom. After all, is not Lynn Andrews hardly off the plane to some exotic locale before traditional medicine people are running to reveal their secrets to her? Earnest seekers who would be enraged at the idea of a freeway through Yellowstone Park expect a four-lane highway to shamanic knowledge. When a more classic tale of experience emerges, they do not even recognize it. A reviewer for *Harvest*, a New England journal of modern Neo-Paganism, was baffled by *Birth of a Modern Shaman*, the biography of Tayja Wiger. Wiger, an Indian, illustrates the classic type of the "wounded healer" who must hit bottom (alcoholism, prostitution, mental illness, hysterical blindness) before she herself can be a healer. She is cured of her blindness at a metaphysical Christian healing service and slowly rebuilds her life, first in a group home and later on her own. Ordained as a Spiritualist minister, she becomes a healer herself. But, finding no astral battles with rival sorcerers and no locales more exotic than Minnesota, the reviewer pronounced the book "murky" and said that "seekers of real mysteries are likely to feel that they've just left a banquet where all the wrong food was served." Perhaps that is because the food was not the usual Coke and pizza to which the seekers are accustomed.

This is an era of special-interest magazines and the shamanism wave has spawned one also, via some people connected with the University of California, Berkeley, anthropology department. *Shaman's Drum*, a quarterly on newsstands everywhere, bills itself as *A Journal of Experiential Shamanism*. One of its major advisors is Michael Harner, an anthropologist who got tired of being on the outside and started teaching shamanism as a practical art, noting rightly that "in our society there hasn't been the opportunity for long-term intensive training in shamanism."[8] *Shaman's Drum* mixes serious researchers with the occasional wide-eyed seeker, at times producing some unintentional humor. A would-be shaman who goes to visit

the Peruvian curandero (healer) Don Eduardo Calderón reports, "The next day I heard that during the ritual, don Eduardo had been hit by some dark, confounding force. He experienced sharp pains in his chest and down his left arm during this episode. A woman healer . . . came to his aid, standing behind him to shield and heal him at the same time."[9]

Evidently it did not occur to her that the shaman, who looks to be a fat man in his forties, might have been having a heart attack. Psychic attack by "dark forces" is certainly more exotic.

If *Shaman's Drum*'s rapid growth and loyal readers are the way things are going, North America is indeed seeing a renaissance of eclectic shamanistic healers. The question is, who will trust these "neoshamans" to heal them? And will the "neoshamans" dare to try? If they are guided by the practitioners of magical autobiography, they may have some surprises coming in the regular kitchen-table world, where rows of priestesses with torches do not march across Mayan pyramids, and not everyone can or will pay $150 per hour for "crystal healing." ∎

[8]Jane English. "An Interview with Michael Harner." *Shaman's Drum*, Summer 1985, p. 15. Available from *Shaman's Drum*, P.O. Box 2636-G, Berkeley, CA 94702.

[9]Debra Carroll. "Dancing on the Sword's Edge." *Shaman's Drum*, Fall 1985, p. 29.

Access to Cults

The golden age of encyclopedists wrestling the world's knowledge into book form is usually associated with eighteenth-century Frenchmen like Diderot or Voltaire. However, in the specialized universe of religious research, such a golden age may still be with us. Certainly, J. Gordon Melton's efforts to track down and describe every religious group in modern America (ranging from major denominations down to eccentric grouplets) stands out as an unparalleled undertaking, and the results have been outstanding.

Every public library should have a copy of Melton's **Encyclopedia of American Religions**. Herein one finds succinct summaries of the distinguishing doctrines and histories of over 1,500 religions ranging from the Holy Ukrainian Autocephalous Orthodox Church in Exile to the Fire Baptized Holiness Church (Wesleyan), from the Urantia Foundation to the Lectorium Rosicrucianum, and from the Vedanta Society to a dozen Shinto sects. Melton's descriptions are generally accurate and evenhanded—an all-too-rare occurrence in books purporting to describe a variety of faiths.

Less sweeping in scope, but similarly useful, are Melton's **Biographical Dictionary of American Cult and Sect Leaders** and his **Encyclopedic Handbook of Cults in America.** The **Biographical Dictionary**'s strength is its inclusion of spiritual leaders located abroad, such as Ramakrishna or Meher Baba, as long as their followers have had organizations in the U.S. The book's biggest drawback is Melton's decision to only include people who died prior to January 1, 1983. Thus L. Ron Hubbard, Rev. Moon, and Rajneesh, to name a few, are regrettably missing. As with the **Encyclopedia**, the information here is accurate and makes for fascinating reading. It is easy to dive into these books to look up one group or leader and end up reading a half-dozen adjoining write-ups out of sheer fascination.

The **Encyclopedic Handbook** zeroes in on about two dozen of the most prominent alternative religions and treats them in more depth, including descriptions of the controversies that have swirled around most of them. Also present are descriptions of "counter-cult groups" and a discussion of the mixed meanings of the term "cult" itself. A valuable, balanced book. —Jay Kinney

• DIVINE LIGHT MISSION. Few new religious movements have grown and spread as quickly as the Divine Light Mission did during its early months in the United States. Beginning in 1971, it had, by 1973, more than 40 centers in North American and was publishing both a monthly publication, *And It is Divine*, and a tabloid, *The Divine Times*. The mission was centered upon the then teenage guru Maharaj Ji (b. 1957) who assumed leadership in 1966 at the time of the death of his father, Shri Hans Ji Maharaj . . .

Shri Hans was considered a satguru, or perfect master, by his followers. His death was considered a great loss; however, at his funeral, in the midst of the mourning crowd, one of Sri Hans' four sons, Prem Pal Singh Rawat, then only eight years old, arose and addressed the crowd, "O You have been illusioned by maya (the delusion that suffering is real). Maharaj Ji [i.e., Shri Hans] is here, very much present amidst you. Recognize him, adore him and obey him." Thus Maharaj Ji proclaimed his lordship and established himself as the new head of his father's mission.

Maharaj Ji had been an unusual child who began meditating at age two and giving discourses at age six. He entered his teen years with a curious mixture of "normal" childhood urges and the meditative life of a satguru. Four years later, on November 8, 1970, at the India Gate in Delhi, Maharaj Ji proclaimed the dawn of a new era, and his followers answered his call to mission. Early in 1971, Maharaj Ji made his first tour of the United States, mixing visits to Disneyland and horror movies with sessions with prospective disciples. A second visit was made to a huge meeting of disciples at Montrose, Colorado, in the summer of 1972. Each trip was accompanied by wide advertisement and mass media coverage.

Following Sant Mat tradition, Maharaj Ji is considered a perfect master and, as such, an embodiment of God. He gives initiation (called the giving of knowledge) into the truth of life. Initiation involves instruction in the four yoga techniques taught to Shri Hans by his guru. They are taught to a premie (follower of the guru) by a mahatma (personal representative of the guru). The first involves placing the knuckles on the eyes, a process which produces flashes of light in the head (by pinching the optic nerve). The second involves the plugging of the ears and concentrating only on internal sounds. The third involves a concentration on the sound of one's own breathing. Finally, the "nectar" is a technique in which the tongue is curled backward against the roof of the mouth. These techniques are practiced daily by premies (lovers of god). Regular daily practice of these techniques allows the premie to become attuned to the sound and light current emanating from the Divine.

In the early 1970s, the Mission suffered greatly from its "Millennium 73" program which proved unable to attract enough people to fill (and pay for) the Houston Astrodome. This disaster was followed by internal dissent within Maharaj Ji's family. A month after the Houston event, Maharaj Ji turned 16. He took personal administrative control of the mission. Then in May 1974, he married his 24-year old secretary. His mother, Mataji, reacted by taking control of the mission in India and declaring an older brother in control. A lawsuit gave Maharaj Ji control of the movement outside of India while the family retained control of the large Indian following. The publicity attendant upon the internal problems, concurrent with attacks by anti-cultists in the United States, led the mission to adopt a low profile. Maharaj Ji ceased to make public appearances and announcements of activities were not made outside of the membership. In the late 1970s both the headquarters of the movement in Denver and Maharaj Ji's residence in Malibu were transferred to Miami, Florida. Recently, Maharaj Ji returned to California.

—Encyclopedia of American Religions

• THE NUDIST CHRISTIAN CHURCH OF THE BLESSED VIRGIN JESUS. The Nudist Christian Church of the Blessed Virgin Jesus grew out of a revelation received by the church's founder, Zeus Cosmos. During 1985, while a student at Iowa State University, he asked direction from God. The Spirit of Jesus Christ was sent to Zeus Cosmos, directing him to the West, where he would meet God. He journeyed to the Canaan Wilderness (which he renamed the Zeus Cosmos Nudist National Wilderness) near the Utah-Arizona border. God and the angel Ephygeneia, both naked, appeared to him, directing him to a cave on a nearby ridge. While engaged in a fast and living in a cave, Zeus Cosmos again met "God the Almighty the Triune God" and an angel. God gave him an additional revelation to be added to the Bible, called the *Book of Zeus*. It was to be placed next to the Book of Revelation.

The *Book of Zeus* begins with an admonishment for the Mormon polygamists to give up their adulterous pagan practices and their beliefs in the inferiority of the black race. Zeus Cosmos was told of the holy land of the Nudist Christian people northwest of the Grand Canyon where a city, Cosmos, would be built. Here men and women would have godly respect for each other, their nakedness, and the wholesome natural body.

It is the belief of the church that the human body is God's creation. Nudity means cleanliness, honesty, family atmosphere, modesty at its best, freedom, and goodliness. Life with nudity reduces sexual hang-ups, problems caused by undue expectations of one's body, pornography, and crime. The church actively seeks the establishment of clothes-optional public areas across the United States.

—Encyclopedia of American Religions (Supplement)

• KENNEDY WORSHIPPERS. Shortly after the death of the charismatic President John F. Kennedy, people began to claim contact with his spirit. They began ascribing healings of many serious diseases, some congenital and/or terminal, to that spirit. By 1970 more than 100 such reports were on file. Coincidental with these accounts of miracles was the emergence of a loosely organized movement in which John F. Kennedy was an object of worship. The first manifestations were home shrines centered

Bhagwan Shree Rajneesh, born Rajneesh Chandra Mohan in a small town in India in 1931 of Jain parents, took seriously the Jain belief in *anekantavada,* the many-faceted nature of the truth. Rajneesh studied the varied major religious traditions from which he absorbed a variety of teachings. He earned his Master's degree in philosophy and began a teaching career. . . . In 1966 he resigned his post at the University of Jabalpur and became a full-time spiritual teacher. . . .

During the 1970s he encountered Western humanistic psychology and absorbed several of its emphases, including the high value on self-expression and the release of inner emotions as a means to personal freedom. These emphases and the techniques used to promote them were integrated into the Indian teachings offered by Rajneesh and became embodied in his most distinctive practice, dynamic meditation. . . .

Rajneesh came to the United States in 1981, and after a short stay in New Jersey, he moved to the 64,000 acre Big Muddy Ranch near Antelope, Oregon. The ranch became the site of a proposed new city, Rajneeshpuram. Older residents and eventually many Oregonians began to oppose the proposed plan to bring four to six thousand people to the new city by the end of the century. As the controversy grew, the entire plan came to an abrupt end when, in 1985, Rajneesh was charged with immigration fraud. He was fined and deported from the United States. His former chief assistant, Ma Anand Sheela (Silverman) was also charged on a number of felony counts. Some of his American followers are also under indictment and awaiting trial. The center in Oregon has been offered for sale, and the goals of Rajneeshpuram abandoned. The movement, however, has remained intact.

—*Encyclopedia of American Religions*

upon pictures of Kennedy. In 1972 Farley McGivern organized a John F. Kennedy Memorial Temple in Los Angeles to provide headquarters for the movement. To believers, Kennedy is thought of as a god. McGivern believed that Kennedy gave his life for his people, to warn them of the evil around them.

The existence of this movement has been known only through the occasional encounters by reporters with people who claim to be a part of it. To most people involved in it, their belief is a very private matter which is rarely shared with others, even close friends. Hence, little information about it exists.

—*Encyclopedia of American Religions (Supplement)*

• NOYES, John Humphrey (September 3, 1811, Brattleboro, Vermont—April 13, 1886, Niagara Falls, Canada); married Harriet A. Horton, June 1838; education: Dartmouth University, 1826-30; Andover Theological Seminary, 1931-32; Yale Divinity School, 1832-34.

John Humphrey Noyes, the founder of the Oneida Community, one of the most successful of the nineteenth-century communes, was born to a prominent Vermont family. His agnostic father, a successful businessman, served one term in Congress before retiring at the age of fifty-three. After retirement he settled in Putney, Vermont. At the age of nine, young John entered a private school. Six years later, in 1826, he began studies at Dartmouth with the idea of becoming a lawyer.

Noyes's law career ended with his conversion in 1831 and his resultant decision to enter the ministry. He entered the seminary at Andover but transferred to Yale after his first year. At New Haven he joined the Free Church and also became attracted to perfectionism, the belief that humans could, in some measure, become perfect in this life. Noyes began to identify with the perfectionists and traveled throughout New England preaching his ideas. In 1836 he settled in Putney and began to gather a group of followers, the first members of which were his own family. In 1837 he started *The Witness,* as a periodical to spread his views. Noyes believed that the second coming had already occurred and that man could thus be perfect; that once saved he could not fall from grace; and that church authority should not be allowed to overrule personal conviction.

Noyes had also developed some radical views on marriage. Some of these appeared in August 1837 in a letter published in *The Battle Axe and Weapons of War,* a periodical published by T.R. Gates. In this letter he declared that in heaven there will be no marriage and that sexual relations would not be restrained by law. The letter made him the center of controversy, and to punctuate his response that he was discussing heaven, not earth, he proposed marriage to a woman who had experienced sanctification while reading one of Noyes's writings. They were married the next year.

The next nine years were spent in spreading his views and gathering a close-knit cadre of followers around him at Putney. He published his first book, *The Way of Holiness,* which contained his collected articles. *The Witness* (1837-43) was followed by *The Perfectionist* (1843-44). In 1841 he created the Society for Inquiry as a covenant group that adhered to Noyes's views. In 1844 they formalized the communal nature of their life together with an incorporation that was widened to include all the adults the next year. Twenty-eight adults agreed to share work, living quarters, and finances.

In 1846 Noyes took the first step toward the complex marriage system he was later to develop. Noyes, his wife, and Mary and George Cragin agreed that it was God's will for them to share marriage partners. Two more couples, Noyes's sisters and their husbands, joined the arrangement before the year was out. Unfortunately, word soon leaked out to the community; in the face of the resulting hostility, Noyes was forced to flee.

Noyes reassembled his followers at Oneida, New York, where another group of his followers had begun a second community. He assumed leadership of what was to become his school for perfecting character. By 1851, under Noyes's theocratic leadership, about 275 people had come to reside at Oneida and its several branch communities.

At Oneida Noyes attempted to put into practice all of his perfectionist ideals, the most controversial of which was his system of complex marriage. Complex marriage involved the controlled sexual relations of a community where each male was considered married to each female. Noyes also developed a practice of birth control that he called "male continence," by which males controlled the emission of semen and prevented the production of unwanted children. (Noyes had been motivated to develop the practice, also known as *kerazza,* after his wife had borne five stillborn children.)

The Oneida community functioned well for one generation and was relatively free of persecution until the mid-1870s. At this time, when Noyes's health, particularly his hearing, began to fail, a group of primarily young adults who no longer believed in Noyes's perfectionist ideas emerged within the community. In the face of a crisis in which those who opposed Noyes's authority joined with outsiders bent upon suppressing the "immoral" community, Noyes fled to Canada in June 1879. A few months later the community voted to abandon complex marriage.

Although he kept in touch, Noyes never returned. He settled on the Canadian side of Niagara Falls and lived out his days surrounded by a small group of his most dedicated followers.

The members of the community settled down into more conventional lives. In 1880 the members reorganized as the Oneida Community, Limited, a joint-stock company, and continued to operate the community's industries, the most well-known being its silverworks.

—*Biographical Dictionary of American Cult and Sect Leaders* ☞

A.C. Bhaktivedanta Swami Prabhupada (1896-1977), a former Indian businessman, brought the Krishna Consciousness movement to the U.S. in 1965. The movement now has fifty U.S. centers and over 3,000 core community members, with an additional 250,000 lay constituents.

• Yogi Bhajan (b. 1929), a well-educated Sikh from Delhi, India, moved to Toronto in 1968 and in December of that year settled in Los Angeles. In 1969 he founded an ashram and the Healthy, Happy, Holy Organization (3HO) to teach kundalini yoga and meditation. . . .

For Sikhs, God is self-existent, immortal, immanent, transcendent, omnipotent, omnipresent, and omniscient. He is experienced through chanting of the Name of God, which in the original language is "Sat Nam" (God's name is Truth) or "Wahe Guru" (Experience of Infinite Wisdom). Chanting God's name is frequently done by repeating the mantra, "Ek Ong Kar Nam Siri Wha Guru" ("There is One Creator and one creation. Truth is His name. He is all Great. He is all Wisdom.") Members normally rise before sunrise each day to chant God's name and meditate.

While not required to do so, individuals associated with the Sikh Dharma are encouraged to seek formal initiation and join the Khalsa, the Brotherhood of the Pure Ones, a fellowship begun by Guru Gobind Singh. New members are baptized with sweetened water stirred with a sword. Members of the Sikh Dharma are then required to keep the traditional practices introduced by Guru Gobind Singh that became the distinguishing marks of the Sikh community, known popularly as the five "k's." All hair, including the beard, is kept uncut (*kesh*) and tied on top of the head in a turban. The hair is kept neat with a comb (*kangha*). Sikhs wear special underwear (*kachera*) originally designed to allow freedom of movement in battle; a steel bracelet (*kara*) symbolic of an inseparable bond with God; and a dagger (*kirpan*) symbolic of a commitment to defend truth, righteousness, and those who cannot defend themselves.

Ministers in the Sikh Dharma also normally wear a long hemmed knee-length skirt (*kurta*) and special pants which are loose at the waist and tight around the legs (*chudidas*). Both are solid white as is the turban.

Health is of prime concern within the Sikh Dharma. Natural foods are preferred and fish, meat, alcohol, and drugs prohibited. A number of members have opened health food restaurants and groceries. Members also prefer natural methods of healing.

The Sikh Dharma observes the traditional holidays of Sikhism, especially Balsakhi Day, the birthday of the Khalsa (April); the Martyrdom days of Guru Tegh Bhadus (November) and Guru Arjun Dev (May); and the birthdays of the ten gurus.

Beyond what is normally considered orthodox Sikhism, Yogi Bhajan also teaches kundalini, laya and tantric yoga, the techniques of which he had mastered prior to his coming to the United States. Kundalini yoga consists of exercises which stimulate and control the energy within man which expands the capacity of the self. Laya yoga is the technique of altering consciousness by sound and rhythm. Tantric yoga is practiced by couples who share energies and consciousness. It must be done in the presence of a master or Mahan Tantric (Yogi Bhajan). . . .

The Sikh Dharma has received some attention from the anti-cult movement, and there have been a few deprogramming attempts. One ex-member left and accused Yogi Bhajan of sexual involvement with several of his staff members, but there was no verification of the charges. Controversy has primarily been focused in other areas.

Tension developed during the mid-1970s as members of the Sikh Dharma began to interact with the older American Sikh community. Sikh Dharma members complained that the Punjabi Sikhs had become lax in their discipline, especially in their adherence to the five "k's." The tension led to an attack on Yogi Bhajan and his followers by Dr. Narinder Singh Kapany, editor of the influential *Sikh Sangar*, the magazine of the Sikh Foundation. Kapany condemned Bhajan's emphasis upon yoga and his strictures on diet. Kapany's criticisms have been echoed by other Sikh leaders in both the United States and India. The issues have never been resolved, and the two communities have remained separate.

Sikh Dharma members have encountered constant conflict over their turbans. As early as 1971, Thomas C. Costello faced a military court-martial for refusing to either cut his hair or remove his turban. His case led to a change in Army regulations granting permission for Sikhs to wear turbans. As recently as 1984, Karta Kaur Khalsa was threatened with loss of her teaching certificate because she refused to take off her turban during classes. In 1985 the Oregon Supreme Court declared the law under which she was suspended to be unconstitutional.

While these tensions remain, the Sikh Dharma has been praised highly for its drug rehabilitation program, and Akal Security, a security guard business formed by a group of members in New Mexico, created in no small part out of the image of the fierce Sikh warrior, has been highly sought for its services. —*Encyclopedic Handbook of Cults in America*

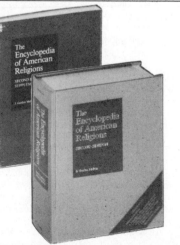
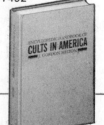

INNER FRONTIERS

Denis Tiani

VOICES FROM BEYOND

The Age-Old Mystery of Channeling

by Ted Schultz

"HAIL. I'M JOHN. . . .WE ARE TAKEN TO FIND ye have investigations. We sense your vibrational condition as such and have familiarity with it." As described in her phenomenal best seller *Out on a Limb,* so began actress-turned-occultist Shirley MacLaine's first session with "John," one of the disembodied entities that speaks through "channel" Kevin Ryerson—and so began 1980s America's infatuation with the mysterious phenomenon called "channeling."

Channeling believers already formed a growing subculture before Shirley, to be sure. Back in the 1960s, the resurgence of interest in all things paranormal had included a renewed enthusiasm for a fellow named Edgar Cayce, whom biographer Jess Stearn dubbed "the sleeping prophet." Between 1910 and 1945, when he died, Cayce, an otherwise ordinary man from Kentucky, gave tens of thousands of "psychic readings" during which he went into a deep trance and advised clients about health, reincarnation, and occult philosophy. Cayce's trance teachings never achieved the extraordinary popularity during his life that was to be theirs in the '60s. Through them, hundreds of thousands of proto-New Agers became acquainted with the concept of "trance channeling."

Then, in the early 1970s, a strange volume called *The Seth Material* appeared. Channeled by an Elmira, New York, novelist named Jane Roberts, the book was the reading public's introduction to "Seth," "an energy personality essence no longer focused in physical reality" who over countless millennia had "known many [existences], both physical and nonphysical." For twenty-one years, until Jane died in 1984, Seth expounded a complex and arcane cosmology that explained individual and group consciousness, the nature of time and space, and the self-creation of reality. Jane Roberts' Seth books rode the cresting New Age wave to become best sellers; over a dozen have been published in the series to date, and the notes she left behind insure that there will be more.

It was thus into a New Age already receptive to the idea of channeling that Shirley MacLaine's *Out on a Limb* entered in 1983. When the TV-movie version of the book appeared in 1987, "channeling" quickly became a household word. Channeling sessions filtered into the middle class like a 1980s metaphysical version of the Tupperware party.

WHO'S THERE?

Channeling is "the process in which a person [the 'channel'] transmits messages from a presumed discarnate source external to his or her consciousness [the 'entity']," to use the definition of William Kautz of the Center for Applied Intuition in San Francisco. Perhaps he should have left out the adjective "discarnate," since some channels (including the psychic spoon-bender Uri Geller) claim to have received communications from outer-space entities who presumably *do* have bodies, though they may be aboard spaceships or inhabiting other planets.

As the authors of the current spate of channeling books are quick to point out, channeling is an ancient phenomenon, as old as religion. The Bible itself is said to be "inspired by God"—channeled, in other words—and instances of channeling are described in its pages. Other religious books, for example the Koran and the Book of

---

Observing the phenomenon of "channeling" can be an eerie experience. As the other-worldly personality takes possession, the "channel's" facial expressions, gestures, and manner of speaking change radically, and you're faced with an undeniably extraordinary occurrence. But unless you're prepared to accept the face-value reality of alien, ultradimensional entities who happily communicate through anybody who takes a channeling workshop and who talk like characters from a Grade-B New Age morality play, you're going to be mighty disappointed with the scanty information available on the subject. The gosh-wow channeling books just didn't do it for me, so I decided to dig a little deeper. Here's the result, which might be called "An Objective Primer of Channeling."

—T.S.

Mormon, are also channeled texts (received via the "channels" Mohammed and Joseph Smith, respectively). Literally tens of thousands of channeled books have been self-published by small groups of believers in the U.S. alone over the last hundred years, and a good case could be made that channeling is an essential element in the formation of any new religion.

Only the most cynical skeptic would charge that all channels are outright frauds. Many channels are obviously reluctant and bewildered by the whole process; one slim volume of channeled material produced in 1978 even bears the title *Why Me?*[1] In many cases the style of speech and writing produced by the channeled entity differs radically from that of the channel's, and the information and philosophy imparted appears, at first glance, to go beyond the abilities of the otherwise rather lackluster human through which the wisdom issues. The mystery that presents itself, then, is where does this material come from? If it doesn't originate from the person whose mouth and tongue are forming the words, then *who is doing the speaking?* The most superficial answer, that a paranormal entity has entered the channel's body, has led millions of people to seek out channels as oracles of divine information.

THE KINDS OF CHANNELING

The oracles most often consulted by seekers in the 1980s employ "automatic speaking," the form of channeling in which entities purportedly speak through a person (the channel) who is in a trance. But automatic speaking is really only a sub-category of the larger psychological phenomenon of *automatisms*—motor behaviors that appear to occur independently of the will—that includes such things as "automatic writing" and "automatic painting."

Automatic Writing. Next to automatic speaking, the most widespread form of channeling is automatic writing. This may be performed when the channel, in a trance, writes out messages with a pen or pencil, or it may be accomplished with the aid of simple devices like the planchette or the Ouija board, which register unconscious movements of the hands. (Similar devices are known to have been used in China and by the American Indians.)

On July 8, 1913, a Ouija board eerily spelled out this introduction to St. Louis housewife Pearl Curran: "Many moons ago I lived. Again I come—Patience Worth my name." At first using the Ouija board, and later using pen and paper or automatic speaking, Patience Worth dictated many poems and stories, including a number of successful novels. In fact, thousands of books have been produced by automatic writing or even, as in the case of the massive *Oahspe: A New Bible,*[2] by "automatic typing."

Automatic Art. Although not as common as automatic

speaking or automatic writing, there are numerous examples of "automatic drawing" or "automatic painting," in which the channel serves as a conduit for deceased artists. Luiz Antonio Gasparetto, a Brazilian who has produced more than 20,000 paintings by the "spirits" of Leonardo da Vinci, Renoir, Michelangelo, Monet, van Gogh, Toulouse-Lautrec, and others, paints in semi-darkness, producing finished works in as little as eight minutes. Sometimes he channels three artists simultaneously, one with each hand and the third with a foot! Many of his paintings bear a strong resemblance to the styles of the supposedly channeled masters, but others are poor matches at best, because, according to Gasparetto, the artists' styles have continued to evolve in the afterlife.

British psychic Matthew Manning has channeled the posthumous work of artists like Klee, Durer, Beardsley, and Picasso (who, as prolific as in life, also works through Gasparetto). In addition, Manning produces written works by deceased poets and philosophers, including the late Bertrand Russell, the famous atheist who, in the afterlife, has been forced to admit he was wrong. Many others continue to write from beyond the veil. An entire book of Emily Dickinson's postmortem poetry has been published, and the late Jane Roberts, of "Seth" fame, produced channeled volumes by Paul Cezanne and William James.

Automatic Surgery. There are even channeled surgeons. The late Arigo (real name: Jose Pedro de Freitas), a Brazilian "psychic surgeon" made famous by the book *Arigo: Surgeon of the Rusty Knife* by John Fuller (author of a number of books on the paranormal), channeled the spirit of a dead German surgeon, "Dr. Fritz." While in trance, Arigo adopted a heavy German accent and performed surgery on patients without the use of anesthetic and under decidedly unsanitary conditions.

PHENOMENA RELATED TO CHANNELING

There are any number of mental states that bear some resemblances to channeling, including possession, glossolalia, past-life regression, and multiple personalities.

Possession. "My name is Legion: for we are many," replies an "unclean spirit" when Jesus commands it to identify itself, in the famous Biblical account of demonic possession. Jesus orders the devils to leave their human victim, so they enter a herd of pigs, which rush over a cliff and drown in the sea. Spirit possession is an age-old belief, common to many cultures. Its similarity to channeling is obvious: in both, a person's normal personality is overwhelmed by an intruding personality (the "entity") that appears to originate from without. In the case of channeling, the entity has been invited in; in possession the intruder is unwelcome.

Glossolalia. Like channeling, glossolalia ("speaking in tongues") is a form of automatic speaking. Glossolalia refers to spontaneous utterances, usually made in a state of religious fervor, that are often incoherent or in a nonexistent "language," or, more rarely, in a real language foreign to the speaker. Mormons, Pentecostals, and other

---

[1] Ji Willow. *Why Me?* Deerfield Enterprises, Inc., 1 Adler Drive, East Syracuse, NY 13057.

[2] Channeled in King James Biblical style by John Newbrough, a New York dentist, in 1881. Today *Oahspe* is the bible of the Universal Brotherhood of Faithists.

North American religious sects practice glossolalia, calling it the "language of heaven."

Glossolalia is not restricted to modern-day North America, however, and is known from many times and places. The Bible describes the glossolalia of Jesus' disciples, when, during Pentecost, they "began to speak with other tongues, as the Spirit gave them utterance." In China, those possessed by the Monkey God speak in an unintelligible language, and, just as in the "language of heaven" of North American churches, an initiated "interpreter" provides the meaning.

Past-Life Regression. In past-life regression, a subject is hypnotically regressed in time, through youth and childhood, through infancy, through birth and the stages of the embryo, and eventually back to a "previous lifetime." Often the subject assumes the personality of the previous life, speaking with an accent and recounting stories rich with details apparently outside the experience of his current lifetime. Thus, past-life regression, like channeling, involves a trance state and the emergence of a separate, seemingly alien personality.

The rise in popularity of past-life regression can be traced to the sensational Bridey Murphy case of 1952. Under hypnosis induced by Morey Bernstein, a Colorado housewife named Virginia Tighe assumed her past-life personality as "Bridey Murphy," a nineteenth-century Irish woman who died in 1864. The book Bernstein wrote, *The Search for Bridey Murphy,* was published in 1956 and became the '50s best-selling equivalent of Shirley MacLaine's *Out on a Limb,* inspiring pop songs like *Bridey Murphy Rock and Roll* and "come as you were" parties. Bridey spoke with a heavy Irish brogue, used many quaint expressions, and recalled potentially verifiable details like the names of her husband and relatives, her husband's occupation (lawyer and professor at Queen's University in Belfast), the street she lived on, how to dance various jigs, and the words to songs.

Since the publication of Bernstein's book, hundreds of other volumes of past-life recollections have appeared, including the popular historical novels of Joan Grant. Since the 1960s, "past-life therapy," in which psychotherapists search for the roots of patients' current problems in previous lifetimes, has become an increasingly accepted form of psychological treatment.

Multiple Personalities. The phenomenon of multiple personalities is fairly well known in psychology, but poorly studied. The public is fascinated with this psychological disorder, as shown by the sales of books like *The Three Faces of Eve* by Corbett H. Thigpen and H. Cleckley (published in 1957, and made into a film starring Joanne Woodward that same year), *Sybil* by F.R. Schreiber (1973), and *The Minds of Billy Milligan* by Daniel Keyes (1981).

In the simplest form of multiple-personality disorder, known as a "fugue," an otherwise normal person adopts an alternative personality in order to escape from an unpleasant situation. In 1890 the great psychologist and student of religion William James described a classic fugue: the case of the Reverend Ansel Bourne of Greene, Rhode Island. One morning Rev. Bourne got up, withdrew $551 from the bank in Providence, and disappeared. Friends of the Reverend became worried and the police conducted a search, but to no avail. Two months later, on March 14, 1887, a man named A.J. Brown awoke in fright in Norristown, Pennsylvania. He called out for his neighbors, begging them to tell him who he was and what he was doing there. Though he could remember nothing about it, he had arrived in Norristown six weeks earlier, rented a shop, stocked it with candy and notions, and carried on a humble trade as an apparently quiet, normal shopkeeper.

Stanley Young

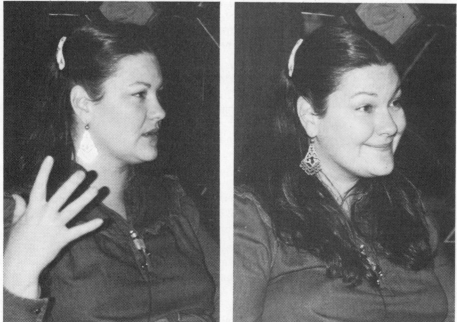

(Left) Jamie Sams, a former country-and-western singer whose life changed when she sighted a spaceship in Pasadena in 1982. (Right) Leah, a sixth-density entity from the planet Venus six hundred years in the future, communicating through Jamie Sams during a channeling session held in the Los Angeles area in 1986.

FROM INDIA TO THE PLANET MARS

Most 19th-century spiritualists channeled "spirit guides" whose origins characterized the exoticism of the day: deceased American Indians, Tibetans, "Hindoos," and the like. In contrast, today's channeled beings mirror our science-fictional times: "entities" from other dimensions, royalty from imaginary civilizations, and beings from outer space. But at least one turn-of-the-century medium scooped everyone by channeling Martians. In his 1901 classic, *From India to the Planet Mars* (New York: Harper), psychologist Theodore Flournoy describes his two-year case study of "Helene Smith" (real name: Catherine-Elise Müller), a particularly dramatic French Swiss medium whose exceptional ability to enter a trance state produced, besides Martians, visitations from earthly personages like Calgiostro, Marie Antoinette, and "Simandini" (a 15th-century Indian princess).

Mademoiselle Smith's rich visions of Mars included "carriages without horses or wheels, emitting sparks as they glided by; houses with fountains on the roof; a cradle having for curtains an angel made of iron with outstretched wings." Lakes were blue-pink, the ground peach-colored, the sky greenish-yellow. Martians, who looked just like humans, wore large robes, flat hats, and sandals. A Martian named Astané used a hand-held flying machine that looked like a carriage-lantern. Through automatic painting, Mlle. Smith produced full-color representations of Martian houses, plants, and animals. Most interesting of all, she spoke and wrote in the Martian language on many occasions.

Flournoy painstakingly recorded and studied the trance languages of Mlle. Smith. Through careful analysis, he demonstrated that, though her "Martian" language sounded and looked quite alien, it was an exact analogue of both written and spoken French, Mlle. Smith's native tongue. Each Martian letter had its equivalent in French, and the syntax was also identical. Apparently, Mlle. Smith's unconscious mind had invented and remembered what was essentially a written and spoken code.

Even though she believed they had been married in a previous incarnation, when Flournoy's book was published Mlle. Smith would have nothing more to do with him. She was outraged by his finding that her phenomena were not "real," but psychological in nature. Mlle. Smith's later life fades into obscurity, but we have Flournoy to thank for an in-depth account of a case of channeling that foreshadowed by eighty years the shape of things to come.　　　　—T.S.

(Above) Paintings of Martian architecture and landscape by the turn-of-the-century medium Helene Smith. (Right) The "Martian alphabet" of Mlle. Smith, along with psychologist Theodore Flournoy's transliteration into French.

He was the Reverend Bourne. As far as James, who investigated the case firsthand, could tell, the Reverend had felt increasingly troubled and harried in Greene, and the fugue was his mind's only way of escaping from these problems.

In Rev. Bourne's case, only two alternate personalities existed, each unaware of the other. In the case of Billy Milligan, there were twenty-four separate but interacting personalities, including males and females of all different ages and "appearances." In the case of "Sybil," there were sixteen. A common feature of most multiple-personality patients is a severely brutal period during childhood, which psychologists theorize may deprive the victims of appropriate adult role models. In the words of Stanford psychologist Ernest Hilgard, for the vicitim of a violent or severely disturbed youth, "the identification figures of childhood do not permit clear identifications and hence do not lead to a satisfactorily integrated personality." Interestingly, Margo Chandley, who wrote a doctoral dissertation on channeling at Southern California's International College, says that most of the channels she has studied were also abused or neglected children. ☛

The sisters who started spiritualism in 1848. From left to right: Leah, Kate, and Margaret Fox.

SPIRITUALISM: CHANNELING, NINETEENTH-CENTURY STYLE

The practice of "spiritualism," or communication with entities—usually dead relatives, friends, and "spirit guides"—through "mediums" (channels), became so popular in the nineteenth century that it eventually resulted in the formation of an influential new religion, the remnants of which still exist today.

Most American spiritualists trace the origin of their movement to the Fox sisters of Hydesville, New York. In 1848, the Fox family began to hear mysterious rapping noises in their home, and soon 12-year-old Kate began to "communicate" with the sounds. Kate, along with her sisters Margaret, 9, and Leah, 23, devised a code by which the rapping designated the letters of the alphabet, and the source identified itself: "Mr. Splitfoot," a spirit entity. News of the Fox sisters spread far and wide, and soon thousands were attending the sisters' seances to seek the spirit's advice. Following the Fox's lead, many more "mediums" appeared in Europe and North America, through which spirits communicated by automatic speaking rather than rapping.

Spiritualism peaked in popularity between 1880 and 1920, when, with the help of spirit mediums, hundreds of thousands of Westerners visited with their departed friends and relatives and received the advice of a wide variety of spirit "guides." The wife of President Lincoln even invited mediums into the White House, one of whom, Nettie Colburn, claimed that her spirit guides influenced Lincoln's decisions about the timing of the Emancipation Proclamation and his visit to the Civil War front lines at Fredericksburg. Thousands of spiritualist churches were formed, and many have survived to this day, united in umbrella organizations like the National Spiritualist Association of Churches in Chicago, the International General Assembly of Spiritualists in Buffalo, and the General Assembly of Spiritualists in New York.

On October 21, 1888, forty years after the Fox sisters produced their first "spirit rappings," Margaret Fox confessed that it had all been a put-on. Writing in the *New York World*, she revealed that the "rappings" had begun as

Divided Consciousness

*Though enigmatic phenomena usually associated with the occult (past-life regression, possession, channeling, automatic writing, visions, etc.) have been ignored by most psychologists, there **has** been scientific inquiry into these areas. **Divided Consciousness**, written by Stanford University professor emeritus Ernest Hilgard, describes some of the very best research that's been done.*

Hilgard's interest is the subdivision of mental functioning—how the mind carries on numerous tasks simultaneously, and how it shifts attention between them or even carries out complex tasks without any conscious attention at all. Using hypnosis as their primary tool, Hilgard and other researchers have been able to easily induce automatisms like automatic writing in order to communicate directly to dissociated portions of the mind, which often exactly resemble the channeled entities of modern occultists. The phenomena they've discovered are all the more incredible because they are indisputably real.

*I got far more thrills per page from **Divided Consciousness** than from all the popular channeling books combined. It's an authoritative tour of the curious states of consciousness associated with possession and mediumship, dreams, imagination and creativity, multiple personalities, age regression, amnesia, and psychosomatic disorders like hysterical blindness and paralysis. The implicit message is that there's far more going on in the unconscious portions of our minds—far more perceiving, remembering, processing, fantasizing—than we give ourselves credit for.* —T.S.

• The instructor was conducting a classroom demonstration of hypnotical deafness. The subject of the demonstration was a blind student, experienced in hypnosis, who had volunteered to serve; his blindness was not related to the demonstration, except that any visual cues were eliminated. After the induction of hypnosis, he was given a suggestion that, at the count of three, he would become completely deaf to all sounds. His hearing would be restored to normal when the instructor's hand was placed on his right shoulder. To be both blind and deaf would have been a frightening experience for the subject had he not known that his deafness was quite temporary. Loud sounds were then made close to the subject's head by banging together some large wooden blocks. There was no sign of any reaction; none was expected because the subject, in a previous demonstration, had shown a lack of responsiveness to the shots of a starter's pistol. He was also completely unresponsive to any questions asked of him while he was hypnotically deaf.

One student in the class questioned whether "some part" of the subject might be aware of what was going on. After all, there was nothing wrong with his ears. The instructor agreed to test this by a method related to interrogation practices used by clinical hypnotists. He addressed the hypnotically deaf subject in a quiet voice, "As you know, there are parts of our nervous system that carry on activities that occur out of awareness, of which control of the circulation of the blood, or the digestive processes, are the most familiar. However, there may be intellectual processes also of which we are unaware, such as those that find expression in night dreams. Although you are hypnotically deaf, perhaps there is some part a game to frighten their mother, but, under the direction of the older Leah, had quickly developed into a lucrative scam. "My sister Katie was the first to observe that by swishing her fingers she could produce certain noises with her knuckles and joints, and that the same effect could be made with her toes. Finding that we could make raps with our feet—first with one foot and then both—we practised until we could do this easily when the room was dark." Two weeks earlier Kate had confessed: "Spiritualism is a humbug from beginning to end. It is the greatest humbug of the century."

CLUES FROM PSYCHOLOGY

Ernest R. Hilgard, professor emeritus of psychology at Stanford University, begins his book *Divided Consciousness: Multiple Controls in Human Thought and Action* with these words: "The unity of consciousness is illusory. Man does more than one thing at a time—all the time—and the conscious representation of these actions is never complete." In other words, conscious attention can be directed toward one task while the mind simultaneously processes others. Everyone has had the experience of daydreaming while reading a book, only to discover that he cannot remember any of the page he's just read (yet, as we shall see, the information may indeed be stored somewhere deep in his mind). Likewise, a pianist may hold a conversation while playing a complex piece of music. These are obvious and somewhat superficial examples, but Hilgard and others have found that this subdivision of mental functioning, known as *divided consciousness,* runs very deep, and operates in ways that are quite extraordinary.

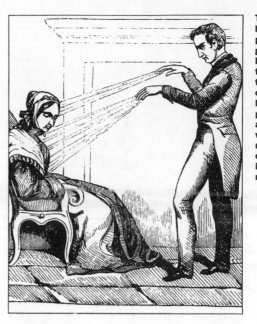

Through hypnosis, psychologists have been able to explore the extraordinary levels of personality associated with channeling and other exotic phenomena.

Around the turn of the century, psychologist Pierre Janet assigned to his hypnotized subject Lucy the task of writing a letter posthypnotically (that is, after she had emerged from hypnosis into normal waking consciousness). Once awake, her hand dutifully wrote out a short letter while, quite unawares, she carried on a casual conversation. When Janet showed the letter to Lucy, she denied having written it, preferring to believe that the doctor had faked her signature. In similar experiments by C.T. Burnett in the 1920s, subjects performed posthypnotic

of you that is hearing my voice and processing the information. If there is, I should like the index finger of your right hand to rise as a sign that this is the case."

To the surprise of the instructor, as well as the class, the finger rose! The subject immediately said, "Please restore my hearing so you can tell me what you did. I felt my finger rise in a way that was not a spontaneous twitch, so you must have done something to make it rise, and I want to know what you did."

• The subject of this informal experiment was a highly hypnotizable student whose story telling was of a high order whether he was hypnotized or not. Although I report a story told under hypnosis, he was quite capable of telling stories of essentially the same vividness when not hypnotized. He came to our attention because, with someone else, under hypnosis he had told a story of early nineteenth century England with such clarity and verisimilitude that he convinced those who heard him—himself as well—that it must have been a case of regression to a prior experience. Only careful depth interviewing proved that he had forgotten memories sufficient to supply the details he had recounted so that the reincarnation concept was not necessary . . .

Inquiry by the hidden observer technique revealed that there was a part of him doing the planning, more like a stage director providing the promptings for the hypnotized part, the actor . . .

The planning aspect in the waking state appears to hold a much larger part of the story telling. Here we find an additional complexity, for we have little difference in the overt experiences while creating in hypnosis and creating in the waking state, but we may have a concealed helper when the story is being created in hypnosis. Jesamyn West believes that much that she writes comes out of her stored memories, even though she does not model her characters after real people. "The bits and pieces you remember should fall down into your unconscious and become compost . . . So, for me, the thing to do in writing is to ask myself questions, not to tell myself answers." Does she perhaps have a hidden observer to organize the material for her?

• It is important to note that the secondary or hidden personality can sometimes be more "normal," better adjusted, healthier than the primary personality. Typically, the secondary personality has the whole set of memories, and therapy is directed to bringing about an integration based on it rather than on the typical personality that at first presents itself as the primary one.

The spirit of Patience Worth, a Puritan girl who had died 300 years before, contacts St. Louis housewife Pearl Curran in 1913. In the ensuing years, Patience would dictate poetry and a number of best-selling novels.

tasks like adding the number of taps the experimenter made with his pencil to the page number of an open book, again without awareness of what they were doing. These and other investigations have demonstrated that automatisms can be experimentally induced, even though they are usually associated with occult phenomena.

Cartoonists like to caricature the agonized sufferer of mental conflict with an angel whispering in one ear and a devil in the other. The experiments of Hilgard and others have shown that in reality our minds may contain many different subdivisions, each operating semi-independently and more or less in agreement with the others. But when, for whatever reason, one of these divisions is perceived as *separate* from the self, *dissociation* is said to occur. A bereaved widow, for instance, may temporarily deny that her husband has died, dissociating and repressing that part of herself that heard and remembers the bad news. Convicted murderers, unable to face their own horrible acts, have been known to dissociate the "evil" parts of themselves, charging that externalized "demons" or "voices" forced them to carry out their crimes. People suffering from multiple-personality disorders are extreme cases of the inability to integrate dissociated subpersonalities.

UNFORGETTABLE CRYPTOMNESIA

Beatle George Harrison got sued for rewriting the Chiffons' "He's So Fine" into "My Sweet Lord." He was the innocent victim of the psychological phenomenon of *cryptomnesia*. So was Helen Keller, the famous blind and deaf woman, when she wrote a story called "The Frost King." After it was published in 1892, she was accused of plagiarizing Margaret Canby's "The Frost Fairies," though Helen had no conscious memory of ever reading it. But, sure enough, inquiries revealed that Canby's story had been read to her (by touch) in 1888. She was devastated: "Joy deserted my heart. . . . I had disgraced myself . . . yet how could it have possibly happened? I racked my brain until I was weary to recall anything about the frost that I had read before I wrote 'The Frost King'; but I could remember nothing."

Cryptomnesia, or "hidden memory," refers to thoughts and ideas that seem new and original, but which are actually memories of things that you've forgotten you knew. The cryptomnesic ideas may be variations on the original memories, with details switched around and changed, but still recognizable.

Cryptomnesia is a professional problem for artists like George Harrison and Helen Keller; it also plays an important role in past-life regression. In the midst of the hoopla surrounding the Bridey Murphy case, the *Denver Post* decided to send newsman William J. Barker to Ireland to try to find evidence of Bridey's actual existence. Unfortunately for reincarnation enthusiasts, careful checking failed to turn up anything conclusive. Barker couldn't locate the street Bridey said she lived on, he couldn't find any essays by Bridey's husband in the *Belfast News-Letter* between 1843 and 1864 (during which time Bridey said he was a contributor), and he couldn't find anyone who had heard of the "Morning Jig" that Bridey danced.[3]

Research by reporters from the *Chicago American* and later by writer Melvin Harris finally uncovered the surprising source of housewife Virginia Tighe's past-life memories. As a teenager in Chicago, Virginia had lived across the street from an Irish woman named Mrs. Anthony Corkell, who had regaled her with tales about the old country. Mrs. Corkell's maiden name was Bridie Murphy! Furthermore, Virginia had been active in high school dramatics, at one point memorizing several Irish monologues which she learned to deliver with a heavy Irish brogue. Finally, the 1893 World's Columbian Exposition, staged in Chicago, had featured a life-size Irish Village, with fifteen cottages, a castle tower, and a population of genuine Irish women who danced jigs, spun cloth, and made butter. No doubt Virginia had heard stories of this exhibition from many of her neighbors and friends while growing up in Chicago in the '20s.[4]

Almost every other case of "past-life memory" that has been objectively investigated has followed the same pattern: the memories, often seemingly quite alien to the life experiences of the regressed subject, simply cannot be verified by historical research; on the other hand, they frequently prove to be the result of cryptomnesia.

In one such case, a young Finnish girl was regressed to a previous life as "Dorothy," an English innkeeper's daughter. The hypnotist, Dr. Reima Kampman of the University of Oulu in Finland, was particularly intrigued by the girl's ability to remember a strange tune she called "the summer song," which she sang in Middle English, a language unfamiliar to her. When Dr. Kampman rehypnotized the girl and instructed her to go back to a time when she might have seen the words or heard the music of the song, she recalled that at age thirteen she had casually taken a book from the shelf in her hometown library in Finland. She'd absent-mindedly flipped through the

---

[3] "The Truth About Bridey Murphy." *Denver Post,* March 11, 1956.
[4] "Yes, Virginia, There Is a Bridey." *Time,* June 18, 1956. See also Melvin Harris' *Investigating the Unexplained* (reviewed on p. 201).

Reincarnation: Pro and Con

Of the authors that contend that reincarnation exists, there is no better researcher than Ian Stevenson. Stevenson, a psychiatrist and professor at the University of Virginia, has spent over twenty-five years tracking down cases of children who claim to remember former lives—in some cases he has even located the families of the "previous incarnation," and compared the "memories" with the facts. The majority of the cases come from India and the Middle East, where reincarnation is a strongly held belief. Some of the cases come from members of the Druse religion, who even attempt, as a matter of religious tradition, to locate the newborn reincarnation of recently deceased relatives (who are usually conveniently reborn nearby). Naturally this suggests the criticism that children of these cultures are prompted or encouraged to spin tales of previous lives, but, to Stevenson's credit, he attempts to address this and other problems as he analyzes the cases.

If it's hard to find reliable books on the case for reincarnation, it's even harder to find any that present the skeptical viewpoint. Three chapters in Melvin Harris' **Investigating the Unexplained** *(reviewed on page 201) provide an excellent skeptical treatment of hypnotic "past-life regressions," discussing both the Bridey Murphy case and the sensational cases of British hypnotherapist Arnall Bloxham. But the best critique of reincarnation I've seen appeared as a four-part series in the Fall 1986 through Summer 1987 issues of* **Free Inquiry** *magazine. The first issue of the series includes an article by Melvin Harris summarizing his research, as well as part one of philosopher Paul Edwards' four-part point-by-point critique of reincarnation. In the series of articles, Edwards outlines the various doctrines of reincarnation and discusses particulars like the Law of Karma, body-mind dualism, the creation of new souls, and where the mind is between incarnations. He concludes with an engrossing discussion of Stevenson's assumptions, methods, and conclusions. —T.S.*

• When Wijeratne was between two and two and a half years old he began to walk around his house in a solitary way talking to himself. His behavior attracted the attention of his mother, who listened to his tale. She overheard him saying that his arm was deformed because he had murdered his wife in his previous life. He mentioned a number of details connected with a crime of which she, until that time, had heard nothing. She asked her husband about the boy's statements and he confirmed the accuracy of what the boy was saying for in fact his younger brother, Ratran Hami, had been executed in 1928 for the murder of his wife.
    —*Twenty Cases Suggestive of Reincarnation*

• Many subjects of these cases have birthmarks or birth defects that correspond, according to the informants and other sources of evidence, to wounds (or other marks) on the body of the related previous personality. In some instances a correspondence occurs between an internal disease of the subject and a similar one from which the previous personality suffered . . .

Birthmarks and birth defects related to the previous personality seem to me to provide some of the strongest evidence in favor of reincarnation as the best interpretation for the cases. They are objectively observable (I have photographed several hundred of them), and for most of them the only serious alternative explanation that I can think of is a psychic force on the part of the baby's mother that influences the body of the embryo or fetus within her. However, this explanation, which is itself almost as mind stretching (for the average Westerner) as reincarnation, can be firmly excluded in about twelve cases in which the child's mother and father never heard of the identified previous personality until after the child's birth.
    —*Children Who Remember Past Lives*

• One of the skeptics is Professor Chari, an Indian philosopher, now retired from Madras Christian University, who is not a Western materialist or positivist but a Hindu and a well-known parapsychologist. Professor Chari does not reject reincarnation, but he believes that Stevenson is incredibly naive and that his reports have no evidential value.

. . . Chari insists that [Stevenson's cases are] cultural artifacts, pure and simple. "A reincarnationist fantasy in the small Asian child," he writes, "starts typically in play or a gamelike situation." It is then promoted (or retarded) by the conscious or unconscious beliefs, attitudes, and responses of parents, guardians, and interested bystanders. Chari calls this fantasy the Asian counterpart of the "imaginary playmate" or "fictitious companion" that has been disclosed in many Western studies of childhood.
    —*The Case Against Reincarnation*

• Ian Wilson has emphasized that Stevenson generally dismisses on the flimsiest grounds the possibility of fraud on the part of the children, their parents, and other interested parties. Stevenson maintains that no motive for fraud exists, when such motives are only too evident. Wilson has pointed out that several of the children remembered belonging to a higher caste in their previous lives and seem to have been motivated by a wish for better living conditions. In one case, for example, a boy asked for one-third of the land of his past-life father, showing no interest in his previous incarnation when this former "father" lost his fortune and became poorer than his father in the present life. Wilson also calls attention to the fact that Stevenson invariably tells us exceedingly little about the character and background of the parents, who are usually vital informants. In many cases, too, there was or easily could have been contact between the parents and persons connected with the "previous personality" about whose life the child had accurate recollections.
    —*The Case Against Reincarnation*

Channeling

As you might expect, there are a lot of channeling books out there right now. At least two others even share the same title as John Klimo's book, but his is the only one I can recommend. Unlike the others, Klimo's makes an effort to present the many sides of this complex subject, including a broad history and at least a little on psychological interpretations and the skeptical viewpoint.

Klimo is clearly convinced that channeling is a supernatural phenomenon, and, unfortunately, much of his book is devoted to freewheeling speculation, glossing over or excusing the obvious inconsistencies between channeled teachings, and promoting his own favorite explanation: the Jungian collective unconscious. But the book's strong point is Klimo's commendable research job, which provides useful thumbnail biographies of modern and historical channels, interesting backgrounds on and excerpts from some of the major channeled texts, and a diversity of viewpoints culled from the literature and from original interviews.　　　　　　　—T.S.

• In 1970, the alleged entity "Michael" first made its presence known to a thirty-three-year-old San Francisco Bay area woman. The channel is called Jessica Lansing (a fictitious name) in the best-selling books by Chelsea Quinn Yarbro, *Messages from Michael* and *More Messages from Michael.* These books have made "Michael" one of the best known of the channeling cases that have come to prominence in the last few years.

Recently, more than half a dozen others in the San Francisco area have been claiming to channel the same "Michael" by various means, including automatic writing, light trance, and full trance. This multi-channeled manifestation of the same supposed source makes the "Michael" material of special interest to us . . .

To those who gather at his sessions, "Michael" refers to channeling as one of the chief methods for growth "by which your false personality is set aside so that there may be inner dialogue with the essence." Yet he often is reported to grow impatient with the petty, private questions of those who seek his counsel, reminding them, at one point, "We are not the Ann Landers of the Cosmos." Apparently wishing to set a more serious and responsible tone, "Michael" added, "We would like to point out to you at this time that many of you are dabblers . . . you dabble in spiritual growth as well . . . Stop for a moment and ask yourself why it is that you search and for what."

After years of channeling "Michael," Jessica asks herself: "Do I believe it? The only answer I can give is: sometimes."

• Perhaps the best-known channel of musical material from supposed spirit sources was London housewife Rosemary Brown, who had no musical education. Brown's autobiographical book *Unfinished Symphonies* chronicles her lifelong association with the supposed spirits of such great composers as Liszt, Beethoven, Debussy, Chopin, Schubert, and Bach. More than four hundred new compositions are reported to have come through her in this manner. She claimed that the spirit of the nineteenth-century Liszt visited her in a clairvoyant vision when she was seven and promised that he would work with her as she got older.

Channeling
Investigations on
Receiving Information
from Paranormal
Sources
Jon Klimo
1987; 384 pp.
$18.95
($20.45 postpaid) from:
St. Martin's Press

Attn: Cash Sales
175 Fifth Ave.
New York, NY 10010
800/221-7945

pages and put the book back, but, amazingly, her unconscious mind had somehow not only retained the words and music, but remembered the book's title and the page number where the song could be found. The song was "Summer is Icumen In," written in medieval English words and published in *Musiikin Vaiheet,* a Finnish translation of *The History of Music* by Benjamin Britten and Imogen Holst. Her unconscious had somehow registered and stored a fleeting perception, only to dredge it up and use it years later in the construction of a past-life fantasy!

Could cryptomnesia be responsible for the material that comes through in channeling? Like past-life memories, most channeled information superficially seems utterly foreign to the experience of the channel. But closer examination often demonstrates otherwise. Edgar Cayce's trance readings on matters of health, for instance, owe a lot to a homeopathic physician named Wesley Ketchum, with whom he associated in his early years, while his readings on occult philosophy stem from his association with Arthur Lammers and other Theosophists who were attracted to him. In turn, many of the pronouncements of the popular modern-day trance channel Kevin Ryerson can be traced to Cayce's teachings, which he is known to have studied at the Association for Research and Enlightenment in Virginia Beach, Virginia.

Helen Schucman, the psychologist who channeled the immensely popular *Course in Miracles,* is personally bewildered by its supposed source: Jesus Christ. But Esalen co-founder Michael Murphy points out: "She was raised on that kind of literature. Her father owned a metaphysical bookshop." And transpersonal psychologist Ken Wilber says: "There's much more of Helen in the *Course* than I first thought. She was brought up mystically inclined. At four she used to stand out on the balcony and say that God would give her a sign of miracles to let her know that he was there. Many ideas from the *Course* came from the new thought or metaphysical schools she had been influenced by. . . . I found also that if you look at Helen's own poetry, you're initially very hard pressed to find any difference between that and the *Course*."

Charles Tart, one of the foremost modern parapsychologists (see page 67), has this to say about channeling: "From my studies with hypnosis, I know that I can set up an apparently independent existent entity whose characteristics are constructed to my specification. And the person hypnotized will experience that as if it's something outside of his own consciousness talking. So there's no doubt that some cases of channeling can be explained in a conventional kind of way. There's nothing psychic involved."[5]

THE DARK SIDE OF CHANNELING

In the '80s we've seen channeled entities whose messages are mostly sweetness and light, with a pinch of fire and brimstone sprinkled in for good measure. For instance, predictions by Edgar Cayce and other channels of vast, destructive earth changes that will destroy much of

---

[5]Murphy, Wilber, and Tart are quoted in *Channeling* by John Klimo; see review, this page.

The appearance of the spirit "Katie King" at a Philadelphia seance in 1874, as depicted in a contemporary engraving. Originally "manifested" through a medium named Florence Cook, Katie has materialized for many psychics, even as recently as 1974. These manifestations contradict Katie's promise, made through Cook, that she would never appear again after 1874.

North America have caused unnecessary anxiety among the populations of the endangered cities (none of these have occurred as predicted; see page 17). Ramtha, the ancient Lemurian channeled by J.Z. Knight, has raised occult eyebrows with his denial of the wrongness of actions like murder ("I do not abhor the act. I have reasoned it. I have understood it. I am beyond it."). Shirley MacLaine's favorite channel, Kevin Ryerson, produces messages instructing AIDS patients to turn to potentially harmful cures like homeopathic compounds derived from the syphilis bacterium, radiation from naturally occurring ore compounds, and moldy bread instead of penicillin.

But there is a more sinister side to channeling. Any number of modern-day murderers have attributed their actions to channeled entities. David Berkowitz, the "Son of Sam" serial killer who murdered six people and wounded seven others, claimed to have acted under orders from a 6,000-year-old entity that spoke through his neighbor's dog. Britain's "Yorkshire Ripper," a man named Peter Sutcliffe who in 1975 murdered thirteen prostitutes, had his first channeling experience in 1967: "I experienced a fantastic feeling . . . I felt for some reason I had been chosen to hear the words of God." In court, he testified that he didn't like having to commit murder, but that "it was the voice of God and God must be right." Mark David Chapman, the murderer of John Lennon, believes that it was demons that made him shoot Lennon, and in prison he heard the voice of God speak to him in "a very small male voice," instructing him to plead guilty.

In a powerful piece entitled "Strip Mining the Psyche," which appeared in the October 1986 issue of *Artifex*,[6] editor Dennis Stillings compares the New Age rush to "develop" the psyche to a rush of land speculators to bulldoze virgin wilderness. He suggests that techniques like channeling give the unprepared and uninitiated access to the unconscious, and, without visionary leaders or cultural values to buffer the effects, the result is often "dissociation and possession by *idées fixés* about UFOs and ETs, the Hollow Earth, and conversations with exotic beings from remote times and places." Stillings points

out that "virtually every psychotic killer is a 'channel' who has heard voices telling him of how evil women are or that the President must be killed or that his wife and children are possessed by evil spirits and should die so their souls might be saved. How individuals respond to the dissociative states involved in channeling can vary greatly and, in some instances, might well lead to destructive consequences."

Finally, Stillings warns that the hidden territories of the psyche are just as likely to harbor "vipers, carnivores, freaks, and monsters" as they are to harbor beings of sweetness and light.

"I BELIEVE IN EVERYTHING"

If, like many channeling enthusiasts, we were to take all of the channeled information at face value, we'd have to believe in many fanciful and contradictory things. We'd have to believe in channeled messages from Bigfoot and the Crystal Skull, in cities on Mars and Venus, in survivors of Atlantis that live in tunnels under Mount Shasta, and in a computer-like intelligence named "Hoova" that controls the world and communicates through Uri Geller. We would have to believe in many contradictory cosmologies, as editor Jay Kinney points out in the Fall 1987 issue of *Gnosis: A Journal of the Western Inner Traditions*:[7] "The [channeled] Books of *Oahspe*, of *Urantia*, and of Alice Bailey, to name just three examples, go into thousands of pages of intricate detail about intergalactic hierarchies and humanity's place in the universe; unfortu-

---

[6]*Artifex* and *Archaeus* are the newsletter and journal, respectively, of the Archaeus Project, an organization devoted to studying holistic health, Jungian psychology, parapsychology, anomalous phenomena, mythology, the psychological effects of electromagnetic radiation, and various other fringe topics. The October 1986 issue of *Artifex*, quoted above, is available for $2.00 from Archaeus Project, 2402 University Avenue, St. Paul, MN 55114.

[7]Available for $5 postpaid from *Gnosis*, P.O. Box 14217, San Francisco, CA 94114. See review, p. 30.

Psychology and the Occult

Carl Jung was known to hold certain occult and parapsychological beliefs—reflected in his ideas about "synchronicity" and the "collective unconscious"—yet his investigations of the "channels" and psychics of his day demonstrate a thorough hard-headedness that makes his conclusions all the more worthy of our attention. This slim volume brings together Jung's writings on the occult, starting with his M.D. dissertation from 1902 and ending with his answers to a questionnaire on parapsychology from 1960. Included are the results of his research into spirit mediumship, divided personality, automatism, heightened unconscious performance, cryptomnesia, and other topics that are essential for a complete understanding of channeling and the other particulars of today's occult explosion. —T.S.

• The psychology of the "Betty Books" differs in no essential respect from the primitive view of the world, where the contents of the unconscious are all projected into external objects. What appears to the primitive to be a "spirit" may on a more conscious level be an abstract thought, just as the gods of antiquity turned into philosophical ideas at the beginning of our era. This primitive projection of psychological factors is common to both spiritualism and theosophy. The advantage of projection is obvious: the projected content is visibly "there" in the object and calls for no further reflection. But since the projection does bring the unconscious a bit nearer to consciousness, it is at least better than nothing.

• [S.W.] once returned from a railway journey in an extremely agitated state. We thought at first that something unpleasant must have happened to her; but finally she pulled herself together and explained that "a star-dweller had sat opposite her in the train." From the description she gave of this being I recognized an elderly merchant I happened to know, who had a rather unsympathetic face. Apropos of this event, she told us all the peculiarities of the star-dwellers: they have no godlike souls, as men have, they pursue no science, no philosophy, but in the technical arts they are far more advanced than we are. Thus, flying machines have long been in existence on Mars; the whole of Mars is covered with canals, the canals are artificial lakes and are used for irrigation. The canals are all flat ditches, the water in them is very shallow . . . Human spirits who get permission to travel in the Beyond are not allowed to set foot on the stars. Similarly, travelling star-dwellers may not touch down on earth but must remain at a distance of some 75 feet above its surface. Should they infringe this law, they remain in the power of the earth and must take on human bodies, from which they are freed only after their natural death. As human beings they are cold, hard-hearted, and cruel. S.W. can recognize them by their peculiar expression, which lacks the "spiritual," and by their hairless, eyebrowless, sharply cut faces. Napoleon I was a typical star-dweller.

• Here I will mention only Binet's experiments, where little letters or other small objects, or complicated little figures in relief, were laid on the anaesthesic skin of the back of the hand or the neck, and the unconscious perceptions were registered by means of signs. On the basis of these experiments he comes to the following conclusion: "According to the calculations that I have been able to make, the unconscious sensibility of an hysterical patient is at certain moments *fifty times* more acute than that of a normal person."

Psychology and the Occult
Carl G. Jung
(translated by
R.F.C. Hull)
1976; 167 pp.

$7.95 (postpaid) from:
Princeton University Press
Attn: Order Dept.
3175 Princeton Pike
Lawrenceville, NJ 08648
609/896-1344

nately, they don't square with each other." And we'd have to believe every word of Madame Blavatsky's *Secret Doctrine,* an essentially racist story of human evolution (for example, Australian aborigines arose from "human fathers and semi-human mothers, or, to speak more correctly, from human monsters," and Tasmanians, some Australians, and certain mountain people of China are "semi-animal creatures").

We would also have to wonder why so many channeled predictions didn't come true, like the coming of the saucer people predicted for 1952 by the entity Sananda, the rising of Atlantis predicted by Edgar Cayce for the late 1960s, or the landing of a fleet of UFOs "some years, or sooner" after 1972, predicted by Uri Geller's entity Hoova.[8] Obviously channeled information is not always true. And this leads to the inevitable question: How do you tell what is true and what is not?

JUNG ON CHANNELING

The great psychologist Carl Gustav Jung, who held many occult and paranormal beliefs,[9] investigated a number of channels during his career. In his M.D. dissertation, he discussed at length the case of "Miss S.W.," an otherwise average turn-of-the-century Swiss girl who had become the channel for a large number of entities, each with its own characteristic facial expression, manner of speaking, and set of gestures. Though Jung observed the channeling of these entities for two years, he concluded that there was no evidence that any of these personalities originated from outside of S.W.'s own unconscious mind. He explained that portions of S.W.'s personality had split off into "complexes," or subpersonalities, which then represented themselves as "spirits," and which had "at their disposal the whole of the medium's memory, even the unconscious portion of it."

Jung theorized that S.W., who was prone to extremes of shyness and boisterousness, was unconsciously "seeking a middle way between two extremes; she endeavors to repress them and strives for a more ideal state. . . . These strivings lead to the adolescent dream of the ideal Ivenes [a calm and poised subpersonality], beside whom the unrefined aspects of her character fade into the background. They are not lost; but as repressed thoughts, analogous to the idea of Ivenes, they begin to lead an independent existence as autonomous personalities."

In an introduction to the 1948 edition of *The Unobstructed Universe* by Stewart Edward White, a book of spirit communications channeled by the author's wife, Jung made clear his non-supernatural explanation for channeling:

> The reader should not casually lay this book aside on discovering that it is about "Invisibles," that is to say

[8] Andrea Puharich. 1974. *Uri: A Journal of the Mystery of Uri Geller.* New York: Doubleday, 1974.

[9] According to William McGuire's introduction to *Psychology and the Occult* (see review, this page), as an undergraduate at Basel University Jung declared in a lecture to a student club that spirits, telekinesis, clairvoyance, second sight, prophetic dreams, and other paranormal phenomena were real.

about spirits, on the assumption that it belongs to the literature of spiritualism. One can very well read the book without resorting to any such hypothesis or theory, and *take it simply as a report of psychological facts or a continuous series of communications from the unconscious*—which is, indeed, what it is really about. . . . *Activated portions of the unconscious assume the character of personalities when they are perceived by the conscious mind* . . . These phenomena exist in their own right, regardless of the way they are interpreted, and it is beyond all doubt that they are genuine manifestations of the unconscious. *The communications of "spirits" are statements about the unconscious psyche,* provided they are really spontaneous and are not cooked up by the conscious mind. *They have this in common with dreams;* for dreams, too, are statements about the unconscious, which is why the psychotherapist uses them as a first-class source of information. [Italics added.]

. . . BUT IT *WORKS!*

If channeling is communication from the unconscious mind rather than from discarnate entities, the information may nonetheless be of great value. In 1865, the German chemist August Kekule (1829-1896), frustrated by the problem of how to join six carbon atoms so that they are all equivalent, dreamed of a snake holding its tail in its mouth. In the morning he awoke to the realization that carbon atoms could be formed into a circle, and discovered the benzene ring. The German-American archaeologist Herman Volrath Hilprecht (1859-1925) once labored for months trying to reassemble the pieces of a broken ancient Assyrian clay tablet. One night a priestess of Bel appeared to him in a dream and showed him how to fit the pieces together. When he awoke, he found that it worked.

Most artists and writers do not know where their ideas come from. Often the best they can do is optimize their working conditions and wait for their "muse." The entities of channeling—warriors and princesses from ancient kingdoms, space brothers from star-spanning galactic civilizations, and godlike beings controlling human affairs—resemble the fictional characters of science fiction, fantasy, and mythology. Can the material that arises in channeling have its origin in the same mental realm that, in writers and artists, produces fiction and imaginary landscapes? Just as Erich *"Chariots of the Gods"* Von Daniken underestimates the ability of ancient humans to construct archaeological wonders, thus drawing fantastic conclusions about ancient astronauts, perhaps we have underestimated the power of our own imaginations, attributing their products instead to external entities possessing more intelligence, creativity, or enlightenment than we credit to ourselves.

THE LAST WORD

Jung concluded a lecture on spiritualistic phenomena delivered in 1905 with the following words:

So far as miraculous reports in the literature are concerned, we should, for all our criticism, never lose sight of the limitations of our knowledge, otherwise something embarrassingly human might happen, making us feel as foolish as the academicians felt over Chladni's meteors,[10] or the highly respected Bavarian Board of Physicians over the railway.[11] Nevertheless, I believe that the present state of affairs gives us reason enough to *wait quietly until more impressive physical phenomena put in an appearance.* If, after making allowance for conscious and unconscious falsification, self-deception, prejudice, etc., we should still find something positive behind them, then *the exact sciences will surely conquer this field by experiment and verification, as has happened in every other realm of human experience.* That many spiritualists brag about their "science" and "scientific knowledge" is, of course, irritating nonsense. These people are lacking not only in criticism but in the most elementary knowledge of psychology. At the bottom they do not want to be taught any better, *but merely to go on believing*—surely the naivest of presumptions in view of our human failings. [Italics added.]

It is now over eighty-five years since Jung made these observations, and we are still waiting quietly for those "more impressive physical phenomena" that will demonstrate that channeling is something other than upwellings of the unconscious. Meanwhile, millions of people seem content to "go on believing" in what philosopher Paul Kurtz has called the twentieth-century version of "spiritualism without the frills." ∎

---

[10] Jung is referring to the stubborn denial of nineteenth-century astronomers to accept Chladni's assertion that meteorites originated in outer space. (See "The Blind Eye of Science," p. 102.)

[11] Jung is referring to the assertion of medical men before the opening of the first German railway that the speed of the trains would cause dizziness in travelers and onlookers, and would sour the milk of cows grazing near the tracks.

The Divining Hand

We started building a house last year. I called the local utility company to come out and mark their underground pipes and wires so I wouldn't dig them up. They sent a dowser, who found them. The same with the phone company. An article in the local paper said a nearby city has three dowsers in their engineering department. One of their tasks is to find "misplaced" sewer and water pipes.

Out here everybody has a water well. Most of my neighbors, or at least my neighbors' well-drillers, have had positive dealings with dowsers. The success of the biggest well-driller in town is based on the ability of its founding brothers to find water by dowsing. The local junior college has a class in dowsing. I took it, and I can tell you this: The movement of the wand, switch, or bent wire is positive, strong, and, most significantly, repeatable. I don't consider myself psychic and I don't knowingly practice magic. The dowsing device, whether a willow fork or a metal rod, is carried to magnify the otherwise imperceptible reaction of the body to a tiny stimulus. And experimental evidence seems to point to minute differences in the earth's magnetic field as that stimulus.

At least that's the conclusion arrived at in **The Divining Hand**, and the organs responsible for sensing the stimulus are even identified: the adrenal gland and either the pituitary or the pineal gland. But that's three-quarters of the way through the book. Before we learn the science we get the history (including the little-known use of dowsing techniques by U.S. Marines to locate Viet Cong tunnels during the Vietnam War), folklore, and myth. There's also plenty of art. Easily the most illustrated and attractive book in a field dominated by limited-budget efforts or academic put-downs, **The Divining Hand** is a comprehensive, plausible, and entertaining exposition of the dowser's art and science.

If someone tells me the earth is flat, I don't believe him because it runs contrary to my personal experience and the evidence I see around me. If someone tells me human senses are limited to sight, hearing, touch, taste, and smell,

The Divining Hand
The 500-Year-Old Mystery of Dowsing
Christopher Bird
1979, 1985; 350 pp.
$15
($16.50 postpaid) from:
New Age Press
Route 2, Box 184
Waynesville, NC 28786
704/926-9355

and that "water witches" are playing us the fool—well, that hasn't been my experience either, and I'll send them to **The Divining Hand.**
—Don Ryan

• During the ongoing process of his research [Dr. Zaboj V.] Harvalik himself has become so expert in remote, map, and information dowsing, the physics of which he cannot yet begin to explain, that he was able while in Australia to perplex and amaze a Sydney Water Board engineer who, skeptical of dowsing, put him to the test. Giving Harvalik the name of one of Sydney's many reservoirs, the engineer asked him in which direction it might lie from where both men were standing and how far away. After dowsing for both answers Harvalik drew an azimuth on a piece of paper fixed to a table and called the distance at 12.6 miles. When the engineer checked his answers on a map, both were correct.

"Can you tell me how deep it is?" he asked.

When Harvalik answered sixty-eight feet, the engineer pulled a booklet from his pocket, flipped a few pages, checked a figure, and said: "Well, you're a little off, but not much. The actual depth is seventy-five feet." The following day, on their way back from a sightseeing tour of the Great Divide, the engineer made a slight detour to show Harvalik the reservoir he had dowsed the day before. When they arrived at its edge he noticed somewhat to his astonishment that the water had dropped from its normal level. Turning to a water board employee he asked: "What's the level of the water today?" "Sixty-eight feet," came the reply.

Water Witching U.S.A.

This is the only book-length scientific study of dowsing, and, perhaps not coincidentally, it stands alone among dowsing books in its conclusions. The authors, an anthropologist (Vogt) and a psychologist (Hyman), carried out their research under the auspices of the Laboratory of Social Relations and the Department of Psychology at Harvard University, working both with dowsers and geologists (one of whom contributed an appendix). In addition to their own investigations, Vogt and Hyman present an overview of history and folklore, and a survey of modern research. They discuss the questions we all wonder about: What makes the rod move? (Their conclusion: the same unconscious muscle actions that move the Ouija board planchette.) Does either the rod or the dowser himself sense some sort of "unknown energy" emanating from the sought-after water, oil, ore, or lost object? (Conclusion: experiments suggest that dowsers are responding to subtle but normal sensory cues in the environment—when these are removed, their performance falls to chance level. And of course, "map dowsers" who perform at locations distant from the site couldn't be detecting such "energies" anyway.) How accurate is dowsing? (Unless sensory cues are present, not very.)

Does this mean that dowsing doesn't work? Not exactly—it works sometimes, but not for the reasons people think, and not any better than geological methods (which often don't work either). Why people continue to "believe" in dowsing, what kinds of people practice it, what the prevailing attitudes are toward it in different regions of the U.S.—all of these form the substance of **Water Witching U.S.A.** Read it for the minority viewpoint on the subject.
—T.S.

• An excellent example of an experiment . . . is the one performed by the American Society for Psychical Research. . . . The field was carefully chosen, so that such cues as surface water, wells, and other indicators of the presence or absence of water were absent. . . . Each diviner witched the field in his own manner . . . All told, the experimenters ran a total of twenty-seven diviners. . . .

As a control, two "experts," a geologist and a water engineer, made estimates of the depth and rate of flow of the underground water at sixteen different points . . . by "relying upon normal utilization of facts about underground water."

Test wells were then sunk at each of the spots assessed by the diviners and experts . . . The results showed that the experts did a good job of estimating the over-all depth of the water as well as the depth of specific points. Neither expert did a good job in guessing the amount of water to be found at specific points, although the engineer made a close guess on the over-all estimate of the rate of flow. The diviners, on the other hand, were complete failures in terms of estimating the depth or the amount of water to be found at their selected spots. . . . This was true not only for the group as a whole but for each diviner as an individual.

Water Witching U.S.A.
Evon Z. Vogt and Ray Hyman
1959, 1979; 271 pp.
$5.95
($6.95 postpaid) from:
University of Chicago Press
11030 South Langley Ave.
Chicago, IL 60628
312/568-1550

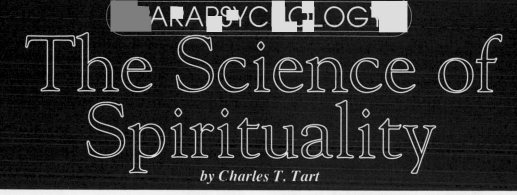

The Science of Spirituality

by Charles T. Tart

An important factor in the current popularity of "New Age" ideas is a reaction against the dehumanizing, despiritualizing effects of *scientism*, the philosophical belief (masquerading as objective science and held with the emotional tenacity of born-again fundamentalism) that we are *nothing but* material beings. To unthinkingly embrace anything and everything labeled "spiritual" or "psychic" or "New Age" is, of course, foolish, for many of these ideas are factually wrong, however noble or inspiring they are. On the other hand, this New Age interest is a legitimate recognition of some of the realities of human nature: people have always had and continue to have experiences that seem to be "psychic" or "spiritual."

Enough has been discovered in scientific parapsychological research to show that the totally material, scientistic view of man is only a partial truth, one that is dangerously misleading in claiming to be complete and thus able to reject, without empirical examination, our psychic and spiritual sides. There is a core of truth in New Age ideas: the human *mind* cannot be limited to the physical *brain*. The mind can sometimes reach out through time and space to gather information about and influence both other minds and the physical world. If minds can directly "touch" each other and the world in this way, is the spiritual idea that "we are all one" merely an abstract concept? This idea has a rational foundation in the reality of telepathy, for example. We still must discriminate the sense from the nonsense in the New Age, but we can use a science like parapsychology as a valuable aid in our quest.

Scientific parapsychology is the proper application of scientific method to understanding the psychic. We must distinguish *scientific* parapsychology, with its rigorous scientific methods, however, from the popular use of the term "parapsychology," which seems to cover anything and everything odd, no matter what the quality of the evidence for it.

In scientific parapsychology we experimentally set up an "impossible" (by known physical standards) situation, such as separating people by long distances; without instrumental aids, they cannot communicate. If one person now tries to mentally "send" randomly selected target information, such as a picture or the order of a deck of shuffled cards, and the other person draws a reasonable facsimile of that picture or guesses the order of the cards to a significantly greater degree than chance would allow, we have a "psychic" or "paranormal" (the two most popular words) or, more accurately, a "paraconceptual" event. Such events should remind us of the tentative nature of all our accepted conceptual systems. *Proper* science then calls for more investigation and/or revision of our conceptual systems. *Pseudo-critics*, who comprise the vast majority of ostensibly scientific critics of parapsychology, ignore parapsychological data or are so emotionally convinced there *must be* something wrong with parapsychological data that they go to extraordinary and quite unscientific lengths to debunk it.

The findings of scientific parapsychology over the last century (more than a thousand parapsychological experiments, carried out in accordance with quite strict scientific methodology) have repeatedly demonstrated that paraconceptual events do happen. Three forms of *extrasensory perception* (ESP) have been thoroughly demonstrated. People can sometimes read others' thoughts (*telepathy*), directly perceive the state of the physical world (*clairvoyance*), or predict a logically unpredictable future event (*precognition*). There is also a form of action at a distance, *psychokinesis* (PK), where mechanical, electronic, atomic, and biological processes can sometimes be altered merely by wishing it. Collectively these four phenomena are currently called *psi* (pronounced like *sigh*) phenomena. No known physical energies can satisfactorily account for them. There may be other kinds of psi, but only these four have been researched to a large enough extent for me to feel extremely confident of their existence.

Parapsychology is a very young, *very* small science. As of 1988, I estimate there are less than two dozen full-time scientific researchers involved in the Western world, with perhaps two to three million dollars a year of research money *for the entire field*; this is a trivial level of scientific activity, given the complexity of psi and the importance of understanding it.

I do not believe that scientific knowledge is the only useful kind of truth, but it is extremely valuable. Questions about our psychic and spiritual natures are too important to be decided by *a priori* beliefs, either pro or con. We should use the best of our scientific resources to give us the most accurate information possible about psi. ■

Do psychic powers exist? This question has been by no means resolved in the halls of science, as other sections of this book make clear. Dr. Charles Tart, one of the world's foremost parapsychologists, is convinced they do. Dr. Tart, who is on the faculty of the University of California at Davis, is the editor of the classic volume Altered States of Consciousness *(New York: Doubleday, 1972) and the author of, among others,* States of Consciousness *(New York: Dutton, 1975),* PSI: Scientific Studies of the Psychic Realm *(New York: Dutton, 1977), and, his most recent,* Waking Up: Overcoming the Obstacles to Human Potential *($14.95 postpaid from Shambhala Publications, Horticulture Hall, 300 Massachusetts Ave., Boston, MA 02115).* —T.S.

Foundations of Parapsychology

Here, amassed into one volume, is the cumulative scientific evidence for the existence of psi. Written by four parapsychologists, **Foundations of Parapsychology** *provides the most thorough survey available of this one hundred-year-old field, including history, experiments, research findings, and theories. Because it was designed to be used as a textbook, experimental design is especially emphasized. Included are sober, scientific discussions of topics more commonly encountered in sensationalistic surroundings, such as premonition, haunting, ESP, psychokinesis ("mind over matter"), survival after death, poltergeists, and such exotic phenomena as "thoughtography" (causing pictures to appear on unexposed film just by thinking it). The section on scientific, philosophical, and social implications ventures into the common ground that some aspects of parapsychology share with religion, including questions of mind-body dualism, reincarnation, and the existence of a "non-material" realm.*
— T.S.
[Suggested by Charles Tart]

Dr. Charles Tart operating his original ten-choice trainer. He is trying to telepathically influence a percipient in another room to press button no. 2 on the percipient's console.

• The cat's homing instinct is proverbial, and stories are fairly common of lost or abandoned dogs, cats, or other pets finding their way back home. It is another matter if an animal is left when a family moves, sometimes hundreds of miles, and some weeks or months later rejoins its 'family' at the new home where it never had been before. The most serious study of such cases was made by J.B. Rhine and Sara R. Feather.

In assessing many such reports that came to the Duke laboratory, they applied the usual criteria for evaluating spontaneous cases. They considered the completeness, consistency, and apparent sincerity of the report (usually by a pet's owner), any supporting statements, and all the individual circumstances (distance involved, condition of the animal on arrival, evidence of its identity, etc.) of each case. After applying these criteria, Rhine and Feather retained 54 cases, involving 28 dogs, 22 cats, and 4 birds, that they considered offered credible evidence of psi-trailing; i.e. of homing achievements that they could not plausibly explain.

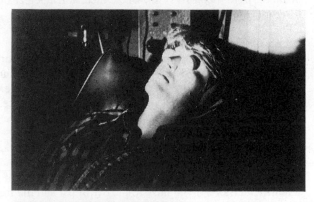

A subject in a ganzfeld experiment [listening only to white noise and seeing only uniform white light] at the Psychophysical Research Laboratories, Princeton, New Jersey.

• Folklore has long attributed haunts to emotionally troubled spirits who are unable to let go of the scenes of their tragic deaths. It has remained for modern psychiatrists to suggest that the troubled spirits are still in the flesh, that the ghosts they see are in some sense reflections of their repressed conflicts. Psychoanalyst Nandor Fodor's account of the 'Ash Manor Ghost' offers a remarkable example of such a psychodynamic situation. A couple and their adolescent daughter, living in an old manor house, were troubled by the lifelike apparition of a repulsive-looking man of an earlier time. They reported that the ghost had appeared repeatedly at the husband's bedroom, being seen sometimes by the wife also, and that loud footsteps had been heard. Fodor observed none of these phenomena, but he recognized signs of severe tensions in the family. His impression was confirmed by the psychic Eileen Garrett when Fodor brought her to Ash Manor to try to evoke the ghost personality. She went into trance and almost at once exhibited the personality and expression of a confused and frightened man who the residents said resembled the phantom they had seen. Fodor's questioning of the 'ghost' developed a dramatic tale of betrayal and murder several centuries earlier. None of the information could be verified, however. Eventually Fodor led the couple to acknowledge their secret problems, centered in the husband's sexual conflict, and to recognize that they had in effect evoked the ghost as a distraction. The apparitions then ceased.

Foundations of Parapsychology
Exploring the Boundaries
of Human Capability
Hoyt Edge, Robert Morris,
John Palmer, and Joseph Rush
1986; 432 pp.
$22.50
($24.25 postpaid) from:
Routledge, Chapman & Hall
29 West 35th St.
New York, NY 10001
212/244-3336

Parapsychology Sources of Information Center

There's a vast literature of parapsychology out there, but it's hard to keep track of. The Parapsychology Sources of Information Center was designed to correct this problem. They publish a wide variety of reference material like **Parapsychology: A Reading and Buying Guide to the Best Books in English** *($12 postpaid),* **On Being Psychic: A Reading Guide** *($15 postpaid),* **Directory of Degrees for Work in Parapsychology** *($10.20 postpaid), and* **Good Books on Parapsychology for Grades 8-12** *(free). They also publish the semi-annual* **Parapsychology Abstracts International** *($35/year), which*

provides summaries of articles from both parapsychology journals and popular magazines like **Omni**, *and even books. Their* **PsiLine** *database provides a search service through the literature of parapsychology.*
—T.S.

Parapsychology Sources of Information Center
Information **free** from:
Parapsychology Sources
of Information Center
2 Plane Tree Lane
Dix Hills, NY 11746
516/271-1243

Parapsychology: The Skeptical Side

*Parapsychology has a problem. It's been around for over a hundred years, yet it hasn't demonstrated the reality of its basic premise that psi exists—at least not to the satisfaction of the scientific community at large. Before parapsychology can cross this hurdle, it must successfully answer the questions raised by its skeptics, and nowhere is the skeptical viewpoint better presented than in the hefty **Skeptic's Handbook of Parapsychology**, which presents the work of over twenty-five authors, some of them parapsychologists and all of whom are concerned with the assumptions and practice of parapsychology. Among the offerings are fascinating historical overviews, beginning with the rise of spiritualism in the 1800s, entertaining discussions of historical and modern hoaxes, and counterexplanations for the phenomena interpreted as demonstrative of psychic forces both in daily life and in the lab.*

*Psychologist C.E.M. Hansel's **ESP and Parapsychology: A Critical Re-evaluation** makes a nice counterpoint companion volume to **Foundations of Parapsychology**, reviewed on the preceding page. It's an experiment-by-experiment skeptical critique of the body of parapsychological evidence, including early psychical research, spiritualism, J.B. Rhine and the modern experimenters, Russian parapsychology, and the recent Uri Geller and remote-viewing work. Marks' and Kammann's **Psychology of the Psychic** zooms in on both Uri Geller and remote-viewing experiments (in which a subject supposedly senses the details of a target site to which another experimenter has traveled). These two psychologists know what they're talking about: they've worked with Geller, and they've replicated the major remote-viewing experiments as well—with decidedly different results.* —T.S.

• Unfortunately, many parapsychologists appear to be committed to belief in psi on the basis of a metaphysical or spiritualist world-view that they wish to vindicate. Charles Tart, a former president of the American Parapsychological Association, admits this motive. Giving an autobiographical account of why he became interested in parapsychology, he says: "I found it hard to believe that science could have *totally* ignored the spiritual dimensions of human existence . . . Parapsychology validated the existence of basic phenomena that could partially account for, and fit in with, some of the spiritual views of the universe."

Of course, parapsychologists will accuse the skeptic of being biased in favor of a materialist or physicalist viewpoint and claim that this inhibits him from looking at evidence for psi or accepting its revolutionary implications. Unfortunately, this has all too often been the case, for some skeptics have been unwilling to look at the evidence. This is indefensible. A priori negativism is as open to criticism as a priori wish-fulfillment. On the other hand, some constructive criticism is essential in science. All that a constructive skeptic asks of the parapsychologist is genuine confirmation of his findings and theories, no more and no less.

I should like to make it clear that I am not denying the possible existence of psi phenomena, remote viewing, precognition, or PK. I am merely saying that, since these claims contravene a substantial body of existing scientific knowledge, in order for us to modify our basic principles—and we must be prepared to do so—the evidence must be *extremely* strong. But that it *is*, remains highly questionable.
—*A Skeptic's Handbook of Parapsychology*

• Claim: In 1951, the Dutch/American clairvoyant Peter Hurkos identified as the perpetrator of a series of arsons near Nijmegan the 17-year-old son of a respected local family whom the police believed to be beyond suspicion. To the utter amazement of the police chief, the boy confessed to the crime when confronted by Hurkos.

Facts: The 17-year-old arsonist, a mentally deranged farmer's son, had been the prime suspect almost from the beginning. He was arrested after the police at the site of one of the fires found candy wrappings of a brand the boy had recently bought in large quantity at the local confectioner's shop. Hurkos's attempts to solve the case began only on the day after the suspect had been arrested and the case had for all intents and purposes been solved.
—*A Skeptic's Handbook of Parapsychology*

• There are many ways of making small objects bend: (1) Distract everybody, bend the object manually, conceal the bend, and then reveal the bend to the now attentive onlookers. This is [Uri Geller's] usual method. The bend is made either by a two-handed tweak, or by levering it in something tough like a belt buckle or the head of another key with a hole in the top. (2) Geller (or an accomplice) pre-stresses the object by bending it many times until it's nearly at breaking point. Later it can be used to dazzle unsuspecting audiences as it bends, appears to melt, or even snaps in two pieces following the slightest pressure from Uri's wiry fingers. (3) Quite often collections of metal objects (e.g., a bunch of keys or a drawer of cutlery) contain one or more items that are already bent. Geller tells you he'll bend something and, when you examine the whole set of objects carefully, the bent item is found and Uri takes credit. (4) When an object is already bent, Geller will often say that it will continue to bend. He may move the object slowly to enhance the effect, or place it on a flat surface and push down on one end. But many people will believe they can see an object slowly bending purely as a result of Geller's suggestion that it is doing so. (5) Substitute objects already bent for the ones provided.
—*The Psychology of the Psychic*

• [In the 1960's, Dr. Helmut Schmidt conducted psychokinesis (PK) experiments] employing cockroaches as subjects. The animals received a shock or not according to the state of the randomizer. In this case the cockroaches, it seems, were unsuccessful in affecting the randomizer so as to avoid shock, but they caused it to produce 109 more shocks in 6,400 generated numbers than would be expected to arise by chance. Schmidt commented: "The magnitude of this deviation suggested that it might be a real effect, even though it raised the question of why a possible PK ability in cockroaches should work to their disadvantage." He did not consider the possibility that there might be any fault in his randomizer or method of data collection, or even that the result might have arisen by chance.
—*ESP and Parapsychology*

CONFESSIONS OF A

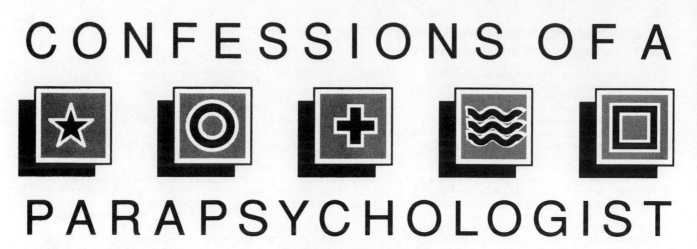

PARAPSYCHOLOGIST

by Susan Blackmore

N 1970, WHEN I FIRST WENT UP TO Oxford, I became fascinated with the paranormal. I joined the student Society for Psychical Research there and ran it myself for most of the three years I was there. We met witches and druids, psychical researchers and parapsychologists, dowsers and occultists of all kinds. I began to learn the basics of parapsychology, its experiments and its claimed phenomena. I came to understand the implications of the paranormal and began to see ever more clearly the deep split between those persons who accepted the paranormal as a natural part of their lives and the psychologists whose science I was learning.

My tutors thought I was dabbling in nonsense and hoped I would soon "grow out of it." Instead I developed a passionate desire to show that they were wrong, that you can't have a complete and workable psychology without taking the paranormal into account. I was determined to study parapsychology, little knowing where it would lead me.

First of all I worked on the idea that the key to memory lay within the paranormal. The physiological basis of memory was then (as now) under dispute. My "solution" was: there is no physiological basis for memory. Rather, I believed that memory is like ESP—that is, all thoughts are stored in some communal store and available as either memories *or* ESP. At that time I (mistakenly) thought this idea was both original and workable.

I understood there were some serious problems with this but then, I thought, all good ideas face problems. The most important question for experimental science is whether a theory is testable and whether the results of those tests support or negate it. Clearly I had to find a way to test my hypothesis.

There are no postgraduate courses in parapsychology in Great Britain. It is possible to work toward a research-oriented Ph.D. at the University of Edinburgh but it is extremely hard to get funding. Also everyone there tries to put you off. Nevertheless I eventually began work for my Ph. D. at Surrey University while teaching part-time at a Polytechnic (roughly equivalent to an American state college) to fund my studies.

I was excited. I was actually going to test my memory theory of ESP. I would find out whether it worked or not. But it was hard to start. You want your first experiment to be so perfect that you never start at all! But by pure chance I found myself able to teach a parapsychology course to undergraduates as part of their general studies program. I had over a hundred students and I couldn't pass up the opportunity to use them as subjects. I set to work testing my memory theory of ESP.

I did three types of experiments based on three predictions. All of them began with the suggestion that ESP is more like memory than perception; it is more like remembering than like a "sixth sense."

(1) If ESP is like memory, then the errors made by those possessing ESP should resemble errors of memory more than errors of perception. I used pictures as ESP targets. The subjects had to guess the identity of concealed pictures. These pictures were placed in sets of three. A key picture, for example a caterpillar, resembled a train in appearance but was more closely associated with a butterfly. I predicted that if ESP were like memory, there should be more errors of *association*; but if it were like perception, there should be more confusion of *appearance*.

There were plenty of errors in my subjects' results. You always compare the number of "hits" with the mean chance expectation in any given ESP test and I got just the number of hits one would expect by chance. That

---

On page 67, parapsychologist Charles Tart tells us why he believes psi exists. Here Susan Blackmore, also a parapsychologist, tells us why she's not so sure anymore. Dr. Blackmore, whose interest in magic, Tarot, and altered states dates back to her years as an undergraduate at Oxford in the early '70s, received a Ph.D. in parapsychology in 1980 from the University of Surrey in England. She's now a Visiting Fellow at the Brain and Perception Laboratory at the University of Bristol Medical School, and a constructive critic of parapsychological research. This article originally appeared in Fate magazine (see review, pp. 81, 83). —T.S.

meant that I could not test my hypothesis about ESP/memory/perception because no evidence at all of psi showed up in my test.

(2) I predicted that the best types of target material for ESP should be those most easily remembered—for example, using words of varying frequency and ready imaging. But again I couldn't test this hypothesis because all my targets were equally bad at eliciting psi!

(3) I predicted correlations between ESP and memory. But one cannot meaningfully look for correlations when one of the measures is of zero reliability. And that was the case for my measure of ESP.

During my two years of research looking for ESP, I chalked up quite an impressive record of failures. All my hopes for my memory theory were disappointed. Instead of making progress in understanding psi, I was thrown up against that perpetual problem: *Does it exist?* This was the last issue I wanted to confront but it was forced on me by my failures.

 F COURSE IT IS POSSIBLE THERE just isn't any such thing as ESP. My own failure to find it, however, couldn't justify such a conclusion. What about the hundreds of other persons who claimed to have found it? I couldn't dismiss them all.

There is also the sticky problem of ESP's being always defined negatively, as in "communication without using the recognized senses." In other words, you can say only what ESP is not, not what it is. That makes it difficult to say that it does not exist! And you can say that you have got ESP only when you have ruled out all other "normal" possibilities. Well, if you don't find evidence of ESP, what can you say? Only that you have failed to find something which, according to science, shouldn't have been there in the first place!

More pressing even than this issue is the fact that no one is surprised when you don't find it. The disbelievers or skeptics just say "told you so," which is exactly what many people happily said to me. And the believers always have some excuse—the conditions of an experiment weren't right, the subjects weren't good enough, or the experimenter's beliefs were wrong.

So what do you do if you actually want to know whether ESP exists or not? My approach was to continue systematically exploring all those "excuses" that might explain where I had "gone wrong."

Possibly I was using the wrong subjects. I had used only my own students; perhaps they weren't psychic enough.

At the same university where I was working, Ernesto Spinelli had been getting outstanding ESP results while testing children between three and eight years old. I tried to emulate his experiments with preschool children in a play group. We did simple ESP experiments in which the targets were colored candies and the children had to guess which color matched the hidden ones. Later I used pictorial targets. The children were delightful to work with and they were convinced they could "guess" the pictures

their friends were looking at. But all our results were close to chance.

I decided I should test people who actually claimed psychic powers. This proved somewhat difficult. At pubs, lectures, or parties I often met individuals who claimed to possess various psychic abilities. But when I invited them to the lab for testing, most of them found reasons why they couldn't come. A small number were willing and eager to come, however, and I proceeded to test them.

I aimed always to find out what they liked to do best and then to design an experiment around their predilections. There is no point in testing for something your subjects don't claim to be able to do.

To take a simple example: A mother and daughter from Scotland asserted they could pick up images from each other's minds. They chose to use playing cards for the tests because that is what they used at home. I let them choose the room in which they would be tested and insured that there was no normal way for the "receiver" to see the cards. They failed. They could not get more right than chance predicted and they were terribly disappointed. They had honestly believed they could do it and I began to see how easy it is to be fooled by your own desire to believe.

I had similar experiences with several dowsers, children who claimed they could move objects psychokinetically, and several who said they had telepathic powers. They all failed. Even now I have a five-digit number, a word, and a small object in my kitchen at home. The place and items were chosen by a young man who intends to "see" them while traveling out of his body. They have been there (though regularly changed) for three years. So far, though, he has had no success.

Of course you can argue that none of these people were really "psychic," but they certainly believed they were. Nor do I have access to any brilliant subjects. Apparently they are few and far between.

An alternate approach, however, is to train people in relevant skills which may lead them to develop psychic abilities. My experience and knowledge of ritual magic, astral projection, and even meditation suggested that the triple skills of relaxation, concentration, and vivid visualization are commonly associated with the awakening of psychic ability. I therefore put together a training group of 10 members and we taught ourselves for many months.

We learned a great deal. We became proficient at previously difficult imagery tasks; we improved our level of mental control, and we had many interesting experiences —including brief out-of-body experiences and sensations of flying or floating. But when we tested ourselves, our ESP scores stayed steadfastly close to chance. This was just one of the findings that gradually caused me to see what a mistake I had been making. I had been equating these interesting experiences, even mystical and peak experiences, with psi. In fact they may have nothing at all to do with psi. Gradually I began to find the experiences themselves more and more interesting—and psi less so.

But I still hadn't discovered why I had failed to find it in my experiments. One further possibility was that the conditions under which I had worked were wrong. I had tested large groups of subjects in boring classroom environments. Perhaps that was the problem.

CHARLES HONORTON, A researcher at Maimonides Medical Center in Brooklyn, had published some highly successful experiments using the "ganzfeld" technique. The idea behind the ganzfeld is to cut the subject off from patterned sensory input by feeding white noise into his ears and placing halved Ping-Pong balls over his eyes. He then lies comfortably for half an hour or more, recounting all the imagery that enters his mind. Meanwhile an agent is looking at a picture in another room and after the session is over the subject tries to select this target picture from among a group of others.

Not only was Honorton successful with this procedure but Carl Sargent at Cambridge was replicating the effect. Perhaps it would be best, I thought, if I placed *my* subjects in this specially psi-conducive setting. So I set about doing my own ganzfeld experiments.

I began getting lots of "hits." In one session, with my brother as agent, I seemed to pick up on almost every detail of the picture he was looking at. But the overall results of the experiments were again at chance. Those close correspondences were, I am sure, just the sort of coincidences you would expect to encounter in a series of such sessions. It is for this reason that we need statistics when evaluating our experiments. My statistics were telling me there was nothing more than chance—and perhaps the illogical human mind—at work.

I now seemed to have exhausted the commonly proposed "excuses" for experimental failure in parapsychology and I was still no nearer to understanding why others got psi in their experiments and I didn't. One last argument was handed to me by the successful experimenters interested in my work. Perhaps it was a "psi-mediated experimenter effect."

This suggests that "psi-conducive" experimenters—those with a good track record in parapsychology—are able to put their *own* psi into their results, regardless of the subjects' capacities. Either they force ESP onto their subjects or they elicit psi from their subjects for psychological reasons. By contrast, a "psi-inhibitory" experimenter suppresses or fails to elicit his subjects' ESP capabilities during an experiment. I was obviously a psi-inhibitory experimenter. But why?

Friends told me it was because I didn't sufficiently believe in ESP. Well, what could I do about that? It was clear to me that I was originally a very strong believer in psi, although, of course, others had only my word for that! Yet my results had been just as close to chance in the beginning as they were now. So that didn't seem to explain it. Nor could I conduct an experiment in which I "believed" for half the subjects and "not-believed" for the other half. There was, however, something I could do. I could test something I *did* believe in.

During this time in my life I had been reading the Tarot cards for about eight years. They seemed to work. Whenever I did a reading for someone, including persons I had never seen before, I found myself telling them things that I couldn't possibly have known. They were often amazed and asked me how on earth I did it. I didn't know. Something was obviously going on and I believed it could be paranormal. So I set up a simple experiment.

I wanted to duplicate as nearly as possible a normal

Out-of-Body Experiences

Nearly 20 percent of all people claim to have experienced leaving their bodies, seeing things from above, and even "flying." Some were relaxing or meditating when this occurred, others were suffering from illness or severe shock, and some were just carrying on with their normal lives. A very few claim to have seen or even to have interacted with things in the physical world at a distance from where their physical body was "parked."

The occult theory of "astral projection" assumes that something—an "astral body," soul, or spirit—actually leaves the body and travels to other worlds, and that this spirit goes on to survive when the body is dead.

Parapsychologists prefer the term "out-of-body experiences" (or OBEs), which doesn't presume any theory, and seek to find out whether anything really does leave the body during OBEs.

Early 20th-century experimenters weighed the bodies of the dying and photographed projected astral bodies, but as research techniques improved the early findings were no longer considered reliable. Recently parapsychologists have concealed targets from people who can have OBEs at will and asked them to observe the targets OB and to describe what they saw. One apparent success was achieved, but generally these experiments have been failures. All kinds of instruments measuring radiation, temperature, or weight have failed to detect any astral body.

The theory of another body is in any case challenged by questioning what it is made of, how it could interact with the physical world (reminiscent of all mind-body problems), how it could see without eyes or affect anything without leaving any traces.

All we now know about OBEs suggests that nothing really leaves the body. In normal perception a model or representation of the world is built by the brain and seems real—likewise, the brain con-

structs a model of self, a "self-image." But what if this image is disrupted in an illness or accident, or even deliberately during meditation? In striving to get back to normal, the brain may need to use an image from memory—but memory images are often in "bird's eye view." If such an image takes over as "reality," then an OBE has occurred. The whole normal world of the senses is replaced by one constructed from memory and imagination.

This explains why objects and situations seen OB often don't match reality and why the astral body is undetectable. It also predicts that OBErs should be especially good at visualizing the world as it would appear from "out-of-the-body"—a prediction that has been confirmed by experiment.

If this view is correct, OBEs provide no evidence for survival after death. They are natural experiences to be enjoyed, not feared. If there is no astral body, you cannot get lost on the astral planes—so enjoy your OBEs!
— *Susan Blackmore*

Tarot reading; otherwise it would not be a fair test. But I had to separate the reader from the subjects, thereby eliminating possible cues from their appearance, behavior and responses. So I got an assistant Tarot reader to lay out the cards in the traditional manner for each of ten subjects. This assistant then gave me the card orders, coded with a letter. From these layouts I wrote out my ten readings. Then the ten subjects had to choose their own reading from among the ten.

It worked! The subjects were able, just significantly better than chance would predict, to pick out their own readings. I was excited—here at least it seemed I had found something, in an experiment in which I believed.

The elation, however, was short-lived. Carl Sargent pointed out that the subjects all knew each other. This made their choices dependent, whereas the statistical test I had used assumed independence of choices. I had to do it all again and when I did, of course, the experiment did not work. Some people argued that it was because I had lost my enthusiasm, or I wasn't close friends with the subjects, or I no longer believed so strongly as I had originally. But these are just *ad hoc* arguments. The fact remains: the first experiment was slightly flawed, so its results cannot be considered valid. The evidence pushed me toward the conclusion that the Tarot works by normal, although interesting, psychological means.

I began to take a much more serious interest in other people's experiments. Whenever possible I visited their laboratories and observed exactly what they were doing. I had access to only a few but my experience was always the same. The further I looked into the details, the more errors or omissions or methodological problems I found there. This forced me to realize the enormous difficulty that exists when the critical student tries to assess the weight of evidence for psi. There is no doubt that most

ESP experiments result in non-significant scoring. The burden of proof rests on just a few studies. Experiments must be watertight to support this burden of proof and I began to wonder how many were.

This issue, added to the fact that my own research had been entirely negative, seriously dented my belief. At one point I even calculated that in 34 independent significance tests I had conducted on my data, only two showed a (statistically significant) probability of less than .05—in other words, a result that would occur by chance one in 20 times the experiment is run. In other words I was getting about as close to chance as you might normally expect.

There could be one final explanation for my failures. Perhaps psi just does not like to appear in laboratory experiments. Perhaps it appears only in real life—in out-of-body experiences, for example, or during poltergeist outbreaks or hauntings. But here too I had the same experiences. The deeper I looked into these reports, the less convincing the evidence seemed. Even famous cases, repeated in book after book, soon lost their initial appeal. When I went back to the original sources and tried to track them down, more often than not the evidence seemed to disappear in a cloud of poor memory, exasperation, and wishful thinking.

 Y NOW I WAS BECOMING thoroughly skeptical, even disbelieving. I began to wonder whether psi exists. I even concluded for a brief period that it could not possibly exist. But there are several reasons why such an extreme skeptical position is untenable.

For one thing, it cannot be tested easily. One of my first responses to my own doubts was to ask whether I

Beyond the Body

One evening during her first year as an undergraduate at Oxford, Susan Blackmore had a particularly vivid out-of-the-body experience ("OBE"). For two hours her "spirit body" soared over housetops, across continents, and to the ends of the universe. The experience was sufficiently long and varied to allow ample opportunity for careful observation and subsequent comparison to the OBEs of others. Eventually Ms. Blackmore went on to receive a Ph.D. in parapsychology. **Beyond the Body** *is the product of over ten years of professional research into OBEs, assembling anecdotal evidence, case studies, cross-cultural traditions, scientific research, and descriptions of related phenomena into perhaps the most even-handed and thorough treatment the subject has ever gotten.*
— T.S.

The "phantom" body connected to the physical body by an astral "cord," from a 1929 book by S. Muldoon and H. Carrington.

•   In his study of shamanism, the eminent anthropologist Mircea Eliade has described how the Siberian and North American shamans prepared for their 'flights'. The Yenisei Ostjak shaman apparently begins by fasting and carrying out a series of rituals, leaping into the air and crying, 'I am high in the air; I see the Yenisei a hundred versts away'.

•   Perhaps [C.E. Green's] most impressive case concerns a woman in hospital who apparently saw, while out of the body, 'a big woman sitting up in bed with her head wrapped in bandages; and she is knitting something with blue wool'. This other patient was as described and was in bed round the corner of the L-shaped ward. Neither woman had been allowed out of bed. But in this case we are not told whether the first woman had to pass by the other bed on her way into the ward when she first arrived, nor whether she could have overheard discussions about the other patient. Nor are we given any kind of corroboration of the story from others present.

could do experiments to test the idea that there is no such thing as psi. I think the simple answer is no, since you can't prove a universal negative.

There are, nevertheless, some close approximations which are quite interesting. One important question is why people should *believe* in psi if it doesn't really exist. This led me to consider the events that typically increase people's belief in psychic phenomena. One's own psychic experiences, especially precognitive dreams, are the most common reason for believing in the paranormal. Like many other psychic experiences, these typically involve a coincidence of some sort—such as a correlation between a dream and a real event. But it is well known that people are very poor at judging the likelihood of a coincidence. I wondered whether people who believe are worse than disbelievers at making such judgments of probability. This might explain how their beliefs came about erroneously.

My husband Tom Troscianko and I tested probability judgments in groups of believers and nonbelievers and found that the believers were worse at many such tasks than the nonbelievers. We also found the believers were more prone to the illusion that they could control something that is in fact a random process. Could these differences explain why the believers see evidence of the paranormal in the world around them, even though it doesn't exist? Maybe—but these finding don't actually prove that the paranormal does not exist. That is impossible.

The other major challenge to the skeptic's position is, of course, the fact that opposing positive evidence exists in the parapsychological literature. I couldn't dismiss it all. This raises a very interesting question: Just how much weight can you or should you give the results of your own experiments over those of other people? On the one hand, your own should carry more weight, since you know exactly how they were done and you know (even if no one else does) that you didn't cheat or make up the results. On the other hand, science is necessarily a collective enterprise. If scientists do not believe each other's results, science cannot proceed at all. So I couldn't use my own failures as justifiable evidence that psi does not exist. I had to consider everyone else's success.

I asked myself a thousand times, as I ask the reader now: Is there a right conclusion?

The only answer I can give, after ten years of intensive research in parapsychology, is that I don't know. If you believe that psychic phenomena exist, you must confront all the problems of illogical human thinking, the negative definitions, the difficulty of finding out anything about psi, and the fact that most laboratory experiments fail to confirm its existence. If you don't believe in psi, you have to face up to all the claims that it exists and the impossibility of proving its nonexistence. If you decide to maintain an open mind, you are in for a tough task, too. Keeping an open mind is far harder work than becoming simply a believer or skeptic. Perhaps it is better never to ask whether psi exists!

But there is a better question. Has belief in the existence of psi actually done any good? Has it progressed our understanding of any phenomena or experiences? Has it ever explained anything that could not be better explained some other way? In other words, has it ever done any scientific work for us? The checkered and controversial history of parapsychology may provide some answers. Aren't we just asking the same questions parapsychologists were asking a hundred years ago? For a hundred years there have been no answers.

My own brief career illustrates this. I began on a quest to understand ESP and memory. Then I turned to exploring out-of-body and near-death experiences. But the psi hypothesis did not help me one bit. Unfathomable and mystical experiences certainly abound, but I don't think the idea of the paranormal helps us to understand them.

My ten years of research have left me an open-minded skeptic rather than a disbeliever, but I have come to one conclusion: The notion of psi is remarkably unhelpful. If we want to understand the higher potentials of human experience, we need a better notion. ∎

Anomalistic Psychology

Faith-healing, fire walking, past-life recall, trance-mediumship ("channeling"), glossolalia ("speaking in tongues"), ESP, dowsing: of all the sciences, psychology is the one most properly equipped to study such phenomena, yet the popular writing on these subjects leaves the impression that they've either been ignored by psychologists or that psychologists have been unable to deal with them. **Anomalistic Psychology** *demonstrates that this simply isn't true. Designed as a college text, this book describes certain little-known, astonishing abilities of mind and perception that help to put seemingly miraculous phenomena in a whole new light. Glossolalia, for instance, can be related to well-studied patterns of speech invention in children. Many cases of "telepathy" have proved, upon examination, to be due to the extraordinary detection of faint sensory stimuli. Cryptomnesia (hidden memory) is often partially responsible for the content of "past-life memories."*

But even though objective investigation has often eliminated supernatural explanations, the authors, both psychologists, are careful not to adopt a debunking tone. Genuine mysteries are not denied, and alternative possibilities are not downplayed. The authors' only assumption is that, however inexplicable, any phenomenon is accessible by the scientific method.

The result is fascinating reading. The genuine psychological phenomena described here are at least as wonderful as the paranormal phenomena they explain. —T.S.

A case of *pareidolia*, projected misperception. Mrs. Maria Rubio and her tortilla image of Jesus.

• [Psychic researcher Harry] Price thought that fire walking could be explained by the short contact time between foot and embers, the low heat conductivity of wood embers, and confidence and steadiness in walking. He discounted or minimized the role of some of the other factors already discussed, such as the chemical preparation of the feet, the spheroidal state, or the need for special preparations.

One of the factors that is not stressed in reports on fire walking is that fire walking is walking, not standing still on embers or stones. There is no recorded instance of anyone's ever having attempted to just stand on red-hot stones or glowing embers for any length of time. The walkers walk rapidly, and it may take them only five or six steps to traverse a 20-foot long trench, for instance. As anyone who has felt the temptation to challenge the flame of a lit candle knows, it is possible to pass one's finger through the flame repeatedly and not get burned, provided one does not linger too long in the flame. It takes a couple of seconds for the skin temperature to reach the point where damage will begin to occur. Rapid walking through the embers, moving one's feet so that no one point is in contact with the embers for more than just a fraction of a second, should not allow the skin temperature to rise enough for burns to occur, even after several steps have been taken. Whatever heat accumulates from the four to six steps taken is dissipated on the cool grass or loose earth around the pit before the walker takes another walk.

• The "true" medium is one who dissociates readily. Proneness to dissociation, repeated practice, and the expectant and supportive atmosphere of the seance room combine to make the medium's performance what it is: a smooth and reliable passage into the trance state and the impressive welling up of autonomous portions of her divided consciousness that are taken as the manifestations of the spirits of the dead.

• In 1903, Professor R. Blondlot, head of the physics department of the University of Nancy, in France, announced the discovery of a new and amazing form of radiation, which he named N-rays. Blondlot reported that N-rays were emitted naturally by several different metals, but never by wood, and that they were faintly visible to the naked eye in a darkened room. Soon, other investigators, particularly in France, were replicating and extending Professor Blondlot's findings. Many other substances giving off N-rays were added to the list (e.g., human tissue, plants, and even a human corpse), but, again, never wood. The prestigious French Academy of Sciences published almost 100 papers on the topic within a year of Blondlot's original discovery, and it announced the decision to award Blondlot a medal and a cash prize for his accomplishment.

However, researchers outside of France were generally unable to replicate Blondlot's findings. Eventually, R. W. Wood, a scientist working in Great Britain, visited Blondlot in his laboratory at Nancy to observe directly the now famous N-rays. But, still unable to detect N-rays even in Blondlot's lab with Blondlot himself conducting the demonstrations, Wood decided that N-rays might be more imaginary than real. Wood proved this by surreptitiously altering some of Blondlot's apparatus. For example, he substituted a wooden roller for a metal file that Blondlot was using as the source of N-rays. When Blondlot reported that he could still see the N-rays, Wood had evidence that N-rays were non-existent because all investigators had reported that wooden objects did not produce N-rays. Several other tests also suggested self-delusion. When Wood's findings and conclusions were reported to the scientific community, the phenomenon of N-rays passed into the history of pseudoscience.

Commentators have generally agreed that the phenomenon of N-rays was not a hoax of the usual sort. Apparently, Blondlot was sincere in his beliefs. He certainly was a qualified scientist in terms of training and expertise. What the saga of N-rays does sadly illustrate is the powerful influence that wishes and extrinsic motivation can have on judgments and reasoning. Blondlot's folly occurred at a time when other strange forms of radiation, such as X-rays, were being discovered. It is likely that Blondlot deluded himself (as did many others) because of the strong desire to participate in the exciting advancements in science being made at that time.

Anomalistic Psychology
A Study of Extraordinary Phenomena
of Behavior and Experience
Leonard Zusne and Warren H. Jones
1982; 498 pp.
$29.95
postpaid from:
Lawrence Erlbaum Publishing
365 Broadway
Hillsdale, NJ 07642
201/666-4110

The Great Mental Calculators

A readable exploration of the lives and abilities of mental calculators, people who perform in their heads arithmetic feats such as finding the date of Easter in the year 3765. The book discusses both those such as the great mathematician Gauss, for whom mental calculation was a minor sidelight, and those for whom it was a center of life, such as the illiterate eighteenth-century Englishman Jedediah Buxton. It illuminates the diverse psychologies and methods of the mental calculators and speculates on the possibility (of questionable value in a world of electronic hand calculators) of teaching everyone to duplicate their feats. —Gerald Feinberg

• We learn our first language not by deliberately committing to memory some set of rules but by hearing examples, on the basis of which we infer a complex system which underlies our ability to speak.

There is at least one case of calculating prodigies who learned to calculate in just this way. Horwitz, Kestenbaum, Person, and Jarvic reported on identical twin calendar calculators. They were self-taught, and their I.Q.'s were at that time in the 60s - 70s. The twins could tell, given a date, the day of the week on which that date fell, or will fall. One of the twins, Charles, was completely accurate only for this century, but his brother George made correct day-date identifications in centuries ranging from 4,100 B.C. to 40,400 A.D. . . .

The twins' ability at calendar calculations was acquired from extensive examination of a perpetual calendar in the

The Great Mental Calculators
The Psychology, Methods, and Lives of Calculating Prodigies Past and Present
Steven B. Smith
1985; 400 pp.
$17.00
($19.00 postpaid) from:
Columbia University Press
136 South Broadway
Irvington, NY 10533
914/591-9370

World Almanac, which George discovered at age 6. By poring over examples, the twins, in some mysterious way, inferred an unconscious algorithm for calendar calculations. Interestingly, they did not incorporate all the data found in the perpetual calendar in formulating their algorithm. The calendar covered the years 1 to 2400 and is correct for the Julian calendar in giving dates before September 14, 1752, when the change to the Gregorian calendar went into effect in the British possessions. The twins were unable to make the correction for the Julian calendar as given in the almanac, even though the Julian calendar is easier to compute.

Something mysterious, though commonplace, is operating here—the mysterious human ability to form unconscious algorithms on the basis of examples. When asked how they did it, the twins' replies were about as informative as one might expect from a man on the street if pressed to explain how he talks: "It's in my head and I do it."

The Adventure of Self-Discovery

Systematic clinical research in the use of psychedelic drugs was a major casualty of the cultural revolution triggered by LSD. The psychiatrist Stanislav Grof, virtually the sole survivor of the original psychedelic researchers, began his research in Prague and moved it to the United States in 1968. The tens of thousands of psychedelic trips he's investigated, as a participant as well as an observer, include thousands of legal LSD sessions with dying patients. His reports of pain-killing as well as spiritually uplifting effects remain a challenge to those who must deal with the dying.

*In **The Adventure of Self-Discovery**, Grof lays out a preliminary cartography of consciousness, relating the "condensed experience" (COEX) structures of psychedelic trips, near-death experiences, and other unusual states. Experiences common to these states include reexperiencing of birth, as well as a range of religious, mythological, and paranormal phenomena. Grof provides a taxonomy of such imagery, categorizing the Hindu gods, Nordic deities, extraterrestrial guardians, and other archetypal entities that abound in psychedelic sessions. Of particular interest is the emergence of a new category of experience that Grof has noted in recent years: the strong, often life-changing experience of the Earth as a living organism, wounded and crying out to be healed.*

—Howard Rheingold

The Adventure of Self-Discovery
Dimensions of Consciousness and New Perspectives in Psychotherapy and Inner Exploration
Stanislav Grof
1988; 321 pp.
$10.95
($14.95 postpaid) from:
CUP Services
P.O. Box 6525
Ithaca, NY 14850

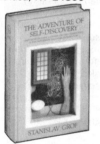

The Ether Demon: **This painting was done after recognizing that an all-pervasive, non-specific sense of nausea, terror, and electric icy cold was related to the anaesthesia used in birth.**

Brain/Mind Bulletin

*Easily the handiest way to stay current with the news and gossip on the soft psychology frontier. Despite success and a burgeoning of subject matter, editor Marilyn Ferguson has admirably kept the **Bulletin**'s format to a terse, packed six pages.* —Stewart Brand

• A nap in time saves nine. That's the conclusion of experimenters who have been studying what might be called "preventive sleep"—optimally timed napping.

Well-placed naps may serve us better than sleep after accumulated "sleep debt." Those anticipating jet lag or all-night studying will be benefited more by napping prior to sleep loss than by napping the next day.

Brain/Mind Bulletin
Marilyn Ferguson, Editor
$35/year
(12 issues) from:
Interface Press
P.O. Box 70457
Pasadena, CA 91107
818/577-7233

Norman Dog

The Mysterious Burning Death

by Kevin Kelly

In certain rare instances, according to some researchers, a human body mysteriously ignites and is largely consumed by fire. There are about two hundred recorded cases of this curious demise, and from these episodes springs enough of a pattern to allow a general description of the phenomenon.

"Spontaneous human combustion" (SHC) fries the body to a crisp, beginning in the torso and often leaving the limbs intact. This contrasts markedly with most burning injuries, in which the limbs are likely to be the first to sear. The burnt body is reduced to greasy ashes—even the bones. There is often no apparent source of flame. Usually, though not always, the victim is a "no-hoper": an elderly person living alone, or someone with depressed spirits. Often, but not always, the victim is an alcoholic. Sometimes SHC happens to younger people, but only

A fire has reduced most of the body to ashes, leaving only parts of the lower legs, the left hand, and portions of the skull. It was intense enough to burn a hole in the floor, yet little damage was done to the surroundings. (Photo: *When the Impossible Happens*)

rarely to children. The singular effect of this phenomenon is the deep internal burning of the body. Human flesh is very difficult to ignite and unlikely to continue to burn like a wooden log, independent of an external source of heat. Tremendous temperatures are needed to set tissue on fire, and even crematoriums must use high temperatures to burn bone. Imagine what it would take to cause a T-bone steak to disintegrate on a grill.

Perhaps less notice would be paid to these odd incidents of SHC were it not for the equally odd circumstance that flammable objects outside the burned area, even just inches away, are untouched by fire. A victim lying in bed might be found reduced to a lump of smelly soot burnt halfway through the mattress, yet the sheet above the body might not be singed.

Naturally the people who hunt down stories of SHC and compile them into books can't help proposing speculative theories. The current favorite says that this selective, intense burning is similar to what might be expected from a sudden localized microwave burst, which would cook watery (especially alcohol-permeated) flesh without marring cloth. But since an external source of microwaves is no more evident in cases of SHC than a source of flames, a shaky logic prevails: Ball lightning is suggested as the culprit, replacing one mystery with another.

I have no reason to believe in spontaneous human combustion other than the evidence of meager second-hand reports and these photographs found in books. (The most complete report is an out-of-print paperback called *Fire From Heaven* by Michael Harrison, 1976; Sidgwick and Jackson, London.)

For the moment I'll file SHC under "unexplained, but not inexplicable." And you?

Kevin Kelly is the editor of Whole Earth Review *(see p. 224) and the general overseer around Point Foundation, the source of all the* Whole Earth Catalogs, *including the one you're reading now. Kevin got all fired up over spontaneous human combustion after reading about it in Reader's Digest's* Mysteries of the Unexplained *(see pp. 82, 84), and dug a little deeper to bring you this grisly but fascinating collection of images.* —T.S.

CAPTIONS: (from top to bottom):

A sketch of the scene of "an unusual death by fire" in Gwent, England, on January 6, 1980. According to John Heymer, a retired Scenes of Crime Officer who was sent to gather evidence for forensic examination, "On the floor about one meter from the hearth was a pile of ashes. On the perimeter of the ashes, furthest from the hearth, was a partially burnt arm-chair. Emerging from the ashes were a pair of human feet clothed in socks. The feet were attached to short lengths of lower leg, encased in trouser leg bottoms. The feet and socks were undamaged. Protruding from what was left of the trousers were calcined leg bones which merged into the ashes. The ashes were the incinerated remains of a man. Of the torso and arms nothing remained but ash. Opposite the feet was a blackened skull. Though the rug and carpet below the ashes were charred, the damage did not extend more than a few centimeters beyond the perimeter of the ashes. Less than a meter away, a settee, fitted with loose covers, was not even scorched. Plastic tiles which covered the floor beneath the carpet were undamaged." (Illustration: *New Scientist* 5/15/86)

The charred remains of a "slim lady, 85 years old, in good health." She was totally consumed, except for one of her feet, in November 1963. Very little of her immediate surroundings was burnt. The case was investigated by Dr. D. J. Gee, lecturer in forensic medicine at University of Leeds. (Photo: *Fire From Heaven*)

An anonymous victim with the apparently unburnt head resting in the fireplace. The lower torso is charred to a residue but the upper part is nearly intact. (Photo: *When The Impossible Happens*)

(Bottom right) Calcined remains of Mrs. E. M., a widow, aged 69, found dead of "preternatural combustibility" in West London, January 29, 1958. (Photo: *Fire From Heaven*)

(Below) Workmen clear away the remains of Mrs. Mary Reeser, a widow of 67 from St. Petersburg, Florida, who was consumed by fire on July 1, 1951. The overstuffed chair she was sitting on was burned down to its springs, there was a patch of soot on the ceiling above and a small circle of carpet was charred around the chair, but a pile of papers nearby was unscorched. Her skull was shrunk by the intense heat. Dr. Wilton Krogman, a forensic scientist specializing in fire death, joined an investigation by the FBI, but had no explanation, saying "I cannot conceive of such complete cremation without more burning of the apartment itself." (Photo: *When the Impossible Happens*)

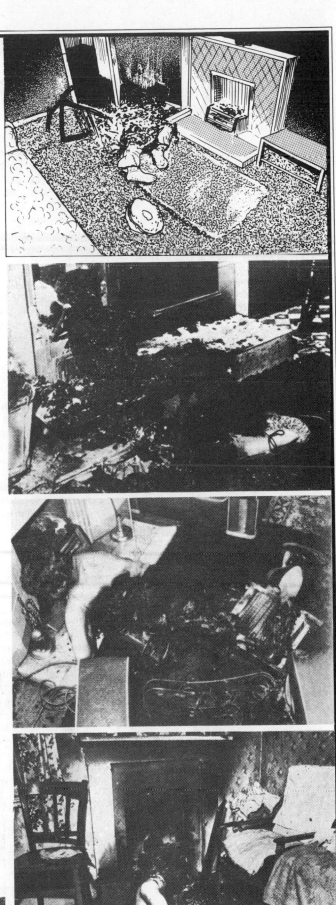

An Explanation?

by Joe Nickell

Dr. J. Irving Bentley, a retired physician, lived on the ground floor of an apartment in Coudersport, in northern Pennsylvania. On the morning of December 5, 1966, Don Gosnell entered the building's basement to read the meter for the North Penn Gas Company and noticed "a light-blue smoke of unusual odor." Going upstairs he found more strange smoke in Bentley's bedroom, but no sign of Bentley. Peering into the bathroom he discovered a large hole burned through the floor to the basement, exposing the pipework below. On the edge of the hole he saw "a brown leg from the knee down, like that of a mannequin" and then fled. (Photo: *The Mysterious World*)

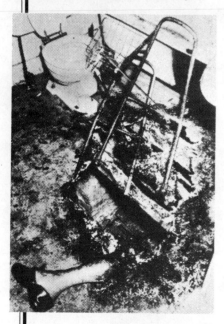

Joe Nickell, who's worked as both a stage magician and private investigator, currently teaches technical writing at the University of Kentucky. He's written for a variety of publications, specializing in strange and unsolved mysteries. His books, Inquest on the Shroud of Turin *and* Secrets of the Supernatural, *are available from Prometheus Press (see p. 202).* —T.S.

Intrigued by the gruesome mystery of "spontaneous human combustion" (SHC), forensic analyst John F. Fischer and I conducted a two-year investigation, comprising 30 historic cases. Our findings (published in the journal of the International Association of Arson Investigators[1]) consistently yielded credible prosaic explanations.

For example, a 1731 immolation was clarified by a detail from an early account: on the floor had been discovered an empty, ash-covered lamp. The 62-year-old woman had apparently fallen on it, the burning oil causing her destruction.

Similar ignition sources were found in nineteenth-century cases: a knocked-over candlestick near one victim's remains, a lighted pipe under the body of another, a hearth across which lay the smoldering corpse of a drunken woman.

Twentieth-century cases included the 1966 death of J. Irving Bentley, a 92-year-old pipe-smoking physician who habitually dropped ashes on his clothes. The fact that Dr. Bentley had shed his robe, discovered charred in the bathtub, demonstrated an external rather than internal source for the ignition.

What has become known as *the* case of alleged SHC, the 1951 death of Mary Reeser, was particularly instructive. Mrs. Reeser's body had been reduced to little more than ashes, a slippered foot, and—reportedly—an eerie, shrunken skull. Yet destruction of her surroundings was minimal.

Our investigation of the case included obtaining original news accounts, the police report, and death certificate, and consulting experts in smoldering combustion and forensic anthropology. The result was an obvious solution to the mystery.

When last seen, Mrs. Reeser was wearing flammable nightclothes, sitting in the overstuffed chair in which she perished, and smoking a cigarette. She had taken at least two sleeping tablets. Mrs. Reeser was a "plump" woman and, once her dropped cigarette started the fire, her own body fat would doubtless aid the destruction (as did partially open windows). In fact, "grease" was discovered where the chair had stood. (By what is known in forensic literature as the "candle effect," some of the melted fat could have been absorbed by the chair's stuffing, thus augmenting the fire which destroyed more of the body and yielded still more fat.)

SHC proponents wrongly compare the destruction of Mrs. Reeser's body to that produced by a crematorium. According to one expert, "Cremation is intended to destroy a body in the shortest possible time and is therefore carried out under extreme conditions, but a relatively small fire can consume flesh and calcine bone if it is allowed to burn for a long time." In the Reeser case nearly 12 hours had elapsed from the time the widow was last seen until her remains were discovered. (Such a lengthy period was typical of the cases of extensive destruction that we researched.)

Our investigation also clarified other elements in the case. The "shrunken skull" was actually unsubstantiated and traceable to an impressionable reporter's story, and Mrs. Reeser's intact foot was explained by a stiff leg which she extended when sitting. Her apartment went relatively unscathed because firemen extinguished a burning beam and because the walls and floor were concrete.

While this example illustrated the need for case-by-case investigation, we were nevertheless able to make some generalizations from our study. There did seem, as proponents suggested, some correlation with drunkenness. However, a person would die of alcohol poisoning long before consuming enough liquor to have even a slight effect on the body's combustibility. Instead, we attributed the correlation to heavy drinkers' carelessness with fire and diminished capacity to properly respond to an accident.

An even more important correlation concerned the amount of destruction of the body. In instances in which that was relatively minimal, the victim's clothes seemed to represent the only significant fuel source. But where the destruction was considerable, additional fuel—chair stuffing, flooring, and the like—was typically involved. (Such materials beneath the body would also have helped retain melted fat to facilitate the "candle effect.")

Our overall conclusion was that while unusual burning deaths certainly occur, special circumstances are invariably involved and we found no evidence for the existence of "spontaneous human combustion."

[1]"Spontaneous Human Combustion" by Joe Nickell and John F. Fischer, *The Fire and Arson Investigator*, March 1984 (Part I) and June 1984 (Part II).

Chroniclers of the Unexplained

by Ted Schultz

STRANGE-BUT-TRUE BOOKS ARE A DIME A DOZEN and, ever since the publication of Frank Edwards's classic *Stranger Than Science* (1959), they've been a bastion of purple journalism. But for those readers persistent enough to wade through the newsstand sludge, the unpolluted headwaters beyond hold a core of delightful material. One must be careful, however: not everything's a mystery that claims to be. It's probably safest to assume that even in the best compilations of strange phenomena, only a small percentage are genuinely inexplicable.

It all started with Charles Fort. Fort, called by one biographer the "Prophet of the Unexplained," spent his life in libraries, enjoying his favorite pastime: systematically combing newspapers, magazines, and journals, and noting down reports of mysterious occurrences like falls of fish and frogs, red snows, blue rains, strange aerial objects, and disappearing planets. He wove his voluminous notes into four books: **The Book of the Damned** (1919), **New Lands** (1923), **Lo!** (1931), and **Wild Talents** (1932), but these texts are more than just grocery lists of anomalous data. Fort poked fun at the scientific establishment and suggested outlandish, tongue-in-cheek theories to explain his "damned facts." Rejecting the mechanistic world view of the science of his time, he proposed instead a playful, prankster universe incomprehensible by logic. "If our existence is an organism, it must be one of the most notorious old rascals in the cosmos," he wrote. Elsewhere he jested, "I am not now saying that God is an Idiot. Maybe he, or it, drools comets and gibbers earthquakes, but the scale would have to be considered at least super-idiocy." Fort's four books have been collected into one volume, **The Complete Books of Charles Fort**.

So prodigious was Fort's research task, and so curious his philosophy, it was probably inevitable that a Fortean "movement" would arise. American novelists Tiffany Thayer and Theodore Dreiser founded the original Fortean Society in 1931, though Fort refused to join. In 1937 they began to publish **Doubt: The Fortean Society Magazine**, which lasted until Thayer's death in 1959. Editor Thayer caustically mocked government, religion, and science at every opportunity, regularly referring to scientists as "dirty yellow bellies." For years, copies of **Doubt** were unobtainable; now, they've been reissued in a six-volume set.

These days the Fortean tradition is carried on in a number of small publications. The undisputed best is **Fortean Times**, which exudes a delightful sense of humor and a healthy excitement for all things strange and wonderful. Highlighted by entertaining editorial commentary, **FT** features mind-boggling surveys of weird events culled from the newspapers of the world, including sea serpents, strange fires, religious miracles, out-of-place animals, ice meteors, etc. In addition, **FT** offers eccentric columnists, odd comic strips, and elegant shoestring design. Great fun to read, and a continuing testament to the strangeness of our world.

Both **INFO Journal** (published by the International Fortean Organization, founded in 1965) and **Pursuit** (published by the Society for the Investigation of the Unexplained, founded in 1966) feature anomaly news items and original articles, including useful surveys of peculiar recurring phenomena. An ambitious newcomer to the field, **Strange Magazine**, made a promising debut in 1987. It's broken new ground with well-researched articles about Fortean elements in popular culture, including historical treatments of mad scientists in the movies and "death rays." Quite a few prominent Forteans are regular columnists and contributors.

The only longstanding Fortean-style newsstand magazine is the venerable **Fate**, which has been around since 1948. Although regular reader-contributed columns like "My Proof of Survival" and "True Mystic Experiences" tend to strain the limits of credibility, **Fate** has over the years managed to publish a lot of genuinely provocative material, some of which, in retrospect, proves to have been ahead of its time. (For example, in the '50s it may have been the first national magazine to publish articles about psychedelic drugs.) Today, between the ghost and miracle stories, **Fate** mixes in reliable articles on parapsychology, dream research, folklore, archaeology, and even debunkings and hoax exposés. And for my money, it's got the most entertaining classified ads of any magazine anywhere.

A contemporary of Charles Fort and a popular radio broadcaster, the Briton Rupert T. Gould had three specialties: marine chronometers, typewriters, and unexplained mysteries. He produced histories of the first two subjects, and two major texts on the last. (He also authored a book on sea serpents and one on the Loch Ness monster.) Gould brought a high level of scholarship to the subject, examining particular topics in depth. **Oddities** (1928) contains fascinating chapters on "the devil's hoof marks" that appeared in fifty linear miles of Devonshire snow one winter morning in 1855, the coffins in Barbados that repeatedly rearranged themselves within a sealed crypt, and islands of the Atlantic that have been sighted, charted—and lost. **Enigmas** (1929) proved a worthy sequel, dealing in depth with legends of giants, mysterious sounds, and the

Horrified witnesses saw Mrs. Olga Worth Stephens suddenly ignite into a "human torch" while sitting in her parked automobile. The car was not damaged by the flames.
—*Mysteries of the Unexplained*

canals of Mars. Gould's books have been in and out of print over the years, though at the time of this writing they're unfortunately "out." They'll be back.

A number of recent books have commendably surveyed the inexplicable. One of the best is **Phenomena: A Book of Wonders** by John Michell and Robert J.M. Rickard (one of the editors of **Fortean Times**). At the outset the authors expound upon "neo-phenomenalism, the science of the future. With nothing to prove, no faiths, theories or taboos to inhibit, we shall look at the universe directly by considering all the evidence of itself it chooses to offer." Then, without further philosophizing, they proceed into the unknown. Two delightfully illustrated pages each are given to over fifty miraculous subjects, including electric people, lightning pictures, images that weep and bleed, stones that move and grow, and children brought up by animals.

Reader's Digest's contribution to Fortean literature, **Mysteries of the Unexplained**, is a large, wonderfully illustrated compilation of inexplicable events extracted from sources ranging from the reliable to the dubious. Not to be outdone, Time-Life has recently released the first three volumes of a projected twenty-volume set, **Mysteries of the Unknown**, that is the most lavishly produced testament to strange phenomena yet. Illustrated with original paintings and obscure photographs, and with a text that consolidates a wealth of obscure historical research, this is an encyclopedia of the popular (if questionable) folklore of the twentieth century: the Bermuda triangle, UFO kidnappings, the hollow earth, ley lines, bizarre psychic powers.

In a 1970s attempt at "statistical Forteanism," two scientists, Michael Persinger and Gyslaine Lafreniere of Laurentian University in Sudbury, Ontario, fed a computer 6,060 weird events extracted from the books of Charles Fort, **Fate** magazine, newspaper clippings, and scientific journals, apparently without regard for reliability. Their goal: to see if the events occurred in "clusters" corresponding to large-scale physical phenomena. The grand solar-geophysical-electromagnetic theory for Fortean events that they propose is appropriately controversial. Their book, **Space-Time Transients and Unusual Events**, is full of beautiful diagrams and is a preeminent example of eccentric scholarship.

You say you just want an inexpensive, reliable introduction to Fortean mysteries? Daniel Cohen's mildly skeptical attitude combined with a genuine love for the material makes his **Encyclopedia of the Strange** the perfect beginner's guide. Ancient mysteries, unknown places, strange people, weird talents, natural mysteries, magic—it's not an exhaustive collection, but it provides enough background history to make you conversant at the next Fortean convention cocktail party.

• An unclothed man shocks a crowd—a moment later, if nobody is generous with an overcoat, somebody is collecting handkerchiefs to knot around him.

A naked fact startles a meeting of a scientific society—and whatever it has for loins is soon diapered with conventional explanations. —*The Complete Books of Charles Fort*

• Clearwater, Minn.: Mound opened. Remains of seven persons, "seven to eight feet tall." Buried heads downward. "Skulls had receding foreheads and teeth were double all the way around, not like those of present race of men." (*St. Paul Pioneer Press*—June 29, 1888) —*Doubt*

• Residents of Whiteface, near Dornach in Sutherland, had some trouble with the water supply after heavy rain fell in February. One man turned on the cold tap and saw a two-inch fish flop into his kitchen sink; another, running the bath, found himself sharing a hot tub with the skeleton of a frog. The problem was blamed on storms causing extensive flooding of the water pipes. *D. Mail* 10 Feb 1987. —*Fortean Times*

• A woman who raised a cobra in the belief it was her dead son reincarnated, died when the snake bit her in Trincomalee, eastern Sri Lanka. S. *Express* 1 July 1984. —*Fortean Times*

The Complete Books of Charles Fort
Charles Fort
1941, 1975; 1125 pp.
$23.95
($25.20 postpaid) from:
Dover Publications
Attn: CRX
31 East Second St.
Mineola, NY 11501

Doubt
Tiffany Thayer, Editor
Volumes 1-5
$16.95 each postpaid
Volume 6
$18.95 postpaid
All from:
Sourcebook Project
P.O. Box 107
Glen Arm, MD 21057

Fortean Times
Robert J.M. Rickard and Paul Sieveking, Editors
$16/4 issues
from:
Fortean Times
96 Mansfield Road
London, NW3 2HX
United Kingdom

INFO Journal
Raymond D. Manners, Editor
$12/year
(4 issues) from:
International Fortean Organization
P.O. Box 367
Arlington, VA 22210-0367

Pursuit
Robert C. Warth, Editor
$12/year
(4 issues) from:
SITU
P.O. Box 265
Little Silver, NJ 07739-0265

- A Phantom Shoe-Chewer has thus far eluded Scottish police who have instigated a nationwide search for the heel. The latest assault occurred in Musselburgh where the victim was relieved of her high heels, then made to stand and watch as the "sole-ful snatcher" munched away.

"It's all very unusual," said a policeman who was working the case. "It seems he takes women's shoes and proceeds to eat them—or at least have a good chew." —*INFO Journal*

- Human blood seeping from the floors of an elderly couple's home has authorities puzzled in Atlanta, Ga.

Homicide Detective Steve Cartwright said there is nothing to indicate any wrongdoing at the home.

"It's an extremely strange situation," Cartwright said. "I've been on the force 10 years, and I've never seen anything like this."

"I don't know what the stuff is" said William Winston, 79. "My wife is upset because she doesn't know where it's coming from. Me, I'm not bothered by it because I'm in bad enough shape as it is."

Minnie Clyde Winston, 77, said she discovered the blood shortly before midnight Tuesday after stepping out of the bathtub to find the floor covered with blood.
SOURCE: AP in *The Plain Dealer*, Cleveland, OH 9/10/87
—*Pursuit*

- A boy, ten or twelve years old, was recently found exhausted, lying on the towpath, near Johnstown. He appeared to be in a dying condition, and a physician was immediately sent for, who promptly administered a powerful purgative. In due time, the medicine had the desired effect, and brought from the boy a double handful of young crabs! [i.e., crayfish]—real bona fide river or brook crabs, with claws, legs, broad tail and all. The mother of the boy explained the circumstances by stating that her son was in the habit of spending much of his time in the water, and that while diving he had swallowed a nest of crab eggs, which had hatched in his stomach. [Daily *Louisville* (Ky.) Democrat, August 12, 1858] —*Strange*

- Broadly speaking, the evidence which I have found shows quite clearly that Brewster was well within the truth when he spoke of a man at Mauritius who could foretell the arrival of ships at the island long before they appeared over the horizon. He might have gone further, and told how this man could determine, by his mysterious gift, whether one ship, or more, was approaching, and how long it would be before it, or they, came in sight—and even state in the same manner, when on board a ship, the distance and bearing of the land when it lay a long way below the visible horizon . . . He had trained himself to see some very faint

Boris Ermolaev, one of Russia's most imaginative young film directors, demonstrates his unique talents only to serious scientists, among them Venyamin Pushkin, a psychology professor at Moscow University, where he started carefully controlled government testing of the psychic as long ago as the early 1970s. —*Fate*

appearance, like an extremely attenuated cloud, somewhere near the sea-horizon, and he found, by experience, that this heralded the advent of a ship. He speaks of the "form" and "colour" of such clouds, and of their acquiring "consistency"; but there can be little doubt that even when most fully developed this appearance was far from easy to see. —*Oddities*

- "Still from his chair of porphyry gaunt Memnon strains his lidless eyes / Across the empty land, and cries each yellow morning unto thee."

If Tennyson, as seems likely, excelled Wilde as a poet, he nevertheless showed himself inferior to the author of *The Sphinx* in accuracy when he wrote: ". . . from her lips, as morn from Memnon, drew Rivers of melodies."

The sounds which are recorded as having been emitted by the famous "vocal statue of Memnon" were neither many nor melodious. Infrequently, but always at sunrise, those who stood near it long ago might hear a thin, strident sound, like the breaking of a harp string. That was all—an aimless cry heard at rare intervals during a relatively short period of two hundred years, a period preceded and followed by many centuries of silence. —*Enigmas*

- In 1900, Greek sponge divers anchored off the island of Antikythera during a storm located a sunken wreck. The report of their initial investigation was enough to bring archaeologists to the scene. They determined that the wreck was that of a commercial vessel, probably Greek, sunk about 65 B.C. while on its way to Rome from either Rhodes or Cos. The cargo was mainly pieces of sculpture, but from the wreckage they pulled what appeared to be a badly corroded piece of machinery. The object remained merely a curiosity for years until it was studied with care by the highly respected academician and historian of science Professor Derek de Solla Price. Professor Price decided that the device, which had been made with bronze plates and complicated gears, had been designed to display the positions of the sun and moon, and possibly the planets. According to British astronomer Colin Ronan, "It was an instrument that gave the positions of celestial bodies in figures—there were pointers that moved over

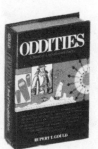

Ball lightning can pass through windows, then exit through the door without doing damage. A storm in Salagnac, France, in September 1845 produced this phenomenon. —*Mysteries of the Unexplained*

the way embarrassing evidence has of getting 'lost', we would be surprised if any other record exists. —*Phenomena*

• In 1926, an elderly Anglo-American caused a sensation with the publication of his first book, *The Lost Continent of Mu*. In this remarkable treatise, Colonel James Churchward claimed to have found irrefutable evidence linking the biblical Garden of Eden to the legendary sunken Pacific continent of Mu.

Churchward wrote that an old Asian priest had taught him to translate the primordial Muvian language, inscribed on certain tablets in India and Mexico. These tablets confirmed that Mu had been the fountainhead of civilization, predating even Atlantis. Several races of early humans had sprung up there, sharing the country with fauna ranging from brilliant butterflies to mastodons . . .

Unfortunately, Churchward reported, this idyllic land rested on a foundation of gas-filled caves. The gas exploded in a great cataclysm 12,000 years ago, and Mu sank beneath the waves. The lucky survivors who escaped to Muvian colonies around the world later inscribed the tablets that Churchward claimed to have deciphered.

No such accounts have ever been found by others, nor have geologists discovered any trace of a sunken Pacific continent. But this has not deterred Churchward's readers: His first and subsequent books on Mu remained in print well into the 1960s. —*Mysteries of the Unknown*

• In the southwestern corner of Pennsylvania, remains have been reported of large humanoid skeletons; local Indian legends describe these creatures with considerable precision. Over the years UFO flaps have passed through or concentrated near these areas and in 1973 an outbreak of ten-foot-tall humanoid sightings was recorded. Certain areas of New York state have been typified by repeated reports over centuries of luminous lights, non-human creatures, and rashes of Fortean events. Along the banks of the Mississippi River, bones remain of prehistoric animals; petroglyphs of these creatures exist along those same banks. There are reports by early explorers that strange flying creatures were seen in a bright day. Today, centuries later, people still report observations of unusual and unclassified creatures.

These kinds of data have prompted many theorists in the area of borderline phenomena to postulate various forms of the repeated or recurrent space theory. Essential to this concept is that unusual events of different categories recur in the same spatial area over time. —*Space-Time Transients and Unusual Events*

dials to indicate the results of its internal calculations . . . In short, this was a mechanical computer, and a complex one at that. Internal evidence also shows that it was a contemporary machine definitely made for everyday use, and not a treasure from some bygone age. We are forced to the conclusion that it pays tribute to a tradition of highly advanced technology in Greece . . . But if there was a tradition of an advanced technology in the ancient world, it did not penetrate into Western Christendom." —*Encyclopedia of the Strange*

• In France, early in 1856, workmen were blasting a tunnel through solid stone as part of the Saint-Dizier to Nancy railway. While they were breaking a large boulder, a monstrous form emerged from a cavity in it, shook its wings feebly and died with a hoarse cry. It was about the size of a large goose, with a hideous head and sharp teeth. Its four long legs were joined by a membrane and terminated in long and crooked talons; its body was a livid black; its skin thick and oily. This living fossil was taken to the town of Gray, where a naturalist, 'versed in palaeontology, immediately recognized it as belonging to the genus [*sic*] *Pterodactylus anas*'. The stone was 'lias' (Jurassic limestone), which accords with the era of these creatures, and the rock cavity formed an 'exact hollow mould of its body, which indicates that it was completely enveloped with the sedimentary deposit.' Our source is the *Illustrated London News*, 9 February 1856, which quoted the original account in the *Presse grayloise*—and knowing

Otherworld Journeys

Otherworld Journeys is about people who die and come back—well, almost die. It compares medieval and modern accounts, showing how the differences are shaped by the imagination and world-view of the individual, which are in turn shaped by the age and culture in which the individual lives. For instance, there's lots of hellish atonement in the medieval stories, but nowadays less accounting for sins is required before you get to feel good. The unchanging feature of both the medieval and modern accounts is that the person who has experienced an "otherworld journey" is profoundly changed by the deep spiritual nature of the experience.   —John Coate

• Although medieval hell and purgatory scenes find scarcely any counterparts in the near-death testimony collected by [Raymond A.] Moody and his colleagues, motifs of paradise topography are much the same in both periods: shining edifices, gardens, meadows, heavenly cities, and so forth. In addition, the ultimate experience of contemplative vision,

Otherworld Journeys
Accounts of Near-Death Experience in Medieval and Modern Times
Carol Zaleski
1987; 275 pp.
$21.95 postpaid from:
Oxford University Press
1600 Pollitt Dr.
Fairlawn, NJ 07410
800/451-7556

though treated only rarely and briefly by medieval otherworld journey narratives, is consistently described as a comprehensive vision of the whole, in which cognitive and affective powers fuse. It is a moment when the dramatic action of the otherworld journey seems to be suspended and unmediated awareness floods in; but an instant later the play resumes, a message is formulated, and the visionary feels compelled, against his desires, to return to life.

The Terror That Comes in the Night

"You are dreaming and you feel as if someone is holding you down. You can do nothing—only cry out. People believe that you will die if you are not awakened." That's how one person described the "incubus," night "mare," "witch-rider," or "Old Hag," all names for the gut-chilling transcultural tradition of supernatural assault-in-the-night that is the subject of folklorist David Hufford's book. Starting with Old Hag accounts from Newfoundland and drawing upon extensive first-person interviews, folk tales, and modern scientific sleep research, Hufford demonstrates that this peculiar belief has a long historical tradition, is widely known in many cultures, and may have a physiological basis in "hypnagogic sleep paralysis."
Sweet dreams . . .   —T.S.

• Well, I had a witch or something ride me once. I don't know what the deuce it was. I heard it before day in the morning . . . It come up on the bed, and I could feel it when it

The Terror That Comes in the Night
David J. Hufford
1982; 352 pp.
$29.95 ($31.90 postpaid) from:
University of Pennsylvania Press
Attn: Order Dept.
418 Service Drive
Blockley Hall, 13th Floor
Philadelphia, PA 19104-6097
215/898-6291

pressed the bed—me and another fellow was in the bed together. And it got up on me, and *I couldn't say a word. I lay flat on my back*, and I commenced a-twisting this a-way and a-whining in my sleep—"ennh, ennh, ennh"—and this boy ketched me. And I heard the thing when it hit the floor, 'bout like a big rat—bip—and out the door it went; you could hear it go on out. I said, "You better go, you devil you." (Laughter.) It was about four o'clock in the morning. That's true.

A Lycanthropy Reader

I'll admit I've known a few flirtatious foxes and some ardent wolves, but a full-moon-baying, graveyard-lurking, raw-meat-eating werewolf has never trotted across my path. Though far more prevalent in medieval and Renaissance times, people suffering from the psychological disorder called "lycanthropy" still exist. This fascinating collection of myths and legends, medieval and modern medical cases, historical trial records and accounts, contemporary sightings, and philosophical and theological interpretations expertly leads you through a macabre world, and provides rich and satisfying reading.   —Susan Erkel Ryan

• A 49-year-old woman [was] presented on an urgent basis for psychiatric evaluation because of delusions of being a wolf and "feeling like an animal with claws." She suffered from extreme apprehension and felt that she was no longer in control of her own fate: she said, "A voice was coming out of me." Throughout her 20-year marriage she experienced compulsive urges toward bestiality, lesbianism, and adultery.

The patient chronically ruminated and dreamed about wolves. One week before her admission, she acted on these ruminations for the first time. At a family gathering, she disrobed, assumed the female sexual posture of a wolf, and offered herself to her mother. This episode lasted for approximately 20 minutes. The following night, after coitus with her husband, the patient suffered a 2-hour episode, during which time she growled, scratched, and gnawed at the bed. She

stated that the devil came into her body and she became an animal. Simultaneously, she experienced auditory hallucinations. There was no drug involvement or alcoholic intoxication.

A Lycanthropy Reader
Werewolves in Western Culture
Charlotte F. Otten, Editor
1986; 352 pp.
$14.95
($16.45 postpaid) from: Syracuse University Press
1600 Jamesville Ave.
Syracuse, NY 13244-5160
315/423-2596

Lycaon transformed by Jupiter into a werewolf, from Ovid's *Metamorphoses* (London, 1717).

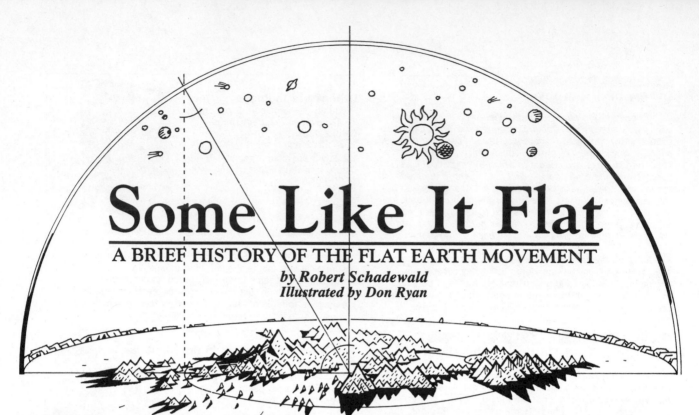

Some Like It Flat

A BRIEF HISTORY OF THE FLAT EARTH MOVEMENT

by Robert Schadewald
Illustrated by Don Ryan

Charles Johnson, president of the Flat Earth Society, is often interviewed by a TV network on Columbus Day. He always explains how Columbus sailed straight across the ocean from Spain to America, thus proving that the earth is flat. Johnson and his followers are the faithful remnant of a much larger movement, which developed in Victorian England and quickly spread throughout the English-speaking world.

Flat-earthism is an ancient Christian tradition. Many of the Fathers of the Church—Lactantius, Diodorus, Severianus, and Chrysostom, to name a few—insisted that scripture teaches a flat earth. In about 548 A.D., the Egyptian monk Cosmas Indicopleustes vigorously defended the Biblical flat earth against the heathen globe in his *Topographia Christiana*. The Cosmas cosmos was shaped like a steamer trunk, rectangular with a vaulted roof. But Cosmas fought a losing battle, and the Ptolemaic system, with its spherical earth, rapidly took over. By the eighth century, flat-earthism was almost dead in the Western world.

The modern flat-earth movement was launched in England in 1849 by an itinerant lecturer who called himself "Parallax." For the next thirty-five years, "Parallax" —his real name was Samuel Birley Rowbotham—toured England, attacking conventional astronomy in public lectures. His flat-earth system is still known to adherents by the name he coined, "zetetic astronomy."

Zetetic astronomy teaches that the known world is a vast circular plane. The north pole is its center and a 150-foot wall of ice marks the "southern limit." The equator is a circle concentric with the pole and the southern limit and lies roughly halfway between them. The sun, moon, and planets circle above the terrestrial plane in the region of the equator. Their apparent rising and setting is an optical illusion caused by atmospheric refraction and the "zetetic law of perspective." The latter law also explains why ships apparently vanish over the horizon when sailing out to sea. The entire universe is enclosed by a solid dome.

Rowbotham called his system "zetetic astronomy" (zetetic from the Greek verb *zeteo*, meaning to search or examine) because he sought only *facts*. In his lectures, he invariably praised facts at the expense of theories. Then he identified conventional astronomy with theories and zetetic astronomy with facts. Rowbotham was a tiger in debates, and newspaper accounts of his lectures often describe how he mopped up the platform with the spherical opposition. While he focused on scientific arguments, he made clear that the bottom line was the Bible.

In 1869, after two decades of "Parallax" lectures, the flat-earthers were still mostly ignored by "respectable" people. In that year, one John Hampden chanced upon a copy of Rowbotham's *Earth Not a Globe*. An Oxford graduate, Hampden considered the book a complete refutation of Copernicus and Newton, and he decided to confront the scientific world with the zetetic facts. He placed an ad in the January 12, 1870, *Scientific Opinion* offering £500 to anyone who could "prove the rotundity and revo-

No matter how universally accepted a consensus opinion may seem, you can be sure a small conclave of stubborn freethinkers exists that supports an alternative notion. There is no better example of this than the flat-earth movement.

Robert Schadewald, a science writer who specializes in the history of fringe ideas, has written for publications like Smithsonian, Science '80, Technology Illustrated, Science Digest, *and* Skeptical Inquirer. *His specialty is the flat-earth movement, and he is currently completing what promises to be the final word on the subject, a book called* The Plane Truth. *Until it's published, your best second choice is the brief history presented here, which was originally written for the* Bulletin of the Tychonian Society, *a journal devoted to yet another alternative to conventional astronomy, geocentrism (see pp. 89, 91).*

—T.S.

lution of the world from Scripture, from reason, or from fact." The famous evolutionist Alfred Russel Wallace accepted the challenge.

The wager was settled at the Old Bedford Canal on March 5, 1870. The experiment proved the curvature of the canal's surface to the satisfaction of the stakeholder, who declared Wallace the winner and handed over the cash. The ensuing controversy spawned a literary output which the flat-earthers never again matched. Hampden launched a pamphlet attack on Wallace, freely using terms like knave, liar, thief, swindler, imposter, rogue, and felon. In January of 1871, Wallace sued him for libel and was awarded £600. He never collected. While Wallace was in court, Hampden signed all his assets over to his son-in-law and declared bankruptcy. More suits and countersuits followed. Believers considered Hampden a hero, a David who boldly attacked Goliath only to be swindled out of his victory.

"The Bedford Canal Swindle" became the zetetic rallying cry. A flat-earth journal, *The Zetetic*, was formed to spread the plane truth, but it soon folded. Hampden kept the zetetics in the public eye, however, and he began to eclipse Rowbotham as the best-known spokesman for flat-earthism. (Many thought he was the famous "Parallax.") From his home, "Cosmos House," Hampden distributed a large selection of flat-earth literature. He founded flat-earth organizations with every other stroke of his pen—the Biblical Science Defence Association, the Biblical Science Institute, the Socratic Society and Biblical Defence Association, the New Geographical Society, the Philosophical Society of Christendom, and the Christian Philosophical Institute. (One suspects he was sometimes the only member.) Hampden also published a series of flat-earth periodicals. His first, *The Truth-Seeker's Oracle and Scriptural Science Review,* was founded in 1876. His last and most successful, *Earth, Scripturally, Rationally, and Practically Described*, ran from 1886 until 1888.

When John Hampden died in 1891, Rowbotham had already been dead for six years. The flat-earth movement had neither a visible leader nor a viable organization. Yet the movement was stronger in numbers than ever before. In 1892, the Universal Zetetic Society (UZS) was founded, and soon afterward its journal, the *Earth—Not a Globe—Review* appeared. Generally known as the *Earth Review*, it was the most ambitious flat-earth periodical ever.

The first issue, dated January 1893, set the pattern. It reported that a paper on zetetic astronomy was read at Breakley Road Chapel in London. The UZS publicly offered £1,000 to the editor of *Science Siftings* magazine for proof of the earth's sphericity. A long poem, "The Song of the Evolutionist," ridiculed Darwinism, geology, and astronomy, suggesting that evolution was part of the spherical plot. Though avowedly nonsectarian, *Earth Review* was hardly sympathetic to liberal religious views.

Within a year, the UZS had members throughout the English-speaking world, and the *Earth Review* had agents in England, Ireland, the U.S., Canada, South Africa, India, Australia, and New Zealand. The UZS published and distributed books, pamphlets, and periodicals attacking the spherical hoax and defending zetetic astronomy. They searched scientific publications for tidbits supporting their views, assembling and continuously recycling a collection of quotations from prominent scientists who made (to them) damning "admissions." A dozen or so freelance lecturers crisscrossed England and Ireland under UZS auspices. When possible, they arranged public debates with the spherical opposition—and they frequently won.

For all the agitation, the distribution of tracts, the free copies of *Earth Review*, the letter writing, ear bending, and arm twisting, the Universal Zetetic Society had limited success. The *Earth Review*, which probably never boasted a thousand subscribers, folded with the April 1897 issue. Its heterogeneous collection of articles, poetry, letters-to-the-editor, and advertisements is the best single source on the flat-earth movement.

Though down, the UZS was not out. There emerged a genteel and tiny tigress, Lady Elizabeth Anne Mould Blount. Daughter of an architect and land surveyor, wife of a wealthy baronet, Lady Blount had been one of the *Earth Review*'s most prolific contributors. She soon founded a new journal, *Earth*, which she edited from January 1900 to November 1904. Aided perhaps by her title and wealth, she persuaded some well-known people to publicly support the UZS, including an archbishop and a theologian still influential today.

The British flat-earthers hoped to convert the Church of England to the plane truth, but their successes were limited. One churchman they *did* convert was Ethelbert William Bullinger, who is still revered among Dispensational Fundamentalists. At first, Bullinger attempted to conceal his flat-earth sympathies. His letter in the June 1873 *Zetetic* was attributed to "E.B." of "the Vicarage." When he subscribed for six copies of William Carpenter's 1877 pamphlet *Delusion of the Day*, it was as "E.W.B." Bullinger finally came out of the closet in 1904 to serve on the UZS Committee under president Lady Blount.

It was no use. The Movement floundered. Lady Blount survived until the 1920s, but the British flat-earth movement seems to have been a casualty of World War I. Meanwhile, however, flat-earthism had taken hold in America.

William Carpenter, a well-known British flat-earther, emigrated to Baltimore in 1880. A printer by trade, Carpenter was an expert in Pitman shorthand, and he opened a shorthand school in his home. "Professor" Carpenter quickly became *de facto* leader of the U.S. flat-earthers. He is best known in this country for his 1885 pamphlet *One Hundred Proofs that the Earth is not a Globe*, which went through a dozen editions. Carpenter sent a copy to Johns Hopkins University president Daniel Gilman, daring him to defend the earth's rotundity. Dr. Gilman ignored him. Carpenter also formed a friendship with the Reverend John Jasper, a former slave famous for his flat-earth sermon, "The Sun Moves."

Alexander Gleason, a civil engineer from Buffalo, New York, was another well-known nineteenth century American flat-earther. Gleason used his knowledge of surveying to make observations on the waters of Lake Erie, which he claimed showed no convexity. He published his results in two editions of *Is the Bible from Heaven? Is the Earth a Globe?* (1890 and 1893). Gleason also produced a beautiful four-color map of the earth as a circular plane.

In terms of numbers, the flat-earth movement probably peaked in Zion, Illinois in the 1920s. Wilbur Glen Voliva, General Overseer of the Christian Apostolic Church of Zion, made flat-earthism a doctrine of the church. He also made Zion a theocracy, notorious for its blue laws and famous for its fig cookies. Voliva had a standing offer of $5,000 to anyone who could prove (to him) that the earth is a globe, and nobody ever collected. Zion had one of the first 100,000-watt radio stations in the country, and Voliva went on the air daily to thunder against "the Devil's Triplets": Evolution, Higher Criticism, and Modern Astronomy. His church claimed tens of thousands of members in the U.S. and it had large missions in Australia and South Africa. Voliva lost power in Zion in the mid-1930s. The Christian Apostolic Church of Zion quickly dropped flat-earthism as necessary for salvation, but there are flat-earthers in Zion to this day.

Charles Johnson, the present head of the Flat Earth Society, corresponded with Voliva just before the latter's death in 1942, but it was not Johnson who revived the modern flat-earth movement. That honor fell to an Englishman, the late Samuel Shenton, who helped organize the International Flat Earth Society in Britain in 1956. Shenton got the Flat Earth Society some press, but most of it was negative. Before he died in 1971, it was Shenton's last wish that the mantle of leadership should pass to Johnson, his most active and enthusiastic member.

Johnson has tried to move flat-earthism away from its Bible-thumping image. *The Flat Earth News*, which Johnson edits, emphasizes *facts*, such as the fact that bodies of still water (like the Salton Sea) are flat. In keeping with zetetic tradition, he also blasts the theory of evolution. Johnson does not, however, align himself with the "scientific creationists"; he considers them hypocrites who claim to defend the Bible while trying to destroy it with the globe. (Worse still are the modern geocentrists—creationists who reject both Copernicus and Darwin but retain the globe!)

The Flat Earth Society still has religious associations. It is also incorporated as the Covenant Peoples Church, which shares the same address (see review, this page). Neither organization proselytizes, however, and people who write to the Flat Earth Society are not inundated with begging letters like those sent by television evangelists. Johnson cares little for money and less about making converts. He recalls that the Bible speaks of Two Witnesses. He and his wife Marjory witness to the world; let them accept who will. ∎

Flat Earth Research Society

*Charles and Marjory Johnson's Flat Earth Research Society is the direct heir to a long tradition of flat-earth organizations. The official Society publication, the **Flat Earth News**, mixes flat-earth "common sense," anti-communism, anti-vivisectionism, and fundamentalist Christianity. It's absolutely and delightfully a one-of-a-kind publication. Eminently quotable, it belongs on the coffee tables of all open-minded "round-ball-earthers."*
— *T.S.*

• . We don't have a "theory" earth is flat... oh no we don't "believe" earth is flat!... oh no! WE KNOW EARTH IS FLAT! how, you say?

We went out and CHECKED IT! How else could we KNOW? Greese ball world is nothing but rubbish myth idle fiction talk... NO PROOF OF ANY KIND EXISTS TODAY 1988 for a Greese Ball whirling in space!

TOTAL PROOF EXISTS FOR THE "FACTS" earth is flat! Your school **religion** "science" tells you... proof earth a Greese ball... as you can see a ship sailing over the edge... we went out checked sea... found sea was FLAT, lakes flat, rivers all... KEEP THE LAWS OF GOD... LAWS OF NATURE used to be called **Laws of Physics**... water seeks its own **LEVEL**... get it? Most of the world is water... right? and all of it **LEVEL**! How about "**SEA level**?" What do you think it means? Sea a **Ball** of water? No, sea **LEVEL**.

A map of the flat earth. The grey area indicates the endless ice field beyond the "southern circumference."

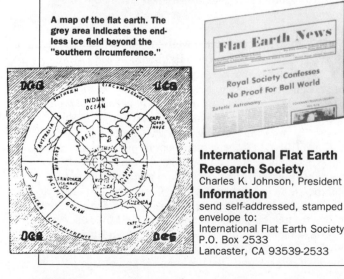

International Flat Earth Research Society

Charles K. Johnson, President

Information

send self-addressed, stamped envelope to:
International Flat Earth Society
P.O. Box 2533
Lancaster, CA 93539-2533

Recommended Reading

For readers wishing to follow up on flat-earth literature, the situation is bleak. Flat-earth literature is extremely scarce. Much that has been written about the flat-earthers is shallow or misinformed. The following are reliable.

Martin Gardner. 1957. *Fads and Fallacies in the Name of Science.* (Second edition.) New York: Dover Publications. Chapter 2 deals with Voliva. (See review, p. 199.)

John Michell. 1984. *Eccentric Lives and Peculiar Notions.* London: Thames and Hudson. One chapter discusses British flat-earthers in some depth and with admirable accuracy. (See review, p. 92.)

Samuel Birley Rowbotham. 1873. *Earth Not a Globe.* London: John B. Day. The second edition of the foundation work of modern flat-earthism.

Robert J. Schadewald. 1978. "He Knew Earth Is Round but His Proof Fell Flat." *Smithsonian*, April 1978, pp. 101-109. A description of the wager between John Hampden and Alfred Russel Wallace.

Robert J. Schadewald. 1981. "Scientific Creationism, Geocentricity, and the Flat Earth." *Skeptical Inquirer*, Winter 1981-82, pp. 41-48. Shows that all three views are grounded in scripture.

Robert J. Schadewald. 1980. "The Flat-Out Truth." *Science Digest*, July 1980, pp. 58-63. Interview with Charles Johnson.

Jumping Geography!

by Ted Schultz

Explorers glimpse the central sun as they sail through the vast polar entrance into the Hollow Earth. —*A Journey to the Earth's Interior* (1920)

The Hollow Earth

In 1818, U.S. Infantry Captain John Cleves Symmes, a hero of the War of 1812, announced his revolutionary theory that the earth is a hollow shell containing four additional concentric spheres, all accessible via polar openings thousands of miles across. Symmes proposed to lead an expedition to the "warm and rich land, stocked with thrifty vegetables and animals" that lay beyond the frozen North, inside the earth. In 1828, at the urging of Symmes's follower Jeremiah Reynolds, Congress actually approved the plan. The secretaries of the Navy and Treasury prepared three ships for the adventure, but the newly elected President Andrew Jackson put an end to the project.

If Symmes's ideas failed to inspire serious scientific investigation, they did inspire works of fiction, including Edgar Allan Poe's *Narrative of Arthur Gordon Pym* and *Manuscript Found in a Bottle*. Meanwhile, in 1869 a man named Cyrus Teed had a revelation. The earth was hollow all right, but we live on the *inside*. Teed, who formed a religion around his theory, traveled around the country gathering followers and in 1894 he founded the Koreshan colony in Estero, Florida. Teed died in 1908, but the Koreshan colony exists to this day. A variation of Teed's idea, known as *Hohlweltlehre*, or Hollow Earth Doctrine, was widely held in Nazi Germany.

In 1906, William Reed's contribution to hollow-earth theory, **The Phantom of the Poles**, appeared. Reed dispensed with Symmes's idea of concentric spheres, describing instead a single hollow globe with polar openings and an undiscovered world of continents and seas within. He explained that the aurora borealis is nothing more than the reflection of forest fires and volcanoes in the earth's interior.

In 1913, Marshall Gardner published **A Journey to the Earth's Interior, or Have the Poles Really Been Discovered**, followed in 1920 by an enlarged edition. While Reed had proposed that the inner earth is illuminated by sunlight penetrating through the polar openings, Gardner believed that it contains its own miniature sun, the light from which causes the auroras. He theorized that Eskimos are descended from inner-earth races, and that the mammoths found frozen in arctic ice originate there. Like Reed, he quoted polar explorers' references to "warm winds," pollen, and plentiful animal life as proof of habitable lands within.

In 1964 Raymond Bernard's modestly titled **The Hollow Earth: The Greatest Geographical Discovery in History** appeared. Borrowing heavily from the works of Reed and Gardner, Bernard expanded the theory to include flying saucers. Ads for the book that appeared at the time asked "Why does one find tropical seeds, plants and trees floating in the fresh water of icebergs? Why do millions of tropical birds and animals go farther north in the wintertime?" and asserted that "Admiral Byrd led a Navy team into the polar opening and came upon this underground region. It is free of ice and snow, has mountains covered with forests, lakes, rivers, vegetation and strange animals." Bernard's book inspired a new generation of hollow-earthers, and has been kept in print by a succession of publishers ever since.

The hollow-earth theory is only one aspect of a more extensive tradition of legends about an interconnecting network of vast caverns under the earth's continents and oceans. The supposed dwelling place of an ancient, advanced civilization, this subterranean world is accessible only through secret entrances at sacred sites around the world. Bruce Walton's **A Guide to the Inner Earth** is an extensive annotated bibliography of such stories, but be forewarned: most of the references are obscure occult magazines and books unlikely to be stocked at your local library. Walton's **Mount Shasta: Home of the Ancients**, on the other hand, reprints in full twenty-five hard-to-find articles, most of which describe an ancient colony of Lemurians living under California's Mt. Shasta. Supposedly their presence is revealed from time to time when hikers observe mysterious lights, encounter strange giants and little people, or stumble across unidentifiable structures that they cannot later relocate.

All of the books mentioned here are available from Health Research, one of the most eccentric publishing houses in the U.S. They offer facsimile editions of obscure, out-of-copyright books like Reed's and Gardner's, and they publish books like Walton's that would never make it in the mass market.

The Geocentric Universe

Gerardus D. Bouw has a doctorate in astronomy from Case Institute of Technology (now Case Western Reserve University) in Cleveland, Ohio. He is also a believer in the literal truth of the Bible. Bouw's careful reading of Scripture has convinced him (as it has many others in history) that the earth is the center of the universe around which

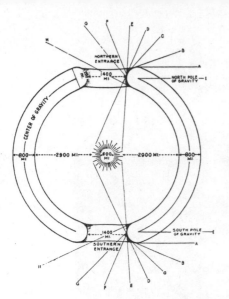

the planets, the sun, and the stars revolve. (Numerous Biblical passages refer to the "rising" or "setting" of the sun and to miracles in which the sun was made to stand still. Others refer to the immobility of the earth.) Bouw has combined his expertise in astronomy and his faith in the Bible to produce two monuments of eccentric scholarship: his journal, **The Bulletin of the Tychonian Society**, and his book, **With Every Wind of Doctrine**.

Since Bouw considers the Bible his ultimate authority, much of his writing deals with the meticulous interpretation of particular Scriptural words and phrases. But at other times he changes gears, spinning complex astronomical scenarios that support geocentrism, or reinterpreting the historical geocentrism vs. heliocentrism debate. Bouw is a geocentrist, creationist—and a gentleman. You won't find here any of the vitriolic prose that issues from some of the other Biblical literalists. The Tychonian Society pleasantly reaffirms that even a disagreement of the most profound nature can be scholarly and polite.

•   Why does the sun not appear for so long a time in winter near the supposed poles? Because during the winter the sun strikes the earth obliquely near the poles. Upon the way round the curve, approaching the interior, the earth being hollow, one sinks a long way in; hence the sun shines over him; it does not show up again until it strikes that part of the earth more squarely and shines down into the basin.   —*The Phantom of the Poles*

•   Meteors are constantly falling near the supposed poles. Why? If the earth be solid, no one can answer this question; if hollow, it is easily answered. Some volcano is in eruption in the interior of the earth, and from it rocks are thrown into the air.
                                        —*Phantom of the Poles*

•   Certainly that animal described by the Eskimo and named by them the arcla, may well be representative of one of the cretaceous animals with a general outline somewhat after that of the kangaroo. These animals were reptiles, however, feeders on vegetable matter and with teeth set in several rows like a tessellated pavement. As birds are well fitted to escape from both geological upheavals and climatic changes by their power of flight we should doubtless find in this refuge some of the very earliest species of birds, such as those with lizard-like beaks in which many teeth were set, birds entirely different from any existing orders on the outside of the globe. If we have an entomologist with the party he will be kept busy collecting insects. There will be the most gorgeous and large butterflies, all sorts of dragon flies, ants of several species, and in fact there will be several thousands of species of insects many of which are not known to exist on the earth today.   —*A Journey to the Earth's Interior*

•   Walters, Richard. WANDERERS AWHEEL IN MALTA, Article in *The National Geographic*, Aug. 1940: A network of caverns under the Mediterranean island of Malta, the entrances to which were closed by the government after a group of school children entered them and never returned. (Also see: Crabb, Riley H. *The Reality Of The Cavern World.*)   —*A Guide to the Inner Earth*

•   Brakefield, Stoney. UNDERGROUND MONSTERS ATE 15 MINERS ALIVE! Article in *News Extra*, a Pennsylvania newspaper, July 14, 1974, reprinted in *The Hollow Hassle*, Vol. 2, No. 1: Disappearance of several coal miners in a mine near Dixonville, PA, in 1944, and the sighting of an unearthly being by the rescue party

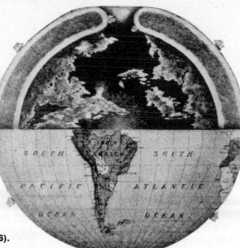

(Facing page, far left) Diagram from Marshall Gardner's *A Journey to the Earth's Interior* (1920) indicates by letters the steps in an imaginary journey to the inner earth; at point "D" the central sun's corona is first glimpsed, while at "E" it is clearly visible (as depicted in the painting reproduced on page 89).
(Facing page, center and right) Photographs of both halves of an actual cutaway scale-model hollow globe that Gardner built and patented, showing the central sun and the interior continents and seas. *(Right)* William Reed's earlier concept of the Hollow Earth, from his *Phantom of the Poles* (1906).

The shell of galaxies appears to move as a whole in this direction relative to the earth at its center.

A two-dimensional analogy for the distribution of galaxies about the earth. —*With Every Wind of Doctrine*

in a previously unknown side tunnel shortly after the disappearances.   —*A Guide to the Inner Earth*

• Several years ago, according to Lovelace, two prospectors were searching for a gold strike in the desolate mountains of southwestern Nevada. The two men were digging in the arid soil when a cave-in revealed a dark opening in the ground. They cautiously entered the newly-formed cavity and soon found themselves in a vast underground tunnel. Following the passageway, they went deep into the heart of the mountain and finally entered a large subterranean room, which they found to be the first in a series of interconnected caverns.

The two astonished prospectors held their torches high and saw that the caves were furnished with chairs and tables, "furniture of an immense size, as if built by giants." Over-sized dishes cast from solid gold and silver were also found on the tables. Other artifacts made from precious metals were also discovered in the caverns, apparently of an imperishable alloy, all having evidence of being undisturbed for countless centuries.

—*Mount Shasta*

• Reports of unusual fires which gave off a blue and white illumination deep in the center of the forests would surface. Between the fire and the observer strange figures could be seen to pass at times. And, if the wind were blowing in the proper direction, strange chantings and singing, accompanied by weird, beautiful music would float or be carried in the direction of one of the small nearby towns.   —*Mount Shasta*

• During the "midnight" ceremonies of these strange people, witnesses claim to have seen several hundreds of individuals around these fires, and at times strange beams of light are seen shining into the sky, sometimes catching a low hanging cloud, or illuminating strange dome-shaped buildings of marble and onyx. A strange stone monolith which had been discovered on the outskirts of the forest was engraven with strange hieroglyphic-type writings *as well* as an English translation which read: "CEREMONY OF ADORATION TO GUATAMA." It was also apparent from the writings that the ceremonies occurred at sunrise, sunset, and midnight and that the word "Guatama" referred to the continent of North America.   —*Mount Shasta*

• The superior scientific culture of the subterranean people, of which their flying saucers are an evident example, is the result of superior brain development and more energetic brains. This is due to the fact that their vital energies flow up to their brain, rather than being dissipated through the sexual channel as among so-called "civilized" surface races. In fact, sex indulgence is completely out of their lives, because of their fruit diet, their endocrines are in a state of perfect balance and harmonious functioning, as in little children, and are not stimulated to abnormal activity by metabolic toxins, as produced by such foods as meat, fowl, fish and eggs and by such aphrodisiacs as salt, pepper, coffee, tobacco and alcohol.   —*The Hollow Earth*

• It is claimed that the earth's crust is honeycombed by a network of tunnels passing under the ocean from continent to continent and leading to subterranean cities in large cavities in the earth. These tunnels are especially abundant in South America, especially under Brazil, which was the chief center of Atlantean colonization; and we may believe they were constructed by the Atlanteans. Most famous of these tunnels is the "Roadway of the Incas" which stretches for several hundred miles south of Lima, Peru, and passes under Cuzco, Tiahuanaco and the Three Peaks, proceeding to the Atacambo Desert. Another branch opens in Arica, Chile, visited by Madame Blavatsky.   —*The Hollow Earth*

• Let me again state my personal stance on geocentricity. Insofar as scientific evidence is concerned, it is a toss-up. Neither geocentricity nor heliocentrism can be proven or disproven from a modern scientific perspective. That has been my stance since the mechanics courses in my undergraduate years in astrophysics, since before becoming a Christian. To show that it is not an oddball or quack conclusion, I shall, Lord willing, reproduce in the next issue of the *Bulletin* several letters from physicists who agree with my early-drawn conclusion. For me, the determining issue is Biblical. If the Bible teaches geocentricity then that tips the evidential scales off neutral. Hence I claim no conclusive scientific argument for geocentricity; nor is there any for heliocentrism. I may not always be right, but the ground whereupon I stand is secure.   —*Bulletin of the Tychonian Society*

• Is relativity the only theory which accounts for the precession of Mercury's orbit? Is it the most accurate of all theories? Both questions are answered in the negative. Perihelion precessions can be accounted for by considering such things as the sun not being truly spherical in shape, or by the existence of matter between the planet and the sun, or by the existence of matter outside the orbit of the planet, or by gravitational shielding (where intervening material weakens the gravitational attraction between the sun and planet), or by considering the advanced potential (where the universe or ether "knows" what is to happen ahead of time).   —*With Every Wind of Doctrine*

Bulletin of the Tychonian Society
Gerardus D. Bouw, Editor
Sample copy **free**
(donation requested)

With Every Wind of Doctrine
Biblical, Historical and Scientific Perspectives of Geocentricity
Gerardus D. Bouw
1984; 288 pp.
$10.95 postpaid

Both from:
Gerardus D. Bouw
4527 Wetzel Ave.
Cleveland, OH 44109

Eccentric Lives and Peculiar Notions

When I picked up this book, I didn't think it would move me to admiration for the people whose stories it tells, or that I might be inspired by them. And, though I'm not ready to run off on a flat-earth crusade, or to begin deciphering the cryptograms woven into every line of Shakespeare's plays, or to single-handedly build a castle out of hand-carved coral rock, I did find something universally human in the struggle of those who think independently, if somewhat erratically, and who stubbornly persist in the face of overwhelming derision. John Michell has performed a wonderful job of eccentric scholarship in compiling the life stories of these colorful characters and the histories of the movements that some of them founded.

Did you know, for instance, that there is a small but vocal movement of "trepanners" who believe you can achieve a permanent psychedelic state by drilling a hole in your head? Me either. A delightful read. —T.S.

• In the latter part of the last century a respectable-looking gentleman could be seen walking about the cities of Britain, gazing intently at young women. He always had one hand in his pocket, and every time he passed a girl in the street the hand would make a slight twitch. There was a perfectly innocent explanation for this: the pocketed hand belonged to Sir Francis Galton, the great man of science, and the purpose of his urban rambles was to gather material for a Beauty Map of Great Britain. Also in his pocket was a piece of paper divided into three sections. Each woman he saw was categorized as either beautiful, middling or ugly, and the judgment was recorded on the appropriate part of the paper by pricking it with a needle mounted on a thimble. No detailed results of these

Eccentric Lives and Peculiar Notions
John Michell
1984, 1987; 240 pp.
$7.95
($9.45 postpaid) from:
Lyle Stuart
120 Enterprise Ave.
Seacaucus, NJ 07094
201/866-0490

Dr. William Price, the revolutionary Welsh Druid, in his ritual outfit of scarlet merino wool with green silk letters in the bardic alphabet he discovered.

researches were ever published, but Galton's general conclusion was that the prettiest girls are found in London and the worst-looking in Aberdeen.

• The most sensational of the projects which [Geoffrey] Pyke submitted to Mountbatten was code-named Habakkuk. Pyke in America had been investigating certain properties of ice and had developed a material, 'pykrete', made from a mixture of ice and wood pulp, which was far stronger than pure ice, more stable and less inclined to melt. A ship made of pykrete would be unsinkable; a torpedo would make only a slight dent in its side, quickly repaired. Pipes circulating cold air within the hull would keep it permanently frozen, and Pyke had worked out how the ship was to be powered and steered and other details.

American Eccentrics

If it's sheer volume of eccentricity you're after, you won't do any better than **American Eccentrics.** *Here, presented in one- to two-page thumbnail biographies, are 140 colorful characters from the 1500s to the present, including flagpole sitters, hermits, religious fanatics, imposters, and many impossible to categorize. Some are famous—Johnny Appleseed, Calamity Jane, "Diamond" Jim Brady, Typhoid Mary—but for the most part, these stories of human unorthodoxy, individualism, and folly are little known.* —T.S.

• For the trifling sum of $750 [John R.] Brinkley would give a man the transplanted glands or testicles of a billy goat ($1,500 for a very young goat). The patient was then supposed to enjoy a complete sexual renaissance. Goat Gland Brinkley, as he came to be called, operating out of the Brinkley Gland Clinic in Milford, Kansas, even allowed patients to pick out the billies of their choice from a backyard pen, thus assuring themselves that they were getting active goats.

Evidently Brinkley qualified for performing this revolutionary scientific advance thanks to his slaughterhouse work for Swift & Co., the meat-packing firm, and a two-month stint in the army (four weeks of which was spent under psychiatric observation).

• [Flagpole sitter Shipwreck Kelly's] props included an eight-inch disk that fitted on the top of the pole, to provide him with a platform. He often fashioned a makeshift chair to sit on. He was able to sleep during his performances by locking his thumbs in bowling-ball-style holes in the flagpole shaft. If he swayed while dozing, the twinge of pain in his thumbs caused him to right himself without waking up. He trained himself to catnap five minutes every hour and found he could last almost indefinitely in that fashion. Some who came to marvel at Shipwreck seemed most intrigued about how he disposed of waste matter; after the performance, they studied the special hose run up beside the flagpole.

Shipwreck Kelly ignored superstition on Friday, October 13, 1939, by standing on his head eating donuts on a plank extended from a Manhattan skyscraper.

American Eccentrics
140 of the Greatest Human Interest Stories Ever Told
Carl Sifakis
1984; 317 pp.
$8.95
postpaid from:
Facts on File
Attn: Order Dept.
460 Park Avenue South
New York, NY 10016
212/683-2244

The Conspiracy Watcher's Field Guide

by Jay Kinney

t is 1975. I decide to check out the San Francisco American Opinion bookstore, one of the national chain of "patriotic" book shops associated with the John Birch Society. Tracking down the address listed in the phone book, I find that the book store is located in a home in the Outer Sunset district—a stuccoed, middle class, residential neighborhood.

I ring the front doorbell and am let in cautiously by a greying woman. The bookstore? It's a little two-shelf bookcase in the front hall. Just what was I interested in? the woman asks. Oh, information and books on the way things are *really* run. You know—the CFR, the Rockefellers, stuff like that, I answer. Squatting in the hallway, I look through the meager selection of paperbacks and pamphlets reprinted from old *American Opinion* magazines, and choose a few of the more promising ones.

By now, apparently convinced of my sincere interest, my hostess takes me into her confidence. You can't be too careful in battling the Insiders, she warns. Why, her next-door neighbors used to have regular nighttime meetings—mysterious gatherings of men who'd arrive by car and meet behind closed drapes, doing *what*, God only knows! You can imagine how shocked her husband and she were to discover that the Illuminati—yes, THE ILLUMINATI!—were holding meetings right next door!

Well! They wasted little time in informing their neighbors that they knew who they *really* were, and by George if it wasn't just a few months later that their neighbors sold their house and moved away!

Somewhat taken aback by this astounding tale of an informed citizenry at work, I offer my congratulations on their small victory against the Conspiracy and leave shortly after, clutching my newly purchased literature.

Nearly fifteen years and countless conspiracies later, I'm still puzzled by that greying Bircher lady with her Illuminati neighbors. Was she merely a paranoid busybody harassing the hapless folks next door or was she actually *onto something*? Of one thing I'm certain: she isn't alone in her certainty that lurking behind the facade of daily life and pulling our strings is a hidden world of power-crazed billionaires and their political henchmen.

Hundreds of thousands (if not millions) of rightward-leaning citizens have found that various conspiracy theories help explain their sense of powerlessness and frustration in the face of world events that seem to grind inexorably on toward some disaster too ghastly to imagine. Some of these conspiracy theories are farfetched, some are laughable, and some are pretty nasty—but all provide maps of reality which clearly point out those to blame for the current mess.

In contrast to the explanations of the Marxist left, where the struggle between impersonal economic classes decides the course of history, the typical right-wing conspiracy theory usually identifies a specific and compact cabal of conspirators as the cause of our misery. In other times these dastardly fiends have been identified as Freemasons, agents of the Vatican, or Elders of Zion, but the favored choice of contemporary conspiratologists is the International Bankers.

Your run-of-the-mill conservative might froth at the mouth over the infiltration of communists into the media and government, but the conspiracy buff knows this is only a red herring (as it were), and that commies are not the *real* threat. No sir. The commies are merely dupes of the financiers who *really* run the show. ☞

Jay Kinney keeps close tabs on the factionalisms and schisms on both the left and right ends of the political spectrum, specializing in fringe groups that are outside the mainstream. His excellent overviews and commentaries have appeared in numerous publications, including the various Whole Earth Catalogs, *the* Whole Earth Review, *and in a now-defunct syndicated newspaper feature called "Cover-Up Lowdown." And, along with Paul Mavrides, Kinney's edited four issues of that celebration of outré politics,* Anarchy Comics *($2.50 each plus $1.50 shipping per order from Last Gasp, 2180 Bryant St., San Francisco, CA 94110). This field guide is a newly updated version of conspiracy surveys that appeared in* Critique *(see p. 96) and* Re/Search *(Re/Search Publications, 20 Romolo St., Suite B, San Francisco, CA 94133).*
—T.S.

The Insiders

GARY ALLEN

This is the basic scenario maintained by the aforementioned John Birch Society [395 Concord Ave., Belmont, MA 02178], *enfants terribles* of the 1960s right wing. The Birchers' name for the conspirators is the "Insiders," a group including not only bankers *a la* David Rockefeller and Wall Street firms such as Lazard Freres, but the top strata of diplomats, advisors, and corporate heads associated with the Council on Foreign Relations (CFR) and the Bilderbergers.

In the single best exposition of this basic theory, *None Dare Call It Conspiracy*, the late Birch author Gary Allen traces the roots of the CFR back to secret Round Tables formed at the instigation of British gold and diamond magnate Cecil Rhodes at the turn of the century. Overlapping CFR circles is the Bilderberg Society, a transatlantic group of the political and corporate elite that supposedly meets in secret once or twice a year to discuss the direction of world affairs, and to push them towards a One World Government.

If the Insiders sound identical to leftist descriptions of the Ruling Class—it's because they are. Paradoxically, if they agree on little else, the far left and the far right often share common enemies in those such as David Rockefeller who, in turn, pass themselves off as defenders of the center. The key difference here is that the left sees Rockefeller *et al* as the logical culmination of capitalist evolution, while the right sees them as smotherers of free enterprise. Ironically, both may be true.

The Birch Society's analysis is the most common conspiracy theory on the right, and the cover of Allen's book boasts "five million in print!" However, the Birchers peaked in popularity in the '60s, and more recently another group, the Liberty Lobby, has grown in influence in conspiracy-spotting circles. [Larry Abraham has published a revised and updated version of Allen's book, now called *Call It Conspiracy*, which is available for $19.20 postpaid from Double A Publications, 18000 Pacific Hwy South, Suite 1115, Seattle, WA 98188; 206/243-9115.]

Bankers & Zionists

The Liberty Lobby's *Weltanschauung*, as expressed in their weekly tabloid *The Spotlight* [$30/year (weekly) from 300 Independence Ave. SE, Washington, DC 20003] (paid circulation over 120,000), is identical to the Birchers' in most respects with one significant difference: the Liberty Lobby adds Zionism to the roster of the secret cabals. In their steady criticism of Israel and their vigorous support for Revisionist historians who argue that most accepted accounts of the Jewish Holocaust have been exaggerated, the Liberty Lobby stops short of

open anti-Semitism, but clearly plays footsie with that milieu.

In the late '70s, the Liberty Lobby made much of apparent hanky-panky between the Rockefellers, the Mafia, Warner Communications, and the Carter administration, while the Reagan years saw it going after "dual loyalists" in the State and Defense departments. *The Spotlight* features regular muckraking exposés that dovetail nicely into the organization's theories. Perhaps more than any other group, the Liberty Lobby has been reponsible for publicizing the role that the Trilateral Commission has played in both Carter's and Reagan's administrations.

What's the Frequency, Mikhail?

Besides the Insiders and the Zionists, of course, there is still the Soviet Union. Most conspiracy theorists are not fooled one bit by *glasnost*, and this certainly goes for C.B. Baker, whose *Youth Action News* [P.O.Box 312, Alexandria, VA 22311] is jam-packed with information about how the Soviets are frying our brains with Extremely Low Frequency (ELF) waves and microwaves, as well as sneaky weather warfare. (Apparently, Eugene, Oregon, for reasons unknown, has been a particularly hard-hit target of microwave zapping. Do the Soviets

know something that we don't?) This distressing news is rendered in tiny six-point type in eight-page issues mailed out at unpredictable intervals (usually twice a year or so). In contrast to some conspiratologists who seem intent on winning as large an audience as humanly possible, Baker warns: ". . . our material is anti-Communist, anti-Zionist and PRO-AMERICAN. If you are an America-laster, Trilateral-supporter or FOREIGN-POWER-LOYALIST, please do not order our material as our intelligence research is for **LOYAL** AMERICANS ONLY." Please take note.

The Crown vs. the Vatican

It may seem like both the British Empire and the Vatican are on the wane, but that doesn't exempt them from playing key roles in the conspiracy theory investigated by *The Project,* a more or less quarterly newsletter published by Lloyd Miller in Michigan. Miller postulates that the British Crown, its associated relatives on the Continent, and the bankers and financiers under their thumbs are engaged in a struggle for world power with operatives of the Vatican. However, this battle is not necessarily as clear-cut as one might think, since Thatcher and Reagan have fallen under the Vatican's influence, while the ubiquitous Masons and Zionists side with the Crown. In addition to publishing *The Project,* Miller sells a selection of conspiracy books at collectors' prices to his readers. [$20/year from A-Albionic Research, P.O. Box 20273, Ferndale, MI 48220.]

Britain and the "Black Guelph Aristocracy"

LYNDON LAROUCHE

Conspiracy theorists like Miller and Baker seem to fit the image of one-man crusades: inspired individuals handing down the "word" to devoted circles of largely passive followers. Lyndon LaRouche, on the other hand, has a well-greased machine of maybe two thousand close supporters, all actively out there gathering and selling intelligence. LaRouche's organization, the National Democratic Policy Committee, first began in 1968 as the National Caucus of Labor Committees, a small faction of renegade SDSers on the East Coast. In the years since, the group's politics have shifted rightward from socialist to high-tech Whig, and its conspiratorial reading of its hated enemies has changed from an early emphasis on the Rockefellers and the CIA to a more mature concentration on the British Royalty, the continental "Black Guelph Aristocracy," the Knights of Malta, and of course the Soviet KGB as would-be wreckers of civilization.

It is not unusual for conspiracy theorists, especially those allied with the John Birch Society, to trace the Conspiracy's shadowy origins to the late 1700s when the Illuminati, a secret occult society founded by Bavarian Adam Weishaupt, allegedly played a manipulative role in both the American and French Revolutions. LaRouche traces things back even farther, however. By characterizing the ongoing, behind-the-scenes struggle as the conflict between a humanist, city-building, progressive philosophy on the one hand and an evil, oligarchist, rural-oriented, zero-growth one on the other, he has dated the Conspiracy's origins to the fourth century B.C.

Of late, LaRouche and company have gained much notoriety by their vociferous stands against drugs and AIDS, and their cheerleading for SDI. Some of LaRouche's troops have succeeded in winning nominations for electoral races as Democrats, although as I write, actual election victory has eluded the LaRouche candidates. Meanwhile, the NDPC has been battling the government over a host of accusations, including violation of election laws and credit-card fraud. Around and around it goes, where it stops, nobody knows.

The Beast: 666

And let's not forget what may be the single most popular conspiracy scenario of all time: the fundamentalist Christian interpretation of the Bible's Book of Revelation. Literal-minded readings of this rather surreal vision of the early disciple John have developed a strict timetable for the (soon to arrive) End of the World.

Events to watch for include the Israelis rebuilding their Temple in Jerusalem, the appearance of the Antichrist masquerading as World Savior, the "Rapture" where all the Christians get whisked off to Heaven, and (if you're still around to watch) seven years of tribulations capped by the Battle of Armageddon.

Devotees of this scenario include millions of down-home folks and TV churchers, but the most colorful proponent has to be Jack T. Chick, publisher of dozens of comic-style tracts and full-color Christian comic books. Chick takes particular glee in depicting foolish souls who have refused to be reborn in Jesus shooting down to Hell after their untimely deaths from drug overdoses and freak accidents. In recent years, Chick has expanded beyond comics into publishing a full line of paperback books with special emphasis on the dastardly deeds of the Roman Catholic Church. All of one's darkest suspicions about the Jesuits, the Pope, and convents, not to mention the rosary, are confirmed and expanded upon in truly unbelievable detail in these volumes. Available in Christian bookstores across the land [or write to Chick Publications, P.O. Box 662, Chino, CA 91710].

The Alien Menace

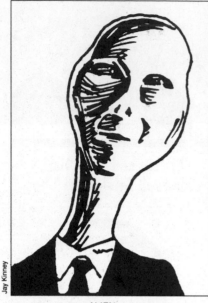

Jay Kinney

ALIEN

Last but hardly least is Cosmic Awareness Communications, a unique group headquartered in Olympia, Washington [P.O. Box 115, Olympia, WA 98507]. The "Cosmic Awareness" in their name refers to the omniscient force that speaks through leader Paul Shockley when he enters his trance states. Besides delivering plentiful New Age-style spiritual teachings, over the past decade Cosmic Awareness has given a running cosmic commentary on social and political events. And what a commentary it is!

For starters, C.A. has the unnerving habit of confirming the accuracy of nearly every conspiracy theory around, including those of LaRouche, the Liberty Lobby, and the headline-writers for the *Weekly World News.* Thus, the earth has been quarantined by the all-powerful Galactic Federation. Luciferian aliens from other star systems are rampant among us—rather like the old TV series, *The Invaders.* The U.S. Government is in the hands of the Rockefellers and the castrato Skoptsis sect, who recently wrested control away from the Bolshevik/Zionist faction. What's more, we've actually had manned missions to Mars since 1962, and that's where all those missing children are!

Much of the space in C.A.C.'s bi-weekly newsletter, *Revelations of Awareness* [$30/year], is taken up with Shockley's trance readings, which manage to iron out many of the contradictions that inevitably arise when aliens, the British, the Illuminati, the Skoptsis, and the Antichrist are all simultaneously to blame.

Luckily, Cosmic Awareness doesn't claim infallibility—insisting that C.A.C. members have to ultimately make up their minds for themselves. Entangled as we may be in the "Web of Conspiracy," we apparently still have some measure of free will!

Conspiracy Books and Magazines

All of the foregoing organizations and individuals pump out enough information and material to warrant their own room at the Library of Congress. Not even the most obsessive conspiratologist has the time, money, or storage space to keep track of it all. What's a conscientious paranoid to do? Until recently there were several active small-circulation conspiracy magazines, including *Conspiracy Digest*, *Conspiracies Unlimited*, and *Conspiracy Tracker*, devoted to keeping tabs on the numerous conspiracy theories afoot. Alas, those worthy publications have all bitten the dust. [Back issues of *Conspiracy Digest* are still available for $3 each, or $35 for all 19 back issues, from A-Albionic Research, P.O. Box 20273, Ferndale, MI 48220.]

This leaves *Critique: A Journal of Conspiracies and Metaphysics* as the primary periodical for researchers into alternate histories and realities. For the last ten years editor Bob Banner has fostered a unique "anything goes" editorial atmosphere that has allowed serious conspiracy buffs, assorted cranks, and lovers of the unusual from all parts of the political and social spectrum to rub elbows. Alien contactees, Birchers, Historical Revisionists, critics of the CIA—they're all likely to turn up in a given issue of *Critique* [$15 for 1 year (3 issues) from: Critique, P.O. Box 11368, Santa Rosa, CA 95406].

For overviews of all the main conspiracy theories and theorists, two books are worth seeking out. *Architects of Fear* by George Johnson [1983; Los Angeles: Tarcher] is a thorough and highly opinionated examination of conspiratology from the early days of the American Revolution down to 1983. Because Johnson is critical of his subject and doesn't consider the possibility that the conspiratologists may be *right*, the book earned a stinging review in *Critique.* It nonetheless remains the single best book-length look at conspiracy theories around, going into far greater depth on personalities such as LaRouche than any other book. Unfortunately, it is currently out of print, so you'll have to look for it at your local library or used bookstore.

Neil Wilgus' book, *The Illuminoids* [1978, 1981; $17.50 postpaid from: Sun Publishing, P.O. Box 5588, Santa Fe, NM 87502-5588], is a more playful jaunt through the conspiracy landscape and a good source for leads to further research. Using the Illuminati conspiracy and all its myriad variations and branches as his starting point, Wilgus provides a detailed chronology of conspiracy-related events down through the centuries. Best of all, *The Illuminoids* is still in print and available.

Over and Out

When all is said and done, there is an exceedingly fine line between discovering conspiracies and seizing upon scapegoats. Yet without a "big picture" within which to fit such a multitude of revelations, most Americans seem to recoil in confusion and cynicism, certain of little except that their trust has been betrayed by *someone*. Accordingly, the congressional inquiry into the Warren Commission's report on the Kennedy assassination could ultimately conclude in 1979 that JFK's death probably *was* the result of a conspiracy after all—surely a staggering revision of recent history—only to be met by yawns, head-scratching, and shrugs.

It is to the credit of the conspiracy buffs that they at least try to give a shape to otherwise isolated events and draw properly indignant conclusions from the evidence of back-room power plays. Yet, this said, it is also the tragedy of most conspiracy theories that their overly simple contours and conclusions repeatedly slide into a reactionary paranoia, which in turn is ripe for exploitation by authoritarian demagogues.

If cancer is the twentieth century's outstanding disease of the body, then paranoia is the favored disease of the mind. Small wonder that those most worried about cancer in the body politic are also the most susceptible to political paranoia and unorthodox cures. Still, it's worth keeping the old saying in mind, "Just because you're paranoid doesn't mean you're not being watched!" ∎

The Journal of Historical Review and Confessions of a Holocaust Revisionist

Declare that the earth is flat, that eyeglasses are actually an obstacle to good eyesight, or that Christ has returned as a Korean munitions-maker, and most Americans will defend your right to your opinion, as hare-brained as they may find it to be. However, most people's patience with unpopular opinions begins to run out about the time that someone gets up and asks "Did six million Jews really die at the hands of the Nazis?" Not only does the question seem superfluous, but it is highly offensive as well.

The **Journal of Historical Review** *has the singular distinction of asking that very question and related ones such as "What actual evidence exists of Nazi gas chambers? How did they supposedly operate? Are some survivor/witness testimonies exaggerated?" Those who delve into such questions call themselves "Historical Revisionists," a label also shared by some historians who have called the popular interpretations of the Cold War into question over the past few decades. For their efforts the* **Journal***'s publisher, the Institute for Historical Review, has had its offices fire-bombed, its conference venues suddenly cancelled, and its books unofficially banned from most bookstores. That's unpopular!*

Who are these Revisionists? Some academics, some amateur historians, some far rightists (and a couple of far leftists), and several libertarians. Are they worth listening to? That depends on your tolerance for having your world turned upside down. Some Revisionists have engaged in careful studies and on-site forensic investigations, and have drawn conclusions that are not easily dismissed even though they fly in the face of conventional history. Other Revisionists, especially the Germanophiles, load their carts with plenty of political baggage and invite you to help pull it. The sum total is a disturbing mix of the ridiculous and the sublime. If you are inclined to write off the Revisionists as pernicious extremists—as most people do—you might do well to read the **JHR** *first and draw your conclusions firsthand.* **Journal** *subscriptions include the* **IHR Newsletter** *which comes out eight times a year.*

For a riveting look inside the mind of a public spokesman for Revisionism, track down **Confessions of a Holocaust Revisionist** *by Bradley Smith. Smith is a libertarian and former bookseller from southern California who was once on trial for selling Henry Miller's* **Tropic of Cancer***. Volume One of Smith's memoirs reveals the episodes and stages that he went through on his way to being convinced that the standard history of the Holocaust may have more holes and contradictions to it than we commonly assume. Smith, who has appeared numerous times on TV and radio talk shows defending Revisionism, emerges here as a down-to-earth sort with a disarming lack of guile and a sardonic (and occasionally tasteless) sense of humor. If the* **Journal of Historical Review** *provides the best overview of the phenomenon of Revisionism, Bradley Smith's* **Confessions** *provides the best underview.*
—Mike Williams

- The truth is that Hitler treated the Jews as his declared enemies, that he wanted to drive them out of Europe, and that he put many of them in labor and concentration camps. Some of the camps had crematoria for burning bodies. None of them had a homicidal gas chamber. The existence of the alleged gas slaughterhouses is impossible for physical, chemical, topographical, architectural, and documentary reasons. The fate of the Jews was atrocious, but not unusually so. Consider the fate of the German children killed or wounded by phosphorous bombs or of those slaughtered at the time of their "transfer" from East to West between 1945 and 1947!
—*Journal of Historical Review*

- If there had been no gas chambers, no programmed extermination of Jews, then the German-Jewish scenario in Eastern Europe, while it would remain a cruel and ugly affair, would make some sense. European Jews would not have acted out then the part of inexplicably pathetic, robotized victims. Jewish mothers then would not have participated passively in the alleged destruction of a million of their children. Millions of Jewish men would not have collaborated with Germans in the mass extinction of their own families without having risen up *en masse* to die defending them. Jewish elders then would not have acted with such stupefied credulity in advising their people.
—*Confessions of a Holocaust Revisionist*

Journal of Historical Review and IHR Newsletter
Theodore J. O'Keefe, Editor
$40/year
(4 Journals and 8 Newsletters) from:
Institute for Historical Review
1822 1/2 Newport Bl. Suite 191,
Costa Mesa, CA 92627

Confessions of a Holocaust Revisionist
Bradley Smith
1987; 123 pp.
$6.95
($8.95 postpaid) from:
Prima Facie
P.O. Box 931089-1
Los Angeles, CA 90093

TABLOID TU
HOUSEWIFE
ZOMBIE!

Librarian reveals all . . .

by Michael H. Randall

Few people in the United States who have passed through a supermarket checkstand have been able to escape noticing tabloids, those small, newspaper-like publications filled with stories of the odd and the sensational. Probably just as few people have never looked inside one of these publications. After all, how many people do not feel some interest in a titillating celebrity scandal or the New Candy Bar Diet? Beyond this casual sort of interest, readers buy over 14 million copies of tabloids every week, and tabloids generate over $380 million in revenues each year. But, despite their phenomenal popularity, the tabloids are reviled and shunned by journalists, critics, and even celebrities, accounts of whose activities provide most of the tabloids' editorial content. The tabloids lack credibility even among their readers; polls show that 75 percent of all readers (the average is a female, age 37, with a $23,000 median household income) do not believe what they read in the tabloids.

Such attitudes are unfair to the extent that they constitute an indictment of all tabloids. While the past (and some current) practices of tabloids have bordered on the underhanded and sleazy, not all tabloids today resort to outright prevarication in their articles to boost sales. In fact, at least one of the tabloids now employs rigorous fact-checking procedures to verify each story before publication. Another tabloid regularly holds seminars for its editors to help them guard against publishing potentially libelous articles. Presumably, these developments have been in response to the flood of lawsuits that have been filed against the tabloids by allegedly libeled celebrities.

Tabloids include numerous service-oriented features on topics of benefit to their readers. They also perform a vital service for the entertainment industry. In fact, this industry probably could not function as it does without the tabloids and their wide publicity value for celebrities and entertainment productions. One writer for the tabloids claims that many entertainment personalities and their publicists make a habit of using the tabloids to further the stars' careers, while publicly denying that they would ever consider doing so.

Although the tabloids are highly popular, as is evidenced by their huge circulation figures, they are faced with strong competition. Tabloids must compete not only with other celebrity-oriented publications like **People** and **Us**, but also with television programs focused on personality news and gossip. Perhaps this competition explains why, in

---

Since nobody reads these little intros anyway, I guess I can make an embarrassing confession: For a while I actually subscribed to the Weekly World News, *which features articles like "First Successful Human Head Transplant!" and "I Had a Space Alien's Baby!" I don't know who laughed harder—me, or the WWN staffers who wrote the stuff. Michael Randall, a University of California research librarian, here applies his skills to this neglected realm of popular journalism, answering some of the questions about editorial and reporting policies that run through my mind whenever I scan the racks at the supermarket checkout counter.* —T.S.

This article originally appeared in the Summer 1985 issue of *Serials Review*, a library journal, and is reprinted here by permission.

1983, all four leading tabloids showed decreases of up to 6.7 percent in total circulation. But tabloids are still in a strong position to retain loyal fans and to attract new readers. This advantage is especially true of those leading tabloids that are entrenched in the coveted display racks located at grocery market checkstands. It is from single-copy sales at checkstands and newsstands that tabloids derive the great bulk of their revenue, a much greater share than other general-interest consumer magazines. For example, in 1983 the **National Enquirer** derived 85 percent of its revenue from circulation (mostly single-copy sales). In comparison, **People** for the same period derived 46 percent of its revenue from circulation—the rest came from advertising. Obviously tabloids are not as dependent upon the goodwill of advertisers and, consequently, tabloid editors do not have to worry about stories and articles offending the conservative or squeamish tastes of big advertisers, as do most other general-interest consumer publications. For this reason, the tabloids are free to publish stories dealing with topics that are popular with millions of readers: mysterious manifestations of the occult, exposés of the indiscretions and details of the deaths of famous people, flying saucer appearances, and eccentric and crackpot theories.

One of the tabloids' business methods that has been most criticized and yet is probably most successful is the use of checkbook journalism, the practice of paying money to obtain information for a story. A payment may range from $50 to a restaurant or hotel employee for a hot tip on a celebrity's activities, all the way up to $15,000 for exclusive details or photographs of a popular subject. For example, in 1984 a baboon heart-transplant operation performed on a human infant who was identified only as Baby Fae drew tabloid reporters to Baby Fae's home town. There, the reporters allegedly circulated through the town, offering thousands of dollars for clues to the identity of the parents. One of the tabloids reportedly placed a local private detective on a $25,000 retainer to obtain information on the story.

This means of obtaining stories has given rise to a complex but effective reporting network. Staff editors and reporters are employed full time by the tabloids to work on assignments. Stringers, part-time employees situated throughout the United States and in other countries (many of whom also work as writers for local newspapers or other publications), are available for special assignments and may also produce stories on their own. Freelance writers

National Enquirer
Iain Calder, Editor
$19.95/year
(52 issues) from:
National Enquirer
Lantana, FL 33464
Circulation:
4,385,000 copies

Star
Dick Kaplan, Editor
$32/year
(52 issues) from:
Star
Order Dept.
P.O. Box 2886
Boulder, CO 80322-2886
Circulation:
3,800,000 copies

Globe
Mike Nevard, Editorial Director
$22/year
(52 issues) from:
Globe International, Inc.
P. O. Box 11
Rouses Point, NY 12979-0011
Circulation:
1,602,723 copies

National Examiner
William Burt, Editor
$22/year
(52 issues) from:
Beta Publications, Ltd.
P. O. Box 711
Rouses Point, NY 12979-0711
Circulation:
1,145,022 copies

Sun
John Vader, Editor
$22/year
(52 issues) from:
Globe International, Inc.
P. O. Box 711
Rouses Point, NY 12979-0711
Circulation:
438,821 copies

Weekly World News
Joe West, Editor
$13.95/year
(52 issues) from:
Weekly World News
600 S. East Coast Ave.
Lantana, FL 33462
Circulation:
600,000 copies

and photographers, while they are not formally connected with the tabloids, know that they can easily sell a juicy story or photograph to a tabloid. And any individual who contacts a tabloid reporter with a lead for a story may be able to get a cash payment.

Following are comments on six widely available tabloids. These remarks may seem to err on the side of charity; however, it should be kept in mind that while critics may fault the tabloids for their sensationalism and extreme simplicity (reporters at one tabloid are told not to write anything that exceeds a fifth-grade reading level), these characteristics are the ones that endear the tabloids to millions of people.

National Enquirer

The **National Enquirer**, founded by William Randolph Hearst, was first published in 1926 with the title **New York Enquirer**. In 1952 it was purchased by current owner Generoso Pope, Jr., for $75,000, reportedly with the help of gangster Frank Costello. Since then Pope has presided over the **Enquirer**'s growth into the nation's most popular and notorious supermarket tabloid. Much of its current success is due to Pope's move in the early 1970s to establish his publication in the middle-class magazine market by placing the **Enquirer** in grocery store display racks across the country. Aside from this circulation strategy, the **Enquirer** cultivates its editorial content by paying a large army of reporters and editors the highest salaries in the tabloid field. While this practice may not result in writing that always measures up to the journalistic standards of a magazine such as **People,** it does allow the **Enquirer** to cover a broad range of topics, and it enables timely responses to events that often result in news scoops. For example, when Elvis Presley died in 1977, scores of **Enquirer** reporters were dispatched to Memphis. **Enquirer** money flowed freely in the town. One result was that a Presley relative photographed Elvis in his casket and sold the picture to the **Enquirer**. The issue with this picture on the cover sold the most copies ever of the **Enquirer**, 6.7 million.

Such sensationalistic tactics may repel some people, but sensationalism is the area in which the **Enquirer** most clearly excels. Millions of readers rely on the **Enquirer** to let them in on the details of the week's hot topics, and the **Enquirer** rarely lets them down.

Star

The **Star**, founded and owned by Australian publishing magnate Rupert Murdoch, is a sister publication of **The Times** of London and numerous other newspapers and magazines owned by Murdoch. While the **Star** does not possess either the renown or the pretensions of **The Times**, it runs a respectable second in tabloid circulation to the **National Enquirer**. In fact, the appearance of the **Star**, with its color pictures, on the tabloid publishing scene in the 1970s prodded the **Enquirer** to adopt color and revamp its graphic design. The **Star**'s formula is largely the same as that of the **Enquirer**, with the usual mix of celebrity stories and service features. An article playing up a spat between a television actress and her country singer husband coexists in one issue with a political analysis column. Other features include gossip columns, advice on personal finance, and recipes for dishes such as "Presidential Popcorn" (just add jellybeans).

Globe

Just tell the story, make the point, and get out with a nice, snappy ending, **Globe** editors urge prospective writers. Owned by Canadian publisher Michael Rosenbloom, who also publishes the tabloids **National Examiner** and **Sun**, the **Globe**'s format remains true to this editorial policy. As with all of the tabloids, celebrity stories and interviews, especially those revealing supposed scandals and embarrassments, are present in the **Globe** (previously titled **Midnight Globe** and **Midnight**). One such recent **Globe** article is "Dark Secrets of the Crystal Cathedral," in which the former daughter-in-law of a prominent television preacher reveals some of the more unflattering aspects of the video cleric's career. Stories describing unusual people and phenomena are also staples in the **Globe**. For example, readers can learn of the "Miracle Chair That Makes Women Pregnant," a piece of eighteenth-century furniture in the custody of a group of nuns in Naples.

In addition to these types of articles, the **Globe** also contains regular features, including special gossip columns covering Hollywood personalities and television soap opera performers. Other recurring features include medical advice and news, how-to articles, and inspirational essays. And of course the **Globe** occasionally prints psychics' predictions, including this startling revelation: "Because of trauma, Michael Jackson will lose all his hair and will drop out of public sight while it regrows."

National Examiner

The **National Examiner**, like its sister publications, **Globe** and **Sun**, has sensationalism on almost every page. Articles on celebrities and unusual people and events fill each issue. Readers expect to be astounded by headlines like "'Man-Boy' Fathers a Child—at Age 7: Doctors Bewildered by Incredible Case History," and "Husband Burns Wife Alive . . . Because She Was Pregnant and Not Rich Enough." Social phenomena are not exempt from the **National Examiner**'s sensationalism; for example, the headline of one article claims that "Women's Lib Causes Wife-Beating." (The article does contain some useful information on spouse abuse, but it also states that efforts to pass the Equal Rights Amendment have driven husbands to violence against their wives.)

Sun

The **Sun** offers a predictable array of stories and pictures covering bizarre events and famous personages. Readers of the **Sun** expect such stories as "He's America's Youngest Dad at Age 13" and "Caged! 2 Women Keep Rapist Prisoner for Five Years as Love Slave." Some of the articles show a semblance of redeeming value. For example, while the article "Drunk Doctors Operate In Our Hospitals" is presented in a sensationalistic manner, it does alert readers to the problem of alcohol and drug abuse among doctors and nurses. Still, there is no question that the majority of articles appearing in the **Sun** are lacking in such redeeming value. "Strange Psychic Power of Cabbage Patch Dolls," a story recounting situations in which telepathic messages from the popular playthings saved human lives and averted tragedies, is more typical of the **Sun**'s offerings.

Weekly World News

This tabloid is a reminder of the sleazy **National Enquirer** of the old days. It is, in fact, owned by **Enquirer** publisher Generoso Pope, Jr. It is the only tabloid reviewed here that is printed entirely in black and white, and its articles and pictures look like rejects from the **Enquirer**: "Ape Gives Birth to Human Baby," "Two-Headed Man Dies at Age 23." In addition to these and other stories celebrating the offbeat, there are several regular feature columns, including Countessa Sophia Sabak's "Weekly Horoscope," and "Dear Dotti," an advice column in which readers seek solutions to emotional dilemmas, and Dotti responds with straightforward answers such as "Dump him" and "Take a cold shower." ▪

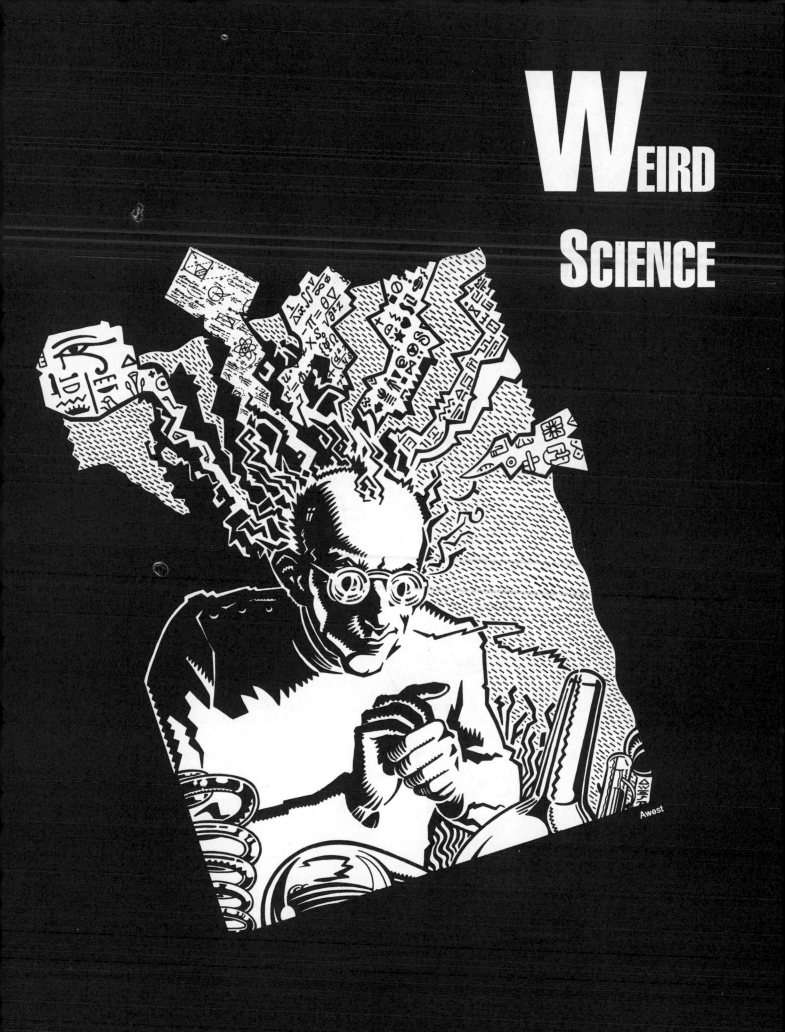

The Blind
Every System of Knowledge Is

by Ron Westrum
Illustrated by Harry S. Robins

For most of recorded history, mankind has been fascinated by *anomalies*, a term that comes from the Greek *a-nomos*, meaning "contrary to rule or law." For us, an anomaly is something in apparent contradiction to scientific law, but this scientific frame of reference is the relatively recent development of the last few centuries. For our ancestors, science was not the key issue.

For the ancients, an anomalous event was a sign or a portent, a miracle, a message from the gods, something not so much interesting in itself but in what it meant for the future, what it *portended*. The word "monster" is derived from the Latin *monstrum*, a portent or warning. Since such warnings from the gods had political implications, the state often insisted on a monopoly on their interpretation. In fact, the Romans had a regular system for the interpretation of "prodigies" to make sure their meaning would come out to the benefit of the state. State and religious powers were supported by conservative interpretations of strange events. As Shakespeare wrote in *Julius Caesar*:

> When beggars die, there are no comets seen
> The heavens themselves blaze forth the death
> of princes.

There were always skeptics such as Epicurus, who doubted the gods were behind such natural phenomena, and who encouraged people not to be frightened by them. Yet the political value of anomalies, as well as

---

Upon scientific examination, many seeming anomalies turn out to be false alarms—misperceptions, hoaxes, and the like. But the reverse also happens: anomalistic claims ignored by science sometimes turn out to be true. As a sociologist and associate director of the Center for Scientific Anomalies Research at Eastern Michigan University, Ron Westrum has devoted much of his life to the study of science's blind side. —T.S.

Eye of Science
Also a System of Ignorance

general popular superstition, kept them mysterious and awesome.

This attitude began to change with the advent of modern science in the 17th century, although the age of reason diffused only slowly to the common people. The motto of the Royal Society of London, founded 1660, was *nullius in verba*, which can be loosely translated as "take nothing on faith." The new scientific philosophy insisted on proof through experiment and investigation, and many of the superstitions of earlier times fell before its onslaught. Signs, wonders, miracles, and portents now were all to be resolved into natural phenomena explainable by natural causes. Furthermore, these natural causes were to be organized within theories of increasing scope.

Every system of knowledge, however, is also a system of ignorance. A great many phenomena did not fit into the newly constructed comprehensive theories, and since these phenomena did not make sense in terms of what was known, they were simply excluded. Signs and wonders had been anomalies because they had departed from the common run of experience. The new meaning of anomaly was something outside the pale of science. As one would expect, the more inaccessible to observation something was, the more it tended to be considered an anomaly. When, in spite of the strictures of the scientific community, people insisted on reporting experiences of anomalous events, science developed a series of strategies for dealing with them.

> ## A Phenomenon
> ## Physically Impossible

One such strategy was ridicule. In the 18th century, there were a great number of reports of stones falling from the sky. Few people connected such objects, often referred to as "thunderstones," to the fiery meteors that occasionally lit up the heavens. From time to time, scientists investigated the thunderstone reports with varying results. For the most

part, if they felt there was anything to the reports, they kept silent. In 1755, for instance, the abbe Domenico Tata became the possessor of a meteorite specimen that five Calabrian shepherds had seen fall. He wrote:

> Since that time, the Prince of San Severo, and the Marquis Mauri, have often tried to persuade me to publish all the details, but other friends dissuaded me. They warned me that the savants and the half-savants (even more to be feared) would attack me on this subject or pretend to be gracious to me while treating me with incredulity. These reasons decided me in favor of silence.

In 1772, a committee of the French Academy of Sciences was able to report that the two specimens of "thunderstones" they examined had no special features indicating an extraordinary origin. The committee, which included the great chemist Antoine Lavoisier, further remarked that "true physicists" had always been skeptical of such reports and saw no reason to change its mind in the current instance. Other savants dealing with these reports suggested that falling stones might be the results of bad observers or bad observations. Museums threw away their precious meteorite specimens.

The skepticism climaxed in 1790, when an area in the southwest of France was virtually inundated by falling stones. On the night of July 24, a huge fireball blazed over the southern skies and exploded over the parishes of Creon and Juillac. Stones rained down everywhere, to the consternation of the peasants who fortunately escaped injury. But the stones knocked branches off trees and shattered roof tiles. Some of the stones ("black as a truffle") weighed twenty pounds.

In the nearby town of Agen, a local professor named St. Amand heard about the strange fall. He could not believe the fall had occurred, but he thought it would be amusing to ask the locals to certify that it had indeed taken place. He wrote to the village and was stunned to receive in return not only a legal protocol signed by the mayor and the village attorney but also a sample of the stones. The affidavit indicated that some 300 people were willing to support the facts in question. Far from convincing St. Amand, the affidavit dismayed him. He sent it to another physicist, Pierre Bertholon, who published it with the following comment:

> If the readers have already had occasion to deplore the error of some individuals, how much more will they be appalled today seeing a whole municipality attest to, consecrate, by a legal protocol in good form, these same popular rumors, which can only excite the pity, not only of physicists, but of all reasonable people . . . . What can we add here to such an affidavit? All the reflections which it suggests will present themselves to the philosophical reader in reading this authentic illustration of an obviously wrong fact, of a phenomenon *physically* impossible.

Others, however, began to take a different view. In 1794, the physicist Ernst Chladni published a daring book that suggested falling stones were dropped by the "fiery meteors" whose nature no one had yet explained. Others, such as English chemist Edward Howard, used the new chemistry of Lavoisier to show that meteorites were indeed not ordinary rocks. In 1803, a meteorite shower 70 miles from Paris created such a stir that it was investigated by the eminent physicist Jean-Baptiste Biot, who showed that there was no doubt the stones had fallen.

This ended most of the incredulity in Europe. But when a meteorite fell at Weston, Connecicut, in 1807, President Thomas Jefferson was not disposed to believe it was real. Pressed by an acquaintance as to his opinion, he said he could sum it up in five words: "It is all a lie." A month later, he expressed a somewhat more moderate opinion in a letter to Daniel Salmon, and suggested that the matter might be looked into by the

American Philosophical Society. His initial reaction, however, is perfectly understandable. And for many scientists, it is the more enduring attitude.

The Self-Constructed Model

In 1819, Ernst Chladni reflected back on his struggles for the recognition of meteorites. While the Enlightenment, the 18th century intellectual movement that examined accepted doctrines of the time, had brought certain benefits, he felt it also brought with it certain intellectual problems. Now scientists "thought it necessary to throw away or reject as error anything that did not conform to a self-constructed model." The very success of scientific experiment and theory had led to a misplaced confidence that *what was real was already within the circle of science.* What was outside, therefore, what did not conform to scientists' theories, could be dismissed by invoking scientific authority and by ignoring or ridiculing observations not supported by it.

More recently, in 1979, the medical researcher Ludwik Fleck noted in his book *The Genesis and Development of a Scientific Fact* a very similar trend. He wrote:

> What we are faced with here is not so much simple passivity or mistrust of new ideas as an active approach which can be divided into several stages.
> (1) A contradiction to the system appears unthinkable.
> (2) What does not fit into the system remains unseen;
> (3) alternatively, if it is noticed, either it is kept secret, or
> (4) laborious efforts are made to explain an exception in terms that do not contradict the system.
> (5) Despite the legitimate claims of contradictory views, one tends to see, describe, or even illustrate those circumstances which corroborate current views and thereby give them substance.

What does not fit the theory is thus excluded. The anomalous event is forced outside the official circle of consciousness into a kind of outlaw existence.

This happened with the unusual luminous phenomenon known as "ball lightning." This form of lightning appears as a luminous ball, usually smaller than a basketball, and is quite short-lived (usually less than a minute). It has a long history of observation, but for many decades was an outlaw event in meteorology. In the 1930s, W. J. Humphreys,

an influential official in the U. S. Weather Bureau, had argued persuasively that ball lightning was probably an optical illusion. There was subsequently little mention of ball lightning in meteorology textbooks, and persons with scientific training who observed ball lightning generally kept quiet about it. When commented upon, it was described as a rare event. One of the reasons that it appeared to be a rare event is shown in anecdotes like the following, which appeared in *The Lightning Book* by Peter Viemeister:

> During the summer of 1937 several technical observers on duty at 500 Fifth Avenue, during the Empire State Building lightning program, saw what might be interpreted as ball lightning, not once but four times. One of the engineers, now the chief technical executive of a large power company, saw a bluish luminescence slowly descend the 38-foot tower of the Empire State Building after four of the ten or eleven strokes that hit the tower that evening. Fearing that his colleagues would regard him as a lightning-ball "quack," he was hesitant to speak about what he had seen, but decided to mention it anyway. Surprisingly several of the others admitted seeing the same things. These observations were omitted from the technical reports since they did not appear on the recording cameras nor on the oscillograph records.

Thus, because there is no *spontaneous reporting* of the anomalous event, scientists may assume that there is no event to be reported. That this might be a self-fulfilling prophecy is hardly considered. Part of the problem, of course, is that no one is *asked* whether they have seen an unclassified phenomenon. When surveys of technical personnel regarding ball lightning *were* done in 1966 at two national laboratories, many meteorologists were surprised to discover that four percent of the potential observers in one laboratory had seen it. This hardly qualifies as a rare event!

The problem with ball lightning is that no one has yet found a satisfactory theory to explain it. It is tempting for physicists to argue, as some in fact have, that since it can't be explained, it probably doesn't exist! (I.e., if it doesn't fit the self-constructed model, it's not real.) So thousands of ball lightning sightings were ruled inadmissible and ignored. In the last decade or so, a much more positive attitude has prevailed, but the phenomenon is still far from completely accepted.

A similar thing happened with "meteor noise." When meteors pass through the atmosphere or explode, they often cause powerful sonic booms, as one would expect.

It is tempting for physicists to argue that since ball lightning can't be explained, it probably doesn't exist!

But some observers, say 20 percent of people who have seen meteors, also report that the meteor made a swishing, crackling, or hissing noise while in flight. Since the meteors are often tens of miles away, these reports seem implausible, since sound only travels about a thousand feet per second. Yet there have been cases in which individuals have first *heard* the meteor and then have gone outside to see it, and many others from credible people which relate the sound heard simultaneously with the meteor observation. Such experiences, because they seemed implausible, were simply dismissed by some meteoriticists. One researcher even suggested there was an inverse correlation between the observer's education and his willingness to make such reports. More recent studies suggest, however, that meteors produce very low frequency (VLF) radiation. Some people (not all) perceive VLF radiation as sound, either because of its direct effects on the brain or because it causes acoustic effects in objects near the observer. Now that an explanation has been found, physicists are more willing to take such anomalous sounds seriously. ☛

The Hidden Event

Study of the social processes of science at work in these examples leads us to the following discovery: If what is contrary to theory is rejected, it is not likely to be reported. If it is not reported, its existence may not even be suspected. Therefore, in some situations, *the anomaly may be a hidden event*, one almost invisible to the society at large. An example of such a hidden event is the battered child syndrome, whose prevalence was virtually unsuspected until the 1950s.

In the 1930s, a radiologist named John Caffey began to suspect that the x-ray films he was handling contained evidence of child abuse. Caffey was later to become one of the founders of pediatric radiology, and his manual *Pediatric X-Ray Diagnosis* (now in its 7th edition) is still the standard reference. As time went on, Caffey's suspicions grew, and in 1946 he published an article entitled "Fractures in the Long Bones of Children with Chronic Subdural Hematoma." This was the first modern article on what would later be called the battered child, but its title and its contents gave only a hint of Caffey's true thoughts. Off the record, he was much more specific, and his two residents Betram Girdany and Frederick Silverman were strongly imbued with Caffey's idea of "multiple unsuspected traumata." In the early 1950s, Silverman and other radiologists began to publish articles in medical journals that were much more direct. Children were being injured, x-rays could detect these injuries, and often the injuries were inflicted by the child's caretakers. But there was little interest in child abuse by the medical community or among the general public.

One of the problems with admitting child abuse as a reality was that physicians, especially pediatricians, simply couldn't accept what was happening. Pediatricians were used to thinking of parents as allies in the treatment of the child, and to see parents as child abusers went against their deepest instincts. "If I thought the parent could abuse the child, I would leave pediatrics immediately!" one pediatrician stated emotionally during a meeting on child abuse.

Even if they did suspect abuse, there wasn't much they could do about it. These social forces conspired to keep child abuse a hidden event. Only after the development of teams that included social workers, pediatricians, and radiologists was intervention generally successful.

The sudden explosion of awareness on child abuse took place because a pediatrician, C. Henry Kempe, became convinced that the problem was widespread. His first brush with the problem was the faulty diagnoses of children's injuries being made by residents under his supervision at the University of Colorado Medical School.

> I was *intellectually* offended at first, before my better instincts took over, by the simply silly diagnoses being made by bright house staff in situations where nothing but child abuse *could* be the diagnosis . . . Having been intellectually engaged in the fact that the wrong diagnosis was being made each day in our hospitals, it was clear that we must do something to help.

And he did. In 1961, as the national program chair for the American Academy of Pediatrics, Kempe organized a panel on child abuse. Along with Frederick Silverman, he invited a social worker, a judge, a psychiatrist, and the director of the Health Law Center of the University of Pittsburgh. The panel was held in the Grand Ballroom of the Palmer House in Chicago, and the packed room held roughly two thousand persons, including the news media. The title of the panel was "The Battered Child Syndrome." The repercussions were powerful, immediate, and enduring. After 1961, there was a steady increase in the coverage of child abuse in medical journals, newspapers, and magazines.

But the key to uncovering the hidden event of child abuse was the establishment of new reporting channels and new laws that mandated reporting. A national survey of hospitals and district attorneys conducted

in 1961 by one of Kempe's students had revealed hundreds of cases. Almost no one at the time suspected, however, that the real figure might be in the hundreds of thousands, or even a million cases annually. What has allowed society to "see" child abuse is not only a novel medical concept, but changed laws, the extension of protective services, interested media and, above all, a widened public awareness.

What Else Is Out There?

We have discussed meteorites, lightning balls, and battered children, and have seen in each case the difficulty that science and society have had in perceiving the anomalous event. An obvious question presents itself: What else is being missed?

In my studies of social flows of information relating to a number of interesting hypothetical anomalies such as UFOs, sea serpents, bigfoot, and spontaneous human combustion, I have found exactly the same kind of reticence to report observations as I have discussed in relation to the real anomalies above. As Ludwik Fleck would have been interested to know, the unusual event is generally not reported; if reported, it is not published; and if it is published, it is usually ridiculed. And so, simply, it is not part of our socially constructed reality.

This does not mean, of course, that every event so hidden is a real anomaly. While some UFO sightings are very difficult to explain, most (about 90 percent) prove upon investigation to be ordinary things that have been misperceived. Most anomaly investigators can relate a large number of cases of mistaken identity, as well as a smaller, but usually quite memorable, number of hoaxes. As such experiences accumulate, investigators become more wary. When I read J. Allen Hynek's excellent book *The UFO Experience* (see p. 161) in 1972, I was surprised that he limited himself largely to cases he had personally investigated. Now I understand why! A great many anomaly experiences thus represent errors.

What I worry about, though, are the anomalies that aren't controversial, the ones that may not even appear in the *Catalogs* of William Corliss (see p. 109). We human beings are relentless experimenters with the world in which we live, but our ability to monitor the results is very modest in comparison to our ability to cause changes. The study of social intelligence

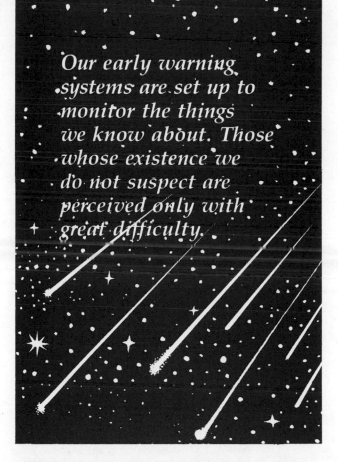

Our early warning systems are set up to monitor the things we know about. Those whose existence we do not suspect are perceived only with great difficulty.

regarding anomalies teaches us that our early warning systems are set up to monitor the things we know about. Those whose existence we do not suspect are perceived only with difficulty and after much struggle. Some years ago, the Smithsonian Institution set up a special network to monitor unusual events, but it described *in advance* what things it wanted to find out about. It was not disappointed; few of the events reported to it belonged to undesignated categories. In recent years, the Smithsonian's network has narrowed the categories reported upon. The "self-constructed model" still guides the research we do. Again, every system of knowledge is likely to have built-in blind spots.

These blind spots are worth studying. They may hide things that are interesting and things that are dangerous. The discovery of the battered child syndrome helped to pave the way for the discovery of other categories of abused persons in society, including sexually abused children. I wonder what kind of environmental problems are hidden from our view because their manifestation seems too implausible to report. I am far from sanguine about the effects of the technologies, physical and biological, that we are introducing into the ecology of the planet and our daily lives. And unless we do a great deal to improve our social intelligence about the unexpected event, we may miss the signals that tell us we have gone too far. ■

The Journal of Meteorology

The daily diary of world weather, with an emphasis on the gargantuan violences to which our atmosphere is prone. Reports of ball lightning, unusually large hail, tornado lightning, and other meteorological anomalies are regularly recorded here, and scholarly articles bearing such titles as "The Mystery of Spiral-Circle Ground Patterns in Crops Made by a Natural Atmospheric-Vortex Phenomenon," "Electrical Aspects of Tornado Theory," and "The Origin of the Extensive Ice-Floes in the English Channel in February 1684" describe frontier meteorological research. —T.S.

• The summer of 1984 was the fifth season in which attention has been given to probing the origin of the mysterious quasi-circular, flattened areas which are sometimes to be found in English cereal fields in the summer months. These flattened areas are circular or nearly circular in outline. Within them, the stalks of the growing cereal crops are laid down clockwise, following a spiral patterns outwards from a central point. Often there is just a single circle. On one occasion (at Cheesefoot Head, near Winchester, in 1981) there were triplets (one large circle flanked by two smaller ones), and on eight known occasions, 1980 to 1984, there have been quintuplets (a large circle attended by four evenly-spaced small satellite ones).

A ringed circle with a plain circle nearby (formed in rye, south Wiltshire).

The Journal of Meteorology
Dr. Terence Meaden, Editor
$40/year (surface mail)
(or $50/year air mail)
(12 issues) from:
Journal of Meteorology
54 Frome Road
Bradford-on-Avon
Wilts, England BA15 1LD

A Geo-Bibliography of Anomalies

This massive 1,115-page volume is an exhaustive guide to the source material for over 22,000 separate anomalistic— "weird" — events from over 10,000 localities in the U.S., Canada, and Greenland. It's a bibliography, which means that the sources (books, journals, and newspapers) are only referenced, not reprinted. It's a geo-bibliography because it's set up to be referenced primarily by locale—state or province, city, town, lake, mountain.

Chances are that your home town is included, followed by listings of UFOs (which predominate), ancient artifacts, anomalous fossils, ball lightning, coal balls, erratic animals, ghost lights, meteorite craters, musical sand, or another of the nearly 100 categories the author, a research librarian, has created to classify anomalies.

Because of the locale reference scheme, I have found this book to be an excellent companion on cross-country driving trips, directing me, with a little research, to some real off-the-beaten-path wonders. —T. S.

•Mojave Desert [California]
—Ancient pyramid
Auburn Placer Herald, 20 Aug. 1853.

A Geo-Bibliography of Anomalies
George M. Eberhart
1980; 1,115 pp.
$85
($87 postpaid) from:

Greenwood Press, Inc.
88 Post Road West
Box 5007
Westport, CT 06881
203/226-3571

•Simcoe [Ontario]
—Genetic anomaly
1889, May/John H. Carter/cow gives birth to lambs
Toronto Globe, 25 May 1889.

•Minneapolis [Kansas]
—Mystery stone spheres
Rock City concretions
Topeka Daily Capital, 31 Aug. 1965.
"Rock City," *Kansas!*, 3d issue, 1970, pp. 29-30. il.

•Saint George [Utah]
—Giant mummies
1947/F. Bruce Russell
L. Sprague de Camp, *Lost Continents* (N.Y.: Dover, 1970 ed.), p. 50.

Ball Lightning and Bead Lightning

This is a good, textbook-style introduction to two forms of lightning so rare that not all atmospheric physicists even agree they exist. Ball lightning is a short-lived, mobile, luminous sphere that seems to appear after a lightning discharge, and bead lightning is a chain of luminous fragments that apparently forms in an imperfect lightning discharge channel. The 1,800-entry bibliography is the best available on this subject, and the author has taken great pains to reproduce virtually every known photo of these two types of lightning; too bad most of them are blurry and indistinct. I guess that's to be expected from snapshots of two of nature's most elusive wonders. —T.S.

Woodcut illustrating the accidental death of Dr. Richmann in St. Petersburg in 1753, reportedly by a ball lightning. The ball lightning is thought to have developed from the experimental apparatus used to measure the electrification of storm clouds.

Ball Lightning and Bead Lightning
James Dale Barry
1980; 298 pp.
$52.50
postpaid from:
Plenum Publishing
233 Spring Street
New York, NY 10013
212/741-6680

An Encyclopedia of Anomalies

THE SOURCEBOOK PROJECT

by William R. Corliss

After more than thirteen years of scouring the scientific and semiscientific literature for anomalies, my major conclusion is that this is an amazingly fruitful activity. In fact, organized science should have been doing the same searching and compiling for the past 200 years. It is simply astounding that a Catalog of Scientific Anomalies does not already exist to guide scientific thinking and research. It is at least as important to realize what is *not* known as it is to recognize the well-explained. My *Catalog* is largely the product of one person's library research, carried forward without grants, contracts, or donations.

Under the aegis of the Sourcebook Project, I have already published 20 volumes, totalling well over 7,000 pages of source material on scientific anomalies. As of this moment, these 20 volumes represent only about 25 percent of my database. New material is being added at the rate of about 1,200 new articles and items per year, about 300 of which are from the current literature. These rates could be easily multiplied several times over by spending more time in libraries. Even after thirteen years, only the scientific journals of the United States and England have received my serious attention. There remain the English-language journals of the rest of the world, those journals in other languages, university theses, government reports, the publications of scientific research facilities, conference papers, untold thousands of books, and an immense reservoir of newspapers. The cataloging task has just begun. The anomalies residing in the world's literature seem nearly infinite in number.

Given this rough assessment of the magnitude of the anomaly literature, one can understand why the *Catalog of Anomalies* will require at least 25 volumes, with master indexes, as only the initial step in providing scientists with ready access to what is not, in *my* opinion, well-explained.

Will the *Catalog of Anomalies* revolutionize science? Probably not — at least not immediately. Quite often the initial reaction to the books of anomalies already published has been disbelief. The data must be in error; the data are mainly testimonial; the data are too old; the supposed anomaly was explained long ago. Germs of truth reside in all these complaints. But for every anomaly or example that can be legitimately demolished, ten more take its place. Nature is very anomalous or, equivalently, nature is not yet well understood by science. Much remains to be done.

—William R. Corliss

How Data and Anomalies Are Evaluated in the *Catalog*

Each anomaly type is rated twice on four-level scales for data "validity" and "anomalousness," as defined below. These evaluations represent only the opinion of the compiler and are really only rough guides.

Data Evaluation Scale

1. Many high-quality observations. Almost certainly a real phenomenon.
2. Several good observations or one or two high-quality observations. Probably real.
3. Only a few observations, some of doubtful quality. Phenomenon reality questionable.
4. Unacceptable, poor-quality data. Such phenomena are included only for the purposes of comparison and amplification.

Anomaly Evaluation Scale

1. Anomaly cannot be explained by modifications of present laws. Revolutionary.
2. Can probably be explained through relatively minor modifications of present laws.
3. Can probably be explained using current theories. Primarily of curiosity value.
4. Well-explained. Included only for purposes of comparison and amplification.

Anomalies that rate "1" on both scales are very rare. Such anomalies, however, are the most important because of their potential for forcing scientific revolutions. As additional *Catalog* volumes are published, the relative proportion of "double-1s" will increase, especially in the fields of biology and psychology.

William Corliss' Sourcebooks are the "Encyclopedia Britannica of the unexplained." Over fifteen years ago Corliss, a physicist and science writer, began to search methodically through the scientific literature, extracting and categorizing reports of anomalistic phenomena. Presented here is a small sampling from his Anomaly Catalog series, which doesn't begin to convey their comprehensive flavor. Corliss has devised the first cross-referenced "taxonomy of anomalies," reflected here by letter-and-number codes like "GLW4" and "X54." You'll find these indispensable when you dive into the Catalogs proper, which can be ordered from The Sourcebook Project, P.O. Box 107, Glen Arm, MD 21057. Ask for a free copy of Corliss' newsletter, Science Frontiers. —T.S.

Diffuse Electrical Discharge Phenomena (GLD)

Aurora-like pillars of light over the Andes.

Key to Phenomena

Everyone is familiar with fast, concentrated discharges of electricity, such as lightning. More rare are the slower, more diffuse flows of natural electricity. In these, the passage of electrical currents is gentle and almost soundless in contrast to the violent thunderbolt. Even so, these slow discharges frequently give rise to luminous, often strangely beautiful phenomena.

Slow electrical discharges usually proceed from projections and sharp points, such as ship masts, radio antennas, and even human fingers held aloft. Pointed structures tend to concentrate electrical fields and, if the fields are intense enough, will encourage a slow flow of electricity from the point into the surrounding air. When these discharges become luminous, they are called St. Elmo's Fire, a well-known bluish electrical glow that occurs on the masts of ships at sea. In damp and stormy weather, high voltage power lines may exhibit eerie luminous discharges around insulators and other structures. These bluish glows are termed "corona discharges." Reports from ships at sea and mountain-top scientific observatories tell of St. Elmo's Fire in the form of cold lambent flames and auras streaming from scientific instruments, guy wires, and even peoples' heads. St. Elmo's Fire also appears infrequently in snowstorms and sandstorms, as the falling and blowing particles transfer electricity between the earth and the air like those Wimshurst electrostatic machines so common in high school physics laboratories.

Corona discharge and St. Elmo's Fire are not particularly mysterious to physicists; they therefore constitute a good starting point for a journey into more controversial territory.

The next stop is a truly spectacular one: the so-called Andes Glow or, to be more general, the mountain-top glow. Since many mountains pierce the atmosphere with sharp projecting surfaces, the appearance of slow electrical discharges from their crests is not especially surprising. It is the scale of the process that is awe-inspiring. The sheets of flame and aurora-like beams of light projecting into the stratosphere may be visible for hundreds of miles. Where does this mountain electricity go? Into outer space? And why are mountaintop glows greatly enhanced during major earthquakes? No one has really studied this phenomenon carefully. It is in essence St. Elmo's Fire on a massive scale.

On a smaller, less-violent scale, intense electrical storms may create ground-level patches or waves of luminous electrical activity that may engulf humans in their paths, electrically shocking them or wrapping them in a garment of St. Elmo's Fire. In some ways, these surface displays resemble the marine phosphorescent displays, particularly the rotating phosphorescent wheels, described elsewhere in the *Catalog*.

Considerably more mysterious are the glowing, enigmatic, floating spheres that observers often compare to toy balloons. These cavorting softly-lit bubbles are certainly not ball lightning and may not even be electrical at all. Whatever they are, modern science has paid little attention to them, perhaps because their explanation is so difficult and their existence so improbable.

These subjects bring us to those strange glows, flashes, and fireballs seen so often near earthquake epicenters. Earthquake lights also take the shapes of auroral beams, mountaintop glows, ball lightning, and moving waves of rock luminosity. Since modern scientific observations demonstrate that earthquake shock waves may penetrate the atmosphere into the ionosphere, it is possible these atmospheric disturbances may help create low-conductivity paths for earth-to-space electrical discharges. The ball lightning, the sheets of flame issuing from the ground, and other localized luminous phenomena may be generated by large-scale piezoelectric effects (i.e., the creation of electricity by stresses in rocks). An alternate explanation of earthquake lights involves the spontaneous ignition of natural gas liberated by the quaking earth.

Violent volcanoes and tornadoes also display unusual lights. Of course, normal lightning and ball lightning are to be expected in violent storms, but whence the peculiar shafts of light reported in tornado funnels and the strange glowing patches in and above storm clouds? The precise role of electricity in tornado action, if any, is highly controversial. Superficially at least, the funnel light columns may, like neon lights, arise from large-scale glow discharges in these naturally formed tubes.

That the earth-as-a-whole is a gigantic electrical machine cannot be doubted. The constant turmoil of the atmosphere, its never-ceasing bombardment by the solar wind, the electrically charged wind-blown dust and snow, and the intense forces squeezing terrestrial rocks, all conspire to create a wide spectrum of curious and poorly understood luminous effects.

Mountain-Top Glows (GLD 1)

Description: Rays, undulating streamers of light, flashes, and steady glows appearing along mountain crests and ridges. The color is usually yellowish white, with green and orange being more rare. This phenomenon is observed in the Andes, the Alps, the Rockies, the Arctic, and probably many other places.

Background: Despite the widespread occurrence of mountain-top glows, science has taken little note of them. Instrumented studies are essentially unknown.

Data Evaluation: Many high quality observations, especially from the Andes and Alps. Rating: 1.

Anomaly Evaluation: Mountain-top glows are probably large-scale discharges of terrestrial electricity into the atmosphere — that is, greatly magnified St. Elmo's Fire. The anomalous aspects are: (1) The very large scale of the phenomenon; (2) The apparent heightening of the displays during earthquakes; (3) The possible periodicity of the flashes; (4) The close resemblance to auroras, which seems to underscore the reality of low-level auroras (GLA4). Rating: 3.

Possible Explanation: Large-scale discharge of terrestrial electricity.

Similar and Related Phenomena: Low-level auroras (GLA4); aurora-related fogs and mists (GLA21); earthquake lights (GLD8).

The Catalog lists over 20 cases of mountain-top glows. Here are a few examples:

X7. June 7, 1954. Madeira. "On approaching Madeira from SW the island was completely covered with low cloud, stratus and stratocumulus. On arriving within 16 miles of the island the cloud rapidly lifted and numerous brilliant white flashes were observed at frequent intervals on various mountain peaks. At the time of these occurrences the cloud was clear of the island, although there was some stratocumulus to NW. After the flashes had continued for some 20 minutes, a low rumbling was heard like distant thunder."
—Robson, G.; *Marine Observer,* 25:95, 1955.

Ship approaching Madeira observes flashes of light on mountains.

X8. General observation. The Andes. "Thunderstorms are rare in Chile, and this fact may possibly be explained on the assumption that the Andes act as a gigantic lightning rod, between which and the clouds silent discharges take place on a vast scale. The visible discharges occur during the warm season, from late spring to autumn, and appear to come especially from certain fixed points. According to Dr. Knoche they are confined almost exclusively to the Andes proper, or Cordillera Real, as distinguished from the coast cordillera. Viewed from a favorable point near their origin there is seen to be, at times, a constant glow around the summits of the mountains, with occasional outbursts, which often simulate the beams of a great searchlight, and may be directed westward so as to extend out over the ocean. The color of the light is pale yellow, or rarely reddish. One striking feature of these discharges is that they are especially magnificent during earthquakes. At the time of the great earthquake of August, 1906, throughout central Chile the whole sky seemed to be on fire; never before or since has the display been so brilliant."
—*"Curious Lightning in the Andes," Scientific American, 106:464, 1912.*
—*"Strange Kinds of Lightning," Literary Digest, 111:22, October 10, 1931.*

X9. General observation. The Andes. "'Andes glow' or 'Andes lights' are terms used to describe illumination seen at night in the vicinity of certain mountain peaks. While the majority of reports have come from the Andes mountains of Bolivia, Chile and Peru, this phenomenon has also been reported in the European Alps, Mexico and Lapland and presumably could occur in many mountainous regions under favourable conditions. While sometimes thought to be lightning, for lack of a more obvious explanation, the interesting property of these light displays is that they can occur under cloudless skies. Sometimes they are but one single flash, while at other times they may persist intermittently for hours. On occasion, a periodicity has been noted in the time between flashes. At their most spectacular they have been described as '. . . not only clothing the peaks, but producing great beams, which can be seen miles out at sea.' They seem to favour particular mountain peaks where often they can be seen during the dry season."
—*Markson, Ralph and Nelson, Richard;"Mountain-Peak Potential-Gradient Measurements and the Andes Glow," Weather, 25:350, 1970.*

General configuration of a typical phosphorescent wheel.

Key to Phenomena

Marine Phosphorescent Displays (GLW)

Ships that ply the Indian Ocean, particularly the waters leading to the oil-sodden lands around the Persian Gulf, frequently encounter dazzling phosphorescent seas. As Kipling described it, the ship's wake is "a welt of light that holds the hot sky tame." Huge globes of light rise from the depths and burst on the surface. Wavetops sparkle, porpoises resemble luminous torpedoes, and broad geometrically precise corridors of light stretch from horizon to horizon. Buckets lowered into these glowing seas prove that marine organisms seem to cause most of the phosphorescent displays.

Phosphorescent ship wakes are mundane and unimpressive compared to the vast rotating wheels of light and the other fantastic luminescent displays encountered from the Persian Gulf, across the Indian Ocean, and into the South China Sea. Ridiculed as wild sailors' tales for centuries, modern ships have reported scores of bona fide geometrical displays. Mariners tell of great spoke-like bands of light seemingly spinning about some distant hub. Occasionally several wheels will overlap, while simultaneously turning in clockwise or counterclockwise senses, creating a vast tableau of moving spokes miles wide. Expanding rings of light and bright whirling crescents (the latter radar-stimulated) may also decorate the ocean surface. Crews that see these fantastic apparitions do not soon forget them. Scientists, alas, have generally ignored these awe-inspiring apparitions.

One's first reaction is to explain the wheels of lights and related geometrical displays in terms of marine bioluminescence stimulated by natural forces that, like the wake of a ship, leave behind glowing evidence of their passage. Sound waves emanating from submarine disturbances have been the most popular type of disturbance in this explanation. But what combination of seismic waves could stimulate overlapping, counterrotating wheels or hundreds of spinning phosphorescent crescents? Furthermore, there are several well-attested cases where the luminous displays were seen in the air well above the sea's surface. This fact plus the persistence of the phenomena (about half an hour) and the complex nature of the displays suggest that we look for other stimuli and nonbiological sources of light.

The physical forces that create the auroras and the Andes Glow may be at work near the ocean's surface, unlikely as it may seem. To illustrate this possibility, the luminous mist seen during some low-level auroras closely resembles the aerial phosphorescence seen in some marine displays. Some ship captains have, in fact, noted the similarities between auroral and marine phosphorescent displays. The curious interaction of radar with marine phosphorescence is also suggestive. Another potential explanation would use the collective behavior of marine bioluminescent organisms. Travelers in the tropics, for example, tell amazing accounts of the synchronized flashing of immense assemblages of fireflies. Could marine bioluminescent organisms indulge in similar cooperative action? If so, how do they communicate pattern geometries and why?

Many other questions can be asked about marine phosphorescent displays. Why are most concentrated in the Indian Ocean and South China Sea when other seas also teem with bioluminescent organisms? Where does the mysterious underwater lightning, called *te lapa* by the Polynesians, fit in? Unfortunately only a few scientists have deigned to notice this fertile field of research.

Marine Phosphorescent Wheels (GLW 4)

Description: Spoke-like bands of light rotating around a central hub. The spokes may be straight, curved, or S-shaped. Rotation is in either direction and may change during the display. In some cases, the outer part of the wheel seems to spin in a different sense from the central part. Illustrating the illusory character of the phenomenon, different observers sometimes see the same wheel rotating in opposite directions. Wheel sizes range from tens of feet to several miles, with spoke widths of 5-50 feet being common. Generally, the sources of light seem to be on or just beneath the surface, but several examples exist of wheels composed of luminous mist spinning well above the sea's surface. Spoke colors are whitish and greenish in most cases. Several wheels may appear simultaneously, rotating in various senses with overlapping patterns. Phosphorescent wheel displays are frequently preceded and followed by displays of moving, parallel bands (GLW2). Like the moving band displays, the phosphorescent wheels are most common in the Indian Ocean, especially the Persian Gulf, and the China Sea. The few wheel-like structures seen in other waters are usually poorly formed and stationary. The duration of a wheel-type display lasts from a few minutes to more than an hour.

Data Evaluation: Scores of well-observed examples. Rating: 1.

Anomaly Evaluation: As with most of the organized phosphorescent displays, the major problem seems to be explaining the origin and long-term stability of rather complex geometrical patterns. If the light source is not bioluminescence, as generally supposed, the anomaly is even stronger. Rating: 2.

Possible Explanations: Certainly bioluminescence is the most likely source of light, although observers frequently remark that the ship's wake is not luminous during wheel-type displays. The aerial wheels of luminous mist, if not illusory, would require air-borne organisms in cases where no wheel is visible in the water proper. Earthquake tremors may stimulate bioluminescence, with the interference patterns created by multiple sources accounting for the complex display geometries. The persistence of intricate geometries over many minutes seems to militate against this theory. Again, as in GLW3, the strong similarity of some marine phosphorescent displays to the so-called low-level auroras (GLA4) is striking. Some wheel observers have noted this, and electromagnetic forces should not be dismissed offhand.

Similar and Related Phenomena: The other marine phosphorescent displays (GLW), low-level auroras (GLA4).

The Catalog lists over 60 cases of phosphorescent wheels. Here are a few examples:

X24. April 24, 1953. Gulf of Thailand. "Faint flashes of light with oscillating movements were observed on the sea. The flashes gradually increased in strength until at 0230 they suddenly changed into rather intensive rays of light moving around centres lying near the horizon. Three groups of rays were present, as shown in the sketch. (a) One on the port bow having a bearing of about 300° with the rays rotating anticlockwise. (b) One on the port bow having a bearing of about 230°, rotating clockwise. (c) One on the starboard bow having a bearing of about 95°, rotating anticlockwise. The beams were curved with the concave side in the direction of the movement, and were passing the ship continuously with a frequency of about three a second; they looked more like glowing shafts than beams of light. Reflections on the ship were clearly visible. . . . The phenomenon lasted till 0250, and it had been clear by the increasing strength of the group ahead and decreasing strength of the group astern, that the ship was advancing through the area of phosphorescence. Soon only the oscillating flashes could be seen and they also disappeared shortly afterwards. At 0300 the situation was normal again."
—*Henney, A., et al.; "Phosphorescent Wheels," Marine Observer, 24:73, 1954.*

X53. March 27, 1976. Gulf of Siam. "At 1917 GMT pulsating bands of parallel light were observed in the sea moving towards the vessel from 045°T. After 2 to 3 minutes the bands took on a definite spoke formation, the centre of which was not seen but which lay in the direction of 315°T. The spokes passed the vessel at an ever-increasing rate, two spokes per second at the fastest. At this time they were about 22 metres in width and there was 22 metres between each spoke. The light given off from the spokes was white to light green in colour, it increased in intensity with the speed of rotation. The direction of rotation was clockwise. By 1925 the centre of the spokes had shifted from 315° to 360°T and gradually reverted back to advancing bands of parallel light. Shortly after this the parallel bands gave way to a counter-clockwise spoke rotation. This was observed in a direction centred along 315°T from the vessel, the spokes moved across the bow to 045°T, at which point they became parallel bands which diminished in intensity. By 1934 they had completely disappeared."
—*Rowntree, C., et al.; "Bioluminescence," Marine Observer, 47:17, 1977.*

X57. March 6, 1980. Arabian Sea. "At 1552 GMT bioluminescence in the form of diffused white light in 'whirlpool' and 'cartwheel' formations was observed; within 3 minutes it completely encircled the vessel and extended to the horizon. The 'cartwheel' formations were brightest at the centre with a halo effect surrounding the outer edges. As the vessel passed over 2 such formations the 'spokes' were estimated to be 2 to 2½ metres in width and the entire concentration, which was more than the width of the vessel (approximately 27 metres), was observed on both sides of the bridge-wing simultaneously. The 'whirlpool' formations, with a distinct central hub, varied from 1¼ to 2 metres in width and from 1 to 15 metres in length. The phenomenon was observed for 40 minutes."
—*Messinger, P.A.; "Bioluminescence," Marine Observer, 51:13, 1981.*

X60. General observation. Light wheels are mostly confined to the continental shelves of Asia and Middle East. They may be caused by earth tremors.
—*"Do Earthquakes Cause Glowing 'Wheels' on the Sea?" New Scientist, 10:528, 1961.*

Three phosphorescent wheels turning simultaneously in the Gulf of Thailand.

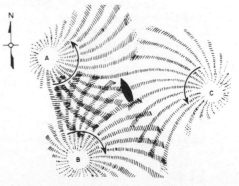

Hailstones formed of crystalline masses.

Irregular hail, England, 1862. Many examples of each type fell.

Spherical hail with raised rims, looking like the planet Saturn, that fell in Guildford, England, on June 25, 1888.

ONE INCH

1.   2.   3.   4.

Irregular hailstones that fell in England in 1893.

Hailstones with Anomalous Shapes
(GWP4)

Key to Phenomena

GWF1	Ice Falls or Hydrometeors
GWF2	Stone Falls
GWF3	Sulphur/Pollen Falls
GWF4	Falls of Miscellaneous Inorganic Substances
GWF5	The Fall of Manna
GWF6	Unusual Falls of Hay and Leaves
GWF7	Gelatinous Meteors or *Pwdre Ser*
GWF8	Prodigious Falls of Web-Like Material
GWF9	Falls of Miscellaneous Organic Substances
GWF10	Fish Falls
GWF11	Falls of Frogs and Toads
GWF12	Insect Falls
GWF13	Bird Falls
GWF14	Falls of Miscellaneous Living Animals

Falls (GWF)

Anomalous rain, snow, and hail are treated in another chapter of the *Catalog*. Beyond these "nearly normal" forms of precipitation are those falling materials that do not belong aloft at all: large chunks of ice, living animals, nonmeteoric stones, and many other nominally terrestrial materials. Charles Fort, who is regarded as the father of anomaly research [see p. 81], made much of falling materials, even though most of them can be explained rationally by appealing to recognized meteorological mechanisms, i.e., whirlwinds, waterspouts, tornados, etc. Fort did have a point, however: any small minority of falling material not succumbing to conventional explanations would require truly revolutionary explanations. Such is the claim of residual anomalies in all areas of science — and this claim is perfectly valid in this chapter.

The overwhelming majority of falls consist of terrestrially derived material and earth-dwelling animals. So-called sulphur falls almost invariably turn out to be wind-blown pollen. The sensationalized falls of fish and frogs, which are well-verified in the literature, are easily explained in terms of whirlwinds, waterspouts, and tornados. Immense falls of hay, leaves, and insects, though startling, are scarcely anomalous. Nature provides ready sources of such material as well as natural vacuum cleaners to snatch up light-weight objects and deposit them somewhere else. Even so, these types of falls present some enigmatic aspects: (1) The descent of some species of animals is so overwhelming in quantity that scientists are hard-pressed to explain where they could have all been collected; (2) The "purity" of the falls, that is, the absence of coexisting species and debris from the falling animals' habitat.

Falls of cobwebs and the so-called gelatinous meteors (or "pwdre ser," which in Welsh means "rot of the stars") introduce a more unsettling factor. While admitting the reality of ballooning spiders, it seems that some of the great web falls involve a substance that may not be insect-produced — it is too strong and quickly evaporates away. It also falls in strands hundreds, even thousands of feet long. Some gelatinous meteors, too, seem to evaporate away strangely. If these properties can be verified, we have something more anomalous than a simple fish fall.

Another pair of phenomena with related characteristics will conclude this introduction: the large hydrometeors and the much-maligned thunderstone. Both phenomena typically occur during thunderstorms. A peal of thunder rings out and something strikes the ground nearby. If one finds a large chunk of ice, a passing plane can always be blamed; but if one find a stone or even a meteor, emotional disbelief takes charge. Yet, no physical reason bars the fall of meteorites during thunderstorms, nor can one deny the possibility of a strong whirlwind picking up a stone of several pounds weight and releasing it during a thunderstorm. After all, some large hailstones reach several pounds, too. The point here is that the possibility of stonefalls should not be dismissed out-of-hand because of any innate distrust of legends carried over from ancient times.

The data presented in this section show rather conclusively that odd things do fall from the sky on occasion. Regardless of the sensationalism usually attached to these falls, most of them are not really very anomalous. A rain of frogs may be rare and certainly Fortean, but meteorology is well equipped to deal with most aspects of this phenomenon.

Ice Falls or Hydrometeors (GWF 1)

Description: Chunks of ice that fall from the sky that are substantially larger than the largest recognized hailstones; that is, more than five inches in diameter or weighing more than two pounds. The ice pieces may fall from a clear sky or they may descend after a powerful stroke of lightning. The chunks may be clear ice, or layered structures, or aggregations of small hailstones. This diversity of structure and meteorological conditions suggests that ice falls may have several different origins.

Background: Today, the fall of large ice chunks is usually blamed on aircraft passing overhead. Certainly, aircraft constitute a likely source, but there are many pre-Wright examples of this phenomenon. Furthermore, aircraft can be ruled out in some modern cases. Nevertheless, it seems that most people are satisfied with the aircraft explanation — perhaps because other origins are difficult to imagine.

Data Evaluation: Some of the older data may seem apocryphal, but there are so many modern ice falls, some investigated by meteorologists, that no one can deny that large ice chunks do fall from the sky on occasion. Rating: 1.

Anomaly Evaluation: Given the fact of ice falls, it seems that large ice chunks weigh so much that the prevailing theory of hail formation in storm cells is inadequate to explain them. The vertical winds in hailstorms do not seem powerful enough to support the large pieces of ice under discussion here. In fact, some modern ice falls are so large that the customary "aircraft" explanation would seem to be wanting. Rating: 2

Possible Explanations: (1) The vertical winds in storm cells are much stronger than generally recognized; (2) Some unappreciated mechanism in hailstorms permits the sudden aggregation of many hailstones; (3) Those hydrometeors that fall after severe lightning strokes may be formed in the lightning discharge channels, possibly as a result of electrostatic forces; (4) Some ice chunks may be true meteors, i.e., from outer space. This last explanation has been ridiculed in the past but some meteorologists are now seriously proposing it, noting in passing that Saturn's rings may be composed of ice chunks.

Similar and Related Phenomena: The fall of meteor-like objects during thunderstorms (GWF2); giant snowflakes (GWP2); giant hailstones (GWP5).

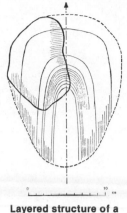

Layered structure of a large hydrometeor.

heavy rainfall was recorded in the area. Inquiries have revealed the pattern of nearby aircraft movements at the time, and it is suggested that the lightning was triggered off by an aeroplane which flew into the storm. No definite conclusion as to the origin of the sample has been arrived at, except that it was composed of cloud water." The ice chunk fell 3 meters from the observer and scattered pieces around. Weight estimate of the composite mass was about 1 to 2 kilograms. One theory proposed that such large hydrometeors may form in the lightning discharge channels with the help of electrostatic acceleration."

—Meaden, G.T.; "The Giant Ice Meteor Mystery," *Journal of Meteorology, U.K.,* 2:137, 1977.
—Meaden, G.T.; "The Giant Ice Meteor or Superhailstone," *Journal of Meteorology, U.K.,* 2:201, 1977.
—Griffiths, R.F.; "Observation and Analysis of an Ice Hydrometeor of Extraordinary Size," *Meteorological Magazine,* 104:253, 1975.
—Crew, E.W.; "Fall of a Large Ice Lump after a Violent Stroke of Lightning," *Journal of Meteorology, U.K.,* 2:142, 1977.
—Crew, E.W.; "Atmospheric Mysteries and Lightning," *Electrical Review,* 199:21, December 17-24, 1976.
—Crew, E.W.; "Origin of Giant Ice Meteors," *Journal of Meteorology, U.K.,* 4:58, 1979.
—Crew, E.W.; "Meteorological Flying Objects," *Royal Astronomical Society, Quarterly Journal,* 21:216, 1980.

The **Catalog** *lists over 50 cases of hydrometeors. Here are a few examples:*

X10. August 1849. Scotland. "A curious phenomenon occurred at the farm of Balvullich, on the estate of Ord, occupied by Mr. Moffat, on the evening of Monday last. Immediately after one of the loudest peals of thunder heard there, a large and irregular-shaped mass of ice, reckoned to be nearly 20 feet in circumference, and of a proportionate thickness, fell near the farm house. It had a beautiful crystalline appearance, being nearly all quite transparent, if we except a small portion of it which consisted of hailstones of uncommon size, fixed together. It was principally composed of small squares, diamond-shaped, of from 1 to 3 inches in size, all firmly congealed together. The weight of this large piece of ice could not be ascertained; but it is a most fortunate circumstance, that it did not fall on Mr. Moffat's house, or it would have crushed it, and undoubtedly have caused the death of some of the inmates. No appearance whatever of either hail or snow was discernible in the surrounding district."
—*"Great Mass of Atmospheric Ice," Edinburgh New Philosophical Journal,* 47:371, 1849.

X42. April 2, 1973. Manchester, England. "A fragment of a very large hydrometeor was analysed in the laboratory where standard thin-section techniques were used to reveal its structure. The ice fell at the time of a severe lightning stroke which occurred in Manchester on 2 April 1973, a day when

X46. January 24, 1975. London, England. A block of ice weighing about 50 pounds fell on an apartment roof.
—Meaden, G.T.; "The Giant Ice Meteor Mystery," *Journal of Meteorology, U.K.,* 2:137, 1977.
—"Large Hail in Britain in 1975," *Journal of Meteorology, U.K.,* 1:261, 1976.

X50. March 1982, Tecumseh, Oklahoma. An ice mass estimated at 30 pounds fell on the land of A.C. Hinson. Investigating meteorologists said that it was not a hailstone but might have fallen from an airplane or even come from outer space.
—"Sky Ice: 30-Lb. Close Encounter," *Boston Herald American,* March 16, 1982, p. 2.

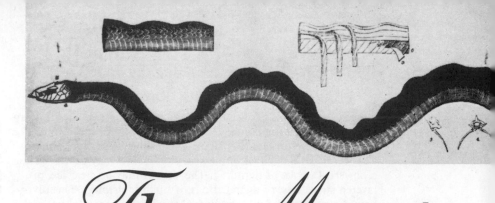

The Monster

THE COELACANTH, A LARGE PREHISTORIC FISH known previously only from sixty-five-million-year-old fossils, was discovered alive off the coast of South Africa in 1939. The African okapi, a "living fossil" in the giraffe family, was identified in 1906. Known only from native legends, the mountain gorilla was not proven real until 1903. Cryptozoologists, the incurable romantics of natural science, point to these and other facts to bolster their premise that large, unclassified animals still exist, known only from folklore and occasional sightings.

The term "cryptozoology" (the science of hidden animals) was coined by the Belgian zoologist Bernard Heuvelmans, whose **On the Track of Unknown Animals**, written in 1955, is still *the* textbook on the subject. Heuvelmans has spent a lifetime collecting reports of unknown animals, and his book is an encyclopedia of the mysterious fauna of land and sea. Many of the animals he describes are known from fossils, like New Zealand's moa (a ten-foot-tall, ostrich-like bird), the Patagonian giant sloth, or African dinosaurs. Others are creatures unknown to science that have been reported by natives and travelers, like the east African Nandi bear, the Sumatran orang pendek (the "little man," an unknown primate), or the Australian bunyip. Heuvelmans' other seminal text, **In the Wake of the Sea Serpents**, provides the most thorough overview written on the surprises that may still await students of marine life.

The most recent American edition of **On the Track of Unknown Animals** was published by MIT Press in 1972, and unfortunately it's long out of print. The good news is

there's a newer book that, though not nearly as exhaustive, provides the same kind of excitement: **Searching for Hidden Animals** by Roy P. Mackal, a University of Chicago biochemist. Mackal, who unashamedly admits to a romanticism "accompanied by a reasoned and balanced credulity," provides a wealth of evidence for unknown sea creatures (including some that may be prehistoric whales called zeuglodons), monstrous Caribbean octopuses, giant Himalayan lizards, living trilobites, and dinosaurs in Africa. It is this last example that has made Mackal semi-famous, for he has conducted three expeditions to the Likouala region of the People's Republic of the Congo to investigate tantalizing reports of a small, brontosaurus-like creature called by the natives *Mokele-mbembe*. The account of his adventures in this remote area are recorded in his book **A Living Dinosaur?** Mackal never saw a Mokele-mbembe, but he collected numerous native accounts of the creature, observed purported Mokele-mbembe trails through the swamps, collected examples of the malombo fruit on which it supposedly feeds, and encountered *something* large and animate that submerged quickly as his boat rounded a bend in the river.

Both Mackal and Heuvelmans are officers in the International Society of Cryptozoology, an organization dedicated to the investigation of "all matters related to animals of unexpected form or size, or unexpected occurrence in time or space." The ISC's board is, in fact, made up of Ph.D. biologists firmly entrenched in academic institutions around the world, so it's hard to dismiss them as crackpots when

---

On the Track of Unknown Animals
Bernard Heuvelmans
1958; 558 pp.
OUT OF PRINT
Hill and Wang
New York, NY
1972; 306 pp. (abridged)
OUT OF PRINT
MIT Press
Cambridge, MA

In the Wake of the Sea Serpents
Bernard Heuvelmans
1968; 645 pp.
OUT OF PRINT
Hill and Wang
New York, NY

Searching for Hidden Animals
Roy P. Mackal
1980; 320 pp.
$39.95
postpaid from:
State Mutual Books
521 Fifth Ave.
New York, NY 10017

A Living Dinosaur?
In Search of Mokele-Mbembe
Roy P. Mackal
1987; 340 pp.
$24.95
($27.45 postpaid)
from:
E.J. Brill
1780 Broadway
Suite 1004
New York, NY 10019
212/757-7628

International Society of Cryptozoology
Bernard Heuvelmans, Pres.
$25/yearly membership
(four newsletter issues and one journal volume) from:
International Society of Cryptozoology
P.O. Box 43070
Tucson, AZ 85733

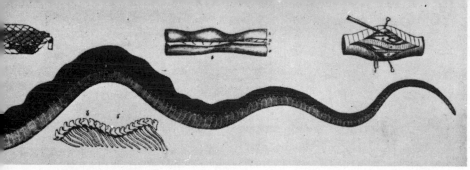

Scollophis atlanticus, the Great American Sea-serpent.
—In the Wake of the Sea-Serpents

Hunters

by Ted Schultz

reading about their efforts to track down a mermaid-like sea mammal called the "Ri" by natives of New Guinea, the Wildman of central China, or the puma-like Onza of Mexico. Following a standard academic format, the ISC produces a yearly journal, **Cryptozoology**, which contains articles, research reports, field reports, and reviews. The ISC also publishes the informal quarterly **ISC Newsletter**, which features fascinating strange-animal news, interviews, reports, and correspondence.

Among the creatures ISC members find interesting is North America's Bigfoot, also known as Sasquatch. Though Bigfoot is a favorite subject of schlock writers, the question of its existence has also received some serious attention. The best books are by John Green, a hardworking journalist and field researcher who has spent over thirty years traveling around the country observing footprints and collecting reports. Green has unearthed numerous nineteenth-century accounts that impressively demonstrate that reports of hairy "wildmen" have been around for a long time. His **On the Track of the Sasquatch** focuses on the Pacific Northwest, where place names like "Ape Canyon" attest to the longstanding wildman tradition; **Sasquatch: The Apes Among Us** deals with both the Northwest and the rest of North America.

Manlike Monsters on Trial reprints a collection of papers delivered at a conference on "Sasquatch and Similar Phenomena" held at the University of British Columbia. The perspectives represented are divided between folklore and natural science. The folklore contributors cover medieval monsters, European wildman myths, and Indian legends, while the naturalists discuss Sasquatch population clines, vocalizations, and feces and hair samples. Like John Green's nineteenth-century accounts, the Indian legends and art demonstrate rather chillingly that, whether Bigfoot is real or not, it's definitely not an invention of twentieth-century supermarket tabloids.

Cryptozoology is only one of the subjects covered by **Living Wonders**, which takes a folklore-oriented approach to its subject. Pets that journey thousands of miles to rejoin their masters, flocks of crows conducting "funerals" for their dead, living toads extracted from cornerstones laid centuries before—these are the kinds of recurrent accounts one encounters in folktales, passing conversations, and throwaway newspaper clippings. **Living Wonders** collates such stories, culled from diverse historical and modern sources, into a thoroughly fascinating collection, wonderfully illustrated with engravings and photos. It leaves the reader with the impression that many an incredible folk belief may have some foundation in natural fact after all.

Finally, for the reader who is serious about surveying the extensive but obscure literature of cryptozoology, there is George Eberhart's **Monsters**. **Monsters** is an exhaustive bibliography of "living animals uncaught and uncataloged by science," and is divided into sections like "Giant Birds, Giant Bats, and Moas," "Mammoths and Mastodons," and "Humanoids in Asia" (e.g., the Yeti). Each section opens with an informative overview, then presents an extensive list of books and articles on the subject. With this book

---

On the Track of the Sasquatch
Books 1 and 2
John Green
1980; 64 pp. each
$5 each postpaid from:
Cheam Publishing
P.O. Box 374
Harrison Hot Springs,B.C.
Canada V0M 1K0

Sasquatch
The Apes Among Us
John Green
1978; 492 pp.
$12.95 postpaid from:
Hancock House
1431 Harrison Ave.
Blaine, WA 98230
206/354-6953

Manlike Monsters on Trial
Early Records and Modern Evidence
Marjorie Halpin and Michael M. Ames, Editors
1980; 334 pp.
$14.95
($18.45 postpaid) from:
University of British Columbia Press
303-6344 Memorial Rd.
Vancouver, B.C.
Canada V6T 1W5
604/228-3846

Living Wonders
Mysteries and Curiosities of the Animal World
John Michell and Robert J.M. Rickard
1982; 176 pp.
$9.95 postpaid from:
Thames and Hudson
500 Fifth Ave.
New York, NY 10110
800/233-4830

Monsters
Including Bigfoot, Many Water Monsters, and Other Irregular Animals
George M. Eberhart
1983; 358 pp.
$33 postpaid from:
Garland Publishing
Attn: Order Dept.
136 Madison Ave.
New York, NY 10016
212/686-7492

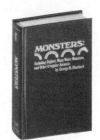

Unknown Antarctic cetacean seen by Edward Wilson in 1902.
—*In the Wake of the Sea Serpents*

and a good library, you'll have cryptozoological reading for years to come.

• Indeed it is not impossible that much larger moas may have survived until today. We know from Maori evidence that they were shy birds that liked to be alone. It has always been supposed that the Dinornithidae, like other running birds, preferred to live in grassy plains. Actually they were a very varied family, large and small, slender and squat. It is very likely that the different kinds had no less different habitats, and that there were slim moas of the plains, little moas of the forests, and heavy moas of the marshes—like the Madagascan Aepyornis. And some of them may well have taken refuge, like the kiwi, in nocturnal habits. Nocturnal moas, living in forests, would have a good chance of eluding all our searches.

The most encouraging tangible evidence is a discovery made by Dr. R. A. Falla in 1949. In a Maori fowler's shelter in a confined valley west of Lake Te Anau in the extreme south–west of South Island, he found the broken dismembered skeleton of a single *Megalapteryx*. There were also unfaded feathers of *wekas*, *kakapos* and *takahes*, preserved flax sandals and *weka* snares, which could not have been more than two hundred years old, and may have been less than a hundred.

—*On the Track of Unknown Animals*

• The Veddahs and the *nittaewo* were constant enemies. The little men had no defence against the Veddahs' bows and arrows, but they made up for it by mischief and cunning. When they found a Veddah asleep they would disembowel him with their claws. But the stronger and better-armed race won in the end. In the late eighteenth century, or so it would seem, the last *nittaewo* were rounded up by the Veddahs of Leanama and driven into a cave. The Veddahs then heaped brushwood in front of the entrance and set fire to it. The bonfire burnt for three days, and the trapped *nittaewo* were all suffocated.

—*On the Track of Unknown Animals*

• Meanwhile the North American sea-serpent, always serpentine, dark in colour, with its head raised out of the water, undulating up and down and showing a string of humps close together, went on appearing as usual. In 1830 three fishermen, one called Gooch, saw it near Kennebec in Maine. In 1831 it was seen not far away in Boothbay harbour by Captain Walden and the crew of the revenue cutter *Detector*, who said it was about 100 feet long. That same year it was seen by some ten people off Boar's Head at Hampton Beach, a favourite spot on Long Island for outings from New York. This time it was reckoned to be 150 feet long, and some thirty to forty little humps, each a foot long, were counted on its back. They also saw something like a horn or a fin near the head. This was quite new, but was to be noticed again later.

—*In the Wake of the Sea Serpent*

• The observations were made by fishermen at Anapkinskaya Bay, just south of Cape Navarin, located approximately 179° W longitude, 62° N latitude. According to Haley, the fishermen were questioned by Vladimir Malukovich of the Kamchatka Museum of Local Lore. The description in translation from the Russian reads: "Its skin was dark, its extremities were flippers, its tail forked like a whale. A slight outline of round ribs was noticeable. We approached the animal, touched it, and were surprised as its head bore an unusual form and its snout was long." Confronted with an illustration of Steller's sea cow, he said that this was the animal in question. As usual there was speculation as to which aquatic mammal may have been mistaken for the sea cow. At least one expert, Edward Mitchell, research biologist for the Canadian Department of Fisheries, stated that the extinct status of Steller's sea cow is a presumption. "There simply haven't been exhaustive inventories of marine vertebrates so that one could state unequivocally that this or any species does not survive." He goes on to suggest that the area should be surveyed by ship. I could not agree with him more.

—*Searching for Hidden Animals*

• The earliest stories with a definite date that have so far come to my attention were from the vicinity of San Francisco, in 1870. The series began with a small article in the San Joaquin *Republican* on September 19, in a column of "Local Brevities," as follows: "WILDMAN—We learn from good authority that a wild man has been seen at Crow Canyon, near Mount Diablo. Several attempts have been made to capture him, but as yet have proved unsuccessful. His tracks measure thirteen inches."

—*On the Track of the Sasquatch, Book 2*

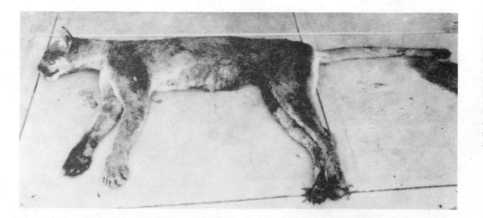

A female Onza shot in January of 1986 by Andres Rodriguez before dissection at Mexico's Regional Diagnostic Laboratory of Animal Pathology, Mazatlan, Sinaloa. It is the first specimen made available to science since the shooting of the Shirk Onza in 1938, which is now lost. The animal is more gracile than a puma, with longer limbs. Comparisons with limb bones of female pumas and electrophoresis of Onza and puma tissues will indicate genetic and evolutionary relationships. —*ISC Newsletter*

- At the end of August, 1958, when the construction crew was roughing out a roadbed some 20 miles north of the Klamath, big tracks started appearing in the dirt overnight. They usually came down from the hillside and crossed the road, going towards the creek. Sometimes they followed the road for a distance, and passed close to parked earth-moving equipment. The prints were like those of a flat-footed human, but huge—16 inches long, seven inches wide at the ball of the foot and only two inches narrower at the heel. Average stride was over four feet. All were made by the same individual. Most of the prints would be obliterated when the machines started to work in the morning, but every few days a new set would be there. After about a month of this a bulldozer operator, Jerry Crew, went to see a friend who was a taxidermist and got some casting plaster and instructions on how to use it. A few days later he appeared at the office of the *Humboldt Times* in Eureka and had his picture taken with a cast of the track. The picture, and an accompanying story, was sent all over the continent by the Associated Press, and "Bigfoot" was born.
  —*Sasquatch: The Apes Among Us*

- The present analysis of reports of alleged eyewitness sightings and tracks of the Sasquatch was undertaken as a result of the increasing seriousness of this anthropological mystery. The preliminary results of our study support the hypothesis that the Sasquatch actually exists, in that population clines in reported body size and track lengths (and apparently coat colour) not only seem to exist but conform to ecogeographical rules. Statistical tests applied to the track and stature data support the assumption that the clines are actual and not a function of sampling bias.
  —*Manlike Monsters on Trial*

- A Rat King consists of a number of rats found inextricably tied together by tails in a central knot. Another name for this fearful conglomeration is the Rat King's Throne. All the reports of Rat Kings agree that black rats only are involved in these mysterious minglings; and one reason for the rarity of the phenomenon today might be the savage depletions of the black rat population by the hordes of brown rats that invaded Central Europe from the region of the Caspian Sea in the eighteenth century.
  —*Living Wonders*

Drawing of the *Mokele-mbembe* based on the concept that it might be a small sauropod dinosaur. —*A Living Dinosaur?*

- South America holds great promise for harboring one or more animals previously thought to be extinct. The giant ground sloth (*Mylodon*) of Patagonia was contemporary with the earliest Indians in the area, and there is some doubt as to when it was actually exterminated. The animal described as *su* by Andre Thevet may well indicate the survival of a giant sloth through the Middle Ages.

  The *iemisch* of the Tehuelche Indians of Patagonia may refer to a variety of the giant otter (*Pteronura*) or extinct saber-toothed tiger (*Smilodon*). The *minhocao* of southern Brazil could be a surviving glyptodont, a huge club-tailed armadillo that lived in the Pleistocene of South America.

  Dinosaurs, or at least large reptiles, may exist in the high plateaus of Guyana. Percy Fawcett repeated stories of similar creatures he had heard in the Mato Grosso, and an odd assortment of monsters is still said to inhabit Patagonia. Whether any of them are based on real animals awaits confirmation. —*Monsters*

Journal of Scientific Exploration

This is the only scientific journal devoted to publishing papers on "1) phenomena outside the current paradigms of one or more of the sciences, 2) phenomena within certain scientific paradigms but at variance with current scientific knowledge, 3) the scientific methods used to study anomalous phenomena, and 4) the study of the impact of anomalous phenomena on science and society in general."

For those who think anomalistics is an up-and-coming discipline, this new journal is welcome indeed. The first issue contains appropriately scholarly articles on factors that influence recollection change in eyewitness accounts (important for the study of UFOs, Bigfoot, etc., that depend on anecdotal evidence), experimental design for investigating psychokinesis (mind over matter), popular beliefs about the Loch Ness monster, and a critical analysis of the U.S. Air Force-commissioned Condon Report on UFOs. —*T.S.*

- The Loch Ness monster rarely needs an introduction—few have not heard of it (or her, under the title of Nessie). The roller-coaster at Busch Gardens in Williamsburg, Virginia, is named in its honor. It is featured in television commercials—for example, a leathery back lifts out of the water a boat-load of kilted and tartan-capped men, in an advertisement for Kellogg's "Raisins, Rice and Rye," shown on U.S. television in 1981. Any serpentine shape coupled with a suggestion of tartan or whisky can, as every cartoonist knows, be used without more explicit identification. And Nessie has been featured in novels and short stories.

Soon after Nessie became international news at the end of 1933, she became closely identified with sea serpents, and has thereafter shared the same public image—of a legendary, mythical, folklorish creature that some gullible people suppose to actually exist. Those who claim sightings are typically ridiculed. Pundits speak of Nessie in the same breath as they do of UFOs, yetis, P.T. Barnum, Atlantis, and so forth. . . .

Nessie has, in fact, become the prototype and stereotype of the aquatic monster. Often, when such a creature is reported, it is described as "a South Pacific Nessie," for example, rather than as a South Pacific monster or sea-serpent (*Newsweek*, 1 August 1977, p. 77); or "Cherokees have own Loch Ness monster" (Asheville [North Carolina] *Citizen-Times*, January 10, 1971) and Nessie's existence serves to validate the search for a similar creature in Lake Champlain . . . A naturalist's sketched impression of a typical sea-serpent is also suggestive; his earlier sketch had resembled the shark-like mosasaurs, but subsequently he pictured the sea-serpent as a Nessie-like plesiosaur.

Journal of Scientific Exploration
Ronald E. Howard, Editor
$40/year (2 issues)
Sample issue free from:
Permagon Journals
Maxwell House, Fairview Park
Elmsford, NY 10523

PERPETUAL M
D

DO YOU THINK THAT THE SEARCH FOR PERPETUAL MOTION ended in failure long ago? You're half right. Failure is perpetual, but the search never ended. The energy shortage that raised its ugly head in the late '70s had doctors, lawyers, and backyard mechanics rediscovering the "overbalancing wheel" and other rusty old ideas discredited a century ago. Time and terms change. The words "perpetual motion machine" cause problems at the Patent Office and scare off investors. Modern experimenters talk instead about tapping energy sources not yet understood or building "over-unity" devices, machines that use energy but produce more than they use.

Despite a long-time historical interest in the pursuit of perpetual motion, I once thought it was a dead issue. My enlightenment came when I personally invented—to hell with modesty—the most ingenious perpetual motion machine ever. I revealed my creation to the world in the April 1978 issue of *Science Digest* in a piece entitled "'What Goes Up'. . . Is Basis for a Breakthrough."

The Schadewald Gravity Engine was designed to take advantage of the theoretical decline of the "universal gravitation constant"—it was essentially a big wheel with a weight on the rim that sped up with every revolution. The tone of my article was slightly immodest, and I compared myself to Descartes, Galileo, and Newton. I railed at the "experts" who sneer at gravity engines, and I defied the Powers That Be to try to suppress my invention. Renouncing material gain, I concluded as follows:

> As of April 1st, 1978, I yield my invention to the public domain, that it may solve the energy crisis and bring peace and prosperity to the world.
>
> I ask only that my initials be inscribed on the wheel of every engine, so that my genius may get the sort of recognition it deserves.
>
> —*Bob Schadewald*

Science Digest illustrated the piece with a small envelope marked, "Do not open until April 1st." Also, contrary to their normal practice, they put the by-line, "Bob Schadewald," immediately following the last sentence of the text. You might suppose that if two references to April 1st and the grandiose and persecuted tone of the piece were not enough, the vision of "B.S." on the wheel of every engine would arouse suspicion.

Before I even knew the magazine was out, a gentleman called from Denver offering to buy my secret. "I've been experimenting with gravity engines for years," he said, "and I could never get one to work." Stunned, I told him that the Schadewald Gravity Engine wouldn't work, either, that it was only an April Fool joke. He was greatly disappointed.

Robert Schadewald is represented twice in this book: here, and as the author of the history of the flat earth movement (see page 86). Schadewald's a rare breed: a historian of eccentric science. He's written for magazines like Smithsonian, Science '80, Technology Illustrated, *and others, including, as you'll soon see,* Science Digest. *For many years, he's made a special study of perpetual motion, traveling to obscure libraries and museums, interviewing inventors, and tracking down antique devices.* —*T.S.*

OTION The Perpetual Quest
by Robert Schadewald

Soon began a flood of mail. An Oklahoma lawyer sent me patent drawings for *his* perpetual motion machine and tried to convince me to write about it. A priest and a violinist lauded me for the unselfish way I gave my invention to the world, instead of trying to make money on it. Some letter writers argued that the machine couldn't possibly work; others wanted more information. Over thirty letters came in all, plus three phone calls.

My experience with the Schadewald Gravity Engine showed me how easy it is to sell perpetual motion, even when you're only trying to make people laugh. I began looking for modern perpetual motion schemes, and I found them aplenty in newspapers, magazines, and television news shows. Before discussing modern schemes, however, a bit of history may be helpful.

Energy shortages are nothing new. The Romans built mills driven by water wheels, and the construction seems to have continued during the Dark Ages. By 1086 A.D., when England's *Domesday Book* (a sort of census report) was written, there were 5,624 water-powered mills in the kingdom. This growth continued, and soon there were no more good mill sites left. The same phenomenon occurred in continental Europe. This dam shortage seems to have inspired the search for perpetual motion.

Many inventors tried to design a water wheel that could both power a mill *and* pump enough water to run itself. In 1618, the alchemist and occultist Robert Fludd described an overshot water wheel that would power a mill and also drive an Archimedean screw-type pump to transport the water back to the flume. The basic idea was common and obvious, and Georg Andreas Boeckler described and illustrated several self-pumping mills in his *Theatrum Machinarum Novum*, published in 1686. No one ever succeeded in making such a mill work, despite numerous attempts. Nevertheless, the hope remains alive to this day, and later we'll look at a modern "self-contained hydroelectric power system" supposed to pump its own water.

Probably no idea is dearer to the hearts of perpetual motionists than the venerable "overbalancing wheel," a vertical wheel equipped with movable weights that are supposed to constantly shift position so that the wheel is always heavier on one side than the other. The earliest surviving description of a perpetual motion scheme, contained in a fifth-century Sanskrit astronomical text, the *Siddhanta Ciromani*, is a variation on this theme. Edward

Somerset, Second Marquis of Worcester (1601-1667), had such an overbalancing wheel built in the tower of London, where he demonstrated it to King Charles I and his court sometime in the 1640s. Somerset later described the demonstration in a book commonly known as *Century of Inventions*, published in 1655:

> They all saw, that no sooner these great weights passed the Diameter-line of their lower side, but they hung a foot further from the Centre, nor no sooner passed the Diameter-line of the upper side, but they hung a foot nearer. Be pleased to judge the consequence.

We are indeed pleased to judge the consequence, and it is nil. (The same cannot be said of other Somerset inventions; he designed an early forerunner of the steam engine.) Numerous schemes have been devised for shifting the weights on an overbalancing wheel as described, and they have one thing in common: they don't work.

A perennially favorite variation is a vertical wheel having curved internal spokes with balls, which can roll between the hub and the rim. The designer—his name is Legion—hopes to produce a constant out-of-balance condition. Analysis of such a device typically shows that at a crucial point in the cycle, each weight has to be "helped over the hump." Once started, momentum does the job

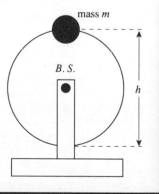

SCHADEWALD GRAVITY ENGINE

The Schadewald Gravity Engine is based on a famous conjecture by the late British physicist P.A.M. Dirac that the "universal gravitation constant" G is in fact slowly decreasing. If true, it follows from high-school physics that g, the acceleration due to gravity at a given point on earth, is also decreasing. Consider then a wheel of diameter h with a heavy weight m attached to its periphery. As the weight rotates from top to bottom, potential energy equal to mg_1h is converted to kinetic energy, and the wheel speeds up. As the weight rotates back to the top, kinetic energy equal to mg_2h is converted to potential energy, and the wheel slows down. But for every revolution, g_2 is less then g_1, so the wheel must gain speed with each revolution.

until friction slows the wheel below a critical speed, when it stops. The permanent lack of balance is an illusion, but a persistent one. Some years ago, I gave a seminar on perpetual motion swindles to the Iowa State University Department of Engineering. Afterward, a student approached me to show me a drawing of his invention—an almost identical overbalancing wheel, except that he had straight spokes set at skewed angles instead of curved spokes! Nothing I had said or could say would shake his confidence in this device.

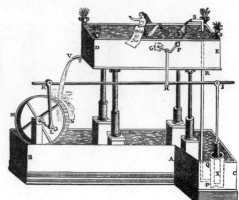

From left to right: The "self-acting pump" of P. Valentine Stansel (1658); the "Wheel of Orffyreus" (1717); astronomer James Ferguson's overbalancing wheel (1770); and the overbalancing wheel of J. Mitz (1658).

The Wheel of Orffyreus

There are, of course, stories of wheels that *did* work. The most famous perpetual motion machine of the classic period was the so-called Wheel of Orffyreus.[1] "Orffyreus" was in fact one Johann Ernest Elias Bessler, who was born in Zittau, Saxony, in 1680. He constructed his pseudonym by writing the letters of the alphabet in a circle; selecting those opposite the letters of "Bessler," he obtained "Orffyre," which he Latinized into "Orffyreus." Beginning in about 1712, he constructed a series of supposedly self-moving wheels, whose mechanisms he always kept concealed.

In about 1717, Orffyreus settled in Hesse-Cassel, where the Landgrave took him under his wing. Bessler was made Town Councillor and provided with work space in the Landgrave's castle near Cassel. By the end of the year, he had built his largest machine, a hollow wheel about 12 feet in diameter and 14 inches thick. The lightly constructed wooden wheel was covered by canvas to keep the interior mechanism from prying eyes. The central axle was about 6 inches in diameter, with each end terminating in a 3/4-inch axle turning in a bearing. If given a slight shove, it would rotate and stop, but if started turning briskly, it would pick up speed, stabilize at about 25 rpm, and continue turning. Under load, it slowed to about 20 rpm. Weights could be heard shifting position as it turned.

On October 31, 1717, Orffyreus was requested to move the machine to a different room of the castle which he did. It was up and running on November 12. The wheel was set in motion and the room sealed up. Two weeks later, the seals were broken and the room opened. The wheel was revolving as when last seen. The room was resealed and not opened again until January 4, 1718. Once again, the wheel was found revolving at its customary rate.

The Landgrave assumed that the wheel had been turning all this time, and he gave Orffyreus a certificate describing the test and the precautions taken. Others were more skeptical. Perhaps they were motivated, as Bessler alleged, by jealousy, but there was also the matter of Bessler's servant girl. She ran away from him and talked, despite a terrible oath of silence he had made her swear. The girl claimed that at certain times she was instructed to turn a small wheel concealed in another room, which she believed powered the large wheel!

At the request of the Landgrave, Professor 's Grave-

1. The most extensive modern treatment of this famous device is by Rupert T. Gould in his 1928 book *Oddities* (see p. 82).

sande of Leyden University made a superficial examination of the Wheel of Orffyreus, as much as the inventor would allow. He paid special attention to the axles and their bearings, but he found no concealed drive mechanism there. (In my opinion, the drive mechanism was in plain sight! Two compound pendulums, one linked to each end of the axle, supposedly regulated the speed. The obvious assumption was that they were driven *by* the wheel. Professor 's Gravesande never seems to have considered that a concealed mechanism might drive the pendulums, which in turn drove the wheel.) Ironically, Bessler destroyed the wheel despite the fact that 's Gravesande gave the machine a clean bill of health.

By the late nineteenth century, a huge and imaginative variety of energy creation schemes had been proposed and attempted. Besides the clanking mechanical wheels, inventors tried to use capillary action to lift water or to drive wheels by magnetic forces rather than gravity. Others tried to achieve unbalanced buoyant forces by wheels or chains of self-wringing sponges. Except for the frauds —and there were plenty of these—nothing worked.

While the perpetual motionists were failing, scientists and engineers were succeeding in understanding what energy is and how it can be controlled. This new field of thermodynamics eventually sharpened the definition of perpetual motion and brought a general consensus that it is impossible.

Kinds of Perpetual Motion Machines

A perpetual motion machine would be a device or system that successfully circumvented one of the laws of thermodynamics. The three laws of thermodynamics can be simply stated: (1) You can't win, (2) you can't break even, and (3) you can't get out of the game.

The first law of thermodynamics is the conservation law, which says energy can be neither created nor destroyed. (Under exotic circumstances, energy can change to matter and vice-versa, but we needn't worry about that here.) The classical overbalancing wheel attempts to produce energy from nothing. But you can't win.

The second law of thermodynamics is the law of entropy. It says heat flows spontaneously from a hot body to a cold one, but not the other way. This obvious idea has subtle consequences. It means energy tends to dissipate, and much of the energy in the universe cannot be harnessed to do useful work. The second law limits the

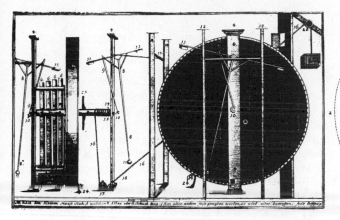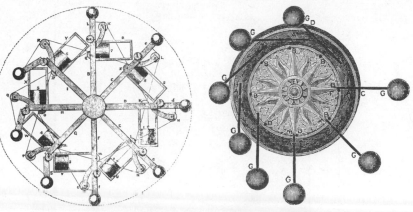

maximum theoretical efficiency of heat engines such as steam engines and automobile engines. Losses are inevitable. You can't break even.

The third law of thermodynamics says nothing can be cooled to absolute zero in a finite number of steps. At absolute zero, wild and wonderful things could happen, including 100 percent efficient heat engines. But you can't get out of the game.

Overbalancing wheels and related devices are therefore called perpetual motion machines of the first kind. Impossible heat engines (discussed later) are perpetual motion machines of the second kind. So far as I know, no one has yet attempted to build a perpetual motion machine of the third kind.

The informed public gradually came to accept that energy is unlikely to be created from nothing. This general understanding, of course, did not end the search for perpetual motion, but it changed the way most perpetual motionists pitched their products. The first and most successful of the new breed was John Ernst Worrell Keely of Philadelphia, America's most successful perpetual motionist.

The Keely Motor

John Keely, born in Philadelphia on September 3, 1837, was six feet tall and extremely muscular. A skillful craftsman, he spent his early adult years as a carpenter and general mechanic. More important than his skill with tools was his skill with words. A charismatic personality, he spoke a mixture of simple English and arcane jargon most listeners found confusing but convincing. Keely's innovation was that he did not claim to create energy from nothing. Rather, he could liberate existing energy from nature.

Keely first gained public notice with his "Hydro-Pneumatic-Pulsating-Vacuo-Engine," which he claimed was powered by the "disintegration" of ordinary water. A beautifully wrought mechanism of brass and copper, the engine had two cylinders, connecting-rods, eccentrics, a flywheel, and miscellaneous appurtenances of unknown function. Investors were impressed by Keely's demonstrations of the motor, and the rights to the invention were assigned to five individuals on February 24, 1872. This partnership evolved into the Keely Motor Company, a joint stock company with a capital of $5,000,000. All the money went to Keely's salary, to building his laboratory,

and to building further demonstration devices—the "Compound Disintegrator," the "Liberator," and so forth.

By 1881, Keely had produced talk and models but no product. Some were beginning to suspect fraud, and Keely exacerbated these suspicions by refusing to reveal his secret technology to anyone. The stockholders revolted, but Keely would not relent. Indeed, he abandoned his disintegration research and left them holding a bag of water vapor. Being musically inclined, Keely began seeking vibratory energy, a new and different technology in which (he claimed) the Keely Motor Company had no rights or interest. (The stockholders took him to court over this, and they lost!) His talk about etheric vibrations and such convinced Theosophists and like-minded people that he had discovered a new and mystical force in nature. (The redoubtable Madame Helena Petrovna Blavatsky endorsed Keely's work in *The Secret Doctrine*, the Theosophical Bible.)

Keely's most enthusiastic and faithful new supporter was Mrs. Clara Bloomfield Moore, a successful poet and novelist who had been left multiple millions by a recently deceased husband. Mrs. Moore promoted Keely's work in Theosophical journals like *Lucifer* and provided large sums for research. Keely provided models of motors, cannons, and miscellaneous devices, all of which operated impressively in his laboratory. Keely would strike a tuning fork and a motor would begin turning, or some such thing. The press reaction was mixed. A. Wilford Hall's *Scientific Arena* described Keely's devices enthusiastically; *Scientific American* described them scathingly. Skepticism abounded, and in February 1896 Mrs. Moore sent the English physicist W. Lascelles-Scott to study Keely's devices and report. A month later, he told the Franklin Institute, "Keely has demonstrated to me, in a way which is absolutely unquestionable, the existence of a force hitherto unknown."

Another physicist, one E.C. Scott, was unconvinced. He and many others suspected that some of the wires and rods on Keely's devices were in fact hollow tubes bearing compressed air. (This Keely vigorously denied.) Scott suggested a simple test. Keely would repeat one of the demonstrations performed for Lascelles-Scott and, while it was in progress, Mrs. Moore would personally cut a particularly suspicious "rod" on the apparatus. Keely haughtily refused, and Mrs. Moore virtually cut off his support. ☞

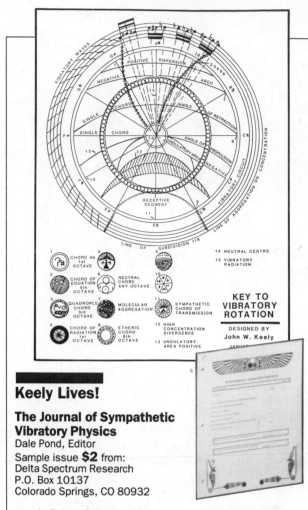

KEY TO VIBRATORY ROTATION

DESIGNED BY John W. Keely

1. CHORD Ab 1st OCTAVE
2. CHORD OF EQUATION 5th OCTAVE
3. QUADRUPLE CHORD 3rd OCTAVE
4. CHORD OF RADIATION 1st OCTAVE
5.
6. NEUTRAL CHORD ANY OCTAVE
7. MOLECULAR AGGREGATION
8. ETHERIC CHORD 8th OCTAVE
9.
10.
11. SYMPATHETIC CHORD OF TRANSMISSION
12. HIGH CONCENTRATION DIVERGENCE
13. UNDULATORY AREA POSITIVE
14. NEUTRAL CENTRE
15. VIBRATORY RADIATION

Keely died on November 18, 1898. The Keely Motor Company immediately took possession of his premises and started investigating. They quickly discovered evidence of massive fraud. The basement contained a huge high-pressure air tank and a water motor. False ceilings and false floors hid compressed air lines and rotating power shafts, which Keely could bring into play with concealed valves and switches. All was duly reported in Philadelphia newspapers, *Scientific American*, and elsewhere. Believers nevertheless remain to this day (see above).

The Garabed

Keely had been in his grave for less than 10 years when Garabed T.K. Giragossian first came before the public in the fall of 1917. An Armenian immigrant living in Boston, Mr. Giragossian claimed to have an inexhaustible source of "free energy" he modestly called the "Garabed." Believing that extraordinary ideas require extraordinary protection, Giragossian hesitated to take his idea to the patent office. With the help of influential friends, he went straight to Congress.

The "Garabed," he told the House Committee on Patents, would power ships, airships, and locomotives, and make the steam engine obsolete. Noting that many pioneers of the past were abused or ignored, Giragossian begged Congress not to let it happen to him.

Giragossian was maddeningly vague about his invention, but prominent Bostonians vouched for his honesty and intelligence. He sought only protection, not money. In early 1918, Congress passed Public Resolution No. 21, offering protection for the Garabed—contingent upon the recommendation of a scientific commission. President Woodrow Wilson signed the resolution and appointed four M.I.T. scientists and an engineer to examine the invention.

The Garabed Commission finally saw the device on June 29, 1918, and the Commission delivered its one-paragraph report the same day. The bottom line: "We do not believe that his (Giragossian's) principles are sound, that his device is operative, or that it can result in the practical development or utilization of free energy."

The Garabed was a massive flywheel! Once set in motion by a burly assistant, a miniature (1/25th horse-power) electric motor would keep the wheel turning. When linked to a brake-type dynamometer, the spinning wheel would briefly produce up to 10 horsepower. Then it stopped. Giragossian thought that he was somehow amplifying the power of the little electric motor 250-fold. In fact, power is a measure of energy flow per unit time. If he could have dumped the flywheel's stored energy into the dynamometer a hundred times more quickly, it would have registered a hundred times more horsepower—for a hundredth as long!

Seldom have so many wasted so much on so little. If this were a fairy tale, I could report that Garabed T.K. Giragossian read a high school physics text and saw the error of his ways, while Congress recognized the folly of rushing in where the patent office refused to tread. Of course, no such thing happened.

Giragossian and friends insisted that the Garabed Commission scientists didn't understand the invention. Congressional supporters held more hearings in 1923 and 1924, and Giragossian told Congressmen that the Garabed would "reshape the destiny of mankind, creating an age of reason and everlasting happiness." Congress voted no further action, but resolutions on Giragossian's behalf were proposed almost annually until 1930.

Stewart Energy Systems

Perpetual motion machines of the first kind all have a "free lunch" aspect that usually makes them easy to spot. But the second law of thermodynamics is not as intuitively obvious as the first, and attempts to violate it aren't always easy to identify.

Suppose you're a farmer shelling out thousands of dollars a year for energy to pump water for center pivot irrigation. You hear about a revolutionary pump engine designed to draw all the energy it needs from the water it pumps. You can purchase a distributorship and get in on the ground floor.

In 1978 and 1979, farmers and investors from all over America bought distributorships for a pump motor being developed by Stewart Energy Systems of Idaho. Stewart's motor was essentially a closed-cycle steam engine, except that it used freon instead of water as a working fluid. Potential investors were shown a working model, but it ran off a conventionally fired boiler. It seems that inventor Robert Stewart had not yet perfected the heat exchanger that was to draw the energy out of the well water by dropping its temperature two or three degrees! Before running afoul of the Securities and Exchange Commission, Stewart Energy Systems took in over three million dollars.

Had the investors consulted a physicist, they would have received some good news and some bad news. The good news is that three BTUs (British Thermal Units), the amount of energy that would be released by lowering the temperature of a pound of water three degrees Fahrenheit, could theoretically lift that pound of water more than 2300 feet. The bad news is that little or none of the three BTUs is available to do useful work.

Heat engines depend on making heat flow. To draw energy from the well water, you would have to make heat energy from the cold water flow to an even colder body (a condenser). How do you cool the condenser? You could build a refrigeration unit, but—you're probably way ahead of me—it would take far more energy to run the refrigeration unit than you'd ever get back.

Ironically, the Stewart motor was identical in principle to a perpetual motion scheme considered by the U.S. Navy a century earlier. In about 1882, John Gamgee went to the Navy with a proposal for a "zeromotor," a device that would power ships with energy drawn from seawater. The essential difference between the Gamgee zeromotor and the Stewart motor was that the former used ammonia and the latter used freon. The output of both was the same: zero.[2]

Jeremiah 33:3

As mentioned previously, some of the oldest perpetual motion schemes involved attempts to make a water wheel pump its own water while doing other useful work. This dream is not dead. In spite of scoffers and legal battles, a Texas inventor tried to develop a "self-contained hydroelectric power system."

Imagine a 100-gallon water tank atop an 18-foot tower. Water from the tank flows down through a coiled "amplification unit" into a turbine. The turbine turns a generator, which charges a battery pack, which in turn powers an AC converter. Water discharged by the turbine flows into a self-acting pump, which returns the discharge water to the tank without consuming any energy.

Inventor Arnold Burke of Temple, Texas, began promoting this system in 1977. Burke claimed his system would eventually retail for about $1500 and would produce 1500 (later 3000) kilowatt-hours per month. Most

---

2. The Gamgee fiasco is described in detail in chapter 10 of Ord-Hume's *Perpetual Motion* (see review, p. 127).

system components could be purchased off the shelf. The key to the system, the self-acting pump, he claimed he had originally invented to drain a gold mine.

Burke initially got financing for his device from a large dairy co-op, but they parted ways after he failed to deliver a working model to the co-op's headquarters. By this time, Burke had christened his machine "Jeremiah 33:3" for the Bible verse—"Call unto me, and I will answer thee, and shew thee great and mighty things, which thou knowest not"—that inspired his invention. He began selling distributorships to individuals, especially Bible Belt investors as impressed by his piety as by his mechanical ingenuity. The Texas attorney general filed suit in the fall of 1979, alleging that Burke and his associates had collected $800,000 in licensing fees under false pretenses.

The Jeremiah trial, held in Belton, Texas, was reportedly a good show. The prosecution called expert witnesses who testified that Jeremiah couldn't possibly do what Burke claimed. The defense called a chemistry professor from Arizona State University who testified that it could. Burke insisted that Jeremiah ran without any external power, and the defense fought a motion to have the machine examined by a court-appointed expert. They lost.

On December 19, 1979, Jeremiah was examined by engineer David Kehl and Assistant Attorney General Roy Smithers. While Kehl was taking Jeremiah's pulse with an electronic stethoscope, Smithers spotted a concealed wire leading from the machine's upper reservoir. It turned

Using advertising like this, Stewart Energy Systems of Idaho took in over three million dollars from farmers before running afoul of the Securities and Exchange Commission.

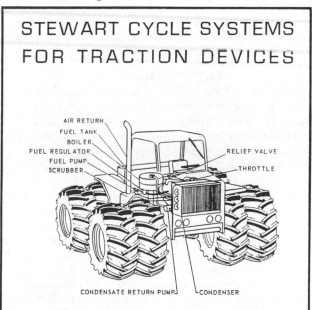

were there. The Kenyon Alternator was turned by a five-horsepower motor, and it produced enough electricity to light a panel of one hundred light bulbs. Solar World personnel monitored instruments and posted figures on a blackboard purportedly showing the motor to be using 5,936 watts while the generator put out 7,512 watts, or nearly 27 percent more than input energy. They denied that the device was a perpetual motion machine, saying its energy source was probably neutrinos. (As neutrinos typically pass through the earth without reacting, it's not clear how they could be harnessed by the Kenyon Alternator.)

Rather than neutrinos, the "secret" of the Kenyon Alternator seems to have been the monitoring instruments and the way they were used. Simple AC voltmeters and ammeters are calibrated for sinusoidal waveforms; if the output of the Kenyon alternator wasn't a sine wave, the instrument readings were wrong. Furthermore, calculations of power must consider "power factor," which depends on the phase relationship between voltage and current. Solar World considered the advertised (not measured) power factor of the drive motor, but they apparently didn't consider the power factor of the Kenyon Alternator itself.

The acid test, of course, would be to hook the output of the Kenyon Alternator up to the input of the motor that drives it. Dr. Kenyon and his associates were aware of this, and talked of building a Kenyon Motor for the experiment. If this obvious and crucial test was ever performed, I haven't heard of it, and the Kenyon Alternator faded away.

The Newman Energy Machine

Joseph W. Newman, an inventor from Lucedale, Mississippi, first got national attention on January 9, 1984, when Dan Rather of CBS News gave a brief report on his "energy machine." The Newman Energy Machine is a direct-current electric motor that differs from conventional DC motors in several respects, including its very high voltage and very low amperage. In his patent application filed in 1979, Newman called it an "Energy Generation System Having Higher Energy Output than Input." Indeed, Newman has claimed that the motor's efficiency is as high as 800 percent. After a long battle, the Patent Office refused to grant a patent, saying the device "smacks of a perpetual motion machine." Newman filed suit.

Newman's case first went to court in mid-1984. After some wrangling, Judge Thomas Jackson appointed a "Special Master," electrical engineer and patent attorney William E. Schuyler, Jr., to investigate. On September 28, 1984, Schuyler reported: "Evidence before the Patent and Trademark Office and the Court is overwhelming that Newman built and tested a prototype of his invention in which the output energy exceeds the external input energy; there is no contradictory factual evidence."

The Patent Office remained skeptical and refused to grant a patent. As with the Kenyon Alternator, there were questions about the test instruments used. The Patent Office recommended that Newman turn the device over to the National Bureau of Standards (NBS) for further test-

out that the wire connected a battery pack under a bunk in an adjoining room to an electric pump in Jeremiah's innards. Burke was arrested and indicted on multiple counts of theft and perjury.

Burke claimed he only installed the electric pump to prevent the disclosure of Jeremiah's *real* secret, and many of his investors kept the faith. In the spring of 1980, while Burke was on trial for one count of fraud, faithful followers raised another $250,000 and bought out disgruntled investors for sixty-six cents on the dollar! The trial ended with the jury hung eleven to one for conviction. That fall, Burke won a directed acquittal on another charge of fraud. At last report, he was back in his laboratory, working the kinks out of Jeremiah's design.

Kenyon Alternator

Jeremiah 33:3 was a classical perpetual motion machine of the type most inventors since Keely have abandoned. The newest wrinkle on the perpetual motion scene is the "over-unity" motor. This is a device that requires an external source of power, but supposedly produces more power than it uses. The Kenyon Alternator was an excellent example.

The Kenyon Alternator was invented in the late 1970s by Dr. Keith Kenyon, then personal physician of former Los Angeles mayor Sam Yorty, and was further developed by Solar World, Inc., a Glendale, California, producer of wind turbines and other alternative energy devices. The Kenyon Alternator was essentially an alternating-current generator that reversed the roles of the usual components. Instead of rotating coils of wire in a magnetic field, it had permanent magnets mounted on the periphery of a wheel and rotated them in an array of coils.

Solar World held a Hollywood-style press conference and demonstration on its premises March 22, 1979. Former Mayor Yorty and ventriloquist Paul Winchell were present, and former astronaut Gordon Cooper was expected but didn't show up. Representatives of five television stations and several radio stations and newspapers ing. As with every aspect of the Newman case, there was much wrangling, but NBS finally tested the device in mid-1986. They measured its efficiency as 27 percent to 67 percent, depending upon the load and other factors. Conventional DC motors commonly achieve 80 percent efficiency, so this is less than impressive.

Newman responded that NBS deliberately rigged the test to make his invention look bad. In December 1986, Newman and the Patent Office were back in court. By this time, about thirty scientists and engineers had endorsed the Newman Energy Machine, most notably physicist Roger Hastings, manager of the Superconductive Electronics Technology Center for Unisys in St. Paul. Hastings and two engineers testified in Newman's favor. The NBS expert was steadfast in defending the NBS tests. In March 1988, Judge Jackson decided in favor of the Patent Office.

Joseph Newman did not wait for the court's decision to express his general displeasure with the proceedings. In 1987 press releases regarding his case, he called Judge Jackson "a criminal of the worst kind," accused the Patent Office of conspiracy, and made rather free use of terms like "fools," "liars," "hypocrites," and "criminals." Newman wanted the judge impeached, the Commissioner of Patents prosecuted, and (for good measure) Ronald Reagan impeached. To ensure that Truth and Justice prevail, Newman announced his candidacy for president on the Truth and Action Party ticket.

The Patent Office calls Newman's device a perpetual motion machine, but he insists it is not. Rather, the Newman Energy Machine converts mass to energy according to Einstein's famous equation, $E=MC^2$. In an updated (apparently 1987) press release, Newman wrote:

> I have persistently stated that this 100% conversion process was achieved by tapping into the basic building block of matter — the energy (gyroscopic particles) comprising a magnetic (gyromagnetic) field. I have disclosed that this energy in a magnetic (electromagnetic) field was literally "a river of energy" that could be tapped for immediate benefit of humanity without pollution to the environment or the human race, would end hunger, would make space travel commonplace, and much more. Also this technology will do more to bring about "World Peace" than all the Kings, Queens, and politicians that have ever lived.

Stating that gyroscopic particles and a conversion process exist and proving it are two different things. (If I state, dear reader, that you have a weightless, odorless, invisible vulture sitting on your left shoulder, you might demand further evidence.) The burden of proof is on Newman, and he has failed. As for his humanitarian sentiments, they are right out of my Schadewald Gravity Engine announcement, except that Newman has obviously no intention of putting the Newman Energy Machine into the public domain.

Not surprisingly, Newman has supporters in Congress, and at least eleven bills have been introduced to force the Patent Office to grant him a patent. None have passed.

And thus has our unbalanced wheel come full circle. Newman claims with Dr. Kenyon to tap a mysterious

Perpetual Motion: The History of an Obsession

Perpetual Motion
The History of an Obsesssion
W.J.G. Ord-Hume
1980; 235 pp.
$5.95
($6.95 postpaid) from:
St. Martin's
175 Fifth Avenue
New York, NY 10010
800/221-7945

If Robert Schadewald's article leaves you thirsting for more, this book is your logical next choice. It is, in fact, the only objective book-length history of perpetual motion. Drawing on antique books and old periodicals, as well as obscure modern publications, Ord-Hume has reconstructed the untold history of perpetual motion from medieval times to the present. Using plenty of contemporary illustrations and photographs, he describes overbalancing and other self-moving wheels, magnetic and steam contraptions, spongewheels, rolling-ball clocks, radium-powered devices, perpetual lamps, and other schemes. The stories of Keely, Garabed, and other colorful inventors are told in detail. And, lest you think that all "perpetual motion" ideas have ended in failure, Ord-Hume describes a number of successes(!), including a "perpetually" ringing bell and the marvelous perpetual clock of James Cox. (Neither of these inventions violates the three laws of thermodynamics, but you'll have to read the book to find out how they work.)
—T.S.

• With the approval of all those present, excepting, no doubt, the exhibitor, [Robert] Fulton began knocking away some pieces of thin wood which appeared to be no part of the mechanism but to pass between the frame of the machine and the wall of the room and serve simply as supports to steady the device. These strips of wood concealed a catgut belt drive which passed through one of the pieces of wood and the frame of the machine to the head of the upright shaft of a principal wheel. The other end of the drive passed through the wall and along the floors of the second story to a back attic some yards from the room where the 'perpetual motion' was to be seen. Here Fulton found the real source of the power which turned Redheffer's machine—an old man with a long beard who displayed all the signs of having been imprisoned in the room for a long, long time. The man had no notion what was happening and sat there on a stool gnawing a crust with one hand and turning the crank with the other.

The crowd turned mob, demolished the perpetual motion machine and Redheffer fled, a stop having at last been put to his deception which had earned him a tidy fortune in Philadelphia and New York. In Scharf and Westcott's *History of Philadelphia* there is a reproduction of the advertising circular which Redheffer used to attract visitors to his exhibition at Germantown, Philadelphia. This reveals that the charlatan had the audacity to charge $5 admission for men, but allowed women to be admitted *gratis*.

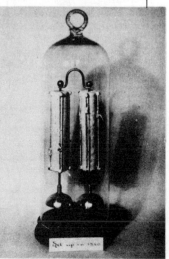

The perpetual chime set up by Singer in 1840 and still in operation today. *Picture by courtesy of Dr. A.J. Croft of the Clarendon Laboratory, University of Oxford.*

force in an unspecified way. Like Giragossian, he seeks patent protection through Congress. Like Orffyreus, he is aggressive, obstreperous, and abusive with skeptics. And like Orffyreus, Keely, Burke, Kenyon, and numerous other inventors, Newman has found people with credible scientific credentials to endorse his invention.

Conclusion

Most people couldn't state the laws of thermodynamics on a bet, but they instinctively know that there is no such thing as a free lunch. When confronted with a Newman Energy Machine, they ask questions like, "Why not hook the motor up to a DC generator, use the output to drive the motor *and* a dynamometer, and get rid of that silly battery pack?"

There is another sort, though, who are perpetually sus-picious of Power and Authority. These people seem to think the laws of thermodynamics are part of the Oil Company Plot to suppress the legendary 200 mile-per-gallon carburetor. If they don't seek perpetual motion themselves, they are eager to endorse someone else's "discovery." I believe the *persona* I assumed in my Schadewald Gravity Engine spoof—earnest, slightly paranoid, altruistic but seeking recognition—is fairly typical of the breed. (Certainly it struck a responsive cord with those readers taken in by the hoax, for they inundated me with letters.)

Nothing changes. Unless I miss my guess, perpetual motion will never be discovered but will ever be sought. Education is only a partial defense, for it cures ignorance, but not delusion. The dream of unlimited energy will keep those who rebel against the laws of physics in perpetual motion.

Perpetual Motion Believers

As Robert Schadewald points out, perpetual motion research is alive and well, though it's been given new names by today's seekers after the inventor's grail. These two books are a good place to start if you want to directly familiarize yourself with this subculture.

The Perpetual Motion Mystery reprints the work of perpetual motionist Irwin R. Barrows, who in 1967 published The Perpetual Motion Handbook and the first of four issues of the Perpetual Motion Journal. The Handbook and all four issues of the Journal are reprinted in the book, as well as fifty extra pages by R.A. Ford, mostly on Orffyreus' Wheel. Don't expect finesse—a lot of the pages were done on a typewriter, and others were copied straight out of old books, magazines, and patent applications. But everything is readable, and the unpolished pages give the book that homemade feel that connoisseurs of fringe theories cherish.

That homemade feel also characterizes The Manual of Free Energy Devices and Systems, which avoids the term "perpetual motion." The Manual is a potpourri of plans, patent descriptions, personality profiles of favorite free-energy inventors (Nicola Tesla is canonized in this world), reprinted articles, fuzzy photographs, and great diagrams. As an added bonus, besides "free-energy" and "over-unity" devices, you'll be introduced to anti-gravity machines as well. —T.S.

• The scientific work of T.J.J. See of the 1930's has been largely unknown and/or ignored by the scientific community for all the years since its first introduction.

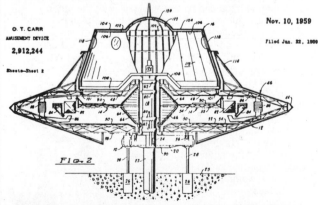

O. T. CARR
AMUSEMENT DEVICE
2,912,244

Sheets—Sheet 2

Nov. 10, 1959

Filed Jan. 22, 1958

FIG. 2

O.T. Carr's Amusement Device, Nov. 10, 1959. The caption reads: "NOTE: This is some kind of "Amusement Device"—one that can be used to explore the worlds around us!!! Wake up you Physicist's" —*The Manual of Free Energy Devices and Systems*

It has been said that See had the unfortunate tendency "to come on too strongly" with his theories which was usually interpreted by astronomer colleagues as being "arrogant egotism" rather than "studied conviction" which it apparently was.

. . . See's anti-gravity theory explains how a rotating body effects gravity, as was vividly demonstrated by John Searl, and Otis Carr in their anti-gravity experiments. According to this theory, when a symmetrical metallic body is rotated at a critical speed, the surrounding ether is set in motion which produces an ether vacuum, which prevents the transmission of gravitational forces to the rotational body.

The well-known psychic, Edgar Cayce identified T.J.J. See "as a scientist with a sound theory to the solution to the riddle of gravitation."

—*Manual of Free Energy Devices and Systems*

• **Advice to Perpetual Motion Inventors**
Because of the many past failures of Perpetual Motion, the author suggests that no one spend more time or money for this search than they are willing to lose. One early inventor tore up his wife's wedding dress to obtain covering for some wire. Your family is your responsibility and should come first. Because the mentally unbalanced do things which set them apart from the general population, the Perpetual Motion inventor should be conservative in his actions and speech. Don't imitate the man who walked into the office of the electric power company and told all the secretaries to quit work because his Perpetual Motion invention would soon put them all out of work. —*The Perpetual Motion Mystery*

The Perpetual Motion Mystery
A Continuing Quest
R.A. Ford
1986; 193 pp.
$9.95
($10.70 postpaid) from:
Lindsay Publications
P.O. Box 12
Bradley, IL 60915-0012
815/468-3668

The Manual of Free Energy Devices and Systems
Compiled by D.A. Kelly
1986; 123 pp.
$12.95
($14.20 postpaid) from:
Adventures Unlimited
P.O. Box 22
Stelle, IL 60919
815/253-6390

Pseudo-Science and Society in Nineteenth-Century America

*Phrenology, the "science" of analyzing character by measuring the bumps on the head, is now all but forgotten. But in the nineteenth century it was as respectable as chiropractic is today. The **American Phrenological Journal**, started in 1838, lasted until 1911; references to phrenology appear frequently in the works of Walt Whitman, Edgar Allan Poe, George Eliot, Charlotte Brontë, Mark Twain, and many of their contemporaries. Phrenology was only one of many pseudosciences that played roles in the art, politics, and society of the 1800s, including hydropathy (the "water cure," which consisted of prolonged bathing and water drinking), mesmerism ("animal magnetism"), homeopathy (enjoying a comeback in the 1980s), spiritualism (also on the upswing, in the form of "channeling"), and electrical cures (including electric belts, corsettes, and hats).*

*In **Pseudo-Science and Society in Nineteenth-Century America**, nine authors (professors of history, English, and religion) describe the strange theories of the day, with special emphasis on their places in the social milieu. The rise of many of these ideas was coupled with social reform movements that promoted women's rights, moral regeneration, and various brands of utopianism. A chapter on sexuality and the pseudo-sciences, for example, describes the popular eugenics movements that recommended "scientific breeding" to produce a superior stock of Americans, as well as "group-marriage" and "free love" movements, and various sex-practice prescriptions like Alice Stockham's "Karezza" (prolonged sex without orgasm). Another chapter argues that mesmerism was the direct precursor of modern psychology.*

The parallels with late twentieth-century America are inescapable. The perspective afforded by a century of time could help us to avoid the same mistakes twice—but I'm not holding my breath waiting for this to happen. How many beliefs that seem like "science" today will be part of the contents when a book like this is written about the twentieth century?
—*T.S.*

• It is difficult to read without a shudder the "cure" offered by a quack in New York for syphilis, or "self-abuse." "The patient sat naked upon a sort of toilet throne, his bare back resting against a metal plate, his scrotum suspended in a whirling pool." The plate and pool were linked by wire to a power source; therapy began when the circuit was completed. While

Harness' Electric Corset, advertised in *The Queen*, March 12, 1892.

this therapy doubtless cured lads of some of the vices in question, normal therapy worked from much the same (albeit less graphic) premises. ["Electrophysiologist" Wilhelm] Erb suggested, for "flaccidity of the testicles" due to sexual excess, "the passage of a moderately strong faradic or galvanic current through the testicles for a few minutes," while the *JAMA* of March 19, 1892, reported that M. Kronfeld of the General Hospital of Vienna treated syphilis with an electric bath. Dommer, in the meantime, suggested treating "sexual neurasthenia" by passing a faradic current between one electrode in the urethra and the other in the rectum.

Pseudo-Science and Society in Nineteenth-Century America
Arthur Wrobel, Editor
1987; 245 pp.
$24
($26.50 postpaid) from:
University Press of Kentucky
P.O. Box 6525
Ithaca, NY 14851
800/666-2211

Diamond Dealers and Feather Merchants

*In this delightful little volume, distinguished chemist Irving Klotz presents a gossipy look into the human side of the scientific enterprise, with an emphasis on follies, eccentricities, and curious behaviors. Included are chapters on the pronouncements of great scientists that turned out to be embarrassingly wrong, a wonderful discussion of the "N rays" discovered and studied for years by Professor Rene Blondlot (over 200 papers were published by many researchers) until it was shown that they didn't exist, the strange case of Russian "polywater" (the inspiration for Kurt Vonnegut's "ice-nine" in **Cat's Cradle**), which also didn't exist, and the "yearning to believe" that can lead to rationalization of contradictory information.*

Klotz's overall message: By viewing how others have become the prisoners of their own mistaken ideas, perhaps we can release ourselves from the "conceptual bottles" into which we have been processed.
—*T.S.*

• When was the decision made that N rays are a delusion? Never. There is no authoritarian hierarchy in science. Science has no vicar on earth to reveal doctrine, no central committee

to proclaim the party line. Actual histories of novel discoveries, except when religious or political authorities have intervened, have followed a pattern best described by an aphorism attributed to the founder of the mathematical theory of electromagnetic waves, James Clark Maxwell. In his introductory lecture on light, Maxwell is said to have remarked:

"There are two theories of the nature of light, the corpuscle theory and the wave theory; we used to believe in the corpuscle theory; now we believe in the wave theory because all who believed in the corpuscle theory have died."

Diamond Dealers and Feather Merchants
Tales from the Sciences
Irving M. Klotz
1986; 126 pp.
$24.95
($27.45 postpaid) from:
Birkhauser
Attn: Order Dept.
44 Hartz Way
Seacaucus, NJ 07094
800/526-7254

BRAIN
BOOSTERS
Road-Testing the New Mind Machines

by Joshua Hammer
Photos by Randy Green

No doubt the brave new day will come when direct electrical stimulation of the brain will be used to produce selected mental states. No more tiresome memorization or years of ascetic meditation; attain genius-level intellect or blissful nirvana with the flick of a switch. According to some, in fact, this day has already arrived.

Joshua Hammer, a Los Angeles-based writer, began his investigation of brain-building devices without any preconceptions, pro or con. Hammer, a former senior writer at People *magazine, has written for* Manhattan, Inc. *and* Esquire, *specializing in business and crime. This piece originally appeared in* California *magazine.* —T.S.

NANCY MALOTT, a former travel agent from Santa Rosa, California, had a problem. After four years of punching up airline schedules on her computer terminal and confronting an endless parade of harried customers, she felt "like my brain was going to explode." Then Malott —a dabbler in a variety of New Age concepts from est to channeling— picked up a copy of the September 28, 1987, *San Francisco Chronicle* and read about a newly opened storefront clinic in Corte Madera that offered "A Quickie Tune-up for Marin Brains." Proponents of the tune-up device claimed to achieve in forty-five minutes from technology what gurus take years to perfect: heightened mental functioning through the meditative state.

"I'd had a hard time getting myself to meditate, and this seemed a perfect shortcut," Malott says. "The beep-beep-beeps, the sound of the ocean coming through my headphones just hypnotized me. The colors I saw through my goggles were so vibrant—I loved them; I could feel them going right through my body."

Linda Jones (a pseudonym), a West Hollywood resident who worked as a secretary in a film studio, was tormented by feelings of insecurity and disdain for the drudgery of her job. Then she heard about Robert Monroe, an "explorer" of human consciousness and potential. Subscribing to the notion that the typical human being uses only one brain hemisphere, Monroe concocted a machine called the Hemi-Sync Synthesizer to bring the two halves into harmonic convergence. Suddenly concentrating on tasks, she says, with both her analytical left brain and her intuitive right brain humming together, Jones felt a transcendent sense of joy. She quit her job and is now working as a freelance word processor. "This was so much better than any type of drug high. I felt calm and energized at the same time."

Welcome to the newest addition to the New Age, wherein growing numbers of people are turning to machines to "tune up" their brains and, they hope, enhance their creativity and intelligence. The phenomenon is known as "brain building," and some proponents claim repeated mental workouts can have the same effect on gray matter that Nautilus equipment has on muscle tone—turning flabby, under-utilized neurons into robust cells rippling with brain power.

Some gadgets, such as the Synchro-Energizer, use high-frequency lights and sounds to bring users into a meditative trance. Others depend on low-voltage zaps of electricity sent directly to the brain. Still others employ electromagnetic fields or cerebellum-stimulating movement. Whatever the methods, the past couple of years have seen an explosion of brain-building gadgetry across California. At the Institute for DeHypnotherapy in the redwood retreat of Soquel, more than 3,500 people have experienced Synchro-Energizer sessions. At the Altered States Float Center in West Hollywood, owners Jeff Labno and Larry Hughes recently installed a MindGym: aficionados can watch their brain-wave patterns crawl across a translucent screen known as the Mind Mirror or spin around on the Graham Potentializer, a massage table surrounded by a two-volt electromagnetic field. At the John-David Learning Institute in Carlsbad, run by an American-born, Congo-educated neuroscientist, several thousand people have signed up for seminars promising to balance cerebral hemispheres, raise IQs, and bring inner tranquility through the application of sixty different sounds aimed at the brain's neurotransmitters. Timothy Leary has become a convert, recently regaling New Agers at the Whole Life Expo in Los Angeles with his lecture entitled "Hi-Tech Methods for Operating the Human Brain."

Dr. Daniel Kirsch, dean of the Graduate School of Electromedical Sciences at the unaccredited City University of Los Angeles and inventor of the electronic Alpha-Stim device, sold by prescription for pain relief, sees Leary's journey as emblematic of the new high-tech zeitgeist. "We've gone from drugs to meditation to devices in the perennial quest for increasing the mind's capacities," he says.

"There is an incredible market out there," explains Denis Gorges, a self-described biomedical researcher who has sold, he estimates, six thousand Synchro-Energizers at $6,500 apiece since 1985. His followers include Carly Simon, Wavy Gravy, Ally Sheedy, and Tina Turner.

Who are the other adherents of the new brain-wave mania? Many are seekers who have previously embraced such movements as est, channeling, crystals, or transcendental meditation. The new movement also has a particular appeal among the high-techies, since the machines blend aspects of mysticism into sleek Silicon Valley technology.

Others say brain building suits the needs of a generation raised on notions of holistic health and self-actualization yet disillusioned by sham holy men and prophets. "We're all tired of fascist gurus such as the Bhagwan," says Randy Adamadama, owner of Universe of You Studios in Corte Madera, California. "Now you're responsible for your own health and consciousness. I call the phenomenon K-Mart spirituality."

Finally, quickie brain tune-ups offer the hope of easy serenity to those who don't have the time to run off to the ashram and sit under a bodhi tree for three years—perfect for the my-time-is-my-money ethos of the 1980s. "When people learn to meditate, their confidence and self-esteem go up, their introversion and tension drop, but only twenty percent of people can achieve meditation," says David Siever, 31, a telecommunications technologist from Edmonton, Alberta, who has sold "about one hundred" of his DAVID 1s (Digital Audio Visual Integration Device) to health spas, flotation centers, and individual users. Using lights and sounds, much like the Synchro-Energizer, "the DAVID 1 is bringing about ninety-five percent of its users into a deep hypnotic state."

Indeed, says Siever, so powerful are the effects of his $3,000 device that he carefully screens prospective owners. "We had a country-music band that wanted to buy a DAVID 1 and hook it up to a microphone in a bar while people were drinking beer. We were worried they might put people in a deep hypnotic trance, then start singing country-western lyrics such as 'Woe is me, my baby left me, I want to jump off a bridge.' And they might do it! People can go under quite hard."

Intrigued by the phenomenon and confident I wouldn't "go under hard," I decided to give it a try. For ten days I had electrodes attached to my earlobes, my temples, my forehead, and my jawbone. At the Los Angeles Invention Convention I sat in a Japanese-designed "brain chair" called the Cerebrex, my head enveloped in a compartment supposedly suffused with mind-enhancing rays and nitrogen-enriched air. I rotated counterclockwise on a platform while a strobe light penetrated my occipital cortex and an electromagnetic field massaged my hypothalamus.

I reclined in a darkened room with a pair of welder's goggles on my head, my eyes blitzed by indicator lights and my ears besieged by rapid-fire beeps. I donned a face mask called the Tranquilite and stared at a translucent blue screen while static, or "pink noise," played through my headphones. I still don't feel more relaxed or more intelligent.

The brain builders are baffled. By now, they say, my synapses should be firing like bottle rockets on Bastille Day. Childhood memories should be bubbling to the surface. Michael Hutchison, author of *Megabrain* (see p. 136), claims in his book that my brain itself should be *growing*, pressing up against my skull like a cheese soufflé expanding over the edges of a cake pan.

Maybe I'm missing something. Maybe I'm just a hardened cynic who is denying himself a genuinely enhancing experience. Maybe my gray matter is so intractable I'm just a hopeless case. Whatever my problem, it is hardly one of consequence to the thousands of satisfied acolytes—or to the handful of promoters and inventors who are currently cashing in on the brain-building boom.

Volker Risto is founder and president of the Enhancement Products Institute in Van Nuys, California (a business with an unlisted phone number), which he runs out of his apartment. Its specialty is "cranial electrotherapy stimulation," or mild electroshock. Risto is a device distributor, and what he sells are commonly known as CES (cranial electrotherapy stimulation) and TENS (transcutaneous electrical nerve stimulus) machines. Despite a variety of names—from the Alpha Pacer II to the Brain Tuner and the BioRest— all of them are pretty much alike: adaptations of a medically approved, low-voltage "black box," or generator, the Alpha-Stim, often used by arthritic patients to alleviate chronic pain. But today they're being promoted by manufacturers and dealers for other purposes. Devotees of these devices, only one of which is currently authorized for sale by the Food and Drug Administration, maintain that repeated applications not only engender deep relaxation but can sharpen memory, mitigate drug addiction, increase intelligence, and perhaps even expand brain cells and tissue.

Ushered into Risto's small Van Nuys office, I sat on a couch, removed my shoes, and settled back for what promised to be a mind-expanding journey. Risto, a lean, mustachioed figure, reached into a leather briefcase and extracted a transistor-radio-sized steel box arrayed with a sophisticated-looking panel of dials, switches, and meters. He attached two electrodes to the hollow spaces between my earlobes and jawbone. Then he twisted one of the dials clockwise, studying my face intently. "Feel anything yet?" he asked.

My skin began to tingle as high-frequency pulses of electricity shot through the wires and into my skull. I felt dizzy, slightly alarmed. For the next fifteen minutes I remained hooked to the Relax Pak while Risto slowly increased the megahertz level with every flick of his wrist.

Dealers and inventors of such machines know they're treading dangerous waters. "I'm on the borderline of getting FDA approval for the Endomax," insists Ted Butler, who manufactures both the $199 Endomax and the $320 Ultron. "We've sold nearly a hundred Endomaxes so far. I've seen incredible results, but I won't say the device stimulates brain growth—you might call the FDA. Still, we're finding it useful for anxiety release, insomnia, and reactive depression."

But in my case it did nothing. I wasn't overcome by euphoria or anything else. Maybe I just don't take kindly to electricity. So perhaps, I thought, a fix of strobe lights and pulsating noises would do the trick.

Randy Adamadama, 54, conducts his business completely in the open—with surprisingly successful results. "It's incredible," said Adamadama, an impish figure wearing a pink, lobster-patterned shirt and blue jeans, as he greeted me at the door of his New Age salon at eleven o'clock on a Satur-

day morning. Crowds were lined up in the lavender hallway in preparation for one of his hourly sessions, each of which attracts as many as thirty people. "When I started Universe of You in September, I couldn't give away sessions. Now I'm grossing more than $1,000 a day."

Adamadama (a "planetary name" he said he adopted last year after deciding Stevens was "male-biased") invested $50,000 in an adaptable, thirty-two-station Synchro-Energizer after a night of intense dreaming following his first experience on the device at the 1986 Whole Life Expo in San Francisco. "I'd suffered nervous breakdowns, but I'd never asked the universe for help," he said. "I was working as a night watchman. I didn't know how to deal with the world. Then at the Expo I saw this machine promising to 'tune up your brain in five minutes.' And I needed it! My brain synchronized itself. I felt relaxed, euphoric—wow! A year later, here I am."

Adamadama's brochure promises that regular use of the Synchro-Energizer will lead to improved memory, increased creativity, deep mental and physical relaxation, and better problem-solving and decision-making abilities. As we walked down a corridor decorated with yin-yang symbols, New Age posters, and collages of Buddhas and Christ figures, Adamadama told me the machine's effects are so powerful and immediate that "some people can't take it the first time. They're so wired up—they start to relax, and they just freak out."

Inside the main studio a Synchro-Energizer session was in progress. A gentle chorus of woodwinds mixed with soothing surf, low beeps, and heartbeats echoed over a quadraphonic stereo system. All I could see in the darkness at first were two dozen pairs of tiny flickering lights, dancing maniacally back and forth. Twenty-four people lay sprawled on beach chairs, their eyes encased in stroboscopic welder's goggles, their ears entombed in metal headphones, their faces bearing expressions of otherworldliness. Adamadama's assistant stood at a stereo console in one corner, the shelf above her head adorned with a pink crystal ball of "plasma energy." ("*Wizard of Oz* decor," said Adamadama.) She was fiddling with dials in an effort to lull her disciples, she explained, into a deeper alpha, or meditative, state.

The Synchro-Energizer does its stuff, according to its proponents, by entraining the brain waves to duplicate specific frequencies imposed by the blinking lights and pulsating noises. Inventor Gorges calls this the frequency-following response: shoot alpha waves in, get alpha waves back. Gorges claims entrainment induces the same nirvanic, trancelike state that yogis labor for twenty years to master. On top of that, it balances the left and right brain hemispheres. And that, according to Adamadama's brochure, "creates an ideal, 'whole-brain' state in which both hemispheres of the brain can be utilized to maximum effect."

Personally, after lying on my back for forty-five minutes with indicator lights flickering against my eyes, I emerged a bit dazed and rather bored. But nearly all of the dozen seekers I interviewed as they staggered out of Universe of You said the $10 cost was well worth it—and pledged to come back for more.

132

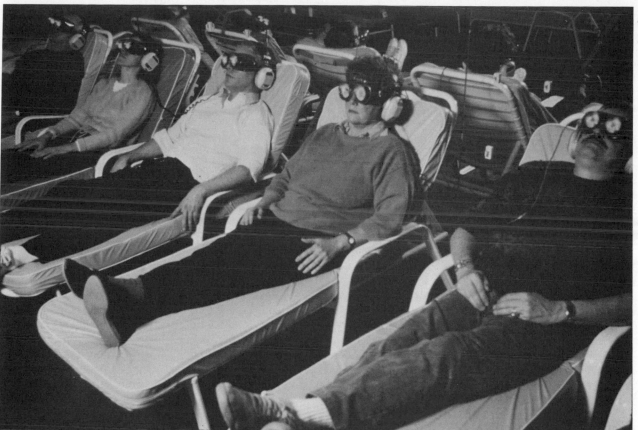

Clients relax at the Universe of You Studio in Corte Madera, California.

Chris Holtz (a pseudonym), 29, a computer programmer from San Rafael, said he is not normally susceptible to the allures of the New Age. But he came here because "my job is stressful and I was looking for ways to alleviate it. The experience was peaceful and calming, without distorting your perceptions," he said. "It's like waking up on a sunny morning during vacation. But I don't think you're tapping into a greater mind." Even so, Holtz said he planned to return—music to the ears of Adamadama, who has begun offering $50 monthly unlimited-use Universe of You memberships. "And if this works out, we're expanding throughout the Bay Area," he said. "Then next the world."

Adamadama is prospering, but he is small-time compared to the Werner Erhard of the mind-tech generation: Carlsbad's John-David, who is perhaps the most successful of the brain builders. I met John-David in the Bodega Bay Lodge north of San Francisco, where he was leading one of his Total Immersion Intensive seminars. Thirty-six people had paid $1,900 each for five days and nights of nonstop self-actualization therapy. When I arrived at the inn, the group was seated in a semicircle in a toy-strewn basement conference room, each person wearing headphones, receiving sounds that were, says John-David, totally repatterning their neural chemistry.

John-David is an exuberant, ample-bellied man in his late forties with curly brown hair and a broad, sunburned face. In his Bermuda shorts, tennis sneakers, yellow-striped shirt, and tinted glasses, he looked like a cuddly version of Polish premier Wojciech Jaruzelski. Emphasizing the attainment of power and self-worth, John-David

has conjured up a New Age goulash of psychojargon and unique theories of neuroscience.

John-David's techniques slightly resemble the Gateway Voyage program of his rival, Robert Monroe, who uses the Hemi-Sync Synthesizer to inject tones of two different frequencies into the left and right brain hemispheres, thus creating a "binaural beat frequency." This purportedly allows the brain to balance itself, heightening powers of concentration. But John-David takes Monroe's Hemi-Sync method one step further. He bases his teaching on his own research and on years spent studying with Tibetan lamas. At the core is his belief that intensive exposure to combinations of sixty sounds—twenty "raw" and forty premixed—will trigger the release of specific, mind-enhancing neurochemicals. These tones, he says, also facilitate the synchronic interplay of both hemispheres. "We can improve the brain's pathways to genius level," John-David claims. "We allow you to enhance language, memory, and sexuality . . . and increase orgasms and erections."

John-David's work has taken him from Zanzibar, where he performed appendectomies and tonsillectomies without a medical license, to Bulgaria, where he studied with the accelerated-learning guru Gyorgi Lozanov, and to Egypt, where he treated brain-damaged soldiers using bells from Tibet. Upon returning to the United States in the mid-1970s, he says, "most of my former college professors at Berkeley wanted to commit me. Some of my work was illegal. So I backed off." He decided to work strictly as an educator, "using tapes to accelerate the learning process." ☛

When I ask John-David for scientific evidence to support his claims, he points to the anecdotal testimony of hundreds of former students, students who've responded to his "Whole or Half Brain?" advertisements in such mainstream publications as *The New York Times*. The John-David Learning Institute opened four years ago and grosses more than $250,000 a month, he says, through tape sales and nation-wide seminars. And in November 1987 John-David opened the first of several brain/mind salons ("your brain's fitness center"), which feature the Synchro-Energizer, the Graham Potentializer, flotation tanks, an Alpha-Chair chamber, and a geodesic dome. "We envision the gray-flannel executive coming in on his lunch hour for a quick brain tune-up," he says.

The seminars sponsored by the John-David Learning Institute are an awesome experience. This Saturday evening, John-David's thirty-six students, including housewives, an inspirational-TV-talk-show host, a bank officer, and a psychologist, were plugged into a seven-minute "sound massage" tape that sounded like fingernails rapping with machine-gun speed against a window pane. The sound was designed to "activate their dendrites and myelinate their axons," says John-David, getting their brains in shape for the rigorous speed-reading drill that would be coming next.

When the tape was over, John-David's disciples were exhilarated. "I feel as if somebody has been caressing my eyeballs!" exclaimed one middle-aged man with a florid complexion.

"It is affecting the optic nerve," John-David replied with a vigorous nod.

"Does it make any sense that it seemed like someone was stimulating my left brain?" someone asked.

"Yes—of course!" cried John-David.

John-David tunes up his brain at the John-David Learning Institute in Carlsbad, California.

Randy Green/Onyx

The group opened copies of Bill Cosby's *Fatherhood* and began running their fingers over the upside-down pages, babbling nonsense.

"Line-line-space-headline-line-line-space. . . ." Known as grokking (a term borrowed from a science fiction novel), this preliminary procedure was intended, said John-David, "to confuse the left brain and focus on the right brain, the intuitive side. You'll soon be comfortable photographing the entire page with your right hemisphere."

At a signal, the students flipped their books right-side up and began scanning the pages.

"Fifteen thousand words a minute!" screamed a teacher in her thirties.

"Twenty-eight thousand words a minute!" one-upped an Indian gentleman seated beside her.

A black-haired New York playwright wearing Tammy Faye Bakker makeup began quivering, tears and mascara cascading down her cheeks. "I can't believe it," she sobbed as John-David massaged her shoulders. "I went through eleven different schools as a child, and I could never even *finish* a book. This is the first time in my life I've ever enjoyed reading." One of John-David's assistants rushed over and pinned a gold star on her blouse.

espite such testimonials and dramatic emotional displays, however, some of John-David's colleagues in the brain-building world don't put much faith in his teaching methods, although that's not really surprising, considering the industry is rent by as much collegial jealousy as academia is. "He's using twenty-year-old technology," says Arnold Stillman, who runs a mind-tech salon called the Transformational Training Center in Encino. "If I had to depend strictly on tapes, I'd be in a lot of trouble."

Since opening his "educational clinic" eighteen months ago, Stillman and his wife, Marcia, who has a Ph.D. in educational psychology, have treated 450 dyslexic adults and children, using a variety of brain-building tools. The first one I tried was the Brain Wave Analyzer, which consists of a plastic band that fits snugly around the head with contact probes touching the scalp and earlobes. The Brain Wave Analyzer, says Stillman, "measures your neural efficiency quotient, which translates into a close approximation of your IQ." The Stillmans use the gadget instead of written tests, which they insist are culturally biased.

Marcia Stillman screwed the device tightly to my skull and clamped two metal pins to my ears. Her husband stood over a computer printer, studying the readout. "Jesus!" he said, whistling softly.

What's going on? I thought. Surely, my seismic brain-wave activity must be classifying me as a genius.

No such luck. "Did you ever experience any reading or writing difficulties in school?" asked Arnold Stillman. "Your IQ is registering about 112. And it seems you're borderline dyslexic."

The Stillmans—who are not licensed psychologists but operate the Transformational Training Center under the auspices of Dr. Ronald Doctor, who *is* licensed—use both the Multisensory Integrator (intended for dyslexia and anxiety) and the Modified Graham Potentializer (for stress). Both are cushioned, four-foot-high platforms that move in a gentle motion. An electromagnetic box placed above the head and strips under the body allegedly induce relaxation on the Modified Graham Potentializer. "As the table revolves," inventor David Graham has explained, "the millions of nerve endings in your inner ear are stimulated, sending out electrical signals that are carried to the cerebellum and throughout the brain. . . . This neural activity causes the neurons to forge new connections. . . . The first thing this does is bring a dramatic increase in your motor and learning abilities."

The Stillmans place patients on the machines for as many as twelve sessions, once or twice a week, charging $85 a session. Offering letters from former clients as evidence, they claim that in eighty-nine percent of their cases "we had a total remission of dyslexia." But Arnold Stillman downplays the effects of the machines when I raise the specter of FDA approval, which neither the Multisensory Integrator nor the Modified Graham Potentializer have. "You have to be careful how you write this," he tells me. "The FDA gets into the picture if we start making medical claims. So we never use the word cure. It's training—only it's training that you won't perceive."

Brain builders have a tendency to back off when asked to provide scientific data to support some of their claims. Nevertheless, most have assembled a voluminous quantity of anecdotal evidence. And the fact is, when confronted with hundreds of first-person testimonials from people who claim the John-David Learning Institute, the Brain Tuner, or the Graham Potentializer "changed my life," one has to be respectful. Some people may honestly believe they've been helped. The devices may act as placebos, giving encouragement to those seeking smarts or inner peace. Some of the machines—such as the Potentializer, the Synchro-Energizer, the DAVID 1—may even be effective relaxation tools. And if they make their users feel good, perhaps they're worth $10, $30, or $85 a pop. For all that, nobody has ever presented a double-blind, scientific study to substantiate claims that stimulation can lead to brain growth, learning enhancement, memory retrieval, serenity, or self-confidence.

Additionally, some of these New Age inventors use pseudoscientific jargon to impart to their devices a sophistication they simply don't have. Take the frequency-following response, which, Gorges insists, duplicates the trancelike state that is achieved by experienced meditators. Dr. Jerome Engel, Jr., professor of neurology at the UCLA School of Medicine, disputes the notion that this is possible. "Using traditional methods to learn to meditate would undoubtedly be good for many people," he says. "But this equipment is claiming to provide a shortcut that is unproven and therefore misleading."

Dr. Robert Heath, emeritus professor of Tulane University's department of neuropsychiatry, scoffs at those such as Gorges who promise to synchronize the left and right brain hemispheres. "I know of no such thing

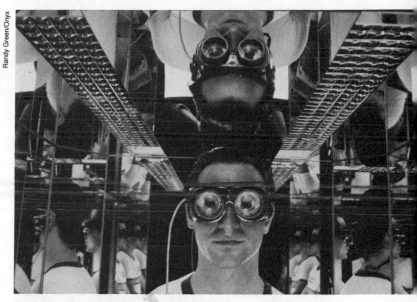

The Synchro-Energizer promises to induce deep relaxation, improve your memory, increase your creativity, and expand your awareness.

that could achieve that balance," he says, "or whether any such concept would be of any value."

"Gorges is making all sorts of claims for the physiological as well as the therapeutic effects," says City University's Kirsch. "If he were making the claims he's making and had registered his device with the FDA, they'd probably crack down on him. But they just don't have the manpower to come out and inspect these devices."

When I call Gordon Scott, public and consumer affairs officer at the Los Angeles branch of the FDA, and read aloud the product brochure distributed by one of the brain/mind salons, his response is unequivocal: "We're dealing with a major case of health fraud here." And when I mention that the brochure includes an FDA endorsement ("this machine has been approved [by the FDA] as a safe and reliable learning/relaxation device"), Scott becomes obviously angry: "Even if we do *approve* devices, we don't permit our agency to be used for promotion of any sort," he says, requesting that I mail him a copy of the brochure.

Researchers are similarly harsh on other claims. Although stimulation of the cerebellum through movement has been used in the past to treat dyslexic children, "no evidence exists that you can repattern the brain of an adult," says Heath. He believes machines promising to repattern the brain are "diffusing facts into quackery."

Clarann Goldring, Ph.D., former president of the L.A. branch of the thirty-eight-year-old Orton Dyslexia Society, which maintains a laboratory at the Harvard Medical School, says, "I have asked the Stillmans time and time again to send me robust, hearty research that their treatment works, and they refuse. . . . They're careful with their wording. If they said they could cure dyslexia I'd go after them in two minutes." Arnold Stillman responds: "She wants the results of a study that we're doing, which has all kinds of positive results. She made all kinds of ac-

Megabrain

Megabrain
Michael Hutchison
1986; 347 pp.
$4.95
($5.95 postpaid) from:
Ballantine/Random House
400 Hahn Road
Westminster, MD 21157

800/638-6460

A gee-whiz reporter for **Omni** *magazine travels around the country trying out various gizmos claimed to elicit altered states of awareness, looking for the action beyond biofeedback. Most of the inventions he examines apply weak electrical currents to the skull. One machine is reputed to emit "love waves"—frequencies that churn up cheery hormones in the user's cortex. Do they work? Well, some of them induce changes in the brain's activity, and the literature Hutchison digs up on each device suggests that some may stimulate the production of neurotransmitter molecules (the appropriate ones?). His own direct experiences suggest that the contraptions, in general, tend toward instilling "alert relaxation." Some would call that simply daydreaming or meditation.*

Too bad his reporting is so uncritical. On the other hand, he deserves attention for his heads-on experimentation. He also supplies manufacturers' references for second opinions. This is the only comprehensive foray into the flaky world of do-your-own brain tuning, and so may be worth a look.

—Kevin Kelly

• Medical researcher Dr. Gene W. Brockopp, who has used the Synchro-Energizer extensively, puts it this way in a recent paper about the device: "Although it is mentioned in some of the promotional literature that research has been done on the synchro-energizer, no research reports are available. Anecdotal information on various individuals who have used the machine is available but nothing even approaching the level of an adequate case study is available at the present time . . . To the author's knowledge, there is no compiled base of theoretical, experimental, or clinical data on the synchro-energizer."

To Gorges, such criticisms are simply too piddling to deal with. Of *course* there isn't sufficient hard scientific evidence to support his claims—but studies like that take a lot of time and a lot of money. Let the machine speak for itself. It works! As he proudly told me, "I've *always* been a heretic and a rebel." Painstaking research holds little interest for him, he said. "I'm interested in *results*!" When asked about the long-term effects of regular use of the Synchro-Energizer, Gorges cries, "Long-term effects? Long-term effects? Who knows about long-term effects? I don't. Nobody knows about long-term effects. This is a new machine, a new technology. Even the doctor doesn't know about long-term effects . . . It's exciting to be a pioneer for science."

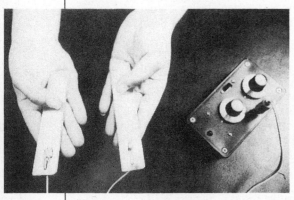

Joseph Light's simple TENS (Transcutaneous Electrical Nerve Stimulation) device is made from "about nineteen dollars' worth of parts from Radio Shack." Many users report that at certain frequency settings, the instrument can increase alertness and concentration, and produce mild euphoria.

cusations. We'll probably end up bringing suit against her."

Perhaps nowhere is the business as rife with potential trouble as in the merchandising of TENS devices. Recent years have witnessed a rash of schemes involving the sale of black boxes promising everything from weight loss to addiction recovery, from the DocTronic Electro-Acupuncture Wand to Dr. Benefit's Slim-Up.

In Ventura County, California, a man named Evans Alex Rapsomanikis was scheduled for trial on fraud charges for allegedly selling 50,000 shares of stock in Electro-Biomorphic, a manufacturer of TENS-like devices that he promised would cure cancer. All this simply underscores the fact, says Dr. Jim Barquest, a biomedical engineer with the California Department of Health Services, "that nobody uses electricity in an approved therapeutic mode, except for electroshock. With TENS devices there's even a chance of burns, chronic headaches, or permanent nerve damage." }

What particularly galls scientists is the disreputable stain some of these hucksters are casting over legitimate cerebral research. Evidence suggests, says a California neurologist, that biofeedback machines such as the Mind Mirror that display brain-wave activity can be useful in teaching a person how to relax and may even help control epilepsy. "But progress in such areas is being greatly hampered by all these wild claims," he says. "It's very hard to get research funding or be taken seriously by one's colleagues."

oes this mean *all* the claims made by brain-building gurus are false? Not necessarily, allows Dr. Richard Jed Wyatt of the National Institute of Mental Health. "There is always a Columbus or an Einstein working outside the mainstream," he says. "But far more often there is somebody getting rich off the rest of us, augmenting his bank account and producing medical disasters in his wake."

The doubts of respected neuroscientists such as Wyatt probably won't make a great deal of difference to brain builders, however, since the machines appeal to a yearning among human beings for novelty and self-improvement, and to the age-old desire of humankind to understand, harness, and manipulate the powers of the brain. From ancient experiments with psychotropic mushrooms on the Indian subcontinent to Sigmund Freud's fascination with cocaine, the drive to control the brain as functionally as we control other parts of the body is timeless, varying only as the philosophy and technology of each age differ.

It seems only natural then that the 1980s would dish up its own version by merging two of the most vital forces of the last two decades—the transcendentalism of the sixties and the high-tech orientation of the seventies, mixing our fascination with meditation and our faith in machines. Add to that the obsession of the eighties—making money —and a movement is born. Brain building as a science may not have arrived, but brain building as a pop phenomenon will not depart until the last possible dollar has been made.

Michael McMillan

THE MAN WHO INVENTED FLYING

by John A. Keel

Carl Jung, who wrote a whole book on flying saucers, called UFOs a "living myth," and said of them, "We have here a golden opportunity to see how a legend is formed." The entire epilogue of Jung's book, Flying Saucers: A Modern Myth of Things Seen in the Sky, *is devoted to the discussion of a book published by Ray Palmer, who John Keel here labels "the man who invented flying saucers." With years of experience in the equally colorful dual worlds of pulp magazine publishing and the UFO subculture, John Keel is uniquely qualified to tell this story of the origins of the flying saucer legend that Jung could not have known.* —T.S.

This article originally appeared in the *Fortean Times* (see review on page 81).

NORTH AMERICA'S "BIGFOOT" WAS NOTHING more than an Indian legend until a zoologist named Ivan T. Sanderson began collecting contemporary sightings of the creature in the early 1950s, publishing the reports in a series of popular magazine articles. He turned the tall, hairy biped into a household word, just as British author Rupert T. Gould rediscovered sea serpents in the 1930s and, through his radio broadcasts, articles, and books, brought Loch Ness to the attention of the world. Another writer named Vincent Gaddis originated the Bermuda Triangle in his 1965 book, *Invisible Horizons: Strange Mysteries of the Sea.* Sanderson and Charles Berlitz later added to the Triangle lore, and rewriting their books became a cottage industry among hack writers in the United States.

Charles Fort put bread on the table of generations of science fiction writers when, in his 1931 book *Lo!*, he

SAUCERS

Robert Gibson Jones/Harry S. Robins

In 1947, the editor of *Amazing Stories* watched in astonishment as the things he had been fabricating for years in his magazine suddenly came true!

assembled the many reports of objects and people strangely transposed in time and place, and coined the term "teleportation." And it took a politician named Ignatius Donnelly to revive lost Atlantis and turn it into a popular subject (again and again and again)[1].

But the man responsible for the most well-known of all such modern myths — flying saucers — has somehow been forgotten. Before the first flying saucer was sighted in 1947, he suggested the idea to the American public. Then he converted UFO reports from what might have been a Silly Season phenomenon into a *subject*, and kept that subject alive during periods of total public disinterest. His name was Raymond A. Palmer.

Born in 1911, Ray Palmer suffered severe injuries that left him dwarfed in stature and partially crippled. He had a difficult childhood because of his infirmities and, like many isolated young men in those pre-television days, he sought escape in "dime novels," cheap magazines printed on coarse paper and filled with lurid stories churned out by writers who were paid a penny a word. He became an avid science fiction fan, and during the Great Depression of the 1930s he was active in the world of fandom — a world of mimeographed fanzines and heavy correspondence. (Science fiction fandom still exists and is very well organized with well-attended annual conventions and lavishly printed fanzines, some of which are even issued weekly.) In 1930, he sold his first science fiction story, and in 1933 he created the Jules Verne Prize Club which gave out annual awards for the best achievements in sci-fi. A facile writer with a robust imagination, Palmer was able to earn many pennies during the dark days of the Depression, undoubtedly buoyed by his mischievous sense of humor, a fortunate development motivated by his unfortunate physical problems. Pain was his constant companion.

In 1938, the Ziff-Davis Publishing Company in Chicago purchased a dying magazine titled

---

[1] Donnelly's book, *Atlantis,* published in 1882, set off a 50-year wave of Atlantean hysteria around the world. Even the characters who materialized at seances during that period claimed to be Atlanteans.

Richard Shaver (left), inventor of the Shaver Mystery, and Ray Palmer (right), the man who invented flying saucers, outside Shaver's house sometime in the 1950s.

Amazing Stories. It had been created in 1929 by the inestimable Hugo Gernsback, who is generally acknowledged as the father of modern science fiction. Gernsback, an electrical engineer, ran a small publishing empire of magazines dealing with radio and technical subjects. (He also founded *Sexology*, a magazine of soft-core pornography disguised as science, which enjoyed great success in a somewhat conservative era.) It was his practice to sell — or even give away — a magazine when its circulation began to slip. Although *Amazing Stories* was one of the first of its kind, its readership was down to a mere 25,000 when Gernsback unloaded it on Ziff-Davis. William B. Ziff decided to hand the editorial reins to the young science fiction buff from Milwaukee, Wisconsin. At the age of 28, Palmer found his life's work.

Expanding the pulp magazine to 200 pages (and as many as 250 pages in some issues), Palmer deliberately tailored it to the tastes of teenaged boys. He filled it with nonfiction features and filler items on science and pseudo-science in addition to the usual formula short stories of BEMs (Bug-Eyed Monsters) and beauteous maidens in distress. Many of the stories were written by Palmer himself under a variety of pseudonyms such as Festus Pragnell and Thorton Ayre, enabling him to supplement his meager salary by paying himself the usual penny-a-word. His old cronies from fandom also contributed stories to the magazine with a zeal that far surpassed their talents. In fact, of the dozen or so science fiction magazines then being sold on the newsstands, *Amazing Stories* easily ranks as the very worst of the lot. Its competitors, such as *Startling Stories, Thrilling Wonder Stories, Planet Stories* and the venerable *Astounding* (now renamed *Analog*) employed skilled, experienced professional writers like Ray Bradbury, Isaac Asimov, and L. Ron Hubbard (who later

created Dianetics and founded Scientology). *Amazing Stories* was garbage in comparison and hardcore sci-fi fans tended to sneer at it.[2]

The magazine might have limped through the 1940s, largely ignored by everyone, if not for a single incident. Howard Browne, a television writer who served as Palmer's associate editor in those days, recalls: "Early in the 1940s, a letter came to us from Dick Shaver purporting to reveal the "truth" about a race of freaks, called "Deros," living under the surface of the earth. Ray Palmer read it, handed it to me for comment. I read a third of it, tossed it in the waste basket. Ray, who loved to show his editors a trick or two about the business, fished it out of the basket, ran it in *Amazing*, and a flood of mail poured in from readers who insisted every word of it was true because *they'd* been plagued by Deros for years."[3]

Actually, Palmer had accidently tapped a huge, previously unrecognized audience. Nearly every community has at least one person who complains constantly to the local police that someone — usually a neighbor — is aiming a terrible ray gun at their house or apartment. This ray, they claim, is ruining their health, causing their plants to die, turning their bread moldy, making their hair and teeth fall out, and broadcasting voices into their heads. Psychiatrists are very familiar with these "ray" victims and relate the problem with paranoid-schizophrenia. For the most part, these paranoiacs are harmless and usually elderly. Occasionally, however, the voices they hear urge them to perform destructive acts, particularly arson. They are a distrustful lot, loners by nature, and very suspicious of everyone, including the government and all figures of authority. In earlier times, they thought they were hearing the voice of God and/or the Devil. Today they often blame the CIA or space beings for their woes. They naturally gravitate to eccentric causes and organizations which reflect their own fears and insecurities, advocating bizarre political philosophies and reinforcing their peculiar belief systems. Ray Palmer unintentionally

---

[2] The author was an active sci-fan in the 1940s and published a fanzine called *Lunarite*. Here's a quote from *Lunarite* dated October 26, 1946: "*Amazing Stories* is still trying to convince everyone that the BEMs in the caves run the world. And I was blaming it on the Democrats. 'Great Gods and Little Termites' was the best tale in this ish [issue]. But Shaver, author of the 'Land of Kui,' ought to give up writing. He's lousy. And the editors of *AS* ought to join Sgt. Saturn on the wagon and quit drinking that Xeno or the BEMs in the caves will get them."

I clearly remember the controversy created by the Shaver Mystery and the great disdain with which the hardcore fans viewed it.

[3] From *Cheap Thrills: An Informal History of the Pulp Magazines* by Ron Goulart (published by Arlington House, New York, 1972).

140

gave thousands of these people focus to their lives.

Shaver's long, rambling letter claimed that while he was welding[4] he heard voices which explained to him how the underground Deros were controlling life on the surface of the earth through the use of fiendish rays. Palmer rewrote the letter, making a novelette out of it, and it was published in the March 1945 issue under the title: "I Remember Lemuria . . . by Richard Shaver."

The Shaver Mystery was born.

Somehow the news of Shaver's discovery quickly spread beyond science fiction circles and people who had never before bought a pulp magazine were rushing to their local newsstands. The demand for *Amazing Stories* far exceeded the supply and Ziff-Davis had to divert paper supplies (remember there were still wartime shortages) from other magazines so they could increase the press run of *AS*.

"Palmer traveled to Pennsylvania to talk to Shaver," Howard Brown later recalled, "found him sitting on reams of stuff he'd written about the Deros, bought every bit of it and contracted for more. I thought it was the sickest crap I'd run into. Palmer ran it and doubled the circulation of *Amazing* within four months."

By the end of 1945, *Amazing Stories* was selling 250,000 copies per month, an amazing circulation for a science fiction pulp magazine. Palmer sat up late at night, rewriting Shaver's material and writing other short stories about the Deros under pseudonyms. Thousands of letters poured into the office. Many of them offered supporting "evidence" for the Shaver stories, describing strange objects they had seen in the sky and strange encounters they had had with alien beings. It seemed that many thousands of people were aware of the existence of some distinctly nonterrestrial group in our midst. Paranoid fantasies were mixed with tales that had the uncomfortable ring of truth. The "Letters-to-the-Editor" section was the most interesting part of the publication. Here is a typical contribution from the issue for June 1946:

Sirs:

I flew my last combat mission on May 26 [1945] when I was shot up over Bassein and ditched my ship in Ramaree Roads off Chedubs Island. I was missing five days. I requested leave at Kashmere (sic). I and Capt. (deleted by request) left Srinagar and went to Rudok then through the Khese pass to the northern foothills of the Karakoram. We found what we were looking for. We knew what we were searching for.

For heaven's sake, drop the whole thing! You are playing with dynamite. My companion and I fought our way out of a cave with submachine guns. I have two 9" scars on my left arm that came from wounds given me in the cave when I was 50 feet from a moving object of any kind and in perfect silence. The muscles were nearly ripped out. How? I don't know. My friend has a hole the size of a dime in his right bicep. It was seared inside. How we don't know. But we both believe we know more about the Shaver Mystery than any other pair.

You can imagine my fright when I picked up my first copy of *Amazing Stories* and see you splashing words about on the subject.

The identity of the author of this letter was withheld by request. Later Palmer revealed his name: Fred Lee Crisman. He had inadvertently described the effects of a laser beam — even though the laser wasn't invented until years later. Apparently Crisman was obsessed with Deros and death rays long before Kenneth Arnold sighted the "first" UFO in June 1947.

A factual article about a saucer-like "circle-winged plane" was featured in this Palmer-edited issue of *Amazing Stories* from September 1946, almost a year before the first "flying saucers" were sighted.

---

[4] It is interesting that so many victims of this type of phenomenon were welding or operating electrical equipment such as radios, radar, etc. when they began to hear voices.

The September 1948 *Fantastic Stories* included this illustration for a "factual" article about a Russian peasant who had been "burned by a ray from a ship from another world."

In September 1946, *Amazing Stories* published a short article by W.C. Hefferlin, "Circle-Winged Plane," describing experiments with a circular craft in 1927 in San Francisco. Shaver's (Palmer's) contribution to that issue was a 30,000 word novelette, "Earth Slaves to Space," dealing with spaceships that regularly visited the Earth to kidnap humans and haul them away to some other planet. Other stories described amnesia, an important element in the UFO reports that still lay far in the future, and mysterious men who supposedly served as agents for those unfriendly Deros.

A letter from army lieutenant Ellis L. Lyon in the September 1946 issue expressed concern over the psychological impact of the Shaver Mystery.

> What I am worried about is that there are a few, and perhaps quite a large number of readers who may accept this Shaver Mystery as being founded on fact, even as Orson Welles put across his invasion from Mars, via radio some years ago. It is, of course, impossible for the reader to sift out in your "Discussions" and "Reader Comment" features, which are actually letters from readers and which are credited to an *Amazing Stories* staff writer, whipped up to keep alive interest in your fictional theories. However, if the letters are generally the work of the readers, it is distressing to see the reaction you have caused in their muddled brains. I refer to the letters from people who have "seen" the exhaust trails of rocket ships or "felt" the influence of radiations from underground sources.

Palmer assigned artists to make sketches of objects described by readers and disc-shaped flying machines appeared on the covers of his magazine long before June 1947. So we can note that a considerable number of people — millions — were exposed to the flying saucer concept before the national news media was even aware of it. Anyone who glanced at the

magazines on a newsstand and caught a glimpse of the saucers-adorned *Amazing Stories* cover had the image implanted in his subconscious. In the course of the two years between March 1945 and June 1947, *millions* of Americans had seen at least one issue of *Amazing Stories* and were aware of the Shaver Mystery with all of its bewildering implications. Many of these people were out studying the empty skies in the hopes that they, like other *Amazing Stories* readers, might glimpse something wondrous. World War II was over and some new excitement was needed. Raymond Palmer was supplying it — much to the alarm of Lt. Lyon and Fred Crisman.

Aside from Palmer's readers, two other groups were ready to serve as cadre for the believers. About 1,500 members of Tiffany Thayer's Fortean Society knew that weird aerial objects had been sighted throughout history and some of them were convinced that this planet was under surveillance by beings from another world. Tiffany Thayer was rigidly opposed to Franklin Roosevelt and loudly proclaimed that almost everything was a government conspiracy, so his Forteans were fully prepared to find new conspiracies hidden in the forthcoming UFO mystery. They would become instant experts, willing to educate the press and the public when the time came. The second group were spiritualists and students of the occult, headed by Dr. Meade Layne, who had been chatting with the space people at seances through trance mediums and Ouija boards. They knew the space ships were coming and were hardly surprised when "ghost rockets" were reported over Europe in 1946.[5] Combined, these three groups represented a formidable segment of the population.

On June 24, 1947, Kenneth Arnold made his famous sighting of a group of "flying saucers" over Mt. Rainier, and in Chicago Ray Palmer watched in astonishment as the newspaper clippings poured in from every state. The things that he had been fabricating for his magazine were suddenly coming true!

For two weeks, the newspapers were filled with UFO reports. Then they tapered off and the Forteans howled "Censorship!" and "Conspiracy!" But dozens of magazine writers were busy compiling articles on this new subject and their pieces would appear steadily during the next year. One man, who had earned his living

---

[5] The widespread "ghost rockets" of 1946 received little notice in the U.S. press. I remember carrying a tiny clipping around in my wallet describing mysterious rockets weaving through the mountains of Switzerland. But that was the only "ghost rocket" report that reached me that year.

writing stories for the pulp magazines in the 1930s, saw the situation as a chance to break into the "slicks" (better quality magazines printed on glossy or "slick" paper). Although he was 44 years old at the time of Pearl Harbor, he served as a Captain in the marines until he was in a plane accident. Discharged as Major (it was the practice to promote officers one grade when they retired), he was trying to resume his writing career when Ralph Daigh, an editor at *True* magazine, assigned him to investigate the flying saucer enigma. Thus, at the age of 50, Donald E. Keyhoe entered Never-Never-Land. His article, "Flying Saucers Are Real," would cause a sensation, and Keyhoe would become an instant UFO personality.

That same year, Palmer decided to put out an all-flying saucer issue of *Amazing Stories*. Instead, the publisher demanded that he drop the whole subject after, according to Palmer, two men in Air Force uniforms visited him. Palmer decided to publish a magazine of his own. Enlisting the aid of Curtis Fuller, editor of a flying magazine, and a few other friends, he put out the first issue of *Fate* in the spring of 1948. A digest-sized magazine printed on the cheapest paper, *Fate* was as poorly edited as *Amazing Stories* and had no impact on the reading public. But it was the only newsstand periodical that carried UFO reports in every issue. The *Amazing Stories* readership supported the early issues wholeheartedly.

In the fall of 1948, the first flying saucer convention was held at the Labor Temple on 14th Street in New York City. Attended by about thirty people, most of whom were clutching the latest issue of *Fate,* the meeting quickly dissolved into a shouting match[6]. Although the flying saucer mystery was only a year old, the side issues of government conspiracy and censorship already dominated the situation because of their strong emotional appeal. The U.S. Air Force had been sullenly silent throughout 1948 while, unbeknownst to the UFO advocates, the boys at Wright-Patterson Air Force Base in Ohio were making a sincere effort to untangle the mystery.

When the Air Force investigation failed to turn up any tangible evidence (even though the investigators accepted the extraterrestrial theory) General Hoyt Vandenburg, Chief of the Air Force and former head of the CIA, ordered a negative report to release to the public. The result was Project Grudge, hundreds of pages of irrelevant nonsense that was unveiled around the time *True* magazine printed Keyhoe's pro-UFO article. Keyhoe took this personally, even though his article was largely

---

[6] I attended this meeting but my memory of it is vague after so many years. I cannot recall who sponsored it.

Pinnacles of pulpdom: Palmer-edited issues of *Amazing* and *Fantastic* from the 1940s.

The first wave: Flying saucer books from the early '50s, including Keyhoe's 1950 classic, *The Flying Saucers Are Real*.

a rehash of Fort's books, and Ralph Daigh had decided to go with the extraterrestrial hypothesis because it seemed to be the most commercially acceptable theory (that is, it would sell magazines).

Palmer's relationship with Ziff-Davis was strained now that he was publishing his own magazine. "When I took over from Palmer, in 1949," Howard Browne said, "I put an abrupt end to the Shaver Mystery — writing off over 7,000 dollars worth of scripts."

Moving to Amherst, Wisconsin, Palmer set up his own printing plant and eventually he printed many of those Shaver stories in his *Hidden World* series. As it turned out, postwar inflation and the advent of television was killing the pulp magazine market anyway. In the fall of 1949, hundreds of pulps suddenly ceased publication, putting thousands of writers and editors out of work. *Amazing Stories* has often changed hands since but is still being published, and is still paying its writers a penny a word.[7]

For some reason known only to himself, Palmer chose not to use his name in *Fate*. Instead, a fictitious "Robert N. Webster" was listed as editor for many years. Palmer established another magazine, *Search,* to compete with *Fate. Search* became a catch-all for inane letters and occult articles that failed to meet *Fate's* low standards.

Although there was a brief revival of public and press interest in flying saucers following the great wave of the summer of 1952, the subject largely remained in the hands of cultists, cranks, teenagers, and housewives who reproduced newspaper clippings in little mimeographed journals and looked up to Palmer as their fearless leader.

In June, 1956, a major four-day symposium on UFOs was held in Washington, D.C. It was unquestionably the most important UFO affair of the 1950s and was attended by leading military men, government officials and industrialists. Men like William Lear, inventor of the Lear Jet, and assorted generals, admirals and former CIA heads freely discussed the UFO "problem" with the press. Notably absent were Ray Palmer and Donald Keyhoe. One of the results of the meetings was the founding of the National Investigation Committee on Aerial Phenomena (NICAP) by a physicist named Townsend Brown. Although the symposium received extensive press coverage at the time, it was subsequently censored out of UFO history by the UFO cultists themselves — primarily because they had not participated in it.[8]

The American public was aware of only two flying saucer personalities, contactee George Adamski, a lovable rogue with a talent for obtaining publicity, and Donald Keyhoe, a zealot who howled "Coverup!" and was locked in mortal combat with Adamski for newspaper coverage. Since Adamski was the more colorful (he had ridden a saucer to the moon), he was usually awarded more attention. The press gave him the title of "astronomer" (he lived in a house on Mount Palomar where a great telescope was in operation), while Keyhoe attacked him as "the operator of a hamburger stand." Ray Palmer tried to remain aloof of the warring factions, so, naturally, some of them turned against him.

The year 1957 was marked by several significant developments. There was another major flying saucer wave. Townsend Brown's NICAP floun-

---

[7] A few of the surviving science fiction magazines now pay (gasp!) three cents a word. But writing sci-fi still remains a sure way to starve to death.

[8] When David Michael Jacobs wrote *The UFO Controversy in America,* a book generally regarded as the most complete history of the UFO maze, he chose to completely revise the history of the 1940s and 50s, carefully excising any mention of Palmer, the 1956 symposium, and many of the other important developments during that period.

Early issues of *Fate* magazine, created by Ray Palmer as a vehicle for articles on the occult and unexplained. The first issue (Spring 1948, far left) devoted 44 pages to flying saucers, at that time a topic only a few months old.

dered and Keyhoe took it over. And Ray Palmer launched a new newsstand publication called *Flying Saucers From Other Worlds*. In the early issues he hinted that he knew some important "secret." After tantalizing his readers for months, he finally revealed that UFOs came from the center of the earth and the phrase *From Other Worlds* was dropped from the title. His readers were variously enthralled, appalled, and galled by the revelation.

For seven years, from 1957 to 1964, ufology in the United States was in total limbo. This was the Dark Age. Keyhoe and NICAP were buried in Washington, vainly tilting at windmills and trying to initiate a congressional investigation into the UFO situation.

A few hundred UFO believers clustered around Coral Lorenzen's Aerial Phenomena Research Organization (APRO). And about 2,000 teenagers bought *Flying Saucers* from newsstands each month. Palmer devoted much space to UFO clubs, information exchanges, and letters-to-the-editor. So it was Palmer, and Palmer alone, who kept the subject alive during the Dark Age and lured new youngsters into ufology. He published his strange books about Deros, and ran a mail-order business selling the UFO books that had been published after the various waves of the 1950s. His partners in the *Fate* venture bought him out, so he was able to devote his full time to his UFO enterprises.

Palmer had set up a system similar to sci-fi fandom, but with himself as the nucleus. He had come a long way since his early days and the Jules Verne Prize Club. He had been instrumental in inventing a whole system of belief, a frame of reference — the magical world of Shaverism and flying saucers — and he had set himself up as the king of that world. Once the belief system had been set up it became self-perpetuating. The people beleaguered by mysterious rays were joined by the wishful thinkers who hoped that living, compassionate beings existed out there beyond the stars. They didn't need any real evidence. The belief itself was enough to sustain them.

When a massive new UFO wave — the biggest one in U.S. history — struck in 1964 and continued unabated until 1968, APRO and NICAP were caught unawares and unprepared to deal with renewed public interest. Palmer increased the press run of *Flying Saucers* and reached out to a new audience. Then, in the 1970s, a new Dark Age began. October 1973 produced a flurry of well-publicized reports and then the doldrums set in. NICAP strangled in its own confusion and dissolved in a puddle of apathy, along with scores of lesser UFO organizations. Donald Keyhoe, a very elder statesman, lives in seclusion in Virginia. Most of the hopeful contactees and UFO investigators of the 1940s and 50s have passed away. Palmer's *Flying Saucers* quietly self-destructed in 1975, but he continued with *Search* until his death in the summer of 1977. Richard Shaver is gone but the Shaver Mystery still has a few adherents. Yet the sad truth is that none of this might have come about if Howard Browne hadn't scoffed at that letter in that dingy editorial office in that faraway city so long ago. ■

Following Ray Palmer's death, his wife Marjorie managed Palmer Publications until a few years ago, when she sold the business. The new owners carry on, still publishing Search *and* Space World *magazines, as well as books about the Shaver Mystery, UFOs, and the paranormal. Their address is Palmer Publications, P. O. Box 296, Amherst, WI 54406. Meanwhile, the Shaver Mystery tradition endures in literature available from Health Research, P.O. Box 70, Mokelumne Hill, CA 95245.*

IN ADVANCE OF THE LANDING

FOLK CONCEPTS OF OUTER SPACE
by Douglas Curran

Project Starlight International, a research complex of lights, radio, and laser gear for signaling UFOs, constructed by the Association for the Understanding of Man near Austin, Texas.

Since its inception, described in the preceding "The Man Who Invented Flying Saucers," the flying saucer mythos has diversified into myriad variations. Here's an excerpt from an extraordinary book that provides an intimate look into this world, described with compassionate insight by author/photographer Douglas Curran. (In Advance of the Landing may be obtained for $18.95 postpaid from Abbeville Press, 488 Madison Ave., New York, NY 10022; 800/227-7210.) —T.S.

All photographs © 1985 by Douglas Curran. Reprinted with permission.

In the fall of 1977 I bought a second-hand yellow Renault 16. I christened it "Giselle," pulled out the rear seat, and fitted a small cupboard-desk in the space behind the driver's seat. The passenger seat folded down into a bed at night, and with the glove compartment open I was able to find room for my feet. With more a hunch than a plan, I began driving, looking for objects that people might have made to express their ideas about outer space and the future. I followed secondary highways through towns and cities, from British Columbia down the West Coast, eventually circumscribing the United States along a counter-clockwise route. Three months and 22,000 miles later, I arrived in Toronto with a rough collection of negatives that became the basis of this book.

By the fall of 1978 I was on the road again, better equipped with a 4 x 5 camera and an emerging awareness of a new mythology of gods and technology as relevant to twentieth-century civilization as Zeus and Apollo had been to the ancient Greeks. Giselle was my home for months at a time for several years. I might wake up in Ontario one morning and not shut the engine off until Kansas, on my way to a flying-saucer convention. I lost track of the miles. One day the speedometer needle fell off, and I was delighted to see the end of its nagging.

Initially I sought information

about backyard rockets and flying saucers from newspaper editors, waitresses, and gas station attendants in the towns and cities I drove through. I would fan out postcards made from some photographs taken during my first trip and say: "I'm studying what people think about outer space. Have you seen anything around here that looks like this?" Many times the discussion that followed would involve the whole newsroom or cafe in a debate over the possibilities of life on other planets and alien visitations to Earth. Eventually much information for the project was to come from an expanding circle of UFO researchers, science fiction buffs, and sociologists, but luck and

driving — the turn of the steering wheel like a roll of the dice — uncovered more than any single researcher.

* * *

On my travels across the continent I never had to wait too long for someone to tell me about his or her UFO experience, whether I was chatting with a farmer in Kansas, Ruth Norman at the Unarius Foundation, or a cafe owner in Florida. What continually struck me in talking with these people was how positive and ultimately life-giving a force was their belief in outer space. Their belief reaffirmed the essential fact of human existence: the need for order and hope. It is this that establishes them — and

O. T. Nodrog sells avocado plants, wheat berries, and honey every Saturday morning at the Weslaco, Texas, flea market. He is also the leader of a small group at the Armageddon Time Ark Base, channelling messages from the Outer Dimensional Forces. Basing their beliefs on the Bible, Nodrog and his followers predict an apocalyptic S-Day, when Yahweh will activate the Sixth Seal of Revelations, and Time Ark Service Modules (fifth-dimensional starships) will rescue only those who have undergone their Survival Training to start the post-apocalyptic Manasseh Free Territory.

me — in the continuity of human experience. It brought me to a greater understanding of Oscar Wilde's observation, "We are all lying in the gutter — but some of us are looking at the stars."

The second annual Unariun Conclave of Light, held in San Diego, California, in May 1981, drew over 400 members from as far away as Milwaukee, Toronto, and New York. Like the Warfield brothers, Brian and Mike (above), and the Bond family (below), everyone dresses in costumes from their past lives on other planets. Kenneth Bond, a successful businessman, and his wife Birgit are bringing up their sons Derek and Stephen according to Unariun concepts.

The Unarius Foundation presents members with a complete and ordered cosmography. Earth, they believe, is "the garbage dump of the universe," the place where unfulfilled souls end up until they achieve enough of a karmic bank balance to bail themselves out. Our planet operates at such a low level of consciousness that it even **vibrates** at a low frequency. To raise that consciousness, to increase that frequency, is the goal of the Unariuns. Such a move, they believe, would send a cosmic "yes" to the Intergalactic Confederation. Thirty-two spaceships — one from each planet of the Intergalactic Confederation — would then "land on Planet Earth to help this rapidly dying world . . . to teach mankind a better, a higher and happier way of life. . . ."

The power for such an ambitious endeavor comes from Ruth Norman, an eighty-two-year-old widow living in El Cajon, California. Unariuns know her as the Archangel Uriel, the present incarnation of a supreme spiritual being who has visited Earth many times before.

The acknowledgment of amassed guilt from past lives is the first part of the healing-enlightenment process. These explorations of the past tend to revolve around Uriel. A student might come to a reading session, as one related to me, and reveal, "I had a

Members of the Aetherius Society charge a spiritual battery during a prayer session in Hollywood, California. The battery is just one of the radionic inventions of Aetherius founder George King, who communicates with Cosmic Masters from many planets. The prayer sessions are part of his larger plan for harnessing and directing healing psychic energies throughout the world.

dream, a realization of my life on the planet Deva where I committed a terrible atrocity. I was a usurper of power. When the king came with Uriel to watch the pageant I blew up the stadium, not realizing in my ignorance that I couldn't truly kill Uriel." After group discussion of such a revelation, one of the senior teachers will correct any points that do not fit in with Unariun cosmological history. The past-life negation is then expunged, and the student is lifted to "a more regenerative position in his scale of life," moving toward that "psychic polarization and oscillation directed by the Perfected Minds on Higher Frequency Worlds." After one session, I watched strong men break into tears as they realized what they had done to Uriel in past lives and how kind she was just to let them appear in her presence now.

The Spiritual Battery, covered with a cloth and mounted on a surveyor's tripod, is the focal point of the room. A choir-robed member sits at a folding camp table to one side. With stopwatch in hand, the time-keeper transcribes into a ledger the precise number of participants and the minutes of prayer energy focused into the battery. Batlike in his robes, with white-gloved hands stretched above his head, Dr. Charles Abrahamson, a senior member of the Aetherius Society, holds a silent count-down to the stroke of 7:30. At that exact moment Abrahamson sweeps his arms downward and the group of 45 charges into the Holy Mantra, "Om mani padme hum . . . OM mani padme Hum . . . OM mani padme HUM." Abrahamson exhorts the group into a rapid, emphatic chant. "Deeper, deeper!" he commands. The response, though spirited, never reaches a level of euphoric rapture. Rather, like most of Aetherius's workings, it remains efficient, almost military in its precision.

Once the group is rolling well

with the mantra, the specially trained Prayer Team advances in single file toward the battery.

The lead team member proceeds alone to within a few feet of the battery and recites the first of the Twelve Blessings. The Prayer Team continues to recite the Twelve Blessings in turn throughout the second and third cycles of the evening.

The Spiritual Battery, nearing its full-charge capacity of 700 prayer-hours, is carefully capped and taken to safe storage. As the battery and its escort make their way through the crowded room, the members cautiously fall back from it. It is felt that with so much power stored in the battery, an inadvertent mishap could have devastating results for life, limb, and karma. Aetherius founder George King maintains that the specialized radionics equipment he has developed is capable of storing this spiritual energy for up to 10,000 years, to be released as needed. Several batteries are kept permanently charged, ready to forestall world crises.

149

(Top) Charles Gaiffe, a retired screw-machine operator and machinist, holds a mold for the propulsion unit of the Bluebird flying saucer, housed in a barn in Detour Village, Michigan. (Bottom) named after a Hopi Indian legend, the Bluebird is 35 feet in diameter and incorporates a three-foot planetary gear transmission valued at $100,000.

Whenever I travel east I make a point of stopping in to see Charles. Peering through the window of his shop out behind his house, I might find him sitting in a wired-together swivel chair, contemplating a machine part, or hunched over the lathe with curls of copper splitting off a new turning. For Charles, the motor, the purpose of his life, and God's will are inextricably tied together. He believes that guardian angels watch over him and that God keeps him alive as long as he works on the motor. The more complex parts of his invention are still made for him in the shops of old friends who long ago deserted the dream of the Bluebird.

In Bellaire, Michigan, John Shepherd has converted his grandparents' home into a UFO-detecting station.

John Shepherd is trying to contact extraterrestrial life. For years now, each morning at ten he has begun broadcasting music and binary signals from Earth Station Radio. The music and signals pulse from a home-built 20-foot transmitter accelerator assembly sunk into the bowels of his facility.

John's station has been in operation for nearly 11 years, constantly changing and growing in sophistication. In a black pit in the center of the room are sunk large hydro transformers scrounged from the local power utility, looped and crossed by heavy cables. Rising out of this well is the accelerator tower, a structure reminiscent of an Edison experiment. Plates and grids bracketed with insulators set up a fierce buzzing as the signal charge crosses over them in a fan of blue arcs into the antennae. The saturated magnetic field ionizes the air, leaving the smell of ozone as after a lightning storm.

Underfoot and along the baseboards run cable bundles the thickness of a man's arm, while overhead hang service boards and modules mounted with UV meters, phase loop converters, signal-strength indicators, manometers, voltmeters, pulse shapers, pulse-shape monitors, potentiometers, switches, patch cords, ICs, LEDs, and ready lights. All of it alive and talking to itself and someone or something, immeasurable miles and galaxies away.

Coupled with the signaling gear is a system for detecting UFOs. In operation 24 hours a day, gravimeters monitor any violent changes in the Earth's magnetic field caused by UFOs. Radio direction-finding gear, coupled with the gravimeters, would attempt to pinpoint such a disturbance and in turn trigger a prerecorded message of peace and goodwill interspersed with binary tone signals automatically ranged over a scale of frequencies by a signal scanner.

John and his grandma live frugally; for example, they do without natural gas service in order to funnel money into materials for the project. Grandpa Lamb used to grumble at the growing incursion of paraphernalia into the living room. Eventually, he and Mrs. Lamb were left with only a small settee scrunched into a corner between whole walls taken up by their grandson's consoles and oscilloscopes. Grandpa Lamb died two years ago. Now John and his grandmother make a good team. Together they built an addition on the house to allow space for John's burgeoning equipment and put a rocking chair in the living room for Mrs. Lamb.

(Above) "The Rocketman" in Houston, Texas. (Below) Clayton Bailey's "Alien Rocket" in Port Costa, California.

It was while rounding a curve on a two-lane highway in Quebec that I found my first rocket. Thrust out over the trees lining the highway, it was held in simulated flight, reflecting the last light of the sun. Deus ex machina! The rocket seemed to strain against its metal pylons, a totem attempting to leap away from the gravity of Earth to the realms of the gods. It was at one and the same time the quintessential product of western civilization, a daydream of technology, and a symbol of transcendence and freedom. It was nostalgia for the future.

CRASHED SAUCERS
The Ultimate Secret?

by Jerome Clark

Harry S. Robins

THE FIRST EXTRATERRESTRIAL SPACESHIP TO crash on earthly soil met its doom long before the words "flying saucer" and "unidentified flying object" entered the terrestrial vocabulary. The event occurred on June 6, 1884, in Dundy County in south-central Nebraska and was witnessed by cowboys, one of whom was permanently blinded by the intense heat emanating from the device. *The Nebraska Nugget*, published in Holdrege 100 miles from the site of the accident, reported that the object was "about 50 or 60 feet long, cylindrical, and about 10 or 12 feet in diameter." Unfortunately, according to the *Nugget's* anonymous correspondent, what remained of the ship dissolved "like a spoonful of salt" during a blinding rainstorm.

The story, of course, was a practical joke, though that wasn't immediately apparent decades later to ufologists who rediscovered the initial newspaper account—but not the follow-up—with its telltale reference to the substance with which readers were slyly advised to ingest the account. In any case, even lifelong residents of the county, investigators found, had never heard of the incident, although an active local historical society kept careful records of notable events in pioneer times.

Likewise, another nineteenth-century story, rediscovered in the 1960s and re-rediscovered in the 1970s, set ufologists' blood racing until it was learned that no, a spaceship did not plow into Judge J.S. Proctor's windmill in Aurora, Texas, on April 17, 1897, despite the assertions of the *Dallas Morning Post* two days later. The *Post* reported soberly that the "badly disfigured" body of a Martian was found in the wreckage. Many years afterwards, ufologists learned that the story was concocted by a local writer seeking to draw attention to a town badly in need of same: the railroad had passed it by and a spotted-fever epidemic had decimated the population.

But stories of crashed spaceships—otherwise known as the "Ultimate Secret"—didn't come into their own until 1947, following the celebrated June 24 Kenneth Arnold sighting which ushered in the UFO age. Two weeks later, when the remains of an aerial object were found on a ranch near remote Corona, New Mexico, newspapers reported that a flying saucer had crashed. Then the Air

Force said it had all been a big mistake; the "saucer" was just a balloon with an attached radar calibration instrument. This, as it happened, was a lie, but it was one that would go uncaught for over three decades.

In 1950, in the most audacious crashed-disc hoax of them all, *Variety* columnist Frank Scully reported in his best-selling *Behind the Flying Saucers* that three spaceships had crashed in the Southwest, and that the military had snatched them along with the bodies of their small humanlike pilots. Scully's sources, as it turned out, were two shady characters who had concocted the story as part of an elaborate scam to peddle a bogus oil-detection device. Scully seems to have been an innocent victim of the swindle, but his book cast a long shadow: for the next two and a half decades, no serious UFO student would pay attention to crashed-disc stories.

That doesn't mean they didn't continue to circulate in popular culture. They became a kind of urban folklore and inspired a slew of science-fiction and suspense novels and movies. Many of the stories centered on a "Blue Room" at Wright-Patterson Air Force Base, where wreckage and humanoid bodies were supposedly stored. In the mid-1960s Senator Barry Goldwater, a major general in the Air Force reserve, asked his friend General Curtis LeMay if he could see what was there. LeMay gave him "holy hell," Goldwater recalled (*New Yorker*, April 25, 1988), informed him that he did not have a sufficiently high security clearance, and warned him never to bring up the subject again.

Ten years later two civilian investigators, writer William Moore and nuclear scientist Stanton Friedman, encountered people who were in Roswell, New Mexico, in July 1947, when the object that the Air Force claimed was a balloon crashed near Corona. In the course of an investigation that continued into the early 1980s, Moore and Friedman interviewed more than ninety persons involved in one way or another with what came to be called the "Roswell incident." These included military and civilian intelligence officers, the family on whose property the material fell, local reporters, and others. The material was described as a strangely light but extremely tough metal and there were, in one witness's words, "strange hieroglyphic typewriting symbols across the inner surfaces" resembling the characters of no terrestrial language. Those involved in the recovery of the material believed it was from an extraterrestrial spacecraft. They also said the weather-balloon identification was a cover story invented by the authorities at Eighth Air Force Headquarters in Fort Worth, where the material was taken immediately af-

---

In the following four pages, two ufologists present capsule histories of three of the most colorful legends in UFO lore: crashed saucers, the men in black, and the humanoids. Jerome Clark is the editor of the International UFO Reporter; *Dennis Stacy is the editor of the* MUFON UFO Journal *(see p. 163 for reviews of both publications).*

—*T.S.*

ter the recovery. It was subsequently secretly shipped to Wright Field (later Wright-Patterson AFB), and that was the last anyone ever heard of it.

Until, perhaps, September 15, 1950, when physicist Robert Sarbacher, a member of the U.S. Defense Department's Research and Development Board (RDB), told Canadian government scientists—who had asked him if there was anything to those rumors of crashed flying saucers—that yes, there was, and that the investigation of same was being conducted by a small group under the direction of Dr. Vannevar Bush, head of the RDB and President Truman's chief science adviser. Sarbacher (who died in 1986) repeated the story three decades later when investigators found him living in Florida retirement, after the Canadian government account was found in official archives. Sarbacher, who had not been directly involved in the project, recalled having been told that the UFO materials were "extremely light and very tough." There were bodies, too, of beings which, despite their humanoid appearance, were "constructed like certain insects."

In the early 1970s, southern California filmmaker Robert Emenegger says he was approached by military officers who asked him to prepare a documentary film that would reveal what had been covered up: not only extraterrestrial visitation but high-level contact with the aliens. The project fell through, but a decade later military intelligence personnel reportedly approached ufologist Bill Moore, television producer Jaime Shandera, and another documentary filmmaker, Linda Howe, with identical stories about the U.S. government's dealings with "extraterrestrial biological entities" (EBEs—pronounced EE-buhs). Shandera was even given a document, allegedly a November 18, 1952, briefing paper prepared for President-elect Eisenhower by onetime CIA director Admiral R.H. Hillenkoetter, detailing the conclusions of an ultrasecret group, "Majestic-12," headed by Vannevar Bush. The "MJ-12 document," as it came to be called, caused a flurry of media interest, even a *Nightline* segment, in mid-1987 but no follow-up investigations by journalists.

Can all this be? Who knows? So far the MJ-12 document has not been successfully debunked (despite some frantic efforts by veteran UFOphobe Philip J. Klass in CSICOP's *Skeptical Inquirer* [see page 198]), and several retired military and intelligence people have since asserted that such a group does exist. And in the spring of 1988 linguist-document examiner Roger Wescott of Drew University, after studying the memo and comparing it to materials known to have been written by Hillenkoetter, declared that Hillenkoetter was indeed the author.

Either belief or disbelief is premature at the moment, but that hasn't stopped speculation among those puzzled by all this but unable to stomach the idea of an Ultimate Secret. They speculate—though, they acknowledge, without supporting evidence—that these disclosures are part of an enormous conspiracy to disinform the KGB. Such an effort, however, could only induce massive paranoia among the intended recipients and probably sabotage arms-control agreements. What nation, after all, would want to disarm if it thought its adversary had access to ET technology?

THE MEN IN BLACK

by Dennis Stacy

SUPERNATURAL LORE IS FULL OF phantom intimidators; so is ufology, with its tales of mysterious men in black (MIB). Such stories date back to at least 1953, when Bridgeport, Connecticut, factory clerk Albert K. Bender, founder and director of the International Flying Saucer Bureau, claimed he had been visited by three men dressed in black suits.

According to Bender, the MIB not only revealed the secret of flying saucers, but they also intimated he'd end up in jail if he told anyone else. Suitably impressed, Bender folded his burgeoning bureau and headed off to Los Angeles. And in the last issue of the group's newsletter, *Space Review*, he cryptically warned "those engaged in saucer work to please be very cautious."

Bender may well have been an eccentric, but his case was hardly unique. Many UFO investigators claim that MIB plague them to this day. "The curious thing," says Peter Rojcewicz, a folklorist who has studied the phenomenon, "is that MIB sometimes show up *before* the witness has had a chance to report a UFO sighting. They often have intimate information about the percipient that only he or a family member would normally have access to. And they customarily identify themselves as military-intelligence officers."

Rojcewicz, now an assistant professor of humanities at The Juilliard School in New York, first became fascinated by MIB stories and the people who told them in the early eighties while researching a doctoral thesis on UFO folklore at the University of Pennsylvania. His studies revealed a series of bizarre, if contradictory, patterns.

"Ninety-nine percent of the MIB are men,"

THE HUMANOIDS

by Jerome Clark

Harry S. Robins

Rojcewicz says. "Invariably they are dressed in black clothes that appear either neatly pressed or like they haven't been ironed in weeks. They customarily come in threes, often arriving or departing in black Cadillacs or other large, dark-colored sedans."

One anonymous source told Rojcewicz of an unsettling encounter that took place in a university library reading room. A singular male figure dressed in a white shirt, black suit, and a "black, Texan-like string-tie" tried to engage the researcher in a casual conversation about UFOs. "I told him I didn't care much whether they were real, physical flying craft or not but that I found stories about them interesting," said Rojcewicz's source. "Well, I thought the guy was going to come unglued! He became highly agitated. 'Flying saucers are the most important fact of the century,' he shouted, 'and you're not interested?'"

Not everyone within the UFO community accepts the existence of men in black. "I've tried everything I know in the last thirty years to get them interested in me, without a nibble," says James Moseley, who publishes the irreverent and iconoclastic broadsheet *Saucer Smear*.

In fact, the likelihood of an MIB encounter does not seem to be directly correlated to the individual's degree of involvement with UFOs. But if it *should* happen to you, Rojcewicz offers the following advice: "Keep a sense of humor about yourself. Don't get upset or take them too seriously. In other words, don't feed the phenomenon."

DO "HUMANOIDS" PILOT UFOS? Have human beings seen them?

The first widely-publicized affirmative answer to these questions appeared in a 1950 best seller, *Behind the Flying Saucers* by Frank Scully. The book alleged, on the say-so of what proved to be extremely unreliable informants, that spaceships containing diminutive Venusians had crashed in the Southwestern desert of the U.S. in 1948 and 1949. A couple of years later George Adamski, whose followers called him "professor" but who might more accurately be called a life-long occult hustler, reported meeting a (normal-sized, handsome-human-looking) Venusian named Orthon in the California desert; soon he was writing books and lecturing on this and subsequent contacts with Venusians, Martians, and Saturnians. The print was hardly dry in Adamski's first book (*Flying Saucers Have Landed*, with Desmond Leslie, 1953) before other, similarly dubious characters, with their own Space Brethren buddies, were working the same circuit.

The newspapers, of course, loved it—and so did UFO debunkers, who represented these con men and their guileless followers as typical flying-saucer true believers. In fact, serious-minded amateurs, who were forming such groups as the Aerial Phenomena Research Organization (APRO), Civilian Saucer Intelligence (CSI), and the National Investigations Committee on Aerial Phenomena (NICAP), did not count Orthon among the possible UFO occupants or Adamski among the "reliable witnesses" whose testimony they were willing to consider. They were appalled by the antics of the "contactees" and spent much fruitless effort trying to persuade scientists and reporters that they, the serious researchers, were not fruitcakes looking for salvation from outer space, but would-be scientists trying to figure out what was behind the UFO reports.

Most of them suspected that what was causing UFO reports was extraterrestrial visitation. Among the credible sighting reports (and sighters included scientists, military and civilian pilots, radar operators, and numerous individuals possessing impeccable middle-class credentials) were many describing metallic, structured discs, some with what were thought to be "portholes." The clear implication was that the objects had somebody inside. But because the public associated all UFO reports with the likes of Scully, Adamski, and others, the "respectable" ufologists were all the more chagrined when persons who in all other ways seemed like typical UFO witnesses began reporting little men. ☛

155

Harry S. Robins

Not "little *green* men," though that didn't deter the press, which soon had a new phrase with which to amuse readers at the expense of silly saucer buffs. But there was, alas, no getting around the reports. Whether or not little men existed, people who seemed sincere and sane were reporting them. Even the Air Force's Project Blue Book, not known for pro-UFO sympathies, was finding, on those rare occasions that it investigated such reports, that they were, uh, puzzling—even the wild ones like that alleged to have occurred near Kelly, Kentucky, on August 22, 1955, when (so the story went) members of a hillbilly family fired on loping, big-eared humanoids as they dashed in and out of sight.

APRO and CSI came to take the "humanoid" reports seriously, seeing no intrinsic reason not to, but NICAP would have nothing to do with them, for reasons having less to do with the quality of the evidence (neither better nor worse than the evidence for many less exotic reports) than with the organization's desire to maintain a nonthreatening image to professionals who might be attracted to UFO study.

Finally, however, an April 24, 1964, report by police officer Lonnie Zamora of two small figures and a landed UFO near Socorro, New Mexico, ended the humanoid controversy within ufology. Even the Air Force acknowledged that the witness was entirely credible and listed the case among the few it was willing to admit, albeit grudgingly, that it could not explain.

Then that same year, when Boston psychiatrist Benjamin Simon hypnotized a New Hampshire couple, Barney and Betty Hill, who were suffering anxiety problems which they believed were related to a UFO sighting they'd had three years earlier, a whole new aspect of the humanoid phenomenon came to ufologists' sometimes-reluctant attention: "missing time," amnesia, and later "recollection" (mostly but not always by hypnosis) of an abduction and physical examination by ostensible extraterrestrials. A new UFO controversy had begun.

If the Hill story were the only one of its kind (as it appeared to be initially), it would have meant little. It could have even been "accounted for"—if one were not too insistent on cleaning up every loose end (such as marks on the Hills' bodies and on their car)—as a psychological episode. But in the years ahead, many similar reports would come to light.

In 1987 (and again in 1988, with the appearance of the paperback edition), Whitley Strieber's *Communion,* a nonfiction treatment of the author's apparent abduction experiences, would top best-seller lists and make "UFO abduction" a staple of popular culture. Strieber's wildly subjective account, however, never makes clear where a possible "real" event ends and the author's imagination picks up. A clearer picture of the abduction phenomenon emerges in two books, *Missing Time* (1981) and *Intruders* (1987) by Budd Hopkins, a New York artist-sculptor who has worked with psychiatrists, psychologists, and physicians in the investigation of these reports. (See reviews, next page.)

Hopkins found numerous patterns in the reports and concluded that the experiences were just what they seemed: kidnappings by aliens. The mental-health professionals with whom he worked wouldn't go that far, but they did acknowledge that, contrary to what their colleagues were declaring from the safety of armchairs, these did not appear to be purely psychological experiences. For example, when abductees were subjected to a series of tests by three New York psychologists, they were found to be "normal." Beyond that, they had one unusual trait in common: an "impaired identity sense," much like that associated with victims of personal assault. "The test findings," wrote Dr. Elizabeth Slate, who had administered the tests blind and only later learned she was dealing with people who claimed to have been abducted by UFOs (she was "flabbergasted," she says), "are not inconsistent with the possibility that reported UFO abductions have, in fact, occurred."

In 1987 Dr. Thomas E. Bullard, a folklorist with a professional interest in UFO beliefs, studied all abduction reports in the literature and found numerous patterns, some of which not even investigators had noticed (one being what Bullard called "doorway amnesia": the abductees' consistent inability to recall passing through the door of the UFO). He also found that consciously recalled abduction stories comprised fully one-third of the total, and these were identical in every regard to those reported under hypnosis. This seemed to lay to rest the frequently-heard debunking argument that "abductions," like "past-life recall," are artifacts of hypnosis, the product of cueing and confabulation.

By the late 1980s many American ufologists—and virtually all mental-health specialists who had involved themselves in direct investigation of the reports—were taking seriously (if not necessarily endorsing) the hypothesis that abductions are physical experiences. European ufologists, on the other hand, were seeking hypothetical psychological mechanisms and drawing on Jungian and other speculations to come up with a "dream theory" of abductions.

At this stage there is little question that the abduction phenomenon—whatever causes it—is a reality. Increasingly sophisticated investigation of it by ufologists, working with growing numbers of scientists and psychologists fascinated by it, should eventually tell us just what that "reality" consists of.

Alien Abductions

Are humans being abducted by creepy little aliens and subjected to nightmarish surgical procedures? Since 1966, when John G. Fuller's book **The Interrupted Journey** appeared, "alien abductions" have become a steadily increasing element in UFO folklore. Fuller's wasn't the first book to describe the humanoids that are most often associated with UFOs, those diminutive, large-headed, gray-skinned creatures with the wrap-around eyes. What was different about the humanoids in **The Interrupted Journey** was that they kidnapped two people (the famous Barney and Betty Hill), forced them to undergo frightening medical "examinations," and induced in their victims an amnesia of the whole incident penetrable years later only through hypnosis.

That amnesic fog liftable only by hypnosis—"missing time," as it came to be called—added a whole new dimension to UFO research. A number of ufologists began to specialize in hypnotic recall, most notably Dr. James Harder, an engineer at the University of California at Berkeley, and Dr. Leo Sprinkle, a psychologist at the University of Wyoming. Then, in the mid-1970s, Budd Hopkins came onto the scene. Hopkins, a New York artist inspired by Fuller's book, used hypnosis to single-mindedly uncover case after case of abduction, surgical invasion, and amnesia. In his book, **Missing Time**, Hopkins published his home address and an invitation for possible abductees to contact him. The best responses became the material for his second effort, **Intruders**.

One of the many troubled people who contacted Hopkins was an imaginative horror writer named Whitley Strieber who, with Hopkins' help, remembered his own numerous and particularly horrendous encounters with aliens going back to his childhood. The account of his lifelong ordeal, **Communion**, received one of the biggest publishing advances ever (one million dollars), and became the first UFO book to hit the best-seller lists.

Critics have pointed out that the only evidence for any of the alien abduction stories is the testimony of the witnesses themselves. Though ufologists point to scars on abductees' bodies where surgical incisions were supposedly made, or scorched patches of ground where the saucers were said to hover, they have produced no indisputable physical evidence. Critics further point out that most of the accounts were produced under hypnosis, usually conducted by a UFO investigator predisposed to the alien abduction idea to begin with. Proneness to confuse fantasy with reality and susceptibility to even the most subtle unconscious suggestions of the hypnotist are well known features of the hypnotic state. Philip Klass's **UFO Abductions: A Dangerous Game**, the only book-length skeptical treatment of the subject, points out these and other flaws in the reports, including the fantasy-prone psychology of the "victims," the questionable methods of Budd Hopkins and other abductionists, and the inconsistencies in the stories themselves.

Finally, folklorists have not failed to notice similarities between UFO-humanoid accounts and traditional stories of the "fairy folk." Like the UFO aliens, fairy folk are a strange mixture of the frightening and the benign. Sometimes, like Hopkins's "intruders," they kidnap your babies. And when the fairies take you for a visit to their world, you might, like Rip Van Winkle, wind up with a case of missing time. The question is: Are fairy stories evidence for alien abductions in the past, or are UFOs simply the modern version of a continuing archetypal myth that is more fiction than fact?
— T.S.

• They touch [me] with these needles, somehow or other. I don't know what they're doing, but they seem to be so happy about whatever they're doing. So then they roll me over on my back, and the examiner has a long needle in his hand. And I see the needle. And it's bigger than any needle that I've ever seen. And I ask him what he's going to do with it . . .

(She is beginning to get upset again.)

It won't hurt me. And I ask him what, and he said he just wants to put it in my navel, it's just a simple test.

(More rapid sobbing.)

And I tell him, no, it will hurt, don't do it, don't do it. And I'm crying, and I'm telling him, "It's hurting, it's hurting, take it out, take it out!" And the leader comes over and he puts his hand, rubs his hand in front of my eyes, and he says it will be all right. I won't feel it.
—The Interrupted Journey

• The next thing I knew I was being shown an enormous and extremely ugly object, gray and scaly, with a sort of network of wires on the end. It was at least a foot long, narrow, and triangular in structure. They inserted this thing into my rectum. It seemed to swarm into me as if it had a life of its own. Apparently its purpose was to take samples, possibly of fecal matter, but at the time I had the impression that I was being raped, and for the first time I felt anger.

Only when the thing was withdrawn did I see that it was a mechanical device. The individual holding it pointed to the wire cage on the tip and seemed to warn me about something. But what? I never found out.

Events once again started moving very quickly.

One of them took my right hand and made an incision on my forefinger. There was no pain at all. Abruptly, my memories end. There isn't even blackness, just morning.

I have no further recollection of the incident. —Communion

• Sandy recalled what she—like Joyce—hoped at the time was only a realistic dream. She remembered that a tube of liquid had been inserted in her ear as part of what seems to have been an implant operation, and when she awoke, she found that her hair and neck were inexplicably wet—wet enough to have dampened her pillow. Her husband, like Joyce's, confirmed these odd physical details. For that matter, Kathie's UFO "dream" experience apparently involving a gynecological examination had a strange physical aftermath—she had gone to bed wearing her panties,

---

The Interrupted Journey
John G. Fuller
1966, 1987; 350 pp.
$3.95
($5.95 postpaid) from:
Dell Reader's Service
P.O. Box 5057
Des Plaines, IL 60017-5057
800/255-4133

Missing Time
Budd Hopkins
1981; 255 pp.
$3.95
($4.45 postpaid)

Intruders
The Incredible
Visitations at
Copley Woods
Budd Hopkins
1987; 319 pp.
$4.95
($5.45 postpaid)

Both from:
Ballantine Mail Sales
201 E. 50th Street
New York, NY 10022

Communion
A True Story
Whitley Strieber
1987; 320 pp.
$4.95
($6.20 postpaid) from:
Avon Books
P.O. Box 767
Dresden, TN 38225
212/481-5600

UFO Abductions
A Dangerous Game
Philip J. Klass
1988; 200 pp.
$18.95
($20.95 postpaid) from:
Prometheus Books
700 East Amherst Street
Buffalo, NY 14215
800/421-0351

Rendering of Steven Kilburn's abductors from his hypnotically retrieved recollections.
—*Missing Time*

but in the morning found them lying neatly outside the covers on top of the bed.
—*Intruders*

• Hopkins is convinced that the extraterrestrial genetic experiment is multifaceted, because some of his male subjects describe having been "raped" by female extraterrestrials. One such "victim" described his sex-partner as having long black hair, while another subject said his extraterrestrial sex-mate had a large *bald* head but was quite voluptuous.

Hopkins does not even consider the possibility that these stories might be sexual dream fantasies, even when they contain obvious contradictions. For example, one male subject reported that after his encounter, his sex partner left the room while "two guys . . . took little spoons and scraped the leftover semen off my penis" and put it in a bottle. But later the subject told Hopkins: "I'm sterile. They didn't even get any sperm. I had a vasectomy a couple of years before this." This prompts Hopkins to recall that after a previous hypnosis session this subject had said that the UFOnauts seemed angry at him. "Now I understood why," Hopkins writes.
—*UFO Abductions*

• When Betty and Barney Hill finished their treatment under Dr. Simon, the experienced psychiatrist assured them that the UFO-abduction tale was simply dream-fantasy. He thereby freed them from the cloud of perpetual fear that they might again encounter such a potentially terrifying experience. And while Betty Hill sub-

sequently claimed that she often saw UFOs in the night sky, neither she nor Barney lived in fear of repeated abductions.

This contrasts sharply with Hopkins's subjects. For example, after one male subject, a New York City policeman, recounted under hypnosis his "rape" by a gruesome-looking extraterrestrial female, he said to Hopkins: "It was a dream, wasn't it, Budd? It had to be a dream . . . This can't be real, can it?" Hopkins says he reassured the subject that it was only a dream, but adds that "as I spoke there were tears in his eyes, and in mine, *because we both knew the truth.*" (Emphasis added.) Hopkins admits that "every single abductee I've ever worked with is sure that it may happen again."

How tragic for those who have sought counsel from a person with no training in psychotherapy who admits that he has shifted his emphasis to "therapeutic considerations—helping the abductee deal with fear and uncertainty." In my opinion, that fear and uncertainty is the completely unnecessary product of Hopkins's own UFO fantasies, which he unwittingly implants in his subjects' minds. When subjects are under hypnosis and thus in an extremely suggestible state of mind, pseudo-memories unwittingly implanted can last a lifetime.
—*UFO Abductions*

• When Strieber was interviewed in the early 1980s by Douglas E. Winter for his book on famous authors of horror-fiction, *Faces of Fear,* Strieber vividly described how he was almost killed by a sniper in a tower at the University of Texas in July 1966. As recounted by Strieber in Winter's book, the mad sniper "shot two girls in the stomach right behind me. And they were lying there in the grass, screaming, begging, pleading for help . . . One was vomiting pieces of herself out of her mouth. And I could smell the blood and the odor of stomachs."

In *Communion,* Strieber admits that "for years I have told of being present when Charles Whitman went on his shooting spree from the tower in 1966. *But I wasn't there.*" (Emphasis added.) However, shortly after his book was published, Strieber again changed his story in an article written for the January/February 1987 edition of *International UFO Reporter (IUR),* published by the J. Allen Hynek Center for UFO Studies, and once again claimed that he was on the scene at the time of the sniper incident.
—*UFO Abductions*

• During an off-the-air commercial break in the *Oprah Winfrey Show,* following mention of my offer to pay $10,000 to any FBI-confirmed UFO-abductee, Hopkins announced that he would pay $20,000 to any FBI-confirmed UFO-abduction victim. In view of Hopkins's claim that he is convinced that more than a hundred of his subjects are "abductees," his offer indicates either that he is eager to pay out several million dollars, or that he very much doubts that an FBI investigation will confirm his claims.
—*UFO Abductions*

UFO's: A Scientific Debate

In 1969, the American Association for the Advancement of Science held a special UFO symposium, chaired by astronomers Carl Sagan and Thornton Page. The papers delivered at that conference are all here, making this the best book to read when asking the question "Are UFOs real?" You may not come away with a clear answer—half the papers are pro, half of them are con, and the authors are all excellent scientists —but you'll be well informed on both points of view. —*T.S.*

• Ever since radar first probed the atmosphere, scientists concerned with the interpretation of the returned signal have been intrigued by mysterious echoes, or "angels," from invisible targets in the apparently clear atmosphere. The nature of these targets as proposed by various investigators falls into four categories: (1) surface and airborne targets below the line of sight which are brought into view by anomalous propagation, (2) insects and birds, (3) direct backscatter from sharp gradients or fluctuations in the index of refraction in the clear air, and (4) unidentified flying objects (UFO's).

• Case 1. South-Central U.S., July 17, 1957
Summary: An Air Force RB-47, equipped with ECM (Electronic Countermeasures) gear and manned by six officers, was followed for a distance of well over 700 miles and for a time period of 1.5 hours, as it flew from Mississippi, through Louisiana and Texas, and into Oklahoma. The object was, at various times, seen visually by the cockpit crew as an intensely luminous light, followed by ground-radar, and detected on ECM monitoring gear aboard the RB-47. Of special interest in this case are several instances of simultaneous appearances and disappearances on all three physically distinct "channels," and a rapidity of maneuvers beyond prior experience of the aircrew.

UFO's: A Scientific Debate
Carl Sagan & Thornton Page, Editors
1974; 344 pp.
$7.95
postpaid from:
W. W. Norton
500 Fifth Avenue
New York, NY 10110

The Great Airship Mystery

The Great Airship Mystery
A UFO of the 1890s
Daniel Cohen
1981; 256 pp.
$10.95
($12.45 postpaid) from:
Putnam Publishers
390 Murray Hill Parkway
East Rutherford, NJ 07073
800/631-8571

The modern UFO wave began in 1947, but there was another, earlier one that began in 1896. Yes, **1896!** For over a year, the North American continent was visited by one or more "mystery airships," which by most accounts resembled some sort of motor-driven dirigible (something that hadn't been invented yet). Theories abounded, including visitors from another planet and the work of a mad inventor. **The Great Airship Mystery** tells the whole fascinating story, reproducing original newpaper accounts, tracing the century-old trail of a possible mysterious inventor, and generally outlining a curious, little-known chapter in American history that has important implications for UFO research today. —T.S.

• The incident described was supposed to have taken place on April 19 [1897], a high point of airship activity in the Texas region. The young man said that he was nearly killed when the airship passed overhead, so terrifying the team of horses he was driving that he was thrown to the ground. The airship then stopped, hovered about a hundred feet from him, and two men came down a rope ladder. "It was decidedly gratifying to find that they were plain, every day Americans like myself, and they were very gentlemanly." The two "plain Americans" apologized for frightening his horses, and offered to take him aboard the airship. One of the men was the airship's owner, a Mr. Wilson, no first name given; the other was his friend, Scott Warren . . .

"I learned that Mr. Wilson (though I doubt if that is his correct name) formerly lived in Fort Worth, but I do not remember to have ever seen him. He is apparently a young man and has the typical face of a genius or an inventor."

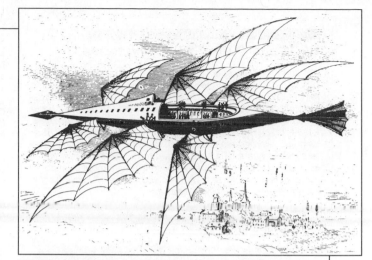

Widely circulated drawing of "Edison's Airship." Edison, however, never worked on an airship and this drawing was a hoax that capitalized on the famous man's name.

• Sometime between the hours of midnight and six A.M. of June 14, 1973, a person or persons unknown sneaked into the cemetery in the tiny Texas town of Aurora, and stole a tombstone with a crudely carved outline of a UFO on it. The tombstone marked the spot at which a "man from Mars" was buried after he had been killed when his spaceship crashed into a windmill in Aurora. The crash took place on April 17, 1897, right in the middle of the mysterious airship flap.

Not content with merely stealing the tombstone, the robber or robbers then used "long, slender, pointed, saw tooth metal probes," to work their way down through the hole left by the stolen marker. In this way they managed to remove metal fragments that were known to be buried in the grave. According to an investigator on the scene, "If they went that far they knew what they were after and also must have tried to get specimen remains of the occupant's body, clothing or something to identify him by." The whole grave robbery, said the investigator, was handled in "a thoroughly professional" manner.

The UFO Controversy in America

The most complete, sober, and objective social history of UFOs. Included is a thorough overview of the little-known presage of the modern UFO era, the "Mystery Airship" wave of 1896-97. Air Force coverups, government investigations, contactees, and UFO personalities populate the cast of this twentieth-century drama. —T.S.

• In 1959 the Office of Naval Intelligence heard of a woman in Maine who claimed to be in contact with space people and brought it to the CIA's attention. Normally the government would have ignored this contactee-like case in which the woman used the common psychic device of automatic writing. But the Canadian government had also heard of this woman, and it sent Wilbert Smith, its UFO expert, to interview her. In her trance the woman purportedly correctly answered technical questions about space flight beyond her knowledge. After learning of this, the navy sent two officers to investigate. The woman persuaded one of the officers to go into trance himself and try to contact the space people. He tried but failed.

When the two officers returned to Washington, they told CIA officials about their experience. The CIA arranged to have the officer who unsuccessfully tried to make contact try again at CIA headquarters. Six witnesses gathered in the CIA office to watch. The officer went into another trance and apparently made contact with space people. The other men in the room wanted proof. The officer in a trance said that if they looked out the window, they would see a flying saucer. Three men rushed to the window and were astonished to see a UFO. Two of these men were CIA employees and the third was with the Office of Naval Intelligence. At the exact same time, the radar center at Washington National Airport reported that its radar returns had been blocked out in the direction of the sighting. The CIA briefed Major Friend on these developments, and Friend sat in on a later trance session. He asked to be kept informed if anything else happened, but apparently nothing did. Friend thought Duke University's parapsychology laboratories should investigate the officer and the woman. But Project Blue Book never analyzed the sighting and what the men actually did see remains a mystery. The CIA did not treat the incident seriously yet took punitive actions against the men involved. It made sure they were transferred to other positions. As far as is known, the government never followed up on the sighting or the radar blackout.

The UFO Controversy in America
David Michael Jacobs
1975; 384 pp.
OUT OF PRINT
Indiana University Press
Bloomington, IN

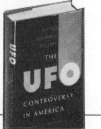

UFOs and Outer Space Mysteries

James Oberg, space-science writer and former NASA employee, is a "sympathetic skeptic" whose genuine fascination for the UFO phenomenon is exceeded only by his stubborn determination to track down the facts behind the reports. He invokes detective-novel thrills as he unravels some of ufology's longstanding mysteries. An expert on both the U.S. and Russian space programs, Oberg includes especially riveting chapters on astronaut UFO sightings and the "missing" Russian cosmonauts who literally have been retouched out of history. His discussion of lunar mysteries and the crank literature surrounding them is equally delightful. —T.S.

• The keystone of Beckley's "saucer sex" story was a newspaper account dated February 12, 1978, entitled "Kidnapped to Venus." Reporter Jerry Burger related how a thirty-one-year-old librarian was found by police as she wandered nude in a town park. She claimed she had been "abducted by Venusians," taken to the "back of the moon," and there "implanted with outer-space semen" before being returned to earth. Beckley reported the case as true and added that "such reports are taking place on a global scale . . . There can be little doubt from the documented evidence that some tremendous event is slated to happen that will guide us to a higher understanding of ourselves and the cosmos . . . The UFOnauts are trying to teach us a lesson—that love is universal and encompasses every living creature, regardless of their planet or dimension of origin." And for those readers who wanted more information, Beckley added that the "saucer sex" story is just one chapter in his new book, *Strange Encounters—Bizarre & Eerie Contacts with Flying Saucers,* available from the author: $6.95 plus postage and handling.

Unfortunately, Beckley's story is even more absurd than it first appears—and that's saying a lot. Houston spaceflight expert Robert Nichols actually unearthed the original of the

UFOs and Outer Space Mysteries

A Sympathetic Skeptic's Report
James Oberg
1982; 192 pp.
OUT OF PRINT
Donning Company Publishers
Norfolk, VA

newspaper clipping quoted by Beckley. The article did not come from a real newspaper at all, but from a 1978 satirical publication, the *Sunday Newspaper Parody* written by the *National Lampoon* staff. Beckley (or somebody on his staff) evidently made some editorial changes to enhance the credibility (such as it is) of the article, changing the original spelling of the saucer rape victim from the highly suspicious "Penelope Cuntz" to the acceptably ethnic "Penelope Kuntz," and altering the name of the newspaper from the rather utopian Dacron, Ohio *Republican-Democrat* to the Toronto *Sunday Sun.* The entire account, then, is a fictional spoof—but the extent of Beckley's role in promoting it and altering it (or merely passing it along credulously) is still undetermined.

• The greatest mystery of the moon remains the reports of lights and shadows on the surface, which come and go unexpectedly. Called 'Lunar Transient Phenomena' (LTP), they consist of hundreds of documented cases of glows, flashes, obscurations, mists, and colored patches. Scientists take them quite seriously and have a number of theories. . . .

The distribution of LTP sightings is not random, showing a preference for the edges of the lunar maria or a few young craters (there are very few reports from the lunar highlands), suggesting a volcanic connection. . . . There are no coincidences between the most active LTP sites and any of the moonquake regions charted by the [Apollo earthquake-detecting] stations . . .

UFOs: The Public Deceived

Recently Budd Hopkins, author of **Missing Time** *and* **Intruders** *(see p. 157), wrote: "Klass must be treated the way one treats any other grossly incompetent investigator. He must be totally ignored. . . . I will never again receive his phone calls and I will return his letters unopened." Though some infuriated UFO believers would agree with Hopkins, those who appreciate constructive criticism are on friendly terms with ufology's reigning arch-skeptic. Klass, former senior editor of* **Aviation Week and Space Technology** *and a founding fellow of the Committee for the Scientific Investigation of Claims of the Paranormal (see p. 197), has spent over 20 years investigating UFO reports. His books demonstrate that seemingly inexplicable cases often have quite prosaic explanations, and that many ufologists are incompetent investigators.* **UFOs: The Public Deceived** *includes a full account of Klass's firsthand, damning exposure of the hoax behind the Travis Walton abduction case, voted the "Best Case of 1975" and awarded $5000 by the* **National Enquirer.**
—T.S.

UFOs: The Public Deceived
Philip J. Klass
1983; 310 pp.
$12.95
($14.95 postpaid) from:
Prometheus Books
700 East Amherst St.
Buffalo, NY 14215
800/421-0351

• On May 9, I wrote Mrs. Chenoweth to tell her of the Minuteman launch from Vandenberg. She replied on May 13 with a letter that began: "You have done me such a huge favor. . . . Thank heavens, inexplicable things have not arrived to taunt us from the heavens . . ." Her reaction stands in sharp contrast to many "UFO sighters," who will go so far as to sharply revise their original description of the incident after a prosaic explanation has been found in an effort to invalidate that explanation and to retain the distinction of "having seen a *genuine* UFO."

• On June 10, 1977, the *Washington Post* carried a short article reporting that a UFO had been sighted by a number of persons two nights earlier on the outskirts of the metropolitan area. One Maryland State Police officer described the object as resembling a "giant jellyfish." He was quoted as saying that the strange object had "disappeared in the southern portion of the sky after hovering for approximately five minutes." If, as one might expect, this law enforcement officer's word "hovering" meant precisely that, clearly this UFO could not possibly be a fixed-wing advertising aircraft.

But the next day's edition of the *Post* said that the UFO had indeed been identified as an advertising airplane. As a result of the previous article, the newspaper had received a telephone call from a Nadine Brown, who said "We are the culprits." She went on to explain that she and her husband operated an advertising airplane, a Cessna-150 with more than three hundred electric lights, controlled electronically to spell out sales messages. Mrs. Brown said: "You can see it from a long ways away, but you cannot read the message unless you are a quarter of a mile on each side of it." For observers watching from a greater distance and more oblique angle, she said, "you see a jellyfish sort of thing."

The UFO Experience

In what is arguably the single best "pro-UFO" book, the late J. Allen Hynek—the man who invented the term "close encounters of the third kind"—attempts to demonstrate that the core of UFO reports that cannot be explained represents an important phenomenon unknown to science. Hynek had credentials that were hard to ignore: an astronomer at Northwestern University and scientific consultant on UFOs to the U.S. Air Force for twenty years, during which he was converted from skeptic to "believer." The UFO Experience is a rational, persuasive book with fantastic implications. Read it and see if you can still say, "There's nothing to the UFO phenomenon."

—*T.S.*

• The markings on the ground are discovered almost immediately in the daytime cases and the following morning in the more frequent nighttime sightings. Natural curiosity draws the

The UFO Experience
A Scientific Inquiry
J. Allen Hynek
1972, 1977; 309 pp.
OUT OF PRINT
Ballantine Books
New York, NY

witnesses to the landing spot, and there they generally find a marking that fits a general pattern: either a circular patch, uniformly depressed, burned, or dehydrated, or a ring the overall diameter of which can be 30 feet or more but which itself is 1 to 3 feet in thickness (that is, the inner and outer diameters of the ring differ by that amount, while the ring itself may be quite large). The most frequently reported diameters are 20-30 feet. It is almost universally reported that the rings persist for weeks or months—sometimes years—and that the interior of the ring or sometimes the whole circle remains barren for a season or two.

William L. Moore Publications

William Moore is a thorough investigator and a controversial figure in ufology, especially for his recent championing of the "MJ-12" documents, purported to demonstrate that the military secretly retrieved a crashed flying saucer and its alien crew in 1947. Moore offers a large variety of unusual publications, books, and even videotapes on some of the more intriguing mysteries of ufology. He also publishes a monthly newsletter, Focus.

—*T.S.*

**William L. Moore
Publications**
Catalog **$1**

Focus
Jimmy Moore and
William L. Moore, Editors
$20/year (12 issues)

Both from:
William L. Moore Publications
4219 West Olive Avenue
Suite 247
Burbank, CA 91505

The Encyclopedia of UFOs

At 500,000 words this is one of the longest UFO books ever published and, though flawed, will have to do as the standard reference until something better comes along. Its entries include the major cases up till the late 1970s, personalities, theories, and essays on relevant issues. These last are the most appealing part of the book; consulting editor Richard Greenwell's entry on the "Extraterrestrial Hypothesis" is (along with Dr. Michael D. Swords's "The Third Option: How They Got Here, and Why," International UFO Reporter, January/February, 1987) as fine a concise analysis of that idea as you're going to find anywhere. Among the least satisfactory entries are some by editor Story himself, a ufological novice who seems not to have fully mastered his material and who manages to make some whopping errors (asserting, for example, that there were no UFO-related humanoid reports prior to 1949, when in fact a number of such accounts are in the literature). His eight-paragraph entry on contactees (persons claiming regular communications with angelic, long-winded spacefolk), a subject meriting far more, is superficial and naive, taking no note, for example, of the pioneering studies of religious scholars such as J. Gordon Melton and the late David Stupple. Much valuable space is wasted on long "position statements" by individuals who have nothing interesting to say.

Still, there is much of worth here and for the most part the speculation is reasonable and the history accurate (if not always complete). It sure beats plowing through scads of books and obscure magazines in search of some elusive cryptofact. By now, however, the Encyclopedia is dated. The 1980s have proven an extraordinarily eventful time in ufology, and a new reference work correcting the old one's shortcomings and covering the intervening decade's developments is sorely needed.

—*Jerome Clark*

• In considering the extraterrestrial hypothesis for UFOs, then, it should be recognized that:

(1) there are many likely locations for the emergence of life in our galaxy, as well as in other galaxies;

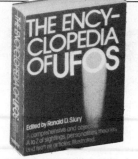

The Encyclopedia of UFOs
Ronald D. Story, Editor
1980; 440 pp.
OUT OF PRINT
Dolphin Books
Doubleday & Company, Inc.
Garden City, New York

(2) the emergence of life does not necessarily imply the eventual evolution of intelligent species;

(3) if such intelligences have evolved in the galaxy, or in other galaxies, they have already existed as such for far longer periods than the existence of *Homo sapiens*;

(4) one can only speculate over the biological, social, or technical development of such hypothetical intelligences;

(5) average distances between stars are enormous, but factors such as moving entire societies, time dilation, suspended animation, biomagnetic levitation, and prolongevity would reduce or even eliminate the distance problem;

(6) our understanding of processes in the Universe is still relatively poor, and it is premature to decide at this time what is "possible" or what is "impossible";

(7) any statement categorically rejecting the *hypothesis* that UFOs may represent some form of interstellar visitation is simplistic and is not based on a critical evaluation and synthesis of all relevant factors;

(8) any acceptance of UFOs as representing extraterrestrial visitation, based on the available evidence, can only be construed as a belief unsupported by established facts.

The emotional commitment on the part of those speculating on the ETH, positively or negatively, is not likely to diminish as long as UFOs continue to be reported, and there is no indication that reports are decreasing with the advent of a better-informed public and a more sophisticated Earth-based technology. (J. Richard Greenwell)

UFOs and the Extraterrestrial Contact Movement

This is the best bibliography of ufology ever published. Nothing else even comes close. Volume One, **Unidentified Flying Objects**, lists 10,990 books, monographs, periodicals, and articles dealing with every aspect of the UFO controversy, including the varieties of encounters, official and popular responses to the phenomenon, history, theories, sonic anomalies, and even ball lightning (believed responsible for some UFO reports). Volume Two, **The Extraterrestrial Contact Movement**, covers saucer literature's wilder and woolier aspects: contactee yarns, ancient astronauts, hollow-earth and Great-Pyramid speculations, men in black and Marian apparitions (vision of the Virgin Mary, which some theorists have suggested are a Roman Catholic version of the contactee experience). Volume Two closes with sections on UFOs in popular culture and speculations about extraterrestrial intelligence. All of this is prefaced with compiler Eberhart's informed and intelligent commentary.

Eberhart, an editor of the American Library Association's **College and Research Libraries News** and a board member of the J. Allen Hynek Center for UFO Studies, sees the literature as a record of ufology's evolution from fringe hobby to protoscience: from, as he puts it, the "era of the 1950s flying saucer buff . . . to [the] interesting mix of the 'amazing facts' and the 'let's get the facts straight' counterbalance of the 1960s . . . [to] the renewed enthusiasm generated by America's last big UFO flap in 1973, with its occupant and abduction cases . . . [to] the new wave of cautious speculation, retrenchment, and increased professionalism of the 1980s." Volume Two, which has little to do with ufology as such, shows the contactee movement to be an evolving Space Age religion with roots in two centuries of occult tradition—not a simple matter of kooks and crooks, as stereotype would have it, although such types are not hard to find within the movement. The bibliography's one limitation is that all its article citations are from sources other than the specialty UFO magazines and bulletins. The compiling of that material—perhaps an even more demanding task than the already heroic one Eberhart here performs—waits for some courageous future bibliophile.

—Jerome Clark

UFOs and the Extraterrestrial Contact Movement
George M. Eberhart
1986; 1,342 pp. (2 volumes)
$97.50
(postpaid) from:
The Scarecrow Press, Inc.
52 Liberty Street
Metuchen, New Jersey 08840

• [Sample listings:]
1785. Callahan, Philip Serna, and R.W. Mankin. "Insects as Unidentified Flying Objects." APPLIED OPTICS 17 (1978): 3355-60.
4108. Matyi, J. Robert. MY GOD, THEY'RE REAL! Port Washington, N.Y.: Ashley, 1979. 147p.
4370. Saunders, Alex. "The Case for an Underwater Civilization." SEARCH, no. 128 (Fall 1976): 9-12.
5880. Mather, Increase. HEAVEN'S ALARM TO THE WORLD: OR, A SERMON WHEREIN IS SHEWED, THAT FEARFUL SIGHTS AND SIGNS IN HEAVEN ARE THE PRESAGES OF GREAT CALAMATIES AT HAND. Boston: John Foster, 1681. 17p.
7469. Kennedy, Robert F. "Unidentified Flying Objects: Extension of Remarks of Hon. Robert F. Kennedy." CONGRESSIONAL RECORD, 90th Cong., 1st Sess., May 25, 1967, vol. 113, pp. A2605-606.
10215. Hynek, J. Allen. THE SCIENTIFIC PROBLEM POSED BY UNIDENTIFIED FLYING OBJECTS. Evanston, Ill.: The author, 1968. 15p.
Reprint of his statement made to the House Committee on Science and Astronautics, July 29, 1968.
10362. McCarthy, Paul. POLITICKING AND PARADIGM SHIFTING: JAMES E. McDONALD AND THE UFO CASE STUDY. Ph.D. diss., University of Hawaii, December 1975. 303p.
11720. Owens, Ted. HOW TO CONTACT SPACE PEOPLE. Clarksburg, W. Va.: Saucerian, 1969. 96p.
11762. The Scientist of Venus [pseud.] VENUS SPEAKS: DIRECT REVELATION REGARDING FLYING SAUCERS AND LIFE ON VENUS. London: Regency [1955, 1958]. 63p.

UFOs and Related Subjects: An Annotated Bibliography

This guide to over 1,600 books, articles, pamphlets, phonograph records, tapes, and other materials was prepared by the Library of Congress Science and Technology Division for the Air Force's Condon Committee investigation of UFOs in 1969. An addendum prepared by the Library of Congress in 1976 lists over 200 additional items. The material is divided into useful sections, including ancient records, contact claims, men in black, radar, ball lightning and fireballs, unidentified submarine objects, and gravity and anti-gravity. Best of all, each item is briefly and excellently described—a nice feature, considering the obscurity of many of the sources.   —T.S.

• Strange effects from EM waves. The UFO Investigator, v.3, Nov.-Dec. 1965: 5.
Experiments and research by Prof. Clyde E. Ingalls, Cornell University, are summarized and seem to indicate that electromagnetic waves can be "heard." Reports of odd effects and EM (electromagnetic) interference concomitant with UFO sightings are briefly surveyed.

• Steiger, Brad. What price silence? Flying Saucers, June, 1968: 31
A private citizen investigates an alleged UFO landing and is given a piece of metal that supposedly fell from the machine. The metal sample is taken away from him during a visit by what seemed to be representatives of "the men in black."

• Creighton, Gordon W. Even more amazing. Flying Saucer Review, v. 12, July-Aug. 1966: 23-27; Sept.-Oct. 1966: 22-25; Nov.-Dec. 1966: 14-16 v. 13, Jan.-Feb. 1967: 25-27; v. 14, Jan.-Feb. 1968: 18-20.
English version of original declaration made by Antonio Villas Boas that on the night of October 15-16, 1957, he was abducted by helmeted, uniformed creatures from his farm near Francisco de Sales, Brazil, onto a landed spacecraft of apparently extraterrestrial origin; there, he was seduced by a naked, fair-skinned, red-haired woman with slanting eyes in what may have been a biological experiment. A translation of the medical report confirms the possibility of the alleged experience.

UFOs and Related Subjects
An Annotated Bibliography
Lynn E. Catoe
1969, 1978, 1979; 411 pp.
$75 postpaid from:
Gale Research Co.
Book Tower, Dept. 77748
Detroit, MI 48277-0748
313/961-2242

UFO Periodicals

*Circulating through the mails to small but devoted subscriberships, UFO magazines have been around since the early '50s. Most of them have only lasted a few years, but some have endured for as long as twenty years. That record-holder is **MUFON UFO Journal,** the official publication of the Mutual UFO Network and the longest-running UFO periodical in the U.S. The MUFON membership includes active researchers who often arrive at the scenes of sightings while the grass is still scorched. You can read their reports here, as well as offerings from Budd Hopkins, William Moore, and others. MUFON also publishes offprints of papers delivered at their annual conferences, which are a good source of crashed-saucer reports and other UFO esoterica.*

*The **International UFO Reporter,** which also features articles by the big guns of the UFO world, is the official publication of the J. Allen Hynek Center for UFO Studies, or CUFOS for short. Hynek, who died in 1986, was the premier "scientific ufologist," a Northwestern University astronomer who was converted from skeptic to believer after working for the Air Force as a scientific consultant on UFOs from 1948-1968. CUFOS carries on in the Hynek tradition, conducting investigations and serving as a clearinghouse and repository for UFO sighting reports. They also publish the **Journal of UFO Studies** and a variety of offprints.*

*Unlike the journals mentioned above, **UFO** (formerly **California UFO**) has only been around for a couple of years. It's a bit more sensationalistic, and casts its nets a little wider to include articles on UFO movies and non-UFO paranormal subjects, as well as interviews with UFO personalities.*

*Finally, there's my favorite, the **UFO Newsclipping Service,** a monthly newsletter of twenty jam-packed legal-size pages that simply reproduces clippings of UFO sightings culled from the world's newspapers. There's something eerily compelling about the sheer volume, repetitive similarity, and small-town honesty of these back-page reports, sans editorializing, that no polished UFO book can equal.*

—*T.S.*

• On February 7, 1988 at approximately 7:00 p.m., Ed's wife was feeding their dog in the backyard. Suddenly a blue beam approximately 28 inches in diameter appeared near her. She called for Ed to come out, but he didn't hear her. Their daughter said loudly, "Daddy, Mommie needs you." As Ed ran to the back kitchen door, he picked up his camera. Ed's wife said the circumference of the beam was "rotating" fast and leaves were being drawn up by this action. When Ed reached the back kitchen door, another "blue beam" appeared near the door, blocking and apparently discouraging Ed from rushing outside to help his wife. (He was very cognizant of his prior experiences with the paralysis in-

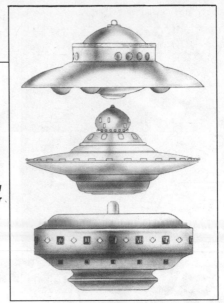

Three disputed "UFOs": From top to bottom, George Adamski's Venusian scoutcraft, Billy Meier's Pleiadean beamship, and "Ed's" Gulf Breeze "unknown of great significance."
—*International UFO Reporter*

duced.) Ed made a photo from their kitchen window of this beam, with his wife attempting to get past it to enter the back door.
—*MUFON UFO Journal*

• After a series of close encounters, a European couple were in a car accident that may result in a ufological coup, according to author Budd Hopkins, who's in contact with the researchers involved.

The identity of the couple is not available, but apparently they have a history of abduction. Hopkins tells *UFO* that after the accident, the man felt a curious sensation in his head, alerting him to something as it fell from his nose.

He found what's described as an object "larger than a BB and smaller than a pea." Now in the hands of investigators who hope to have it analyzed, the object is thought to be the nasal implant the aliens had placed in the man's head during an abduction.

As a curious sidelight, the couple once reported seeing a group of small humanoid aliens standing around their ship, dressed identically in plaid shirts and bib overalls. —*UFO*

• The searchers anticipated seeing the wreckage of a plane. What they found instead was a large acorn-shaped metallic object which appeared to be embedded in a 25- to 30-foot long ditch apparently created by the impact. The ditch was several feet wide and 7 to 8 feet deep at one end. . . .

"We all assumed it was a plane but when a plane crashes there are pieces all over." He described it as circular in shape with a bumper around the radius that bore raised markings that reminded him of ancient Egyptian hieroglyphics. The metal, which he described as grayish pale gold in color, was crumpled much like a deflated beachball. "It was a color you just don't normally see," he says.
—*UFO Newsclipping Service*

MUFON UFO Journal
Dennis Stacy, Editor
$25/year
(12 issues) from:
MUFON UFO Journal
103 Oldtowne Road
Seguin, TX 78155-4099

International UFO Reporter
Jerome Clark, Editor
$25/year
(6 issues) from:
International UFO Reporter
2457 West Peterson Ave.
Chicago, IL 60659

UFO
Vicki Cooper and
Sherie Stark, Editors
$18/year
(6 issues) from:
UFO
1800 S. Robertson Blvd.
Box 355
Los Angeles, CA 90035

UFO Newsclipping Service
Lucius Farish, Editor
$55/year (12 issues)
$5/single issue from:
UFO Newsclipping Service
Route 1, Box 220
Plumerville, AR 72127

THE GREAT PHONOGRAPH IN THE SKY

NEAR FORT LAUDERDALE, FLORIDA, ONE ENTIRE WING of an out-of-the-way military hospital is sealed off and heavily guarded. For over four decades, the wing has housed a single patient, well tended by doctors and nurses who are sworn to secrecy. He is a victim of one of the strangest episodes in naval history: the Disappearance of Flight 19.

Unless you've been in a coma for the past forty years, you've probably heard the story of Flight 19. On December 5, 1945, five Grumman Avenger torpedo bombers carrying a total of fourteen men took off on a routine training flight off the coast of Florida. Even though they were equipped with radar and the latest in navigation gear, they all managed to get lost. Later that same day, a Mariner flying boat with thirteen men aboard went searching for them. It vanished too. In the weeks that followed, a massive search by air, sea, and land was conducted, covering many thousands of miles. But not a trace of Flight 19 or the Mariner was found. No floating debris, no oil slicks, nothing. Forty-two years later, in 1987, a single Avenger plane was found under thirty feet of water a few miles from the Florida coastline, but it has not been positively identified as a participant in Flight 19.

Rumors about Flight 19 have circulated for four decades and have served as the fodder for many books. The earliest tale cropped up in Florida shortly after the big search was abandoned, claiming that a ship had actually rescued a solitary survivor floating on a raft. He was babbling mindlessly about horrible things and the Navy put him in a hospital where they have been keeping him prisoner ever since.

As rumors go, the hospital story is a good one because it endorses the acute paranoia of those who collect unsolved mysteries. It has been repeated many times in many places over the years. A similar rumor alleges that a solitary UFO witness is living in a closed-off section of a hospital in San Diego, California. Yet another victim of a paranormal event is lolling about in luxury in a hospital in Boston. In 1967, a mystery man turned up in England, wandering through the streets of a London suburb stark naked. He's had his own private wing in a British hospital for over two decades now.

In the subculture of fringe beliefs, rumors run rampant. They are often wonderful and mysterious stories, though ultimately unverifiable. As you read this article, bear in mind that John Keel has heard them all. Since his first-person account of the mysteries of the Orient, Jadoo, *appeared in 1957, Keel has been a central figure in outré journalism. Canonized by many UFO enthusiasts, Keel is the author of such diverse cult classics of UFO and Fortean lore as* UFOs: Operation Trojan Horse *(1970),* Strange Creatures From Time and Space *(1970),* Our Haunted Planet *(1971),* The Eighth Tower *(1975), and* The Mothman Prophecies *(1975). His bemused look at the New Age,* Disneyland of the Gods, *has just appeared from AMOK Press (P.O. Box 875112, Los Angeles, CA 90087; $11.95 postpaid).* —T.S.

by *John A. Keel*
Illustrated by Kim Deitch

Where do these rumors come from and how are they perpetuated? As in most folklore, there must be just enough basis in fact to make the stories believable despite persistent embellishments. And believers of a rumor must suffer from total suspension of disbelief. This is a kind way of saying that they must be gullible as hell.

Take the case of the "Philadelphia Experiment," a rumor so prevalent that it was even the subject of a major motion picture. It's been the theme of several books, too, and is based upon three facts: 1) A section of the Philadelphia Naval yard was sealed off during World War II. 2) Strange scholarly civilians carrying briefcases were seen entering and leaving the restricted area (one of whom was clearly recognized as Albert Einstein). 3) A weird newspaper article that was published during the war years described how sailors had been terrified aboard their ship by eerie electrical phenomena. These three facts resulted in a rumor that the Navy was experimenting with a system to cause ships—and their crews—to dematerialize.

One lone man set this rumor in motion when he mailed a cryptic document to a popular UFO researcher. His name was Carl Allen, a.k.a. "Carlos Allende." Whenever the cultists showed signs of losing interest in the rumor, he would stir things up again with letters to cult leaders revealing new evidence of the government conspiracy to hide the truth from the public.

Mr. Allen had been a seaman during the war and he had spent some time in Philadelphia. Like all the sailors there, he was fascinated by the Off Limits area of the Naval Yard and the comings and goings of the oddball professorial types. And he wondered about all the wires and weird equipment seen aboard some of the ships docked there. A rumor was circulated among the seamen that these ships were being degaussed (i.e., demagnetized so they wouldn't attract magnetic mines). After the war, the truth came out. *That closed area was a part of the Manhattan Project*, part of the effort to build the atomic bomb. Cloud chambers and cyclotrons were on board the ships that the scientists, including Einstein, visited. The degaussing story was actually put into circulation by the security people guarding the Manhattan Project.

The third element of the rumor—the newspaper article—was hard to pin down. Researchers spent years wading through Philadelphia newspapers looking for the item Allen swore he had read. Only recently has a leading Fortean researcher, Michael T. Shoemaker, stumbled across the story in *The Philadelphia Inquirer* of August 1, 1904. That's right, *1904* !

According to the article, the British steamer *Mohican* ran into a mysterious "magnetic" cloud that July. Here is the Captain's description (his name was Urquhart) which was "vouched for by every man of the crew":

It was shortly after the sun had gone and we were in latitude 37 degrees 16 minutes and longitude 72 degrees 48 minutes. The sea was almost as level as a parlor carpet and scarcely a breeze ruffled the water. It was slowly growing dark when the lookout saw a strange gray cloud in the southeast. At first it appeared as a speck on the horizon, but it rapidly came nearer and was soon as large as a balloon. . . . Suddenly the cloud enveloped the ship, and the most remarkable phenomena took place. The *Mohican* suddenly blazed forth like a ship on fire, and from stem to stern and topmast to keel everything was tinged with the strange glow. The seamen were in terror when they found themselves looking as if they had been immersed in hell fire. Their hair stood straight on end, not from fright so much as from the magnetic power of the cloud.

They rushed about the deck in consternation, and the more they rushed about the more excited they became. I tried to calm them, but the situation was beyond me. I looked at the needle (compass) and it was flying around like an electric fan. I ordered several of the crew to move some iron chains that were lying on the deck, thinking that it would distract their attention. But what a surprise to find that the sailors could not budge the chains, although they did not weigh more than seventy-five pounds each. Everything was magnetized, and chains, bolts, spikes and bars were as tight on the deck as if they had been riveted there.

The cloud was so dense that it was impossible for the vessel to proceed. I could not see beyond the decks, and it appeared as if the whole world was a mass of glowing fire . . . After we had been in the cloud for about ten minutes, we noticed that it became difficult to move our arms and legs, in fact, all the joints of the body seemed to stiffen . . . I tried to talk, but the words refused to leave my lips. The density of the cloud was so great that it would not carry sound. ☞

Rumor! and More Rumor!

Rumor!
Hal Morgan and Kerry Tucker
1984; 158 pp.
$3.50
($6.50 postpaid)

More Rumor!
Hal Morgan and Kerry Tucker
1987; 206 pp.
$3.50
($6.50 postpaid)

Both from:
Penguin Books
Attn: DMO
299 Murray Hill Parkway
East Rutherford, NJ 07073
800/631-3577

Did you ever hear that Walt Disney was frozen when he died? (Not true.) That Mrs. Fields charges $250 for her cookie recipe? (Not true.) That the Procter and Gamble trademark is a Satanic symbol? (Not true.) That the liquid in golf balls is a powerful explosive? (Not true.) That B.F. Skinner's daughter spent her infancy in a "Skinner box"? (Not exactly true.) That "Ring Around the Rosy" refers to the 1606 Black Plague of London? (Not true.) That there are alligators in New York's sewers? (Possibly true.)

For those who worry excessively about the veracity of such stories, **Rumor!** *and* **More Rumor!** *may be the key to a full night's sleep at last. Not unexpectedly, most of these popular rumors fall into the category of "not true," but some very interesting ones turn out to be "true," or, in the case of invisible Navy ships and crashed flying saucers, "unconfirmed" or "unverifiable." Provided you've done your homework in advance, you'll probably earn back the purchase price of these two volumes the first time you use them to settle a bet.* —T.S.

• Albert Einstein's brain now sits in a cider box in the corner of a doctor's office in Wichita, Kansas. (1978)

True. Or at least that's where the brain was when Steven Levy, a reporter from *New Jersey Monthly* magazine, tracked it down in 1978. Einstein had requested that, after his death, his brain be used for research. When he died on April 18, 1955, the most celebrated brain of our time was carefully removed from Einstein's body and preserved. The rest of the body was cremated.

The brain fell under the care of Dr. Thomas S. Harvey, the pathologist at the Princeton, New Jersey, hospital where Einstein had died. Dr. Harvey made plans for a team of experts to study the brain to try to unlock the mystery of its genius. But after his first examination of the tissue he commented: "It looks just like anybody else's."

Microscopic sections were taken and distributed for closer study, but, when the New Jersey reporter tracked down Dr. Harvey in 1978, no findings had been published. Dr. Harvey, by then a supervisor at a biological testing laboratory in Wichita, offered to show the reporter the pieces of the brain that remained. The reporter was spellbound as the doctor reached into a cardboard cider box in the corner of his office and pulled out a Mason jar holding the specimen:

"I had risen to look into the jar, but now I was sunk in my chair, speechless. My eyes were fixed upon that jar as I tried to comprehend that these pieces of gunk bobbling up and down had caused a revolution in physics and quite possibly changed the course of civilization. *There it was!*" —*Rumor!*

• If you put a troll doll in the freezer its hair will grow. (1963)
Not true.
—*More Rumor!*

Suddenly the cloud began to lift. The phosphorescent glow of the ship and the crew began to fade. It gradually died away . . . In minutes the cloud had passed over the vessel and we saw it moving off over the sea. It loomed above the water as a great gray mass, spotted like a leopard's back with bright, glowing patches.

Linguist and writer on paranormal subjects Charles Berlitz has interviewed modern witnesses who claim to have encountered similar magnetic clouds in the area now known as the Bermuda Triangle. But no one, including the young Carl Allen, knew of such things in the 1940s. The 1904 *Inquirer* story was reprinted several times and it finally turned up, with some rather vivid additions, in a Sunday newspaper supplement called *The American Weekly*. During the 1930s and '40s, *The American Weekly* was edited by a Fortean named A.A. Merritt. Each issue was filled with stories of vampires, ghosts, and items gleaned from the works of the "Father of Anomalies," Charles Fort (see page 81). Merritt, who was a famous science fiction writer, did not hesitate to make his factual yarns more entertaining by adding a bit of the blarney. The impressionable Mr. Allen was greatly influenced by Merritt's treatment of the *Mohican* account and since Philadelphia was mentioned, he must have assumed the magnetic cloud was directly related to the strange goings-on at the Naval Yard. He put everything together in his own way and came up with the now-legendary Philadelphia Experiment.

Rumors of the Philadelphia Experiment have endured since World War II simply because none of the believers can accept the well-established facts of the situation. They regard the many published accounts of the Manhattan Project's activities in the Philadelphia Naval Yard as part of a massive government coverup. There is no truth, you see, except the Truth accepted by cultists. They don't want to be confused with facts when there are so many delicious rumors available. This is, in fact, one of the major features of a good cult rumor: It can't be proven, nor can it be disproven, so it must be true! The more the rumor is denied, the more the cultists are certain of its veracity. They are especially certain of rumors that conform to their particular belief systems. This attitude has kept the Flat Earthers in business for a long time: Everyone who denies the flatness of the Earth is, naturally enough, part of the conspiracy. Any NASA scientist who claims the Earth is really round is obviously lying through his teeth.

Take the Aztec, New Mexico, affair, for another example. That's where a flying saucer supposedly crashed in 1947, spilling out a number of bodies, all very small (about three feet tall), which the Air force whisked away to Ohio and pickled in bottles. The rumor of the little bodies has been floating around ever since, and it is periodically revived. The cyclical recurrence of these revivals is more interesting in many ways than the story itself. It's as if someone somewhere wants to keep this rumor alive. Every few years a new set of alleged government documents appears in the mailbox of some cult leader. The origin of these phoney documents is a mystery, though they are usually so poorly executed that only the Incurably Gullible (I.G.) would even consider them. The "pickled little men" story has enjoyed several such revivals in the 1950s and '60s, and in 1987 it was again occupying center stage at UFO conventions around the country.

The Aztec story began in the pages of *Variety* in 1949, when humorist Frank Scully filled some of his columns with rumors of crashed saucers in Mexico and New Mexico. He followed up with a book, *Behind The Flying Saucers*, which was one of the best sellers of 1950. His "source" was "Dr. G.," who turned out to be a TV repairman. (Apparently the Air Force had called in a TV repairman to examine the bodies of the little men!) The tale snowballed from there. Today, the I.G.s believe that outer space corpses are permanently installed in a hangar at Wright-Patterson Air Force Base in Dayton, Ohio. The more the Air Force denied that it was harboring corpses of little spacemen, the more convinced the I.G.s were that the rumors were true. In 1980, a book titled *The Roswell Incident* [1] appeared. It was written by one William Moore, who had earlier assembled a believer's book on the Philadelphia Experiment.[2] Moore and his colleagues visited New Mexico and interviewed people in the city of Roswell who claimed to remember a saucer crash there in 1947 (not in Aztec which was far to the north). What their stories boiled down to was that they had seen a truck filled with junk that it had picked up on a nearby ranch. Since Roswell is less than a hundred miles from the White Sands Missile Range, the debris may not have been as mysterious as these "eyewitnesses" have tried to make it.

Because hardcore ufologists (numbering about two thousand in the United States) have no substantive evidence of extraterrestrial visitants, they must accept rumors, hearsay, and, frequently, schizophrenic delusions as proof of their beliefs. Indeed, the tight little world of ufology has all the underpinnings of religion. Ufological fundamentalists believe that there are countless other planets out there in the universe and that entities from many of them visit Earth on a regular basis, but without establishing formal contact with us. This belief is reinforced by pilgrimages to distant UFO sites where significant extraterrestrial (E.T.) events allegedly occurred years ago. Very few ufologists have any knowledge of science or astronomy—most are not even acquainted with high school physics—so they have accepted "scientists" (usually college professors) as their high priests. Scientism—the worship of science—is a key component of the UFO religion, provided, of course, that the "scientist" says what the ufologists want to hear. Astronomer Carl Sagan is an enemy because he scoffs at the basic tenets of the UFO religion, but the late J. Allen Hynek, also an astronomer, was a high priest because he introduced the holy mantra, "Where there's smoke, there must be fire."

Actually, where there's smoke there must be a smudge pot. Acrid fumes have been beclouding the UFO scene for a very long time and they show no signs of dissipating. In the 1980s, a whole new generation led by actress Shirley MacLaine is embracing the E.T. cosmic order under the label of the New Age. That smudge pot is burning smokier than ever. The first New Age was launched about four thousand years ago when an Egyptian named Osiris announced that he was a god. It wasn't long before there were "gods" all over the planet, preaching darkly magical things about crystals, reincarnation, channeling, and all the accoutrements of modern MacLaineism. It's as if there is a phonograph up there in the sky with a broken record that cranks out the same message over and over to generation after generation. An examination of the New Age literature of the 1800s produces a *déjà vu* because so much of it is being repeated, almost mindlessly, in the New Age literature of the 1980s.

New Ages are not only old-fashioned, they are monotonous. In the past forty years alone there have been six New Age explosions. After the public became aware of the UFO phenomenon in the 1940s, thousands of

[1]Charles Berlitz and William L. Moore. 1980. *The Roswell Incident.* New York: Grosset and Dunlap. (Out of Print.)

[2]William L. Moore. 1979. *The Philadelphia Experiment.* New York: Fawcett. ($4.50 postpaid from: Random House, 400 Hahn Rd., Westminster, MD 21157; 800/638-6460.)

people began to have real or imagined experiences with the saucers and their bewildering array of occupants. Some were called "contactees," while others—"abductees"—insisted they had been kidnapped, usually in isolated areas. By the mid-1950s there were over fifty thousand contactees and abductees in the United States, many of whom started or joined New Age organizations. Believers and I.G.s clustered around them. One '50s convention at Giant Rock, California, drew more than ten thousand people.

The abductee phenomenon extends back to the beginning of history. Ancient manuscripts found in Russia tell what is possibly the earliest story of an abduction by aliens. Here's how the father of Methuselah, Enoch, describes his experience:

> On the first day of the first month I was in my house alone and was resting on my couch and slept. And there appeared to me two men, exceeding big, so that I never saw such on earth; their faces were shining like the sun, their eyes too were like a burning light . . .

These two luminous giants gathered Enoch up and took him on a tour of other worlds. He was gone for months and when he returned he suffered a bit from the partial amnesia or "missing time" commonly reported by modern UFO abductees. According to the Bible, Enoch did not die. He just disappeared one day: "God took him."

Several thousand years later, a horror novelist named Whitley Strieber woke up in his cabin in the Catskill Mountains and found some equally strange visitors in *his* bedroom. Though these were *little* men who did *not* glow, he was off on an Enochian adventure that he quickly turned into a best-selling book, *Communion* (see p. 157). Unfamiliar with UFO lore, he didn't realize that thousands of people shared his experiences and many of them had also laboriously written books, though often these abductees spent their life savings to self-publish

them. Some deserted their families, quit their jobs, and even changed their names in order to become UFO evangelists, proselytizing the doctrines of the space brothers. Mr. Strieber was not much different from William Denton, for example, a contactee who stumped the country and published books in the 1860s. And you can be sure that one hundred years from now, a man in the post-nuclear age will wake up in the middle of the night to see frightening phantoms in the darkness of his cave.

The "aliens" have always been with us, inspiring myths and theologies as they impersonated representatives of "powers and principalities." Century after century, generation after generation, men and women have stood on hilltops, watching in wonder as brilliant multicolored lights danced against the night sky. Having witnessed such unshakeable evidence of another world, they descended and joined the ranks of the Incurably Gullible, embracing the rumors that outfly the saucers. According to them, our hospitals are filled with prisoners who "know too much." Crashed saucers are everywhere. Bottles of pickled little men are undoubtedly hidden at some Air Force base although no one has ever seen them—except perhaps for a lone TV repairman. And the gigantic governmental conspiracy continues. Meanwhile, an anonymous prankster somewhere out there will send the newest batch of childishly phoney documents to the next wave of I.G.s, and the rumors and myths will be perpetuated forever.

That great phonograph in the sky continues to grind away, sending out its messages of hope and hopelessness. And a large part of the burgeoning human race will continue to worship it. When our currently deteriorating civilization has crumbled altogether, that phonograph will still remain and the survivors will still gather on those hilltops to gaze in wonder at mysterious lights, and to listen in mesmerized fascination to that phonograph's single monotonous melody. ■

WHAT IS REALITY?

Bill Griffith

Beyond True & False

by Robert Anton Wilson

A Sneaky Quiz with a Subversive Commentary

DIRECTIONS: The following quiz has been designed to undermine the unstated and often unconscious assumptions that inflame most arguments or discussions about heretical ideas and turn debate into heated quarrel. With no further explanation (at this point), I invite you to jump in and measure your S.N.Q. (Semantic Naivety Quotient) by judging each of the following assertions.

TRUE FALSE

❏ ❏ 1. Francis Bacon wrote *Hamlet*.

❏ ❏ 2. Ronald Reagan wrote *Hamlet*.

❏ ❏ 3. F=ma (Force equals mass times acceleration)

❏ ❏ 4. *pq=qp*

❏ ❏ 5. Water boils at 100° Centigrade.

❏ ❏ 6. There is a tenth planet in our solar system beyond Pluto.

❏ ❏ 7. All propositions are either true or false.

❏ ❏ 8. All propositions are true in some sense, false in some sense, true and false in some sense, and neither true nor false in some sense.

❏ ❏ 9. When blessed by an ordained Catholic priest, a piece of bread becomes the body of a Jew who died about 2000 years ago.

❏ ❏ 10. All gremlins eat red lemons.

❏ ❏ 11. The Pope is infallible in matters of faith and morals.

❏ ❏ 12. Charlie Manson was responsible for several murders.

❏ ❏ 13. A court found Charlie Manson responsible for several murders.

❏ ❏ 14. The Nazi government killed six million Jews.

TRUE FALSE

❏ ❏ 15. The Federal Reserve Bank is controlled by the Bavarian Illuminati.

❏ ❏ 16. Colorless green ideas sleep furiously.

❏ ❏ 17. The Smithsonian Institute has John Dillinger's legendary 23-inch penis in a jar, but they only show it to friends of government officials and deny its existence to people like you and me.

❏ ❏ 18. A boy has never wept nor dashed a thousand kim.

❏ ❏ 19. Beethoven is a better composer than Mozart.

❏ ❏ 20. The electron is a wave.

❏ ❏ 21. The electron is a particle.

❏ ❏ 22. *Lady Chatterley's Lover* is a pornographic novel.

❏ ❏ 23. *Lady Chatterley's Lover* is a sexist novel.

❏ ❏ 24. All men are created equal.

❏ ❏ 25. All humans are created equal.

❏ ❏ 26. All entities are created equal.

❏ ❏ 27. God told me to tell you that what you want is sinful.

❏ ❏ 28. I became one with God.

❏ ❏ 29. The following sentence is false.

❏ ❏ 30. The previous sentence was true.

❏ ❏ 31. The Darwinian Theory of Evolution has been conclusively proven.

❏ ❏ 32. The Darwinian Theory of Evolution has been conclusively disproven.

❏ ❏ 33. UFOs exist.

Skepticism is a two-edged sword. The same attitude that can lead to suspicion of fringe theories can lead to suspicion of orthodoxy as well. Robert Anton Wilson is perhaps best known for his Illuminatus! *trilogy, coauthored with Robert Shea, a set of novels that paints a picture of a history- and globe-spanning conspiracy that is both a paranoiac's nightmare and delight. A former* Playboy *editor, Wilson's the author of many other books, including science fiction and fantasy novels, historical novels, and nonfiction volumes of "futurist psychology" and "guerilla ontology." He's recorded a comedy record* (Secrets of Power) *and a punk-rock record* (The Chocolate Biscuit Conspiracy), *and regularly conducts seminars at Esalen and other New Age centers. His play,* Wilhelm Reich in Hell, *was recently performed by the Edmund Burke Theater in Dublin, Ireland.*

—T.S.

INCE TECHNIQUES OF JUDGING THE TRUTH value of propositions are still in heated dispute among logicians, mathematicians, scientists, and philosophers, I am not about to give "correct" answers to this quiz. Instead, I will offer a commentary on why *some* uncertainty attends all the preceding propositions and why the uncertainty about some of them is vast and abysmal.

Proposition 1, "Francis Bacon wrote *Hamlet*," is believed by a small but vehement minority and regarded as not only "false" but patently absurd by academic orthodoxy. No scientific way exists to test such propositions, and, since historians frequently have disputes over what constitutes "real" historical evidence, *some* doubt must attend a theory of this nature. I would suggest that the amount of doubt should be greater than in the case of the proposition "Franklin Delano Roosevelt was President of the United States from 1933 to 1945," certainly less than in the case of "Ronald Reagan wrote *Hamlet*," and might be perhaps equal to that in the case of "Francis Bacon definitely did not write *Hamlet*."

Personally, I tend to believe Will Shakespeare of Stratford wrote *Hamlet*, but since I can't prove it scientifically and am not an expert on Elizabethan conspiracies, I am not 100 percent sure, and prefer to listen to the Baconians politely rather than arouse their (quickly aroused) hostility by dogmatic denial of their Faith.

Proposition 2, "Ronald Reagan wrote *Hamlet*," only *seems* clearly false. We would only evade a possible trap if we more carefully worded this as "Ronald Reagan wrote the version of *Hamlet* usually attributed to Shakespeare." After all, Ronnie might have written his own version in youth and prudently decided not to publish it . . .

Proposition 3, about force being mathematically equal to mass times acceleration, seems absolutely true to everybody—except a few very philosophical scientists. Nobel laureate P.W. Bridgman, for instance, held the position that such scientific laws should better be considered "useful" than "true," and that what appears "useful" will change with time as knowledge increases. Logician Anatole Rapoport (and many others) would describe such "laws" as *valid* rather than "true," on the grounds that we can prove their mathematical consistency (inner validity) but can only observe that they *seem* to work experimentally thus far and can't know they will always work. Sir Karl Popper, philosopher-physicist, offers the most devastating criticism of all, arguing that no scientific law has ever been proven, but some have been dis-

proven. Popper's argument is that it would take an infinite number of experiments to prove a law strictly, and we haven't had that much time yet, so science actually advances by disproving inadequate theories and pragmatically "making do" with the ones that have thus far resisted disproof.

I do not aver that the criticisms of Bridgman, Rapoport, Popper, and others of that ilk have been conclusive, but only that many learned persons share such views and the matter of scientific "truth" still remains in dispute. Some minds cling to certitude, not because it can be clearly justified, but evidently because such minds have an emotional need for certitude.

Proposition 4, "*pq = qp*," again appears to belong to mathematical validity rather than demonstrable certainty. It is, in fact, a rule of commutative algebra, and, however useful you may find it in the grocery store, there are alternative algebras, one of which, known as Hamiltonian or non-commutative algebra, is just as valid (internally consistent) and has been found as useful in quantum mechanics as ordinary algebra is in shopping. The Hamiltonian algebra holds that *pq* is *not* equal to *qp*.

Examples like this (and the co-existence of Euclidean, non-Euclidean, and Fullerian geometries) demonstrate why many mathematicians do not any longer assert "truth" or "falsity" for mathematical systems, but only "validity" or "non-validity."

Proposition 5, "Water boils at 100° Centigrade," appears true on this planet, to people living at sea-level. *Even* on this planet, it appears clearly and demonstrably false to people living or doing research in the Rocky Mountains, the Alps, the Himalayas, etc.

The Cosmological Principle holds that scientific laws should be true everywhere in space-time, but we do not know if any of our current "laws" are cosmological in that sense. We only know that they seem to work thus far in the space-time we have explored thus far. When we and/or our instruments probe further, many cosmological laws will probably be disproven and replaced by different "laws" (better approximations).

Proposition 6, about the planet beyond Pluto, is believed by many astronomers on the basis of strong inference, but such a planet has not been observed yet. Dr. Rapoport would class such assertions as "indeterminate," rather than true or false, until actual observations are reported and repeatedly confirmed.

Incidentally, would you care to guess how many of your favorite religious, political, or economic beliefs would be classed as "indeterminate" by the Rapoport standard?

Proposition 7, "All propositions are either true or false," is still valiantly defended by the Jesuits, Martin Gardner, the disciples of Ayn Rand, and ideologists of all schools of political frenzy, but is increasingly doubted by modern logicians and scientists. One reason for this increasing doubt is that many propositions appear "indeterminate" in Rapoport's sense, and we will confront other reasons as we advance. For now, it is enough to note that the Formalist school of mathematicians regard all logical-mathematical systems as being more like Game Rules than scientific "laws," and, in this case, we should consider "All propositions are either true or false" as a Game Rule of Aristotelian logic. (Alfred Korzybski, G. Spencer Brown, and John von Neumann, among others, have invented non-Aristotelian logics that are as valid as non-Euclidian geometries.)

Similarly, 8, "All propositions are true in some sense, false in some sense, true and false in some sense, and neither true nor false in some sense," can be considered a Game Rule in Mahayana Buddhism (and in some philosophical interpretations of quantum mechanics, it seems).

9, about bread becoming flesh during a magical ritual, is fervently believed by Roman Catholics, denied by Rationalists, and considered "meaningless" by Logical Positivists. The grounds for considering such propositions meaningless are that no event in space-time (no act, no sense impression, no scientific measurement) can prove or disprove such allegations. For example, one could say that the ritual actually turns the bread into the hide of the Easter Bunny, and even though Catholics would probably join Rationalists in rejecting such a statement, it is on par with the idea that the ritual turns the bread into human flesh. When propositions do not refer to existential events that humans may encounter and endure in space-time, it seems that the Logical Positivists have some reasonable grounds for employing the label "meaningless." (Finding technical problems in this label, Bridgman suggested the alternative and obviously colloquial term, "footless propositions.")

10, about gremlins and red lemons, seems also "meaningless" by this Logical Positivist (and Operationalist) standard. (But how about statements about "the National Debt?")

11, about Papal infallibility, appears false to Rationalists, but at this point some may prefer the label "meaningless," since there is no operation to test the Pope's omniscience. Or is Papal Infallibility best considered a Game Rule of Catholicism, like "the umpire's decision is binding" is considered a Game Rule of baseball?

12, about Manson's guilt, would be considered "legally true" by lawyers, since a jury, a judge, and a higher court all found Charlie guilty. However, since even the American Bar Association admits that around five percent of all convicted "criminals" are innocent, it appears that legal truth does not guarantee absolute factual truth. That's why there are books challenging the court's verdict in almost all the famous trials of history, and one can safely guess there will someday be books challenging the court's decision on Manson.

13, "A court found Charlie Manson guilty of several murders," seems safer than 12. It will be challenged only by those who are also willing to assert that all (or most) documents relevant to the trial are forgeries created by some enormous conspiracy . . .

14, concerning the Holocaust, confronts us with exactly that problem, alas. Some people claim all the evidence of murder in 6,000,000 cases has been faked by a huge conspiracy. I will explain below why I think that instead of simply calling such all-embracing conspiracy theories "false," we might more profitably label them "Strange Loops." For now, I merely observe that a conspiracy that can deceive us about 6,000,000 deaths can deceive us about *anything*, and that it takes a great leap of faith for Holocaust Revisionists to believe World War II happened at all, or that Franklin Roosevelt did serve as President from 1933 to 1945, or that Marilyn Monroe was more "real" than King Kong or Donald Duck.

15, Illuminati control of banks, also creates a Strange Loop. If we believe in a conspiracy of that size, we cannot fully believe in anything else, *including the evidence that led us to believe in such a conspiracy.*

16, "Colorless green ideas sleep furiously," seems to be a classic "meaningless" statement in the Logical Positivist sense, since we cannot hope to encounter colorless green ideas or observe their sleeping habits. However, this proposition is not meaningless in another sense. It comes from Noam Chomsky and has meaning in linguistics, because it demonstrates that we can recognize a correct grammatical structure without knowing what the sentence containing it is asserting. This is one reason for doubting that the Logical Positivist label of "meaningless" is going to solve all hard cases for us . . .

17, the Dillinger penis in the Smithsonian, I would classify as purely meaningless in the Logical Positivist sense. The proposition indeed is carefully worded to tell us that any attempt to prove or disprove it will lead us to be deceived, and hence like all mega-conspiracy theories this verges over from meaningless into a total Strange Loop.

18, "A boy has never wept nor dashed a thousand kim," certainly appears meaningless by almost any criteria, but it was evidently urgently meaningful to the gentleman who said it. He was Dutch Shultz, and he had a bullet in him and a high fever (due to the bullet), and he was doing the best he could, under the circumstances, to tell the police what had happened. We will have to consider this "failed communication" unless we are bold enough to call it Great Poetry.

19, Beethoven's "superiority" to Mozart, also seems meaningless by strict Positivist standards. I would prefer to call it *self-reflexive*, on the grounds that it refers to the nervous system of the speaker and is a clumsy formulation of the more accurate report "Beethoven seems better than Mozart to me, at the current stage of my musical knowledge and ignorance."

20, "The electron is a wave," once seemed "true," but now quantum physicists tend to regard it as instrumentally self-reflexive. That is, it should be considered a bad formulation of the more accurate report "Using certain instruments we constrain the electron to appear as a wave."

21, "The electron is a particle," similarly should be considered a bad formulation of the accurate report "Using other instruments we constrain the electron to behave like a particle."

22, about the "pornography" of D.H. Lawrence's best-known novel, was once legally "true" and is currently legally "false." I suggest that such statements should be considered self-reflexive in the sense explained above. One set of judges, using the only instruments they had (their nervous systems), registered pornography; a later set of judges, with other instruments (nervous systems), did not register pornography.

23, about the "sexism" of the same novel, also seems self-reflexive to me; I think it describes events in the nervous system of the speaker. However, many people, who will agree that statements about musical merit or pornography "are" self-reflexive, still insist that statements about sexism "are" as objective as statements about the number of apples in a barrel. I therefore continue to *suggest* only and do not insist on anything. Maybe somebody will invent a Smutometer or Chauvinoscope someday and we will be able to measure "pornography" or "sexism" . . .

24, "All men are created equal," once seemed true (Jefferson thought he was writing an anthropological law), and is currently not only indeterminate but sounds a bit reactionary to most of us. I suggest we call it a Game Rule of Jeffersonian Democracy.

25, "All humans are created equal," thus appears a Game Rule of current post-Jeffersonian Democracy, just as Papal Infallibility appears a Game Rule of pre-Jeffersonian Autocracy.

26, "All entities are created equal," appears to be a Game Rule of Buddhism, and is becoming a Game Rule of Moral Ecology (as distinguished from scientific ecology).

27, "God told me to tell you that what you want is sinful," appears true to many devout fans of Fundamentalist Evangelism, and is regarded as imposture by scoffers and skeptics. I personally regard it as impertinence, but, anyway, it might best be called a bad formulation of the instrumentally self-reflexive report "I have had such an astounding experience that the only terms I know that can describe it are to assert that God told me to go out and correct the rest of you bastards." This does not contradict the fact that other people have other terms for the experience, including paranoia and megalomania.

28, "I became one with God," similarly seems to me a sloppy formulation of the report "I had such an astounding experience that the only model I know that describes it is to say God and I are one." This does not contradict the fact that other people have other models, including "I and the universe became one" and "my right brain hemisphere began to merge with my left brain hemisphere" (and others).

29, "The following sentence is false," appears neither true, nor false, nor indeterminate, nor meaningless, but *incomplete*. We cannot judge it at all until we can judge the system of which it is part. (Most theological and political arguments are about such incomplete statements, which are discussed as if they had true-false ratings, or "meaning," outside the system which contains them.)

30, "The previous sentence was true," completes the incomplete system, which now can be judged. As is immediately obvious, this system is true if and only if it is false, and it's false if and only if it's true. Douglas Hofstadter calls such systems Strange Loops, and (without using that term) anthropologist Gregory Bateson has demonstrated that the Game Rules of many societies and sub-cultures cause believers to appear like lunatics when seen from outside the system. Before judging any proposition as true or false, you should not only ask if it might better be called indeterminate or meaningless or self-reflexive or a "local" Game Rule, but also if it is part of a Strange Loop that may make you appear crazy if you try to live with it. All conspiracy theories beyond the local and temporary—for example, "The city council was bribed by the oil company"— *tend* to produce Strange Loops because they create the possibility that no data is untainted by conspiratorial manipulation, and the larger an alleged conspiracy is

supposed to be, the greater is the tendency of believers to enter the Strange Loop of paranoid schizophrenia.

31 and 32, asserting that Darwinian evolutionary theory has been proven or disproven, I personally would classify as None Of The Above. I regard such assertions as propaganda in the Cold War between Darwinians and Creationists. The Darwinian theory has more or less stood up for over a hundred years, has flaws which most biologists now admit, and may need considerable revision in the near future, but remains, as Popper has often argued, not in the same ball park at all as the "laws" of sciences like mathematical physics. (Personally, I don't see any better biological model around than Darwin's, but considering the criticisms recently raised within biology I strongly suspect a better model will arrive shortly — and will probably be equally offensive to Creationists . . .)

33, "UFOs exist," seems to me the trickiest proposition on the list. I regard it as a simple empirical observation, as

"true" and/or "false" as any other sense impression. People are always seeing things in the sky that they can't identify; right now, it is fashionable to call such glitches "unidentified flying objects." But people also are forever seeing things on the ground that they can't identify; should we call them "unidentified terrestrial objects?"

This last example simply illustrates that when a feud lasts long enough, people lose track of what they are arguing about. "UFOs exist" does not assert the same thing as "Alien spaceships exist"; it is merely the heat of intellectual warfare that causes both sides to frequently lose sight of that simple distinction. It would be miraculous if no unidentified flying objects existed; that could only indicate a sudden evolutionary quantum jump in which human perception and reasoning both increased to near perfection. Personally, I often encounter unidentified objects in my own closet . . . and sometimes my wife doesn't know what they are or where they came from, either.

It is a wonderful convenience when we can reduce an argument to simple "true or false," without fudging the data or conveniently "forgetting" ambiguities and uncertainties. In such cases, Aristotelian-Boolean logic quickly solves the question. The main reason so many issues in science, philosophy, religion, and politics are still in dispute, however, is not that everybody is "unreasonable" except for you and your friends, but that, *at any given time*, most theories remain merely internally valid or phenomenologically indeterminate or meaningless, or are merely self-reflexive or are local Game Rules or contain paradox-and-paranoia-engendering Strange Loops. Or else, in many cases, we simply haven't yet collected enough data to settle the matter. ∎

The New Inquisition and Wilhelm Reich in Hell

*When I learned that **The New Inquisition** was a critique of the style of skepticism practiced by the Committee for the Scientific Investigation for Claims of the Paranormal, I didn't expect to like it very much. I've always had a soft spot for the underdog, and the CSICOP/skeptical point of view is grossly underrepresented in the popular literature of the paranormal. But I was wrong about this book. It's witty, contentious, and in its own way rigorously skeptical of everything, including the "Fundamentalist Materialism" of **some** (but not all) of the CSICOP-style skeptics. Wilson's obviously sympathetic to a whole range of fringe ideas, but he's careful to maintain a healthy skepticism about these as well.*

*The most appealing thing about **The New Inquisition** is that, except for the first chapter, it's written in a perfect imitation of Charles Fort's quirky style (see p. 81). This makes it a particular delight for Forteans, all the more so because Wilson drags in a grab-bag of weird facts and fringe theories in order to illustrate the relativism of our assumptions about reality.*

***Wilhelm Reich in Hell**, a play that's been performed at the Edmund Burke Theatre in Dublin, Ireland, is a simultaneously hilarious and poignant example of Wilson's fiction writing. The setting is an absurdist Hell, and the characters include Reich (the scientist whose books were burned in the '50s), Satan, the Marquis de Sade (as a clown), Baron von Sa-*

cher-Masoch (also a clown), Marilyn Monroe, Ouspensky, "Abbyjerry Hoffrubin," Playboy bunnies, a punk-rock American Medical Association, and Calley Eichmann, a cabbage. — T.S.

• I live in Ireland, a country where the majority of the population, according to a recent poll, believes that Jesus Christ was conceived parthogenetically and rose from the dead after being buried. They do not bump into walls, and they drive their cars about as well as Londoners or New Yorkers, and they do not seem particularly mad to me. Their reality-tunnel seems to work well enough, most of the time—as most reality tunnels seem to work tolerably well, most of the time.

It seems to me that existence—at this point I have doubts about "the" "universe"—is a lot like a Rorschach ink-blot. Everybody looks at it and sees their own favorite reality-tunnel.
—*The New Inquisition*

The New Inquisition
Irrational Rationalism and the Citadel of Science
Robert Anton Wilson
1986; 240 pp.
$9.95
($10.95 postpaid)

Wilhelm Reich in Hell
Robert Anton Wilson
1987; 165 pp.
$9.95
($10.95 postpaid)

Both from:
Falcon Press
1605 E. Charleston Blvd., Suite 147
Las Vegas, NV 89104
800/545-3266

"There were these Japanese scientists in the '50s who left potatoes out every day for these wild monkeys on Koshima Island and then watched what they did.

One of these monkeys learned to wash the potatoes and began teaching this to the others. Then, when a certain number had learned, maybe a hundred —scientists call this a 'critical mass'—an amazing thing happened. Suddenly, all the monkeys knew how to wash potatoes, even monkeys on other islands hundreds of miles away! Scientists consider this to be conclusive proof of a telepathic 'group mind'. **"**

You've probably heard the story. It's been repeated in scores of books and magazine articles— even a movie. Most people seem to regard it as "just another amazing scientific fact," even though the story implies that telepathy in monkeys has been accepted by science since the 1950s—a staggering assertion. In fact, the "Hundredth Monkey" story was first told by a writer on paranormal subjects named Lyall Watson in his 1979 book, *Lifetide*. But the popularity of the tale is due largely to Ken Keyes, Jr., a human-potential guru whose 1982 book *The Hundredth Monkey* has been through ten printings and sold over a million copies.

The odd and discouraging feature of the many published retellings of Watson's paranormal tale is that not one of the writers bothers to ask "Did this story really happen?"—probably the first question to cross most people's minds upon hearing it. The first published skeptical evaluation of this modern myth was written by psychologist Maureen O'Hara, who criticized the story in the July 1983 *Association of Humanistic Psychology Newsletter* and again in the Winter 1985 *Journal of Humanistic Psychology*. The response from many of her colleagues was one of hostility. They regarded her concern for objective truth as petty; their counterreplies paraphrased the New Age axiom "if it feels good, it must be true."

We've chosen to give the Hundredth Monkey story a thorough scrutiny, not only because it is extremely widespread in human potential, New Age, and even nuclear freeze circles (Keyes' book is primarily a proposal for using Hundredth Monkey-style telepathic consciousness to prevent nuclear war), but also because it represents the tip of an iceberg of growing confusion between speculation and proven fact, prevalent, as we shall see, even in scholarly circles. This confusion is often deliberately reinforced by writers and public figures whose motivation is to push a particular theory or belief system, and by publishers who have found that representing sensationalistic claims as science sells books and magazines.

We begin with Ron Amundson's definitive answer to the question, "Did the Hundredth Monkey phenomenon really happen?"—followed by a response from the inventor of the story himself, Lyall Watson. Then Maureen O'Hara, the psychologist who first questioned the story, presents her analysis of the current trend toward pseudoscience and superstition in the humanistic community. By combining the testimony of these three expert witnesses, we can begin to construct a composite portrait of this literally mythic beast that has become one of the most enthusiastically received symbols of the New Age. —*T.S.*

The books that started it all: Lyall Watson's Lifetide *(1979) and Ken Keyes'* The Hundredth Monkey *(1982). The latter has been through ten printings and sold over a million copies.*

THE HUNDREDTH MONKEY DEBUNKED

by Ron Amundson
Illustrated by Norman Dog

CLAIMS OF THE PARANORMAL are supported in many ways. Personal reports ("I was kidnapped by extraterrestrials"), appeals to puzzling everyday experiences ("Did you ever get a phone call from someone you had just dreamed about?"), and references to "ancient wisdom" are a few. Citations of actual scientific results are usually limited to ESP experiments and a few attempts to mystify further the already bizarre discoveries of modern physics. But the New Age is upon us (we're told) and New Age authors like Rupert Sheldrake (*A New Science of Life*) and Lyall Watson *(Lifetide)* support their new visions of reality with scientific documentation. Sheldrake has a bibliography of about 200 listings, and Watson lists exactly 600 sources. The sources cited are mostly respectable academic and scientific publications. The days of "[unnamed] scientists say" and "Fred Jones, while walking alone in the woods one day . . ." are gone. Or are they?

I teach college courses in epistemology, in the philosophy of science, and in pseudoscience and the occult. Students in these courses naturally bring to class examples of remarkable and paranormal claims. During the past few years, one such claim has become especially popular: the "Hundredth Monkey Phenomenon." This phenomenon was baptized by Lyall Watson, who documents the case with references to five highly respectable articles by Japanese primatologists Kinji Imanishi, Masao Kawai, Syunzo Kawamura, and Atsuo Tsumori. Watson's discussion of this phenomenon covers less than two pages. (Except where noted, all references to Watson are to pages 147 and 148 of *Lifetide.)* But this brief report has inspired much attention. Following Watson, a book by Ken Keyes, an article in *The Brain/Mind Bulletin,* and a film by Elda Hartley have each been created with the title "The Hundredth Monkey." In addition, we find an article entitled "The 'Hundredth Monkey' and Humanity's Quest for Survival" in the *Phoenix Journal of Transpersonal Anthropology,* and an article called "The Quantum Monkey" in *Science Digest.* Each relies on Watson as the sole source of information on the remarkable and supernatural behavior of primates.

The monkeys referred to are indeed remarkable. They are Japanese macaques (*Macaca fuscata),* which live in wild troops on several islands in Japan. They have been under observation for years. During 1952 and 1953 the primatologists began "provisioning" the troops — providing

---

Ron Amundson is a professor of philosophy at the University of Hawaii at Hilo, where he specializes in the philosophy of science. He spent the 1985-86 academic year on sabbatical at Stephen Jay Gould's laboratory in the Museum of Comparative Zoology at Harvard, studying the historical influence of the theory of evolution on the development of experimental psychology. Intrigued by the extraordinary implications of the Hundredth Monkey story, he decided to investigate for himself. The result is this article, which originally appeared in the Summer 1985 issue of the Skeptical Inquirer (see review, page 198).
—T.S.

Imo was a "monkey genius," Watson tells us, and potato washing is "comparable to the invention of the wheel."

them with such foods as sweet potatoes and wheat. This kept the monkeys from raiding farms and also made them easier to observe. The food was left in open areas, often on beaches. As a result of this new economy, the monkeys developed several innovative forms of behavior. One of these was invented in 1953 by an 18-month-old female that the observers named "Imo." Imo was a member of the troop on Koshima Island. She discovered that sand and grit could be removed from the sweet potatoes by washing them in a stream or in the ocean. Imo's playmates and her mother learned this trick from Imo, and it soon spread to other members of the troop. Unlike most food customs, this innovation was learned by older monkeys from younger ones. In most other matters, the children learn from their parents. The potato-washing habit spread gradually, according to Watson, up until 1958. But in the fall of 1958 a remarkable event occurred on Koshima. This event formed the basis of the "Hundredth Monkey Phenomenon."

The Miracle on Koshima

According to Watson, all of the juveniles on Koshima were washing their potatoes by early 1958, but the only adult washers were those who had learned from the children. In the fall of that year something astounding happened. The exact nature of the event is unclear. Watson says:

> One has to gather the rest of the story from personal anecdotes and bits of folklore among primate researchers, because most of them are still not quite sure what happened. And those who do suspect the truth are reluctant to publish it for fear of ridicule. So I am forced to improvise the details, but as near as I can tell, this is what seems to have happened. In the autumn of that year an unspecified number of monkeys on Koshima were washing sweet potatoes in the sea. . . . Let us say, for argument's sake, that the number was ninety-nine and that at eleven o'clock on a Tuesday morning, one further convert was added to the fold in the usual way. But the addition of the hundredth monkey apparently carried the number across some sort of threshold, pushing it

through a kind of critical mass, because by that evening almost everyone was doing it. Not only that, but the habit seems to have jumped natural barriers and to have appeared spontaneously, like glycerine crystals in sealed laboratory jars, in colonies on other islands and on the mainland in a troop at Takasakiyama.

A sort of group consciousness had developed among the monkeys, Watson tells us. It had developed suddenly, as a result of one last monkey's learning potato washing by conventional means. The sudden learning of the rest of the Koshima troop was not attributable to the normal one-monkey-at-a-time methods of previous years. The new phenomenon of group consciousness was responsible not only for the sudden learning on Koshima but for the equally sudden acquisition of the habit by monkeys across the sea. Watson admits that he was forced to "improvise" some of the details — the time of the day, the day of the week, and the exact number of monkeys required for the "critical mass" were not specified in the scientific literature. But by evening (or at least in a very short period of time) almost everyone (or at least a large number of the remaining monkeys) in the colony had suddenly acquired the custom. This is remarkable in part because of the slow and gradual mode of acquisition that had typified the first five years after Imo's innovation. Even more remarkable was the sudden jumping of natural boundaries, apparently caused by the Koshima miracle.

Documentation

To be sure, we must not expect too much from Lyall Watson's sources. Watson has warned us that the complete story was not told and that he was "forced to improvise the details." But we should expect to find some evidence of the mysteriousness of the Koshima events of 1958. In particular, we should expect to find evidence of an episode of sudden learning within the troop at this time (though perhaps not in one afternoon) and evidence of the sudden appearance of potato washing in other troops sometime soon after the Koshima event. We also have a negative expectation of the literature; it should *fail* to report certain important details. It will not (we expect) tell us the exact number of monkeys washing potatoes prior to or after the event of 1958, nor will it provide us with an explanation of how the post-event Koshima learners were able to acquire their knowledge. After all, it is Watson's claim that the event produced *paranormal* learning of potato washing. These three expectations will be tested against the literature. Was there a sudden event at Koshima? Did acquisition at other colonies follow closely the Koshima event? Does Watson

improvise details *only* when the cited literature fails to provide adequate information? The following comments will be restricted to the literature on macaques actually cited by Watson.

Almost all of the information about the Koshima troop appears in a journal article by Masao Kawai in 1965; the other articles are secondary on this topic. Kawai's article is remarkably detailed in its description of the Koshima events. The troop numbered 20 in 1952 and grew to 59 by 1962. (At least in the numerical sense, there was never a "hundredth monkey" on Koshima.) Watson states that "an unspecified number" of monkeys on Koshima had acquired the potato-washing habit by 1958. Actually this number was far from unspecified. Kawai's data allows the reader to determine the dates of acquisition of potato washing (and two other food behaviors), as well as the dates of birth and geneological relationships, *of every monkey in the Koshima troop from 1949 to 1962.* In March 1958, exactly 2 of 11 monkeys over seven years old had learned potato washing, while exactly 15 of 19 monkeys between two and seven had the habit. This amounts to 17 of 30 noninfant monkeys. There is no mention in this paper (or in any other) of a sudden learning event in the fall of 1958. However, it is noted that by 1962, 36 of the 49 monkeys had acquired the habit. So both the population and the number of potato washers had increased by 19 during this four-year period. Perhaps this is what suggested to Watson that a sudden event occurred in the fall of 1958. And perhaps (since one can only surmise) this idea was reinforced in Watson's mind by the following statement by Kawai: "The acquisition of [potato washing] behavior can be divided into two periods; before and after 1958."

So Kawai does not give a time of year, a day of the week, or even the season for any sudden event in 1958. But he does at least identify the year. And is Kawai mystified about the difference between pre- and post-1958 acquisition? Is he "not quite sure what happened?" Is he reluctant to publish details "for fear of ridicule?" No, he publishes the whole story, in gothic detail. The post-1958 learning period was remarkable only for its normalcy. The period from 1953 to 1958 had been a period of exciting innovation. The troop encountered new food sources, and the juveniles invented ways of dealing with these sources. But by 1958, the innovative youth had become status quo adults; macaques mature faster than humans. The unusual juvenile-to-adult teaching methods reverted to the more traditional process of learning one's food manners at one's mother's knee. Imo's first child, a male named

According to Watson, a sort of group consciousness had developed among the monkeys.

"Ika," was born in 1957. Imo and her former playmates brought up their children as good little potato-washers. One can only hope that Ika has been less trouble to his Mom than Imo was to hers. Kawai speaks of the innovative period from 1953 to 1958 as "individual propagation" and the period after 1958 as "precultural propagation." (This latter term does not indicate anything unusual for the monkey troops. The troops under normal circumstances have behavioral idiosyncrasies and customs that are passed along within the group by "pre-cultural" means. The expression only indicates a reluctance to refer to monkey behavior as genuinely "cultural.")

So there was nothing left unsaid in Kawai's description. There was nothing mysterious, or even sudden, in the events of 1958. Nineteen fifty-eight and 1959 were the years of maturation of a group of innovative youngsters. The human hippies of the 1960s now know that feeling. In fact 1958 was a singularly poor year for habit acquisition on Koshima. Only two monkeys learned to wash potatoes during that year, young females named Zabon and Nogi. An average of three a year had learned potato washing during the previous five years. There is no evidence that Zabon and Nogi were psychic or in any other way unusual.

Let us try to take Watson seriously for a moment longer. Since only two monkeys learned potato washing during 1958 (according to Watson's own citation), one of them must have been the "Hundredth Monkey." Watson leaves "unspecified" which monkey it was, so I am "forced to improvise" and "say, for argument's sake" that it was Zabon. This means that poor little Nogi carries the grim metaphysical burden of being the "almost everyone in the colony" who, according to Watson, suddenly and miraculously began to wash her potatoes on that autumn afternoon.

Watson claims that the potato-washing habit "spontaneously" leaped natural barriers. Is there evidence of this? Well, Japanese primatologists Masao Kawai and Atsuo Tsumori

177

report that the behavior was observed off Koshima, in at least five different colonies. Their reports specifically state that the behavior was observed only among a few individual monkeys and that it had not spread throughout a colony. There is no report of when these behaviors occurred. They must have been observed sometime between 1953 and 1967. But there is nothing to indicate that they followed closely upon some supposed miraculous event on Koshima during the autumn of 1958, or that they were in any other way remarkable. In fact there is absolutely no reason to believe in the 1958 miracle on Koshima. There is every reason to deny it. Watson's description of the event is refuted *in great detail* by the very sources he cites to validate it. In contrast to Watson's claims of a sudden and inexplicable event, "Such behavior patterns seem to be smoothly transmitted among individuals in the troop and handed down to the next generation," according to Tsumori.

Methodology of Pseudoscience

The factual issue ends here. Watson's claim of a "Hundredth Monkey Phenomenon" is conclusively refuted by the very sources he cites in its support. He either failed to read or misreported the information in these scientific articles. But Watson's own mode of reasoning and reporting, as well as the responses he has inspired in the popular literature, deserve attention. They exemplify the pseudoscientific tradition. Consider the following:

1. Hidden sources of information: Watson informs us that the scientific reports leave important data "unspecified." This is simply false. But, more subtly, he tells us that most of the researchers are still unsure of what happened and that those who "do suspect the truth are reluctant to publish it for fear of ridicule." In one fell swoop Watson brands himself as courageous, explains why no one else has dared report this miraculous phenomenon, and dis-

courages us from checking the cited literature for corroboration. Watson got the real story from "personal anecdotes and bits of folklore among primate researchers." Those of us who don't hobnob with such folks must trust Watson. The technique was effective. Of the commentaries I have found on the Hundredth Monkey Phenomenon, not one shows evidence of having consulted the scientific sources cited by Watson. Nonetheless, each presents Watson's fantasy as a scientifically authenticated fact. Nor is additional information available from Watson. I have written both to Watson and to his publishers requesting such information and have received no reply.

2. Aversion to naturalistic explanations: The fact is that potato washing was observed on different islands. Watson infers that it had traveled in some paranormal way from one location to another. Like other aficionados of the paranormal, Watson ignores two plausible explanations of the concurrence of potato washing. First, it could well have been an independent innovation — different monkeys inventing the same solution to a common problem. This process is anathema to the pseudoscientist. The natives of the Americas simply *could not have* invented the pyramid independently of the Egyptians — they just didn't have the smarts. In more extreme cases (Erich von Daniken, for example) a *human being* is just too dumb to invent certain clever things — extraterrestrials must have done it.

Watson assumes that Imo was the only monkey capable of recognizing the usefulness of washing potatoes. In his words, Imo was "a monkey genius" and potato washing is "comparable almost to the invention of the wheel." Monkeys on other islands were too dumb for this sort of innovation. But keep in mind that these monkeys didn't even *have* potatoes to wash before 1952 or 1953, when provisioning began. Monkeys in at least five locations had learned potato washing by 1962. This suggests

From Keyes one gets the image of spontaneous mass orgies of spud-dunking.

to me that these monkeys are clever creatures. It suggests to Watson that *one* monkey was clever and that the paranormal took care of the rest. A second neglected explanation is natural diffusion. And indeed Kawai reports that in 1960 a potato washer named "Jugo" swam from Koshima to the island on which the Takasakiyama troop lives. Jugo returned in 1964. Watson does not mention this. The Japanese monkeys are known to be both clever and mobile, and either characteristic might explain the interisland spread of potato washing. Watson ignores both explanations, preferring to invent a new paranormal power.

3. Inflation of the miracle: As myths get passed along, everyone puffs them up a bit. The following two examples come from second-generation commentaries that quote extensively from Watson. Nevertheless, even Watson's claims are beginning to bulge. First, the primatologists' reports had mentioned that only a few isolated cases of off-Koshima potato washing were observed. Watson reports this as the habit's having "appeared spontaneously . . . in colonies on other islands." Not actually false, since the few individuals were indeed *in* other colonies (though only individuals and not whole colonies adopted the behavior). Following Watson, Ken Keyes reports that, after the hundredth Koshima monkey, "colonies of monkeys on other islands . . . began washing their sweet potatoes!" From Keyes, one gets the image of spontaneous mass orgies of spud dunking. A second example: Regarding the primatologists' attitudes toward the events of 1958, Watson reports only that they are "still not quite sure what happened." But the primatological confusion quickly grows, for *Science Digest* reports "a mystery which has stumped scientists for nearly a quarter of a century." In these two particular cases, Watson's own statements are at least modest. They're not what one would call accurate, but not exorbitantly false either. By the second generation, we find that "not quite sure what happened" becomes

"stumped for nearly a quarter of a century," and the habit that *appeared in* individuals within colonies of monkeys becomes a habit *of* colonies of monkeys. Please keep in mind that the second generation relies *only* on Watson for its information; even Watson's none-too-accurate report has been distorted — and not, needless to say, in the direction of accuracy.

4. The paranormal validates the paranormal: The validity of one supernatural report is strengthened by its consistency with other such reports. Watson's commentators show how this works. Keyes supports the Hundredth Monkey Phenomenon by its consistency with J. B. Rhine's work at Duke, which "demonstrated" telepathy between individual humans. "We now know that the strength of this extrasensory communication can be amplified to a powerfully effective level when the consciousness of the 'hundredth person' is added." Elda Hartley's film *The Hundredth Monkey* invokes Edgar Cayce. And in a remarkable feat of group consciousness, *four of the five* secondary sources emphasize the similarities between Watson's Hundredth Monkey Phenomenon and Rupert Sheldrake's notion of the "morphogenetic field" (a mysterious patterning field generated by a natural system that organizes subsequent, similar systems). The spontaneous recognition of the similarities between Watson and Sheldrake seems to have leaped the natural boundaries between the four publications! Now *there's* a miracle! (Surely independent invention or natural diffusion couldn't account for such a coincidence.)

Conclusions

I must admit sympathy for some of the secondary sources on the Hundredth Monkey Phenomenon. This feeling comes from the purpose for which the phenomenon was cited. Ken Keyes' book uses the phenomenon as a theme, but the real topic of the book is nuclear disarmament. Arthur Stein's article in the

We can only hope that Santa Claus and the Hundredth Monkey are not our best chances to avoid nuclear war.

Phoenix Journal of Transpersonal Anthropology and (to a lesser extent) the Hartley film are inspired by Keyes' hope that the Hundredth Monkey Phenomenon may help prevent nuclear war. The message is that "you may be the Hundredth Monkey" whose contribution to the collective consciousness turns the world away from nuclear holocaust. It is hard to find fault in this motive. For these very same reasons, one couldn't fault the motives of a child who wrote to Santa Claus requesting world nuclear disarmament as a Christmas present. We can only hope that Santa Claus and the Hundredth Monkey are not our best chances to avoid nuclear war.

Watson's primary concern is not prevention of war but sheer love of the paranormal. His book begins with a description of a child who, before Watson's own eyes, and with a "short implosive sound, very soft, like a cork being drawn in the dark," psychically turned a tennis ball inside out — fuzz side in, rubber side out — without losing air pressure. Just after the Hundredth Monkey discussion, Watson makes a revealing point. He quotes with approval a statement attributed to Lawrence Blair: "When a myth is shared by large numbers of people, it becomes a reality." This sort of relativist epistemology is not unusual in New Age thought. I would express Blair's thought somewhat differently: "Convince enough people of a lie, and it becomes the truth." I suggest that someone who accepts this view of truth is not to be trusted as a source of knowledge. He may, of course, be a marvelous source of fantasy, rumor, and pseudoscientific best-sellers.

I prefer epistemological realism to this sort of relativism. Truth is not dependent on the numbers of believers or on the frequency of published repetition. My preferred epistemology can be expressed simply: Facts are facts. There is no Hundredth Monkey Phenomenon. ■

Lyall Watson Responds...

I find the cavils of self-appointed committees for the supression of curiosity very tedious.

And I am deeply suspicious of those who feel the need to set themselves up as defenders of the scientific faith.

But I have to say that I admire Ron Amundson. His analysis of the Hundredth Monkey Phenomenon is lucid, amusing and refreshingly free of the emotional dismissals that characterize much of the usual output of the Committee for the Scientific Investigation of Claims of the Paranormal.

Lyall Watson, the originator of the Hundredth Monkey story, is a hard man to track down. As I worked to locate him so that he could respond to Ron Amundson's critique, I became increasingly intrigued by what I learned secondhand of this mysterious and elusive character. Aside from authoring a series of best-selling books on the occult and the paranormal (Supernature, Lifetide, Gifts of Unknown Things), *he is also a BBC television producer, an inveterate world traveler, the Seychelles representative to the International Whaling Commission (where he is an influential campaigner against commercial whaling), and the author of the definitive* Sea Guide to Whales of the World, *a book based on his ten years of cetacean study aboard the* MS Lindblad Explorer. *He holds degrees in anthropology, ethology, and marine biology. His newest books are* Dreams of Dragons *and* The Water Planet. *Clearly, Watson is not your typical occult theory-monger. Needless to say, I finally got hold of Lyall Watson, and found him quite happy to respond to Amundson's analysis of his monkey tale. As he put it, "I enjoyed Amundson's argument and I have tried to reply in similar good humor."*
—*T.S.*

I accept Amundson's analysis of the origin and evolution of the Hundredth Monkey without reservation. It is a metaphor of my own making, based — as he rightly suggests — on very slim evidence and a great deal of hearsay. I have never pretended otherwise.

I take issue, however, with his conclusion that, therefore, the Hundredth Monkey Phenomenon cannot exist.

It might have come to be called the Hundredth Cockroach or Hairy Nosed Wombat Phenomenon if my travels had taken me in a different direction. As it happened, I was already interested in the nonlinear manner in which ideas and fashions travel through our culture, and the notion of quantum leaps in consciousness (a sort of punctuated equilibrium of the mind) was taking shape in my own mind when I arrived in Japan. It was off-the-record conversations with those familiar with the potato-washing work that led me to choose a monkey as the vehicle for my metaphor. And I still contend that there is more to those studies than meets the eye or reaches Hawaii in scientific journals.

I based none of my conclusions on the five sources Amundson uses to refute me. I was careful to describe the evidence for the phenomenon as strictly anecdotal and included citations in *Lifetide*, not to validate anything, but in accordance with my usual practice of providing tools, of giving access to useful background information.

I freely acknowledge a tendency to get excited by ideas, sometimes without good and sufficient reason, but I remain convinced that there is something like the Hundredth Monkey Phenomenon in action in nature, even if it remains unproven on Koshima. There seem to me to be mechanisms in evolution other than those governed by traditional natural selection, and a growing need to identify and describe such processes. The Hundredth Monkey is my way of drawing attention to the possibility of critical mass in social behaviour and of stimulating discussion about it. And Amundson is living proof that I have succeeded in doing so, even if he persists in criticising an idea on grounds that were never offered in its defence.

Amundson concludes that there can be no Hundredth Monkey Phenomenon. "Facts are facts," he says, hoisting the banner of epistemological realism over a collection carefully selected to prove his point. "The factual issue ends here."

But does it?

Science, as Ron Amundson well knows, decides what is possible by reference to its definition of reality. Anything that fits the definition is acceptable. Anything that doesn't fit is impossible and must be rejected. And the problem here is that the concept of collective consciousness in any form stands in direct confrontation to the current definition. So the issue, when it ever reaches open debate, is reduced to a choice between rival facts. The normal versus the paranormal. Science versus what Amundson relishes in describing as pseudoscience. And of course, science always wins — even if it has to go through extraordinary contortions to do so.

What is usually ignored in such discussion is the point that the scientific definition of reality is a theory, not a fact. We don't know exactly how things work. All we have is a reasonably good hypothesis. There is no need to force a choice between rival sets of facts. The debate concerns discordant information or ideas and their relationship to a theory of how things happen. All that is at stake is the validity of a working hypothesis. And all that is necessary to reconcile the new notion with the old theory is an admission that the theory might be incomplete — that information might be communicated other than through the accepted channels. There is no assault on the laws of nature or the principles of science, and no need for protectors of the scientific faith or charges of heresy.

The Hundredth Monkey Phenomenon is a plea for a broader definition of reality. One that includes the possibility of certain things happening when minds, perhaps even relatively simple ones, are involved. It is, and remains, an admission that being alive is being a part of something very much larger — a global ecology of mind in which even Japanese macaques are small, albeit well-washed, potatoes.

—Lyall Watson

OF MYTHS & MONKEYS

A CRITICAL LOOK AT CRITICAL MASS

by Maureen O'Hara
Illustrated by Kathleen O'Neill

THE HUNDREDTH MONKEY provides us with a case study through which to examine the deterioration in the quality of thought and scholarship among those people who participate in what has become known as the "New Age" or "human potential" community. I believe that this deterioration may ultimately result (if it has not already) in discrediting humanistic science altogether, leaving us with nothing more than faddism and a rag-bag of pseudoreligious and pseudoscientific superstition. Because I believe that a humanistic view of persons and their communities has never been more necessary in order to counterbalance the galloping alienation in human life, I view this trend toward superstition with real alarm.

Lyall Watson does not tell us the monkey tale in his book *Lifetide* because he is interested in studies of behavior propagation in macaques — he is merely using the story to support his conviction about human consciousness, that when a certain "critical mass" of people believe in something, suddenly the idea becomes true for everyone. There can be no doubt that ideas and attitudes can spread rapidly through a community from time to time. Evidence of this exists everywhere. Perhaps this monkey story and the rapidity with which it passed from pseudoscientific speculation, through dubious editing, word of mouth transmission by superstars in the human potential movement, into popular New-Age superstition, makes a far better case study of the very phenomenon that the monkey research putatively demonstrates.

Inspired in the 1960s by the works of Abraham Maslow, Carl Rogers, Gregory Bateson, and others, Maureen O'Hara cut short a career in biology and became a humanistic psychologist in order to participate in "the creation of a precise humanistic science" with the goal of "a humane global collective, composed of free, responsible, rational people capable of purposeful action, critical thought, creativity, and individual conscience." Today she is alarmed by the way her profession, intertwined as it is with the human potential and New Age communities, has embraced the trappings of pseudoscience and become prone to accept and amplify "bad myths," of which the Hundredth Monkey story is only one example. As a specialist in mass psychology and cross-cultural phenomena, she is particularly qualified to comment on the "critical mass" concept idealized in the Hundredth Monkey myth, and to provide us with an insider's view of the reasons behind the rise of superstition in humanistic science.

—Ted Schultz

stead a monolithic ideology in which what is true for a "critical mass" of people becomes true for *everyone*? The idea gives me the willies.

PSEUDOSCIENCE, SCIENCE, AND AMBIVALENCE

How could such a profoundly nonhumanistic idea become so popular among people who consider themselves the harbingers of a "New Age"? I think the answer lies, at least in part, in the renewed infatuation with science and its shadow, pseudoscience. In the past ten years or so, we have seen the image of nuclear physicists shift from Dr. Strangelove-like creators of the most terrifying death devices in history to their present status as darlings of the so-called "new paradigm" consciousness. When we saw the physicists as on "their side," we rejected everything they did. Now that they are on "our side," we quote them at breakfast. Books like Fritjof Capra's *The Tao of Physics* have the New Age community convinced that physics is just some kind of Taoism with numbers.

This new infatuation with science is a shallow one, easily swayed by tricks of the pseudoscience trade such as theorizing wildly in scientific-sounding language, sprinkling speculative discussion with isolated fragments of real data regardless of relevance, confusing analogy with homology, breaking conventional rules of evidence at will, and extrapolating from one level of reality into others wherein different principles operate.

I do not wish to imply that pseudoscience necessarily stems from a conscious effort to deceive. More often than not, crossing the line from science to pseudoscience comes from ignorance and inexperience, and the popularity of pseudoscience is with an audience equally ignorant and inexperienced. Because this audience is not equipped to evaluate claims of scientific validity, they instead accept them on faith.

One standard trick of the pseudoscience trade, for example, is to emphasize whatever affiliations to established science the writers have or had. It is to great advantage if the writer can be referred to as a scientist associated with a prestigious university with a wide reputation for scientific excellence. It matters not to the purveyors of pseudoscience whether or not the "scientists" referred to have been in a lab for years, or if, when they were, it was in a field even remotely relevant to the subject at hand.

An August 1981 *Brain/Mind Bulletin* account of the Hundredth Monkey story refers to Lyall Watson as a biologist: the monkey story follows. The bibliography of Watson's book contains not one reference to any scientific research, biological or otherwise, that he has published, yet his other books, on the occult, are listed. It is not difficult

This process is widely known and effectively manipulated by those wishing to influence large numbers of people. Hitler was terrifyingly successful in convincing an entire people (at least a critical mass) of the reasonableness of his "final solution." Teenage culture in our own country offers nonstop demonstration of new fads that emerge, spread through the group to become a critical mass, and disappear, all in a matter of weeks. Madison Avenue advertisers pay high salaries to those psychologists who become adept at manipulating the mass psyche to form critical mass, as do the Defense Department and politicians running for office. The means by which critical mass is achieved, however, is not in any way mysterious. It is a matter of telecommunications, not telepathy.

There are major contradictions in the present idealization of critical mass — seen not only in the Hundredth Monkey story, but in the ideologies of such organizations as est, Bhagwan Rajneesh, and the "Aquarian conspirators." In promoting the idea that, although our ideas are shared by only an enlightened few (for the time being), if we really believe them, in some magical way what we hold to be true becomes true for everyone, proponents of the critical mass ideal ignore the principles of both humanism and democratic open society. The basis for openness in our kind of society is the belief that, for good or ill, each of us holds his or her own beliefs as a responsible participant in a pluralistic culture. Are we really willing to give up on this ideal and promote in-

183

to imagine a rather different response from the reader if *Brain/Mind Bulletin* had introduced the monkey story by referring to Watson as a writer on the occult.

Another example of "authority transfer" can be found in Tom Cooper's review of the film, *The Hundredth Monkey*, which appeared in the May 1983 issue of the *Association for Humanistic Psychology Newsletter*. In asserting that the Hundredth Monkey thesis is "substantiated" he says, "Rupert Sheldrake, the Cambridge scientist, reports that when one group of rats was taught . . ." The implication here is clear and misleading. The statement conveys the impression that Sheldrake (a) is currently on the faculty at Cambridge; (b) does scientific research there; (c) knows a lot about rats; (d) is "reporting" on his own research.

If we look at Sheldrake's own book, *A New Science of Life*, we find that he was once a scholar at a Cambridge College, and is described as currently a consultant at an international research institute in India. His research is on the physiology of tropical plants. Again, the impact would be very different if Cooper had written, "Rupert Sheldrake, tropical plant physiologist in an Indian crop research center, says that when one group of rats . . ." This kind of "credentialeering" is obviously intended to give credibility to scientific-sounding propositions. Such authority-borrowing works because institutions such as Cambridge University and disciplines such as biology have, despite occasional, widely publicized aberrations, lived up to their reputations for reliability.

Another characteristic of pseudoscience is its profound ambivalence toward the scientific establishment. Despite his identification as a biologist, Watson's work carries within it clear evidence of his ambivalence. On one hand, he uses research findings to try to support his conviction about critical mass theory in human

events. On the other hand, he suggests that the scientific community is less than honest when he tells us that these same researchers were reluctant to publish what they suspected was the truth. He panders to the popular distrust of science by suggesting that this reluctance was due to fear of ridicule by, one assumes, the scientific community.

Those who engage in pseudoscience want it both ways. They want the authority of science but are unwilling to abide by the rules by which the scientific community earned its authority in the first place. Pseudoscientists and their publishers may actually use criticism of their ideas by the scientific community as evidence that they are important because they are controversial. They seem to reason that because Einstein was controversial, anyone who is controversial must be an Einstein. On the jacket of the U.S. paperback edition of Sheldrake's *A New Science of Life* is the proud claim that the British scientific journal *Nature* had suggested that the book was "the best candidate for burning there has been for many years." As the designers of trade-book jackets are well aware, such outbursts by the scientific establishment only enhance a work's attractiveness to a generation of lay people fed up with the excesses of "more orthodox than thou" attitudes of the scientific establishment.

This ambivalence toward establishment science strikes an immediate and comforting chord in the minds of a public that is not only ambivalent about science, but largely ignorant. It is difficult for the uninitiated to distinguish between good science, bad science, and pseudoscience. Appraisal becomes especially difficult when isolated pieces of scientific knowledge are abstracted from their contexts within the broad, interwoven fabric of scientific thought. It is context that makes knowledge out of data. This is true not only for sciences, but for all areas of advanced knowledge such as

184

Pseudoscientists want the authority of science but are unwilling to abide by the rules by which the scientific community earned its authority in the first place.

art, zen, medicine, psychotherapy, and so on. This makes a book like Capra's *Tao of Physics* almost impossible to evaluate adequately. Those adept at physics don't understand orientalism; those well versed in Taoist philosophy can say little about the physics. The people who swallow Capra's speculations usually can critique neither. If they like what they read, they accept it as fact.

One concrete consequence of this ubiquitous ambivalence toward science can be seen in the rejection of training in science and logical thinking by some would-be humanistic psychologists and other aspiring agents of change. Without such training these people, regardless of their heart-felt commitment to transformation, have practically no basis on which to evaluate claims made in the name of science. Anyone — crackpot, charlatan, genius, or sage — must be dealt with in the same way (believed or disbelieved) solely on the basis of personal opinion. Personal opinion then becomes equated with knowledge and can be asserted without embarrassment.

The result is that the human potential movement has come dangerously close to creating the conditions for the establishment of yet another orthodoxy resting on unproved articles of faith and taken-for-granted definitions, axioms, and concepts. Humanistic science loses ground each time it hands over authority to pseudoscientists and speculative myth builders.

GOOD MYTHS AND BAD MYTHS

On two occasions (both gatherings of humanistic psychologists) when the monkey story was told, I tried to raise some of the issues raised here. When I suggested that the Hundredth Monkey story lay in the realm of mythic thought, not scientific, the response was the same; the speakers were unimpressed. "Myths are as true as science," was the response. "It's a metaphor" was another. P.B. Walsh's comment in the November 1983 *Association for Humanistic Psychology Newsletter* was characteristic: "Science or myth, the Hundredth Monkey is a metaphor that exactly fits . . ." and, later, "As metaphor it speaks to our empowerment."

As to the assertion that myths are as true as science, I take the point. But there is more that has to be said, for although they might both be "true," they are not true in the same way. These respondents either do not know this or do not think it matters much. But, of course, it matters a great deal and I believe that it is urgent that we learn to recognize the difference. Casually interchanging myth, science, and metaphor robs each of these realms of its unique power to deepen our understanding of the world, to orient our science, and to inform our actions. Women and ethnic minorities well know the consequences of wrapping a myth together with science. It is especially pernicious, as any Nazi holocaust survivor can confirm, when a bad myth is wrapped up with bad science.

My objection to the Hundredth Monkey Phenomenon, then, is not that it is myth, but that it is bad myth, and that it draws its force not from the collective imagination, but by masquerading as science. It leads us (as I have tried to show) in the direction of propaganda, manipulation, totalitarianism, and a worldview dominated by the powerful and persuasive — in other words, business as usual.

Perhaps the best use for this myth has already been found by the publishers of the *New Age Journal*. After giving me in their mass mailing a streamlined and even more anthropomorphized version of the monkey story, after flattering me with the thought that I am a person with a more advanced consciousness, after telling me that "test after test" by "behavioral scientists" has shown "conclusively that when a critical number of learners reach a new awareness, this new awareness may be spontaneously communicated from mind to mind," they tell me that now is the time to get a good deal on their magazine. So sure of their ground are they, they conclude, "There's no doubt about it. (I am their) Hundredth Monkey."

When I was first drawn into humanistic science, I was well aware that I was attracted to its myth. I knew of very little actual "data" that could support a belief in the possibility of a humane global collective, composed of free, responsible, rational people capable of purposeful action, critical thought, creativitiy, and individual conscience. Of course I knew this to be an idealized myth standing in sharp contrast to the indignities that are the actual daily experience of all but a privileged few. Even so, I think it is a good myth and has the psychological power to mobilize us and to orient our search for knowledge about ourselves. ☛

185

> ## Casually interchanging myth, science, and metaphor robs each of these realms of its unique power to deepen our understanding of the world.

Over the past 15 years, this myth has guided my studies and those of my colleagues (and at times has required acts of faith as great as any religion would demand) as we have tried to discover, as all science does, if this mythic possible world could, in fact, be an actual world; and if not, why not? So far we have discovered little that, in my judgment, gives much grounds for the current New Age optimism that the transformation is just around the corner. It is a testimony to the sustaining power of the humanistic myth that we did not give up our research long ago and open a restaurant.

In contrast, I most emphatically cannot agree that the "Hundredth Monkey myth empowers." In fact, I believe it to be a betrayal of the whole idea of human empowerment. In this myth the individual as a responsible agent disappears; what empowers is no longer the moral force of one's beliefs, not their empirical status, rather, it is the number of people who share them. Once the magic number is reached curiosity, science, art, criticism, doubt and all other such activities subversive of the common consensus become unnecessary or even worse. Individuals no longer have any obligation to develop their own worldview within such a collective — it will come to them ready-made from those around. Nor are we called on to develop our arguments and articulate them for, by magic, those around us will catch them anyway. This is not a transformational myth impelling us toward the fullest development of our capacities, but one that reduces us instead to quite literally nothing more than a mindless herd at the mercy of the "Great Communicators." The myth of the Hundredth Monkey Phenomenon is more chillingly Orwellian than Aquarian. ∎

THE HUNDREDTH MONKEY: A SELECTED BIBLIOGRAPHY

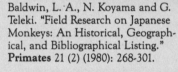

Baldwin, L. A., N. Koyama and G. Teleki. "Field Research on Japanese Monkeys: An Historical, Geographical, and Bibliographical Listing." **Primates** 21 (2) (1980): 268-301.

Brain/Mind Bulletin (August 1981). (Available from Brain/Mind Bulletin, Box 42211, Los Angeles, CA 90042).

Brain/Mind Bulletin. "The Hundredth Monkey." In Updated Special Issue: "A New Science of Life" (1982).

Cooper, T. "The Hundredth Monkey by Elda Hartley: Film Review." **Association for Humanistic Psychology Newsletter** (May 1983).

Eaton, G. "Snowball Construction by a Feral Troop of Japanese Macaques (*Macaca fuscata*) Living Under Seminatural Conditions." **Primates** 13(4) (1972): 411-414.

Flasher, B. Letter to the editor. **Association for Humanistic Psychology Newsletter** (November 1983).

Hartley, Elda (producer). **The Hundredth Monkey** (film and videotape). Hartley Film Foundation, Inc. Cos Cob, Connecticut.

Hiraiwa, M. "Pebble-Collecting Behavior by Juvenile Japanese Monkeys." **Monkey** 195-6 (1975): 24-25. (In Japanese.)

Huffman, M. A. "Stone-Play of *Macaca fuscata* in Arashiyama B Troop: Transmission of a Nonadaptive Behavior." **J. of Human Evolution** 13: (1984) 725-735.

Imanishi, Kinji. "Social Behavior in Japanese Monkeys." In **Primate Social Behavior.** Charles A. Southwick, Ed. Toronto: Van Nostrand, 1983.

Itani, J. and A. Nishimura. "The Study of Infrahuman Culture in Japan: A Review." In **Precultural Primate Behavior** (pp. 26-50). E. W. Menzel, Ed. Basel: Karger.

Kawai, M. "On the Newly Acquired Behavior of the Natural Troop of Japanese Monkeys on Koshima Island." **Primates** 5 (1962): 3-4.

Kawai, M. "Newly Acquired Pre-Cultural Behavior of the Natural Troop of Japanese Monkeys on Koshima Islet." **Primates** 6 (1962): 1-31.

Kawamura, S. "The Process of Sub-Cultural Propagation Among Japanese Monkeys." In **Primate Social Behavior** (pp. 82-99). Charles H. Southwick, Ed. Princeton, NJ: Van Nostrand Reinhold.

Keyes, Ken, Jr. **The Hundredth Monkey.** Coos Bay, Ore.: Vision Books, 1982.

O'Hara, M. M. "The Hundredth Humanistic Psychologist." **Association for Humanistic Psychology Newsletter** (July 1983).

O'Hara, M. M. "Of Myths and Monkeys." **Journal of Humanistic Psychology** 25 (1) (1985): 61-78.

Scheuer, J. and B. Thierry: "A Further Food-Washing Tradition in Japanese Macaques (*Macaca fuscata*)." **Primates** 26 (4) (1985): 491-494.

Science Digest 8 (1981): 57. "The Quantum Monkey."

Sheldrake, R. **A New Science of Life: The Hypothesis of Formative Causation.** Los Angeles: J. P. Tarcher, 1982.

Stein, Arthur. "The Hundredth Monkey and Humanity's Quest for Survival." **Phoenix Journal of Transpersonal Anthropology,** 7 (1983): 29-40.

Tsumori, Atsuo. "Newly Acquired Behavior and Social Interactions of Japanese Monkeys." **Social Communication Among Primates.** Stuart Altman, Ed. Chicago: University of Chicago Press, 1967.

Walsh, P. B. **Association for Humanistic Psychology Newsletter** (November 1983).

Watson, Lyall. **Lifetide.** New York: Simon and Schuster, 1979.

Reality Shopping

A Consumer's Guide to New Age Hokum

by Alan M. MacRobert and Ted Schultz

RECENTLY ON DISPLAY in bookstores throughout America was a flashy paperback entitled *Somebody Else Is On the Moon*. The cover depicts an astronaut coming upon huge tracks in the lunar soil and pipes sticking out of a crater. "For 200 years astronomers have suspected — now we know!" proclaims the blurb. "Incredible proof of an alien race on the moon! The evidence: Immense mechanical rigs, some over a mile long. Lights, flares, vehicle tracks, towers, pipes, conduits."

To the connoisseur of crank literature, this book is a delight. It is the rambling narrative of how author George H. Leonard, a retired public health official, has identified amazing things in photographs of the moon that he gets by mail order from NASA. (NASA, of course, is part of a governmental conspiracy to cover up Leonard's findings. The only reason the Apollo astronauts visited the moon was to study its inhabitants, and everything else is a government hoax that "dwarfs Watergate.") The chapters of Leonard's book bear such titles as "A Motor As Big As the Bronx" and "Service Station in a Crater?" Thirty-five pages of moon photos illustrate with circles and arrows the marvels discussed in the text. But the circles and arrows point to nothing unusual at all. The photos are just ordinary moonscapes of hills, plains, and craters.

The most interesting thing about *Somebody Else Is On the Moon*, however, is not its contents. It's the publisher's marketing strategy. The book was placed in bookstores among the offerings for "New Age" readers, including those like myself who like to think that we are in the vanguard, exploring important new ideas and philosophies. There, in fact, is where all sorts of crank literature has migrated. That's where it sells.

In times past, purveyors of fringe and paranormal ideas bitterly charged that they were being censored out of print by conspiracies of publishers and orthodox scientists. No more; all holds are off. Firewalking, sunken continents, astrology, psychokinetic spoon-bending, psychic readings, channelling, aura reading, remote viewing, psychic archaeology, scores of dubious holistic health systems, and a thousand other paranormal ideas have been getting a hearing like never before. And my generation, the supposedly "skeptical" generation, is eating it up.

The very abundance of such claims has made the "Search," as I like to call it, more difficult than ever. This Search is a tradition in my family. My grandfather was a devout Spiritualist. He held seances with the great mediums of the day — Arthur Ford, Eileen Garrett — and he took my mother and father to all the main Spiritualist camps. My parents were somewhat more skeptical. My father joined the American Society for Psychical Research and became one of its directors, investigating haunted houses, poltergeists, clairvoyants, and telepaths long before such investigators were guaranteed a spot on the *Merv Griffin Show*. Up in the attic we still have a set of fake spirit photographs a medium tried to pass off on him; spirit

If there were a Consumers' Union for the paranormal marketplace, Alan MacRobert could be its Ralph Nader. As the heir to three generations of Spiritualism and psychic investigation, he's learned to harmonize the dual traits of fascination with the unknown and healthy, uncompromising skepticism. His article is a guided, grounded tour through the carnival of paranormal claims. MacRobert is an editor at Sky and Telescope magazine, and a former editor at Vermont Vanguard Press, where a substantially different version of this article originally appeared.
—T.S.

Physicist John Taylor published this photo in his 1975 book Superminds as proof of psychokinesis. This seven-year-old boy was one of several children who fooled Taylor into believing that they could bend silverware with paranormal powers.

photography was the popular equivalent in those days of psychics' key-bending stunts now.

Some of my earliest reading materials were the "psychic books" that filled my family's bookcases. In one of them, I ran across an engraving of my great-grandfather, Emerson J. MacRobert, a Spiritualist in London, Ontario. At a time when such activities were scandalous and possibly illegal, he had held seances in a top-floor room of an old house with velvet tacked over the windows. Word got out and he was nearly forced from his post on the London School Board by righteous churchgoers. In my childhood reading, I also ran across an old reference to something called a "Treborcam Ethereal Healing Machine." The name is my own spelled backwards.

Descended from two generations of Spiritualists, my father was always noncommittal. He had run across plenty of frauds and exaggerations, but, even at its best, the Society for Psychical Research seemed only able to draw blanks. Under close scrutiny, psychics failed because they were "having a bad day" or because their powers were impeded by the presence of skeptics. Modern parapsychologists excuse the "nonrepeatability" of their experiments with much the same rationale.

This lifetime exposure to the paranormal has left me somewhat disillusioned and impatient with the intellectual credulity of my generation — no improvement on that of my grandfather's. Still, I'm ready for the day when UFO creatures land on the White House lawn and are interviewed by Dan Rather, or when one single psychic somewhere can predict the future or reliably levitate paper clips so that anyone can see it's so. In the meantime, here, culled from all the time I've spent in the Search, are some guidelines by which to evaluate the flood of paranormal claims. These guidelines, carefully applied, should help eliminate the claims that are worthless — at least 98 percent of them — and will provide grounds for evaluating anything that's left.

Almost everyone with a paranormal theory to tout, I have discovered, is *unwilling to scrutinize the phenomenon*. Whatever the claim, chances are he won't examine it closely even when he gets an excellent chance to do so. I get the impression that, deep down, paranormal claimants are afraid they'll see there's nothing there. Because science, *the art of looking carefully to determine the truth*, is precisely what they're afraid of, they'll reject its ability to assess their claim, perhaps with a snide reference to the inadequacy of "linear, left-brain, Western science."

Somebody Else Is On the Moon contains a fine example of this fear of scrutiny. All of Leonard's moon constructions are at the very limit of photo resolution. When he had a chance to get better photos and to see the same terrain more clearly, he didn't.

On the other hand, you might expect John Taylor, a physicist the *New Scientist* called one of the top 20 scientists in the world, to be suspicious of psychics who attempted to avoid his close scrutiny. Yet his 1975 book *Superminds* enthusiastically described his experiments with "Geller children," kids who could bend forks and spoons "psychokinetically," just like Uri Geller. The trouble was, they could only do it when no one was looking. Taylor even gave this aversion to scientific scrutiny a name: the "shyness effect." He accomodatingly designed "sealed" tubes with the objects to be bent placed inside, and sent them home with the children. When they returned bent the next day, still sealed in the tubes, he considered this proof of psychic abilities.

Taylor refused to see the magician, the Amazing Randi, who felt he could explain the shyness effect in more prosaic terms: cheating. Perhaps Taylor himself had become afraid of close scrutiny. Randi called on him anyway, disguised as a reporter, and found Taylor particularly easy to fool. In his book *The Truth About Uri Geller*, Randi describes having no trouble at all opening and closing the crudely sealed tubes in Taylor's presence, even managing to bend an aluminum bar while Taylor was momentarily distracted, scratch on it "Bent by Randi," and replace it among Taylor's collection undetected!

The final blow to Taylor's shyness effect occurred when an alternative team of scientists decided to replicate Taylor's findings. Six of his metal-bending prodigies were tested in a room with one observer, who noticed no cheating even though "psychokinetic" metal-bending occurred repeatedly. But a hidden camera recorded the truth about the shyness effect, as reported by the investigators in the September 4, 1975, issue of the scientific journal *Nature:* "A put the rod under her foot and tried to bend it; *B, E,* and *F* used two hands to bend the spoon . . . while *D* tried to hide his hands under a table to bend the spoon." Today, Taylor has retracted many of his 1975 claims.

When my father was investigating mediums, they often claimed that the spirits would stay away if there was a skeptic in the room. So if an investigator frisked the medium for gadgets, the spirits would fail to materialize. This is a very convenient explanation for why paranormal phenomena disappear when someone looks closely, and it is invoked in many ways by New Age theorists. The Amazing Randi is strongly disliked by the modern parapsychological community, and quite unwelcome at psychic demonstrations because of this "skeptics effect." A simpler explanation for why something isn't there when you look carefully is that it isn't there at all. Beware of anyone who says you mustn't look closely.

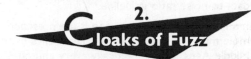

2. Cloaks of Fuzz

This next guideline grows out of the first. Watch out for paranormal phenomena that are cloaked in *noise.*

"Noise" in this sense means any kind of confusion, static, or fuzz that obscures what you're looking for. Leonard's moon marvels are an example, lost as they are in the graininess of his photographs at the limits of resolution, where everything gets fuzzy and random.

Another example comes from the *Journal of the American Society for Psychical Research* on my father's bookshelves. One psychic investigator theorized that psychokinesis, the mind's alleged ability to move objects by will power, might depend on what elements the objects were made of. Zinc might respond differently than zirconium. The straightforward way to test this would be to suspend a piece of each element in such a way that the slightest force would move it, then sit back and concentrate on each one to see which moves in response. Of course, the objects would probably sit there and do nothing. The experimenter seemed to unconsciously realize this, so he instead fashioned dice out of different elements and rolled them thousands of times down a sloping board, concentrating on what numbers he wanted to turn up.

Obviously, the amount of force needed to influence bouncing dice is far greater than the force needed, say, to deflect a needle suspended on a string in a vacuum. But the rolling dice added statistical noise to the experiment, giving the researcher something to work with. His results were not clear-cut, but with a statistics-based experimental design a researcher can fiddle around endlessly, matching good and bad runs to mood, the weather, phases of the moon, sunspots, and so on, making a nice thick report for a psychical research journal.

Dr. J. B. Rhine of Duke University pioneered the

THE CASE OF ILGA K.

In 1935, the Director of the Forensic Institute of the Latvian State University in Riga, Dr. F. von Neureiter, published a monograph describing his experimental observations of a 9-year-old mentally retarded (I.Q. of 48) Latvian girl, Ilga Kirks, who supposedly was able to read the thoughts of her teacher and mother, as well as other individuals. Even though she had great difficulty reading Latvian from a book, she could read Latvian as well as foreign languages rather fluently if these were read silently by another person. Von Neureiter thought that the girl had genuine telepathic ability, and the case of Ilga K., as she is referred to in the literature, became well known both in Latvia and abroad. In 1936 and 1937, a specially formed Commission, made up of 13 professionals representing psychology, physics, medicine, and speech and hearing disorders, conducted and extensive series of tests of Ilga K. Some of these were conducted in a soundproof room and in a Faraday cage (an insulated cubicle that keeps out electromagnetic waves). In their report, the Commission concluded that no paranormality was involved in Ilga's ability. When the agent was Ilga's mother, the word that the mother was thinking of was "sent" to her daughter by breaking it down into separate phonemes and tacking these onto the ends of the words of encouragement uttered by the mother. Ilga would pick them out and put them together into a whole word. When the mother was made to keep quiet or was isolated in a soundproof room, Ilga failed to receive, or else was only partly successful by using the highly expressive gestures and lip movements of the mother. Ilga was most successful with individuals who strongly moved their lips, tongue, and larynx while thinking or reading, which was the case with her teacher who had first brought Ilga's ability to the attention of the scientists. She could learn nothing from her mathematics teacher, whose subvocal speech was very weak, but a special teacher assigned by the Latvian Commission to tutor Ilga at home learned the communication method that Ilga and her mother were using and was able to replicate and even better the mother's performance. Ilga's ability was apparently one that she had developed on her own to compensate for her rather severe intellectual deficit. In spite of the fact that the Latvian Commission's work leaves not the slightest doubt as to the true nature of Ilga K.'s phenomenon, and the additional fact that von Neureiter was one of the Commission's members, some parapsychologists still present her case as a genuine case of telepathy, ignoring the Commission's report altogether.

—from Anomalistic Psychology
*by Leonard Zusne and
Warren H. Jones*

Two of the many photos from George Leonard's crank masterpiece, *Somebody Else is on the Moon.* (Above) According to Leonard, the arrow here points to a "vehicle resting inside anomalous rayed crater in Oceanus Procellarum." (Below) Leonard claims the arrows in this photo indicate "several small craters in the process of being worked with marking crosses on their lips and spraying drones inside."

statistical [ESP] experiments. This suggests to me a very strong indication that a nonrecognized source of systematic errors may have been involved."

This data-to-noise ratio can be applied to many popular paranormal claims, such as the Shroud of Turin. The Shroud is an ancient cloth bearing the image of a mournful looking man. It is widely claimed to be the burial cloth of Jesus, imprinted by a miracle, though it turned up in a church in the 14th century and is not known to have had a prior history. A team of modern Christian scientists has produced volumes of analyses of the Shroud in an attempt to demonstrate its extraordinary characteristics. But recently, secular researchers found that the image contained a red pigment commonly used by 14th-century artists (a conclusion that few newspapers bothered to report — the public always prefers a mystery). Even before this discovery, the Shroud could have been evaluated by the data-to-noise ratio guideline.

An immediate cause for suspicion is the presence of whole museum loads of clearly false relics from the Middle Ages, when practically every church had to have a wood chip from the True Cross, a plate from the Last Supper, or one of Jesus' sandals — any single item of which would be as hard to evaluate as the Shroud itself. The Shroud appeared in the middle of all this noise. Ray N. Rogers, a leading Shroud advocate, once said that he could hardly think of a better way for the deity to prove His existence to a skeptical modern world than to leave us the Shroud. I can think of plenty of better ways, perhaps something clean and clear like materializing as a figure 50 miles tall and speaking loud enough to rattle the earth. The Shroud was a pretty forlorn miracle by comparison, lost in the trivia of the Middle Ages like a needle in a haystack — a speck of dubious data extracted from a sea of noise.

Cloaks of noise by themselves are not proof of the Shroud's inauthenticity — nor that mind power doesn't occasionally tilt a zirconium die, nor that the moon is not covered with artificial objects just a little smaller than the best photographs can show. "Noise" in information theory means, literally, that you just don't know. Data swamped in noise are unworthy of belief, and it is suspicious that evidence for the paranormal is consistently cloaked in this way.

3. Believers

Watch out for "believers." Watch out for stories told and retold. Francis Bacon said, "Man prefers to believe what he prefers to be true." A believer doesn't have to be a zealot. Anyone qualifies who possesses imagination enough to get excited at the idea that the mysterious crashing sounds in the woods just beyond the campfire might be Bigfoot.

statistical approach to the study of psychic phenomena in the 1930s, and it still dominates the experimental design of modern parapsychologists, who seem to delight in devising new ways to make their experiments more complex and the results more confusing. As Albert Einstein wrote of Rhine's experiments in 1946: "I regard it as very strange that the spatial distance between the [telepathic] subjects has no relevance to the

Or that Venus sparkling in the clear dawn sky might be a flying saucer. Our beliefs may predispose us to misinterpret the facts, when ideally the facts should serve as the evidence upon which we base our beliefs.

Garden-variety flying saucer sightings based on such misperceptions clutter up the UFO literature. Some UFO investigators, like the late astronomer J. Allen Hynek, have concluded that after the garbage is sorted out, a few unexplainable cases still remain. Others, like *Aviation Week and Space Technology* magazine editor Philip J. Klass, don't agree. "In twelve years of investigating some of the most famous and highly acclaimed UFO reports," says Klass, "I have yet to find one that could not be explained in prosaic terms . . . I'm not skeptical on principle, just on evidence."

Often a paranormal claim gets thoroughly debunked but continues to travel far and wide. Belief, not evidence, supplies the fuel. Lawrence Kusche, a pilot and investigator for the Committee for the Scientific Investigation of Claims of the Paranormal, scrupulously examined every allegedly mysterious disappearance in the so-called "Bermuda Triangle," for example, and found nothing really mysterious

about any of them. He reported his findings in two books, *The Bermuda Triangle Mystery — Solved* and *The Disappearance of Flight 19*. These books have sold very poorly compared to sensationalistic works like Charles Berlitz's *The Bermuda Triangle*. "I assumed that people who read the weird books would naturally want to read the other side of the story and find out the truth," he commented. "I was wrong." Bermuda Triangle lore continues to percolate through American popular culture. A movie on the Triangle was released a couple of years ago, claiming to be factual. Its television ads were filled with flying saucers, underwater horrors, time warps, and planeloads of screaming people.

Some skeptics have concluded that every last paranormal mystery can be accounted for by these twin forces of true believers and tales amplified in the retelling.

T he Past is Prologue
4.

Check out the history of the claim. The past can put a currently popular paranormal belief in a

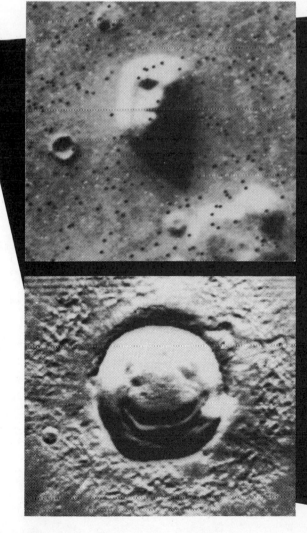

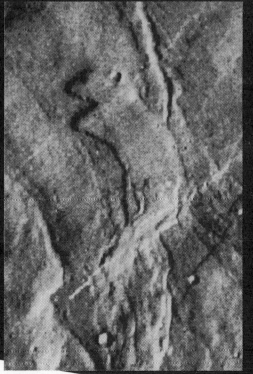

THE FACE ON MARS
(Left) Four books and numerous magazine and newspaper articles have been written interpreting this mile-long feature of Martian geography as a great stone "face" carved by an ancient Martian civilization. NASA officials, who believe that the subject of this Viking 1 photograph is attributable to purely natural geological processes, were happy to supply two other photographs of curious Martian features: a five-mile-wide Happy Face and a lava flow in the form of Kermit the Frog! Pop Culture of the Gods?

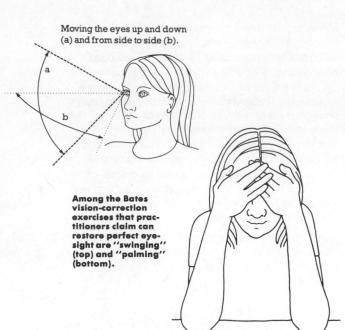

Moving the eyes up and down (a) and from side to side (b).

Among the Bates vision-correction exercises that practitioners claim can restore perfect eyesight are "swinging" (top) and "palming" (bottom).

perspective that can be gained in no other way.

Many of the paranormal claims and movements of the '80s actually have long and colorful histories. One example that has made the rounds in New Age circles in recent years is the Bates vision-correction system, billed as a new, holistic way to treat poor eyesight with a series of easy exercises.

Dr. William Horatio Bates was born in 1860 and graduated from medical school in 1885. His medical career was disrupted by spells of total amnesia, but this did not prevent him from publishing, in 1920, his great work, *The Cure of Imperfect Eyesight by Treatment Without Glasses.* Bates claimed, contrary to reality, that the eye does not focus by changing the shape of the eye lens. He said that the lens never changes shape at all, and that the problems orthodox doctors attribute to imperfect lenses are actually caused by an "abnormal condition of mind" or "a wrong thought." He invented a series of exercises to correct these problems, such as "palming" the eyes with the palms of the hands, "shifting" and "swinging" vision from side to side, and reading under difficult conditions such as in dim light or on a lurching streetcar. He also advocated staring directly at the sun for brief moments (which can cause genuine eye damage).

Bates died in 1931, but disciples kept his theories alive. Dozens of popular books were published on the Bates method, and "Throw away your glasses!" became the rallying cry of an international movement in the '30s and '40s. Thousands of people sincerely believed the Bates exercises had cured them of nearsightedness, astigmatism, cataracts, and glaucoma. Unfortunately, medical tests did not bear this out.

One of the most prominent converts to the Bates system was Aldous Huxley. His corneas had been scarred since childhood, but he believed the Bates exercises had repaired them. He wrote a book about it, *The Art of Seeing,* hailed as a vindication by Bates sympathizers responding to criticisms from opthalmologists. But Huxley could be an embarrassment, too. Bennett Cerf wrote this account of the time Huxley addressed a Hollywood banquet in the April 12, 1952, *Saturday Review:*

> When he arose to make his address he wore no glasses, and evidently experienced no difficulty in reading the paper he had planted on the lectern. Had the exercises really given him normal vision? I, along with 1200 other guests, watched with astonishment while he rattled glibly on . . . Then suddenly he faltered — and the disturbing truth became obvious. He wasn't reading the address at all. He had learned it by heart. To refresh his memory he brought the paper closer to his eyes. When it was only an inch or so away he still couldn't read it, and he had to fish for a magnifying glass in his pocket. It was an agonizing moment.

Eventually the Bates movement ran its course. In 1956, a Manhattan optometrist, Philip Pollack, wrote the definitive book exposing its failures, *The Truth About Eye Exercises.* "It is a rare occasion indeed when anyone so well informed troubles to take apart a pseudoscientific cult in such a thorough and painstaking manner," wrote Martin Gardner in his 1957 book, *Fads and Fallacies in the Name of Science.* But today the Bates method has been resurrected, minus some of Bates' more obvious blunders and clothed in New Age "holistic" rhetoric. Meanwhile, the Pollack book sits forgotten on library shelves.

The pattern is common: a new paranormal claim turns out to be a very old one, debunked long enough ago for the debunking to have been forgotten. The rate at which such old, disproven, and forgotten theories are being revived shows a certain unimaginativeness in the field, as if new paranormal theories cannot be invented fast enough to meet the New Age demand. And every time they are revived, these theories gain a little more venerability. It is important to remember that tradition and venerability aren't necessarily related to *credibility.*

A few years ago I attended a natural living festival in Connecticut and noticed an iridiagnostician on the program. An iridiagnostician! I felt like a biologist discovering a living fossil.

Iridology was invented around 1880 by Ignatz Peczely of Budapest. He declared that every human disease can be diagnosed by studying the iris of the eye. He claimed — no one knows why — that the iris is divided into 40 zones that correspond to the different body parts. The zones run clockwise in one eye, counterclockwise in the other. Peczely gained disciples, and in 1904 his works were translated into English. Orthodox doctors ridiculed iridiagnosticians, who failed to treat diseases accurately when tested. (Pranksters had their day, too. The *Textbook of Iridiagnosis,* fifth edition, 1921, carefully explains how to recognize glass eyes in order to avoid being caught making lengthy diagnoses of them.) The method never produced any results, and so it slowly faded away around the time of my grandfather.

I expected the iridiagnostician at the natural living festival to be a doddering old man in his eighties, full of reminiscenses about Henry Lindlahr, J. Haskell Kritzer, and other bygone greats of the movement. But no. He was a young, hip-looking fellow as enthusiastic about iridology as if it were brand new.

Since then, iridology has become entrenched in the holistic health scene, believed in (and financed) by thousands who never bothered to check out its full history. It has, in fact, been around long enough in its current incarnation to have undergone another round of debunkings. In 1979, University of California at San Diego researchers A. Simon, D. Worthen, and J. Mitas tested three iridologists, including Bernard Jensen, the author of the modern textbooks on the subject. The iridologists scored no better than would be expected by chance at making correct diagnoses of the illnesses of 143 patients. And in 1981, D. Cockburn at the University of Melbourne in Australia had iridologists evaluate before-and-after photos of the irises of patients who had developed acute diseases. Not only did the iridologists fail to diagnose any of the illnesses, they could find no changes in the eyes whatsoever!

A similar resurgent alternative health practice is zone therapy, based on the belief that every organ of the body is connected to a different spot on the bottom of the foot, the roof of the mouth, and the hands. Zone therapy is often linked by its practitioners with acupuncture and shiatsu massage, an association from which it derives venerability, but the truth is that, like iridology, zone therapy was another turn-of-the-century invention, by a Dr. William H. Fitzgerald of St. Francis Hospital of Hartford, Connecticut. Zone therapy flourished for a while, aided by testimonials of spectacular cures. But the cures somehow didn't endure the test of time, and the practice slowly faded out. By 1950 it was nearly extinct. Now it has been resurrected as reflexology, and poster charts of the bottom of the foot can be found in health food stores everywhere. It is currently practiced without some of Dr. Fitzgerald's more unusual treatments, like the application of tight rubber bands and spring clothes pins to various fingers and toes.

Many other past systems of bygone medical quackery have been revived in recent years, including chromotherapy (healing with colored lights), colonics (enemas), and homeopathy (where medicinal tinctures are made so dilute that not one molecule of the active ingredient remains). ☞

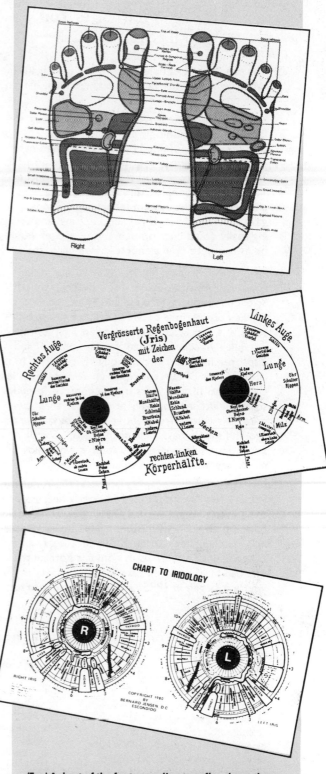

(Top) A chart of the foot according to reflexology, the modern version of zone therapy. Practitioners claim that each region corresponds to a specific organ or portion of the anatomy, and that treatment of bodily ailments can be achieved by the application of pressure to the proper area of the foot. (Middle) Ignatz von Peczely's original iris chart and (bottom) its modern counterpart by iridologist Bernard Jensen. Like reflexologists with feet, iridologists claim that areas of the iris specifically correspond to organs and parts of the body, and that complex diagnoses can be made by the examination of the eye alone.

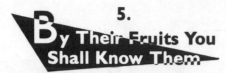

5. By Their Fruits You Shall Know Them

The preceding examples lead to the next guideline: Watch whether the field of study remains barren over time.

In the end, the most telling argument against the Bates system, iridology, and zone therapy was not that they were founded by cranks or were based on spurious theories, but that they bore no fruit. The Bates exercises had every chance to succeed. Thousands of people "threw away their glasses" and practiced the system religiously. Millions more gave it briefer tries. If palming, shifting, and swinging really could cure poor eyesight, glasses would be as obsolete now as horse-drawn carriages.

As physicist Rolf M. Sinclair pointed out at an American Association for the Advancement of Science meeting in 1980 in San Francisco, one of the key distinctions between science and pseudoscience is that science changes rapidly. New ideas are quickly accepted once they are proven, and disproven ideas are likewise quickly rejected. Most of the focus of current research involves ideas less than ten to fifteen years old. In contrast, pseudoscience clutches doggedly at ideas for their own sake. "Astrology froze about two thousand years ago and simply hasn't changed much," Sinclair said. "That unchanging character is what allows me to say astrology is a pseudoscience."

My father finally became inactive in the American Society for Psychical Research partly because nothing ever seemed to lead anywhere. At home we have a shelf lined with issues of the Society's *Journal,* marching back through the decades. Unlike other scientific journals, it contains nothing that one can build upon. In essence, the Society is just where it began in 1885, and where its precursor, the London Society for Psychical Research, began before that. It has yet to demonstrate that psychic powers exist at all, much less learn anything about them.

6. Crank-Watching

If someone making paranormal claims compares himself to Einstein, Galileo, or Pasteur, dismiss him right away. Real geniuses usually let their work speak for itself. If he believes he is being conspired against by the A.M.A., "orthodox oxen," and "would-be scientists" with "frozen beliefs" and "hi-de-hi mathematics" (to quote George F. Gillette, discoverer of an incomprehensible something called the "spiral maximote"), then you may safely ignore him. Paranoia is a frequent refuge of the incompetent.

The crank usually works in isolation from everyone else in his field of study, making grand discoveries in his basement. Many paranormal movements can be traced back to such people — Kirlian photography, for instance. If you pump high-voltage electricity into anything it will emit glowing sparks, common knowledge to electrical workers and hobbyists for a century. It took a lone basement crank to declare that the sparks represent some sort of spiritual aura. In fact, Kirlian photography was subjected to rigorous testing by physicists John O. Pehek, Harry J. Kyler, and David L. Faust, who reported their findings in the October 15, 1976, issue of *Science.* Their conclusion: The variations observed in Kirlian photographs are due solely to moisture on the surface of the body and not to mysterious "auras" or even necessarily to changes in mood or mental state. Nevertheless, television shows, magazines, and books (many by famous parapsychologists) continue to promote Kirlian photography as proof of the unknown.

VON DANIKEN DEBUNKS VON DANIKEN

In 1978, the PBS *Nova* television science program examined the claims of "ancient astronaut" theorist Erich Von Daniken, whose series of books beginning with *Chariots of the Gods* has sold a stunning 36 million copies. The *Nova* interviewer, pressing Von Daniken to confess that he had not really explored an artifact-filled South American cave as he had claimed in *Gold of the Gods,* obtained the following admission:

> No that did not happen, but I think when somebody writes books in my style and in my sense, which are not scientific books, we call it in German "sachbucher." It's a kind of

popular book but it's not science fiction, though all the facts do exist but with other interpretations. Then an author is allowed to use effects. So some little things like this are really not important because they do not touch the facts. They are simply stimulating the reader, and one is allowed to do this.

Nonetheless, Von Daniken's books are sold in America as "nonfiction." As James Randi (the magician, "The Amazing Randi") points out in his book *Flim Flam!:*

> [Von Daniken] at no point calls to our attention the miracle known as Chartres Cathedral, the Parthenon

in Greece, or even Stonehenge — that most remarkable astronomical construction — *because these wonders are European,* built by people he *expects* to have the intelligence and ability to do such work. He cannot conceive of our brown and black brothers having the wit to conceive or the skill to build the great structures that they *did* leave behind. Instead, to satisfy what appear to be his personal prejudices, he invents some sort of divine/extraterrestrial/supernatural intervention that he maintains was necessary to enable the inferior races to put stone upon stone or place paint upon a cave wall.

—T.S.

And finally, of course, there are plenty of outright fakes.

A fake often gives rise to a movement that endures long after the fakery is exposed. Spiritualism, the religion of my family for two generations, began in 1848 when 12-year-old Margaret Fox of Wayne County, New York, became the world's first medium. People sitting with her in a darkened room asked questions of the spirits, and unexplained rapping noises would reply. More and more people came to witness this marvel, and soon Margaret and her sisters went on tour. Much later, in 1888, she confessed it was all a hoax; she did it by snapping her big toe joint against the floor. But by now Spiritualism had grown far beyond the "spirit rapping" stage, and seances were full of flying spirit trumpets, spirit voices, gauzy figures appearing in the dark, and mediums foaming ectoplasm from all their body orifices. Spiritualists continued to revere Margaret Fox as the founder of their religion, even after her confession. Once, my grandfather took my parents to visit the Fox sisters' cabin, preserved as a sort of Spiritualist shrine. My mother remembers sitting in Margaret Fox's chair. She also learned to do the toe-snapping trick, and she can still do it. She demonstrated it for my grandfather once, but "he was very out of patience with us for being so skeptical."

The Self-Defeat of the New Age

In the whole panoply of the paranormal, is there anything at all that an intelligent person can believe in? Perhaps *belief* is not the issue. The *possibility* is always there. Maybe a few of the Spiritualists did get messages — no one can prove otherwise. Maybe the saucers will finally land next month and show up the skeptics once and for all. "If we are only open to those discoveries which will accord with what we already know," said Alan Watts, "we might as well stay shut." And that is as far as an honest person can go.

The real significance of the paranormal boom is that so many of us take it so uncritically. It is as if the question "Is this so?" has become irrelevant — and has been replaced by the attitude, "If it feels good, it must be right for me." This is a very fundamental shift. That an objective reality exists outside of our internal feelings and viewpoints, and that this objective reality is worth studying, is a relatively new idea in the history of the world. It did not gain a firm foothold until as late as the Renaissance, and though it rapidly led to the sciences that have transformed the world, perhaps this idea is more alien to human nature than we might think.

Today, nowhere is the rationalist paradigm "Is this

In the New Age, the inventions of basement cranks can mean big money. The slick and glossy catalog from Supersensonic Energy Technologies of Boulder Creek, California, reads like a "Sharper Image" for yuppie occultists. Their Pi-Ray Coffer (above left) is supposed to "amplify the Pi-Ray field and filter out the negative green field," and can be used to "charge objects like watches, rings, and crystals." At $149.95, it's sure to filter out the green field in your wallet. For the cabalist on the go, their Magnetron XT (above right) is built into a briefcase. It "aligns the magnetic field of the Earth" for you for only $99.95. The Supersensonic Extractor Sink (below) "amplifies the natural process of excreting residual toxic vibrations through your subtle energy field." Price: $249.95.

so?" more roundly attacked, and its replacement, "If it feels good, it must be right," more self-consciously advocated, than in the movements that go collectively under the name "New Age." I believe this paradigm has served us poorly. It has led countless good people to squander years of their brilliance and energy on shabby falsehoods. It has been responsible for trapping others in vicious cults. It may have even short-circuited just the sort of quantum leap in human thought that our theorists keep saying is just around the corner.

Historically, paranormal movements have drawn more adherents from the right wing than from the left. No nation has a more extensive crackpot

	1919	1925	1934	1945	1950	1966	1973	1974	1975	1978	1979	1985
UFOs						48%	54%	46%		57%	59%	43%
Telepathy/ESP		36%	8%		10%			39%		51%	54%	
Precognition	20%		30%					26%		37%		
Astrology		15%	6%	18%	6.5%			25%	22%	29%		40%
Disbelieve human evolution				39%								50%
Lucky/Unlucky numbers	13%		26%					14%				40%
Fortune-telling	11%	1%	13%	1%	2%			6.5%			14%	
Palmistry		8%	15%	20%	2%			3.3%				
Faith-healing		9%		6%	5.5%			34%				
Ghosts								16%		11%		
Phrenology		40%		18%	3%			0%				
Angels										54%		
Devils										39%		

Over 50 years of American belief in the paranormal are represented in this table, based on surveys of college students and adults. The figures indicate the percentage that endorsed each of the beliefs listed. The figures for 1966, 1973, 1978, and 1985 indicate cross-sections of the U. S. adult population; the rest represent college students. It's difficult to elicit trends, especially from the older data, because of the difference in the phraseology of the questions in the various surveys. The most recent survey, conducted in 1985 by the National Science Foundation, indicates that 43 percent of the adult population believes that UFOs are alien spacecraft, 40 percent feel that astrology has scientific credibility, 50 percent disbelieve that humans evolved from earlier species of animals, and 40 percent agree that "some numbers are lucky for some people."

literature than Germany, and never did paranormal beliefs of every kind get more of a hearing than as in that country between the two World Wars. The Nazis' racial theories were only a small part of the pseudoscience that overran Germany.

One of the most widespread beliefs was the World Ice Doctrine (Welt-Eis-Lehre, or WEL), which held that the Milky Way was not made up of stars but of blocks of ice spiralling toward the earth. This pseudoscience was somehow connected with Aryan racial superiority, and the WEL acted almost as a political party. So successful was it that the Propaganda Ministry was obliged to announce, "One can be a good National Socialist without believing in the WEL." Another Nazi doctrine was that the earth is the interior of a hollow sphere, so that a line directed straight up into the sky would hit the other side of the world. The sun and stars were thought to be optical illusions in the middle. This idea was so widely accepted that a military party of 10 was dispatched to the Isle of Rugen to photograph the British fleet by pointing an infrared telescope 45 degrees up into the sky!

The sight of intelligent, educated people walking around with pyramids on their heads, a sight you are liable to witness at any New Age festival, is comical. Perhaps the next irrational movement will not be so funny.

Certainly the New Age will make no lasting progress, nor will it gain any more credibility, until we accept the fact that nature gave us heads as well as hearts. Maybe we were given heads for a good reason. Maybe it is because, in the end, only the truth can set us free. ■

THE ARMY'S PSI STUDY

In 1932 Charles Fort, the "Prophet of the Unexplained," predicted a day when psychic soldiers would wipe out enemy regiments psychokinetically, causing troops to "burst into flames," or smashing them under cliffs "teleported from the Rocky Mountains." According to a U.S. Army-commissioned study conducted by the National Research Council (NRC), of all the military nightmares in our future, this vision of psychic war, thankfully, is one that may not come true. Completed in 1988, the two-year, $425,000 study concluded that there is "no scientific justification, from research conducted over a period of 130 years, for the existence of parapsychological phenomena."

Entitled "Enhancing Human Performance," the NRC study intensively surveyed psychic research, including ESP and psychokinesis, partially because a number of military officers felt that the U.S. was lagging behind the Soviet Union in developing military applications. Some even suspected that the 1963 sinking of the nuclear submarine Thresher might have been the result of a Soviet psychic attack.

The study cited improper statistical methodology and failure to design experiments that preclude fraud as two of parapsychology's outstanding problems. According to University of Oregon psychologist Ray Hyman, who led the study's parapsychology committee, "Until [parapsychologists] clean the defects up, there's no reason for scientists to take what they say seriously."

The NRC researchers checked out other frontiers of human potential as well, including accelerated learning, biofeedback, and neurolinguistic programming (NLP). NLP, which postulates connections between behavior and neurology and claims to train students to "read" others by noting their eye position and choice of language, was also dismissed as having a social rather than a neurological basis. Another disappointment was "Hemispheric Synchronization," a process that promises to somehow align the left and right hemispheres of the brain.

But not everything fared poorly under the NRC's scrutiny. Sleep learning seemed to speed the absorption of certain types of information, including languages and codes, and mental imagery techniques showed potential for enhancing acquisition of routine mechanical skills. —T.S.

SCRUTINIZING
THE PARANORMAL

ACCESS TO SKEPTICAL BOOKS AND MAGAZINES

by Ted Schultz

SENSATIONALISTIC PARANORMAL CLAIMS sell books and magazines. Sober, sensible assessments of those claims do not. Consequently, the body of "skeptical" literature has remained small, supported by a negligible percentage of the reading public's money. Personally, I find the good skeptical publications at least as much fun to read as the paranormal stuff—usually lots better. The good skeptical writers are as fascinated by paranormal claims as the credulous journalists, but—unlike the "true believers"—the skeptics get to the bottom of things through careful examinations of history and facts. I have found more solutions to puzzling anomalies in the few years that I have been reading the skeptics than in the considerably greater number of years I've spent reading the mystery mongers.

Skeptical writers, scientists, and scholars united for the first time in 1976, calling themselves the Committee for the Scientific Investigation of Claims of the Paranormal (CSICOP, known as the "psi-cops" by their detractors). They started a journal, the *Skeptical Inquirer,* which be-

came a major vehicle for skeptical writing. In spite of the lack of public support, CSICOP took on the job of combating what it perceived as a dangerously rising tide of superstition and irrationality, spawned perhaps by a deterioration in the quality of education in both science and critical thinking. After spending its first ten years addressing the claims of disparate paranormalists, CSICOP expanded its investigations to include the single most significant threat to rationalism today: certain highly organized, powerful Christian fundamentalist groups that are exerting considerable economic and political pressure in order to compromise science education in public schools. And more recently, it's also set its sights on the many absurdities that congregate under the banner of the "New Age."

Many paranormalists, Bible scientists, and New Agers would like to see CSICOP wither up and fade away. But what fun would that be? Instead, I look forward to seeing this feisty bunch persevere, like a David against a Goliath, in their battle against unreason.

Science and the Paranormal

If you just wanted to read one book of skeptical literature, this would have to be it. Twenty experts, most of them scientists, take the time to study the evidence for various paranormal claims within their areas of expertise. Botanist Arthur Galston discusses the failures to replicate "plant consciousness" research published in the sensationalistic **Secret Life of Plants**. *Astronomer Carl Sagan examines the Biblically inspired catastrophist reinterpretation of solar system history proposed in Immanuel Velikovsky's* **Worlds in Collision**. *Surgeon William Nolen reports on his extensive investigation of psychic healing. The magician James "The Amazing" Randi demonstrates his duplications of psychic "miracles." The lyrical closing chapter by M.I.T. physicist Philip Morrison redirects the reader to the genuine fountains of wonder that are the basis of all great science. This book is an intelligent, informed analysis of some of the most widely held paranormal beliefs, and a lesson in critical thinking to boot.* —T.S.

• As an experienced surgeon I immediately recognized what I had previously suspected from viewing the films: These so-called operations were simply feats of legerdemain. I managed to persuade Joe Mercado, one of the best-known psychic surgeons, to operate on me, explaining that I had high blood pressure (true) and that high blood pressure might be caused by kidney disease (also true). He operated on me while I stood by the side of the altar in his church (at six foot one I was too tall to lie down on the altar on which he operated on most of his patients). Looking down on his hands, I could easily see as he began the "operation" that he had palmed the intestines and fat of a small animal. I watched him carefully as he pushed against me and it was apparent, both visually and

from the way his hands felt as they pressed on my abdominal musculature, that he had not penetrated my abdominal wall. When he "removed" the fatty tissue, he held it up for all the spectators to see and said, "Evil tissue." He immediately tossed it into a can of flaming alcohol kept behind the altar.

• Next Gauquelin placed an advertisement in a Paris newspaper offering: "Completely Free! Your ultra-personal horoscope; a ten page document. Take advantage of this unique opportunity. Send name, address, date and birthplace . . . "

There were about 150 replies. To each correspondent Gauquelin sent the same horoscope—the one he had received for Dr. Petiot. With each he sent a self-addressed envelope and questionnaire asking about the accuracy of the reading. Ninety-four percent of the respondents said they recognized themselves (that is, they said they were accurately portrayed in the horoscope of a man who murdered several dozen people and dissolved their bodies in quicklime), and for 90 percent this positive opinion was shared by their families and friends.

Science and the Paranormal
George O. Abell
and Barry Singer
1981, 1986; 432 pp.
$12.95
postpaid from:
Charles Scribner's Sons
Macmillan Order Dept.
Front and Brown Streets
Riverside, NJ 08075
800/257-5755

The Skeptical Inquirer

*For years paranormalists complained: "Why don't scientists investigate this?" Now that scientists regularly take up the challenge in the pages of the **Skeptical Inquirer**, the true believers howl "Debunkers!" and run the other way. For ten years, this journal of the Committee for the Scientific Investigation of Claims of the Paranormal has been a lone voice in a sea of irrationality. High-quality articles with plenty of references thoroughly survey and analyze all kinds of paranormal claims. Sure, there's plenty of debunking—usually right on target. Anyone who reads from the extensive literature of the paranormal has to read the **Skeptical Inquirer**, if only for balance. I purchased a complete set of back issues; you can't get this information anywhere else.* —T.S.

• Matthew's chest pains disappeared. His relationships improved with his wife, his children, his coworkers, and his community. If I were a pro-reincarnation therapist, I might argue that his cardiac neurosis was related to his death in a previous lifetime and that his recovery was made possible by recalling the event in hypnosis. However, because my thinking is more in tune with contemporary psychology, I emphasize that Matthew, like many psychosomatic patients, was under a significant degree of stress but lacked the means to express his emotions adequately. He was aware of this problem and traced its origin to his father's strict discipline. Age regression in hypnosis permitted some aspiration of pent-up emotion, but a deeply therapeutic abreaction did not occur until he "regressed" to the alleged past life of Jacques Trecaulte. The further he got from reality, in other words, the more he was able to show emotion. Past-life regressions may be therapeutic not because they are real but precisely because they are not. They create distance from reality and allow the expression of otherwise taboo thoughts and emotions.

• Stephen Barrett "sent a healthy four-year-old girl to five chiropractors for a 'check up.' The first said the child's shoulder blades were 'out of place' and found 'pinched nerves to her stomach and gall bladder.' The second said the child's pelvis was 'twisted.' The third said one hip was 'elevated' and that spinal misalignments could cause 'headaches, nervousness, equilibrium or digestive problems' in the future. The fourth predicted 'bad periods and rough childbirth' if her 'shorter left leg' were not treated. The fifth not only found hip and neck problems, but also 'adjusted them' without bothering to ask permission." Completely inconsistent findings were also diagnosed in two adult women.

(Left) Do you see the demon in the Queen's hair? Some did, and the Canadian dollar bill had to be re-engraved as a result.

(Right) Physicist Bernard Leikind demonstrates that no special preparation, belief, or miracles are required to "fire-walk" across hot coals without injury.

The Skeptical Inquirer
Kendrick Frazier, Editor
$22.50/year
(4 issues) from:
The Skeptical Inquirer
P.O. Box 229
Buffalo, NY 14215-0229

Science Confronts the Paranormal

*Here's an anthology of some of the best articles to appear in the **Skeptical Inquirer** (reviewed above) between 1981 and 1986. Included are pieces on parapsychology, the psychology of misperception, psychic detectives, poltergeists, astrology, palmistry, UFOs, fringe archaeology, and creationism. In general, the authors bring a high level of expertise to their subjects, giving the side of the story you seldom hear, but can't make an informed decision without.* — T.S.

• An anecdote cited by American journalist Jack Harrison Pollack is an almost burlesque example of the lengths to which determined believers will go to make the outcome fit the prediction. Pollack is the author of a full-length biography of the Dutch clairvoyant Gerard Croiset, which Tenhaeff helped

Science Confronts the Paranormal
Kendrick Frazier, Editor
1986; 367 pp.
$16.95
($18.95 postpaid) from:
Prometheus Books
700 East Amherst St.
Buffalo, NY 14215
800/421-0351

him with and vouched for. Consulted in a 1950 Arnheim rape case, Croiset "saw" that the rapist had "an abnormally big genital organ." When the police arrested a suspect, they had a good look at his private parts but found them to be standard size. Never mind, says Pollack, "They learned that he was a twenty-year-old cook who occasionally used a big, red basting syringe in the kitchen, which prompted Croiset's image of an abnormally large genital organ."

• C.R. Snyder, a psychologist at the University of Kansas, and his colleagues drew up a personality description that incorporated the characteristics they found most people believed they possessed. They showed this description to three groups of people, each of whom was asked to rate, on a scale of 1 to 5, how well they were described by it. The individuals in the first group were told it was a universal personality sketch, and the average rating was 3.2. Individuals in the second group were asked for the month in which they were born and were then told the statement was a horoscope for their signs. On the average, they rated it 3.76. The individuals in the third group were asked for the day on which he or she was born and were told that the description was his or her *personal* horoscope. This group rated the same description an average of 4.38. Apparently those who want to believe will do so!

Fads and Fallacies in the Name of Science • Science: Good, Bad, and Bogus • The New Age

*Martin Gardner is a well-known science writer who for years authored the "Mathematical Games" column in **Scientific American**. His **Fads and Fallacies in the Name of Science**, first published in 1952, is **the** classic of skeptical literature. In this volume, Gardner displays some of the best qualities of a skeptical author: good writing, good research in an area fraught with obscurity, and genuine fascination for pseudoscience and crankery of all kinds. His book is a parade of eccentric people and eccentric theories: hollow and flat Earth, bizarre physics, Lysenkoism, the Bates vision-correction system, Reich's orgonomy, general semantics, parapsychology, and medical quackery (always a fertile field). You'd have to spend years haunting libraries and writing away for pamphlets to assemble half of the histories and biographies that Gardner presents here in a thoroughly sane, good-humored style.*

*Gardner has not been idle since **Fads and Fallacies** appeared. He's written many essays on pseudoscience for diverse publications, which have now been assembled into two volumes. **Science: Good, Bad, and Bogus**, which appeared in 1981, is a feisty collection that questions a wide range of topics from the edge of science, including such current controversies as human-ape communication, "physics consciousness," catastrophe theory, and Bible science. **The New Age: Notes of a Fringe Watcher** is an especially entertaining, gossipy book, featuring chapters on Margaret Mead's occult beliefs, Shirley MacLaine, creationism, Rupert Sheldrake, the face on Mars, L. Ron Hubbard (the founder of Scientology), and channeling. Both collections contain damning indictments of modern parapsychology. Needless to say, parapsychologists despise Gardner.*

—*T.S.*

• Since [Albert] Abrams' day, hundreds of similar electrical devices have reaped fortunes for their inventors. In Los Angeles, for example, Dr. Ruth B. Drown is currently operating an Abrams-type machine which diagnoses ailments from the "vibrations" of blood samples. She keeps a huge file of blotting papers on which are preserved samples of the blood of all her patients. By placing a sample in another machine, she can tune the device to the patient, then broadcast healing rays to him while he remains at home!

—*Fads and Fallacies*

• Some idea of the worth of homeopathic medicines may be gathered from the fact that one of them (no longer used) was called *lachryma filia,* and consisted of tears from a weeping young girl. Other curious remedies are made from such substances as powdered starfish (*asterias rubens*), skunk secretion (*mephitis*), crushed live bedbugs (*cimex lectularius*), powdered anthracite coal, powdered oyster shells, and uric acid (*acidum uricum*) obtained from human urine or snake excrement.

—*Fads and Fallacies*

• Geologists find strange things in the ground, but none so strange as the "fossils" unearthed by Johann Beringer, a learned professor of science at the University of Wurzburg. . . . Professor Beringer had an unusual theory. Some fossils, he admitted, might be the remains of life that perished in the great flood of Noah, but most of them were "peculiar stones" carved by God himself as he experimented with the kinds of life he intended to create.

Beringer was ecstatic when his teen-age helpers began to dig up hundreds of stones that supported his hypothesis. They bore images of the bodies of dead insects, birds and fishes never seen on earth. One bird had a fish's head—an idea God had apparently discarded. Other stones showed the sun, moon, five-pointed stars, and comets with blazing tails. He began to find stones with Hebrew letters. One had "Jehovah" carved on it. . . .

In 1726 Beringer published a huge treatise on these marvelous discoveries. . . . Colleagues tried to convince [him] he was being bamboozled, but he dismissed this as "vicious raillery" by stubborn, establishment enemies.

No one knows what finally changed the professor's mind. It was said that he found a stone with his own name on it! An inquiry was held. One of his assistants confessed. It turned out that the two peculiar stones had been carved by two peculiar colleagues, one the university's librarian, the other a professor of geography.

Poor trusting, stupid Beringer, his career shattered, spent his life's savings buying up copies of his idiotic book and burning them. —*Science: Good, Bad, and Bogus*

• Pam McNeeley spent more than $10,000 on Ramtha and is now one of his most vocal critics. Pam is single, 32, and works for a computer firm in Sausalito. She was horrified by what she heard the Ram say in 1985. He predicted that in three years there would be a great holocaust in which cities would be destroyed by disease before the coming of "Twelve Days of Light." A trio of gods—Yahweh, Ramtha, and Id (How did Freud's id get into J.Z.'s mind?) will then arrive in great ships of light to battle the evil Old Testament god Jehovah. AIDS, said Ramtha, is nature's way of eliminating gays. In addition to disease, there will be major earthquakes. "Don't live on a fault line," the Ram said, "It's a zipper." Ramsters were urged to buy pigs and chickens, move to the Northwest, and start farming. Ramtha warned his listeners that if they told anyone about all this he would destroy them. —*The New Age*

• To me the most interesting aspect of [Shirley MacLaine's *It's All in the Playing*] is the disclosure that Shirley is teetering on the edge of solipsism, the ultimate in self-absorption. If each of us creates his or her own reality, she writes, then "objective reality simply does not exist." Could Gerry be nothing more than a creation in her dream? "Perhaps he didn't exist for anyone else at all!"

She seems serious. At a New Year's Eve party, a crystal was passed around, and everyone, when they held it, told what they wanted for the new year. Shirley began by saying she was the only person alive in her universe. Shock waves went around the table. Since everything is her dream, Shirley went on, the best way she can improve the world is to improve herself. When scandalized guests raised objections, Shirley felt she was "creating them to object . . . I hadn't resolved myself. In other words I *was* them. *They* were *me.*"

—*The New Age*

Flim-Flam! • The Truth About Uri Geller • The Faith Healers

The magician James "The Amazing" Randi, a direct descendant of Harry Houdini's crusade against the fraudulence of spiritualism, was awarded a 1986 MacArthur Foundation "genius" prize for his investigations. You may have seen him on the **Tonight Show** with Johnny Carson in February 1986, exposing the Christian faith healer Peter Popoff, who used a radio receiver disguised as a hearing aid to receive "miraculous" knowledge about congregation members transmitted from his wife backstage. Besides faith-healers, Randi is a nemesis of self-styled psychics, duplicating all of the feats (spoon-bending, driving while blindfolded, etc.) that have been pronounced "genuine" by prestigious but gullible parapsychologists. In fact, his book **The Truth About Uri Geller** is a chronicle of the credulity of scientists who were taken in by Geller. Especially revealing is a 1974 exposé article from an Israeli magazine, which Randi reprints in full, that describes Geller's scandalized career as a stage magician. To eliminate the future possibility of fraud, Randi contends that parapsychological experiments should be designed with the help of a magician and, indeed, whenever he's been consulted before the testing of a psychic, the "miracles" have failed to occur. Uri Geller refuses to perform in his presence.

More so than scientists, as a magician Randi is a lifelong expert when it comes to human credulity, chicanery, self-deception, and the will to believe. His book **Flim-Flam!** is an excellent overview of paranormal claims that analyzes medical humbugs, psychic photography, Transcendental Meditation, ancient astronauts, UFOs, and others. Plentiful photographs catch hoaxers in the act. His newest book, **The Faith Healers**, tells the full, gossipy story of the Peter Popoff exposé, as well as the sleazy stories of Oral Roberts, Pat Robertson, W.V. Grant, and others who fleece the faithful while claiming to heal. In all three books, Randi comes off as a spirited, engaging showman who has found his noble purpose: stripping away the flim-flam to expose the truth.

—T.S.

• "When Nasser of Egypt died, Uri was in the midst of his performance and we notified him of this news through the curtains at the back of the stage. The audience, naturally, did not know a thing about it. As soon as we conveyed the news to him, he exploited this information in most theatrical manner. He appeared to be fainting, and called for a doctor. A doctor volunteered from the audience and came up on the stage. Uri asked him to take his pulse right in front of the crowd of seven hundred people. Uri said to him, 'I feel terrible. Very, very bad. I feel bad because I think Nasser is

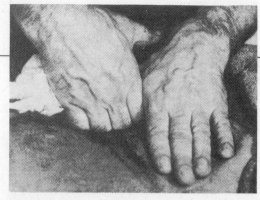

"Psychic surgery": The author's hands apparently enter the body of the subject. The fingers of the right hand are merely folded under to create the illusion that the body is being penetrated. The copious flow of blood was obtained from a piece of balloon (seen on the left), which was extracted from the liquid as if it were a tumor. —*Flim-Flam!*

dying right now. Right this minute.' Naturally, immediately after the performance the audience left the theater and found out about Nasser's death. Thousands of people were once again convinced that Uri Geller was a prophet."
—*The Truth About Uri Geller*

• [Pat] Robertson handed the public a real whopper when he claimed on one TV broadcast that during a crusade in China he delivered his sermon in English, as usual, and was pleased to learn that his audience was miraculously able to understand every word because God had arranged for them to individually hear Robertson's words *in their own regional dialect of Chinese.*
—*The Faith Healers*

• Ex-convict and faith-healer Leroy Jenkins, in full makeup, stuffed into a flashy powder-blue suit and crowned with a rather bad hairpiece, was asked in June 1987 on a CNN-TV interview about the Bakker's reported extravagance and misuse of the ministry's money. He defended them vigorously by explaining how he handles his funds:

"The contributors didn't ask where [the money] was goin'. They don't ask *me* what I'm gonna do with the money, and if they did I'd tell them, 'None of your business!' I'd say, 'You gave it, and that's as far as we go. God blessed you for givin' and He didn't bless you for tellin' *me* what to do with it.'"

At least Leroy tells it like it is: The evangelists take the money and spend it. There's a lot of it, and a lot more where it came from. It's as simple as that. —*The Faith Healers*

(Left) A TM [Transcendental Meditation] student "levitating" while meditating. This is an official photo issued by the TM Ministry of Information. (Right) Steven Zeigler, with no TM instruction whatsoever and no gymnastic training, bounces on a mat in the lotus posture to duplicate the levitation stunt. This unretouched photo was illuminated by a strobe flash. —*Flim-Flam!*

Investigating the Unexplained

Some people consider "debunkers" to be party poopers, out to spoil their favorite mysteries. For them I recommend Melvin Harris, who proves that mystery-solving can be just as much fun as the best of the pro-paranormal books. In the course of his work as a writer, broadcaster, and researcher for the BBC, Harris has investigated the Amityville horror, strange disappearances, psychic detectives (including Robert Lees, who "solved" the Jack the Ripper case), Nostradamus and other prophets, and the regiment of angels supposedly seen by thousands of World War I Allied soldiers. There's perhaps no better demonstration that it's impossible to take the wonder out of life than Harris' discussion of hypnotic past-life regression, in which he replaces a false mystery with a genuine one: cryptomnesia. It's worth the price of the book alone.

—T.S.

• People have long toyed with the idea that physical laws can be set aside by willpower or by specially developed forces within the body. This age-old dream has inspired the publicity behind a number of stage acts, so much so, that less than a century ago audiences were convinced that they were actually witnessing "the negation of the iron laws of nature."

First to succeed with this deception was the "amazing magnetic girl," Lulu Hurst, also known as the "Georgia Wonder." She was the fourteen-year-old daughter of a Baptist deacon of tiny Cedartown, Tennessee. The public was told that her strange powers emerged after a severe electrical storm and a spate of poltergeist-style happenings. Her public demonstrations, however, at no time involved the activities of unseen entities. In full light, using nothing but her hands, Lulu made strong, burly men look like puny weaklings. She presented them with a broom-handle or long pole and calmly defied them to control it against her wishes.

Investigating the Unexplained
Melvin Harris
1986; 222 pp.
$19.95
($21.95 postpaid) from:
Prometheus Books
700 East Amherst St.
Buffalo, NY 14215
800/421-0351

Paranormal? Or parlor tricks?

In one of her feats, two men grasped the pole at its center using both their hands. Lulu then simply placed her open palms on either end of the pole, and after a few slight movements the pole began to twist vigorously up and down, and the men found themselves staggering around the platform guided by the tiny laughing girl

Another, visually more spectacular, feat, involved an attempt by two men to force the pole down onto the stage. The men held the pole vertically while Lulu stood away from them, nonchalantly stretched out her arm and encircled the pole with her open palm. When the word was given the men pushed downwards with all their strength. They struggled away until the sweat rolled from their faces, but the pole stayed in the air with Lulu looking on amused and unruffled!

Pseudoscience and the Paranormal

Terence Hines, a psychologist, begins his book by stating that he agrees with paranormalists that their claims should be evaluated. And he proceeds to do just that, in an exciting, enlightening, information-dense volume. **Pseudoscience and the Paranormal** *is essentially a skeptically minded survey of the full gamut of pseudoscience: psychic powers, life after death, UFOs, ancient astronauts, alternative health practices, and much more. Hines crams his pages full of excellent summaries of unusual ideas, always referring the reader to both the pro and con source material. And he doesn't restrict himself to the usual fare—he critiques fad diets, faith healing, psychoanalysis (to Hines, it's a pseudoscience), and other subjects often ignored by skeptics. Especially enlightening are Hines' discussions of cognitive illusions constructed by the mind and the "falsifiable hypothesis" required to scientifically evaluate a claim.*

—T.S.

• [Wilson Bryan Key, author of *Subliminal Seduction*] claims that advertisers are making common use of sexually arousing patterns and designs embedded in print ads in such a way that they are perceived only subliminally unless one looks for them carefully. He condemns this practice which, naturally, advertising agencies deny using. What evidence does Key use

Pseudoscience and the Paranormal
A Critical Examination of the Evidence
Terence Hines
1988; 372 pp.
$16.95
($18.95 postpaid) from:
Prometheus Books
700 East Amherst St.
Buffalo, NY 14215
800/421-0351

to argue that such embedded sexually arousing stimuli are really being used? He can find them everywhere, in almost any print ad he looks at. He even found an entire sexual orgy, complete with a donkey, in a picture of a plate of clams on a Howard Johnson's restaurant menu. The presence of this subliminal orgy explained why everyone with him ordered clams. This is clearly not evidence; it is merely seeing faces in the clouds.

• Proponents of reincarnation sometimes claim that individuals can speak languages they have not learned in their present life. This is said to occur especially under age-regression hypnosis. S. Thomason, a linguist, has investigated three such cases. As far as I know, these are the only three such cases to have been investigated by a qualified linguist. In the first of the three cases, a hypnotist claimed that one of his patients was speaking Bulgarian while hypnotized. The hypnotist himself did not know any Bulgarian and apparently made the judgment based on the general "sound" of the patient's utterances. In fact, the "language" was not only not Bulgarian, but wasn't any language at all. It was merely run-together sets of syllables that had a Slavic sound. The second case was similar. A patient claimed to be speaking Gaelic and to be a fourteenth-century Frenchman. Analysis of his speech showed that it combined modern French and Latin in a hodge-podge. Further undermining this patient's claim to regression to a past life are the facts that Gaelic was never spoken in France and the patient made many historically incorrect statements about fourteenth-century France while under hypnosis. The third case was of a woman who claimed to have been an Apache in a previous life. Her speech was almost all Hollywood-style pidgin English, for example: "He rides ponies for white man. I no care. He [white man] spoil my Dwaytskem [her husband]. I no like. He scout for white man. I go to happy hunting ground."

Scientists Confront Creationism
and **Creation/Evolution**

"Bible science" and "creation science" are large movements with a lot of clout. Though they are gaining ground, these Christian fundamentalists have so far been unsuccessful in legally achieving equal status for their views in public science education; nonetheless, they've been able to intimidate many science teachers and to influence the rewriting of textbooks by exerting pressure on publishing companies. Bible scientists push their views of "flood geology," creationism, anti-evolutionism, revisionist astronomy (e.g., the universe is only six thousand years old), and even geocentrism not as religion, but as science, claiming as much evidence for their views as secular scientists have for theirs. By so claiming, they enter the realm of empiricism, where their ideas can be tested.

And tested they are, in what is probably the best of the few books that have answered the creationists' challenge, **Scientists Confront Creationism.** *Excellent chapters written by top-notch evolutionary biologists and other scholars address the history of the "Bible science"-vs.-"mainstream science" debate, the age of the universe, the origins of life, the fossil record, biological systematics, and human evolution. How wonderful to get a layman's tutorial in evolution and a refutation of creationism to boot!*

Creation/Evolution *is an excellent little journal put out on a shoestring and written by scientists and educators who have taken the time to analyze Bible-science claims. They help to correct erroneous interpretations of nature and to describe the overwhelming evidence from paleontology, biochemistry, biology, geology, and astronomy that supports evolution and the great age of the universe. They also keep readers up to date on the latest intrusions of religion into the areas of textbook publishing, public education, and public policy.* —T.S.

• Lois Arnold, senior science editor at Prentice-Hall, said, "We don't advocate the idea of scientific creation, but we felt we had to represent other points of view," and another editor whose book presents creationism said, "After all we are in the business of selling textbooks in the 1980s." The resurgence of creationism in major textbooks in the 1980s is a reaction to political and economic pressures, not a changing scientific evaluation of evolution. —*Scientists Confront Creationism*

• The earth's fossils are known to occur in an almost completely exceptionless sequence of order. That is, specific fossils are found only in rocks of a certain age. Trilobites, for instance, an ancient form of shelled sea animal, became extinct

about 300 million years ago, so they are only found in older, generally deeper rocks. Other forms of shellfish are more modern and only appear in younger rocks, higher in the geologic column. [Creationist Henry] Morris has argued the upwelling waters of the flood sorted them by hydraulic drag. For objects of similar shape and density, however, the hydraulic drag force is proportional to cross-sectional area, while the gravitational force is proportional to volume. A rational creationist would therefore expect trilobites to be sorted according to size, with the large ones always deeper than the small ones. This is decidedly *not* the case, and one wonders how Morris, who has a Ph.D. in hydraulic engineering and a background in geology, could seriously advance an explanation based on hydraulic drag. In fact, if the great majority of the world's fossils were buried in the span of a single flood, as the creationists maintain, the mixing of life forms would have been absolutely phenomenal, and no orderly pattern could hope to emerge!

—*Scientists Confront Creationism*

• Creationists are quick to point out error by scientists, and ridicule it. They go on to argue that error and disagreement among specialists are indications that the fabric of science is coming apart, and that it will eventually collapse, with creationism reigning triumphant after Armageddon.

But what creationists ridicule as guesswork, and trial and error, and flip-flopping from theory to theory, are the very essence of science, the stuff of science. Error correction is part of the creative element in the advance of science, and when disagreement occurs, it means not that science is in trouble but that errors are being corrected and scientific advances are being made. Creationism comes on the scene arguing that the Bible is inerrant as a source of scientific truth and that "creation science" cannot admit of error because it simply does not exist. —*Creation/Evolution*

Carl Baugh's Creation Evidences Museum near Glen Rose, Texas.—*Creation/Evolution*

Prometheus Books

Perhaps you've noticed the name of Prometheus Books listed rather frequently in the last few pages. The single best source for skeptical literature, Prometheus keeps books such as those by The Amazing Randi in print while the general public spends its money on more sensationalistic fare. Skeptical works on parapsychology, UFOs, astrology, ancient astronauts—they're all here. Prometheus also publishes books on secular humanism, philosophy, sexuality, and education. A company worth supporting. —T.S.

THE CENSORING PARANORMAL

by Jerome Clark

Writer Charles Fort called them "the damned." Debunkers call them superstitious nonsense that threatens to undermine the fabric of science. Christian fundamentalists call them satanic manifestations that undermine faith in God. Other people simply call them anomalies.

Anomalies are things, or alleged things, that don't fit. They can be minor oddities, of no interest to anyone except a scientist in a highly specialized discipline. Or they can be something else, something hinting at dramatic possibilities and attracting widespread attention and controversy: a UFO sighting, a psychic experience, an encounter with a poltergeist, a report of an unusual animal not known to conventional zoology. Anomalies are nothing new. As long as there have been human beings, people have claimed experiences with phenomena that, according to the prevailing religious or scientific orthodoxy, were not supposed to exist. Some, such as those unfortunates who made such claims during the Inquisition, were burned at the stake for it. Today the burning goes on, if only metaphorically.

In 1977 a group of prominent academics and journalists—few of whom had firsthand experience with anomaly research—formed the Committee for the Scientific Investigation of Claims of the Paranormal (CSICOP). The committee, whose members included such luminaries as Cornell astronomer Carl Sagan and Harvard zoologist Stephen J. Gould, declared as their mission nothing less than the salvation of Western civilization from "irrationality" and "dangerous sects," which, because they accepted the reality of anomalies, opposed science—or so CSICOP charged.

Not long afterward CSICOP complained to the Federal Communications Commission about an NBC documentary that treated paranormal phenomena more sympathetically than the debunkers liked. Although CSICOP alleged that the point of view the documentary represented was harmful to the public, the FCC, unimpressed, refused to act.

In one strange incident CSICOP official Philip J. Klass, learning of a forum on anomalies research that the University of Nebraska was sponsoring, called the school to protest that CSICOP's views were not being represented and that, moreover, in questioning the United States government's word on the nonexistence of UFOs, speakers at the conference were seeking "what the Soviet Union does—to convey to the public that our government cannot be trusted, that it lies, that it falsifies . . . As a patriotic American, I very much resent [this]." After Klass threatened legal action against the university, it canceled its sponsorship of future conferences of this kind. Klass withdrew the threat and pronounced himself satisfied with the university's action.

Since then satellite groups of debunkers have proliferated all around the country, determined to do battle with "pseudoscience," real and imagined. Not content simply to argue the issues on their merits, they have harassed colleges and universities into dropping (usually non-credit) courses in parapsychology, conducted vituperative campaigns against anomaly proponents, and done—in the words of Philadelphian Drew Endacott, one of their number—"anything short of criminal activity" to get "the point across to people who have no demonstrated facility to reason."

As the anti-anomaly hysteria has escalated, even some skeptics have begun to express alarm. Psychologist Ray Hyman, a respected critic of parapsychology, speaks of a "frightening fundamentalism" in all this, a "witch-hunting" mentality that has nothing to do with real science. CSICOP cofounder Marcello Truzzi, a sociologist who left the organization when he grew concerned that it was becoming an "inquisitional body," says that some debunkers have gone "berserk."

In fact, many scientists do not share these skeptics' certainty that all anomalies are bogus. In 1969 the Parapsychological Association was accepted as an affiliate of the American Association for the Advancement of Science (AAAS). Ten years later the AAAS's newly elected president, Kenneth Boulding, declared, "The evidence of parapsychology cannot just be dismissed out of hand." In recent years polls of scientists and academics have revealed a considerable degree of open-mindedness on the subject. And in 1976, when physicist Peter Sturrock polled the members of the American Astronomical Society, fully 80 percent agreed the UFO phenomenon deserves scientific attention. Several of the astronomers described their own UFO sightings.

If history is any guide, most supposed anomalies will eventually be explained in conventional terms, either as delusions or as misinterpreted mundane events—and a few will prove rather more interesting than that. Meanwhile, it's time to defuse the hysteria and get back to the serious business of dispassionate investigation. ■

The skeptics of the Committee for Scientific Investigation of Claims of the Paranormal (CSICOP; see p. 197) have not made many friends among paranormal true believers, the more extreme of whom have (perhaps predictably) accused them of being agents in a government conspiracy to discredit the paranormal. Far more moderate than this, Jerome Clark, editor of both the International al UFO Reporter *(see p. 163) and* Fate *magazine (see pp. 81, 83), first aired his own complaints against CSICOP, reprinted here, in the February 1987 issue of* Omni. —T.S.

Skeptics and Pseudo-skeptics

by Marcello Truzzi

Over the years, I have decried the misuse of the term "skeptic" when used to refer to all critics of anomaly claims. Alas, the label has been thus misapplied by both proponents and critics of the paranormal. Sometimes users of the term have distinguished between so-called "soft" versus "hard" skeptics, and I in part revived the term "zetetic" because of the term's misuse; but I now think the problems created go beyond mere terminology, and matters need to be set right. Since "skepticism" properly refers to doubt rather than denial—nonbelief rather than belief—critics who take the negative rather than an agnostic position but still call themselves "skeptics" are actually *pseudo-skeptics* and have, I believe, gained a false advantage by usurping that label.

In science, the burden of proof falls upon the claimant; and the more extraordinary a claim, the heavier is the burden of proof demanded. The true skeptic takes an agnostic position, one that says the claim is *not proved* rather than *disproved*. He asserts that the claimant has not borne the burden of proof and that science must continue to build its cognitive map of reality without incorporating the extraordinary claim as a new "fact." Since the true skeptic does not assert a claim, *he has no burden to prove anything*. He just goes on using the established theories of "conventional science" as usual. But if a critic asserts that there is evidence for disproof, that he has a *negative hypothesis* (*e.g.*, the conjecture that a seeming psi result was actually due to an artifact), he is *making a claim* and therefore also *has to bear a burden of proof*. Sometimes, such negative claims by critics are also quite extraordinary (*e.g.*, that a UFO was actually a giant plasma or that someone in a psi experiment was cued via an abnormal ability to hear a high pitch others with normal ears would fail to notice), in which case the negative claimant also may have to bear a heavier burden of proof than might normally be expected.

Critics who assert negative claims but who mistakenly call themselves "skeptics" often act as though they (as would be appropriate only for the agnostic or true skeptic) have no burden of proof placed on them at all. A result of this is that many critics seem to feel it is only necessary to present a case for their counter-claims based upon plausibility rather than empirical evidence. Thus, if a subject in a psi experiment can be shown to have had an opportunity to cheat, many critics seem to assume not merely that he probably did cheat but that he *must* have, regardless of what may be the complete absence of evidence that he did so cheat (and sometimes ignoring evidence of the subject's past reputation for honesty). Similarly, improper randomization procedures are sometimes assumed to be the cause of a subject's high psi scores even though all that has been established is the *possibility* of such an artifact having been the real cause. Of course, the evidential weight of the experiment is greatly reduced when we discover an opening in the design that would allow an artifact to confound the results. Discovering an opportunity for error should make such experiments less evidential and usually unconvincing; it usually disproves the claim that the experiment was "airtight" against error, but it does not *disprove* the anomaly claim. Showing evidence is unconvincing is not grounds for completely dismissing it. If a critic asserts that the result was due to artifact X, that critic then has the burden of proof to demonstrate that artifact X can and probably did produce such results under such circumstances. Admittedly, in some cases the appeal to mere plausibility that an artifact produced the result may be so great that nearly all would accept the argument (*e.g.*, when we learn that someone known to have cheated in the past had an opportunity to cheat in this instance, we might reasonably conclude he probably cheated this time, too); but in far too many instances, the critic who makes a merely plausible argument for an artifact closes the door on future research when proper science demands that his hypothesis of an artifact should also be tested. Alas, most critics seem happy to sit in their armchairs producing *post hoc* counterexplanations. Whichever side ends up with the true story, science best progresses through laboratory investigations.

On the other hand, proponents of an anomaly claim who recognize the above fallacy may go too far in the other direction. Some argue, like psychiatrist Cesare Lombroso (1836-1909) when he defended the mediumship of Eusapia Palladino (1854-1941), that the presence of wigs does not deny the existence of real hair. All of us must remember science can tell us what is empirically unlikely but not what is empirically impossible. Evidence in science is always a matter of degree and is seldom if ever absolutely conclusive. Some proponents of anomaly claims, like some critics, seem unwilling to consider evidence in probabilistic terms, clinging to any slim loose end as though the critic must disprove all evidence ever put forward for a particular claim. Both critics and proponents need to learn to think of adjudication in science as more like that found in the law courts, imperfect and with varying degrees of proof and evidence. Absolute truth, like absolute justice, is seldom obtainable. We can only do our best to approximate them. ∎

Zetetic Scholar

The above piece appeared as an editorial in the August 1987 issue of the **Zetetic Scholar**. ("Zetetic" means "skeptically inquiring.") This judicious journal is published on an irregular schedule by the Center for Scientific Anomalies Research, headquartered at Eastern Michigan University. The CSAR stands somewhere between the uncritical "Fortean" press represented by the **Fortean Times** (pp. 81, 82) or **Fate** (pp. 81, 83), and the debunking-prone skepticism of the Committee for the Scientific Investigation of Claims of the Paranormal's (CSICOP's) **Skeptical Inquirer** (p. 198). In fact, **Zetetic Scholar** editor Marcello Truzzi edited the first few issues of CSICOP's journal before starting his own. The **Zetetic Scholar** encourages responsible, open-minded scientific inquiry into paranormal claims. Some **ZS** articles examine such claims, but the bulk of the journal is devoted to discussion of strategies for dealing with anomalous claims in an atmosphere suggestive of the planning stages of a fledgling science. And in the extensive "Dialogue" section, intelligent, articulate folks with varying reasons for being interested in anomalistics carry on lively conversations.

—T.S.

Zetetic Scholar
Marcello Truzzi, Editor
$15/year
(2 issues) from:
Zetetic Scholar
Department of Sociology
Eastern Michigan University
Ypsilanti, MI 48197

AM I PSYCHIC YET?

by Paul Krassner
Illustrated by Bill Griffith

EVERYBODY needs a metaphor to deal with the mystery of life. Personally, I used to believe in reincarnation, but that was in a previous lifetime. There are those who say that even an aborted fetus *chooses* parents who will not carry the pregnancy to term. Well, maybe I decided to be born, but I was circumcised against my will. And now there is another, more subtle form of child abuse, described in the June-July '86 issue of *The Psychic Reader*. The item is about a man who took his daughter into a store:

> She got caught stealing a package of cigarettes. When asked why, she said, "Because my father wanted them." He laughed and called her a liar. The truth was the father was trying to quit smoking and was emoting so much energy of wanting to smoke that his daughter went over and picked up the cigarettes to give to him. She was not even aware that she had stolen the cigarettes.

The explanation?

> When sensitive family members are affected by a strong male, a very important function happens: He takes control over the brain.

When a very angry male climbs into the space of a very sensitive wife or a very sensitive daughter with his energy, it is just as bad as striking them physically or violating them physically.

As a child, it was always very important to me *not* to believe in ESP. Adults might control many aspects of my life, but they could never exert power over what I thought. I indulged in the most bizarre fantasies, completely confident that they were not able to read my mind.

As an adult, I have tried to keep that mind open by maintaining what I consider a healthy skepticism. For example, at the Berkeley Psychic Institute in Berkeley, California, there is a clairvoyant training program — I had predicted there would be — and there is a clause in the application which states that students may cancel and receive full refunds if they do so in writing within two weeks. One would think that the registrar would have anticipated such an occurrence.

People *magazine called Paul Krassner the "father of the underground press," to which he replied, "I demand a blood test." Recently he's revived his legendary publication,* The Realist *(see page 208), which between 1958 and 1974 delighted the irreverent and outraged the straightlaced. I subscribed to it as a high school student in the late '60s, with mutagenic consequences. These days Krassner sandwiches stints as a stand-up comic between bouts of writing. If you've never seen his act, by all means go if you have the chance. Meanwhile, this is the next best thing.*
—T.S.

I WAS ONCE a guest on the *Long John Nebel Show*, an all-night radio program in New York. We were discussing psychic phenomena in general and telekinesis specifically. I put a dime on the table and said that if it could be moved by sheer will power I would immediately become a convert. The other guests ridiculed me. These were powerful gifts, not to be toyed with, they said. You could not move a dime just like that; you had to work up to it.

"All right, let's start with a penny . . . "

The Amazing Randi was also a guest on that show. In 1986, more than a quarter-century later, he was a guest on the *Johnny Carson Show*, demonstrating by film and special audio techniques how a prominent faith-healer "miraculously" received personal information about his patients from his wife, concealed backstage, transmitting to a radio receiver hidden in his ear. I wondered if Ronald Reagan's hearing aid was also actually a receiver for data from Nancy on legislators so that the absent-minded president could "remember" how to blackmail them into voting for aid to the Contras.

I N THE FILM *Rosemary's Baby*, Mia Farrow spelled out the name of her neighbor with Scrabble letters, and when she mixed them around, they spelled out the name of a warlock she had been reading about in a book on witchcraft. Similarly, if you spell out the name of former Vice President Spiro Agnew with Scrabble letters and then mix them around, they spell out GROW A PENIS. This is so appropriate that it defies ordinary standards of coincidence, for when Senator Charles Goodell came out against the war in Vietnam, it was Agnew who called him "the Christine Jorgensen of the Republican Party," thereby equating military might with the mere presence of a penis.

When Mike Wallace interviewed me for *Sixty Minutes* and asked about the difference between the underground press and the mainstream media, I told him about the above anagram, pointing out: "The difference is that I could print that in *The Realist*, but it'll be edited out of this program." Once again, my uncanny ability to forecast events accurately was dramatically demonstrated.

In 1963, during a standup performance at Manhattan's Town Hall, I said that the androgynous singer Tiny Tim would someday get married on the *Johnny Carson Show*. Six years later it happened. I thought I had

merely been projecting into the future a certain cultural trend of co-option, but Baba Ram Dass has called this an example of astral humor. "The connections are all out there," he said, pointing to the heavens. "It's just a matter of plucking them."

I guess one person's logic is another person's astral humor. More recently, I've said on stage that an AIDS victim would be charged with attempted murder when he spat at someone, and that came true. I've also said that since facial stubble has become fashionable by the grace of *Miami Vice*, some entrepreneur would market a razor that *left* facial stubble, and *that* came true.

This is comedy voodoo, and we mustn't let it fall into the wrong hands. I've recently said on stage that the next baboon-to-baby heart transplant would take place as soon as another baboon was in an auto accident and the proper release papers were signed by its parents. Does this mean there will soon be a rash of auto accidents involving baboons?

I N 1970 I took a workshop with John Lilly at Esalen. He was attempting to explore mysticism by the scientific method. We were not allowed to use such words as "project," "fantasize," "daydream," or "rationalize." For the purpose of the workshop we had to accept any experience as reality.

I communicated with my old friend Lenny Bruce, who had died four years previously. Lilly had been talking about not publishing the book he was working on, *The Deep Self*, and Lenny told me to tell him that it was his responsibility to publish it. But Lilly was consistent. "That's Lenny's problem," he said. Nevertheless, the book was published.

Later on, this contact with the grave continued, but I was now allowed to rationalize that I was using Lenny as a touchstone, projecting how I thought he would feel about something. I told his widow, Honey, about this, and she said that she communicated with the spirit of Lenny, too. I asked, "How do you know you're not just projecting?" She replied, "I *know*." Who could argue with that?

I N 1972, six weeks after the Watergate break-in, I presented the printer with a manuscript by assassination researcher Mae Brussell, titled "Why Was Martha Mitchell Kidnapped?" While the mass media still referred to the incident as a "caper" and a "third-rate burglary," her article delineated in detail the conspiratorial aspects, naming L. Patrick Grey, John Mitchell and Richard Nixon. Called crazy at the time, nine months later she was vindicated.

However, the printer wanted $5,000 cash — in advance. I didn't have it. I left totally confident, yet with no reason to feel that way. When I got home, the phone rang. It was Yoko Ono. I had met her in the '60s when she was an avant garde artist, and I had put all my savings into her absurdist project, where folks would get into big black burlap bags on a wooden platform at a macrobiotic restaurant, and people would pay to watch them move around. I think it had something to do with my guilt about money.

Now, Yoko was married to John Lennon. They were visiting San Francisco, and did I want to have lunch with them? Suffice it to say that I brought the galleys with me, and we all ended up going to the bank and withdrawing $5000 cash. My mind was thoroughly blown. I could rationalize to bits the process by which we had come together, but the timing was so exquisite that for me coincidence and mysticism had become the same process.

At that time, the Nixon administration was afraid that Lennon would entertain protesters at the upcoming Republican convention, and there was a strong attempt to deport him. The FBI refuses to release the portion of his file for that period when he was under such heavy surveillance. And, caught somewhere between information overload and political paranoia, I went slightly bonkers myself.

On a bus to Santa Cruz, I was convinced that the man sitting in front of me was a CIA operative. In order to confuse him, I used my ball-point pen as a walkie-talkie: "Calling Abbie Hoffman. Calling Abbie Hoffman . . ." Abbie was freaking out himself around the same time, and it occurred to me that I might have actually *reached* him in this unorthodox manner. Recently I asked him about that.

"Oh, yeah," he replied. "I got your call but I didn't accept it 'cause you were calling collect."

PERHAPS I have simply become too hard up for mystical experience for my own good. But why do those creatures from outer space always make their presence known to *others*? Why don't they ever come to *me*? I would give them publicity or granola or whatever they wanted.

Only once was I convinced that I was about to have a close encounter with beings from another planet. From a cliff above the beach I could see them, dark figures with no ears. They were marking up the ocean floor, dividing it into latitudinal and longitudinal lines, just like on a globe. I was so excited. At last! Only, they turned out to be a few guys in wet suits, and they were digging for clams. Oh, well.

When *Hustler* publisher Larry Flynt got converted to born-again Christianity by Ruth Carter Stapleton, the evangelist sister of then-President Jimmy Carter, he hired me to reform his magazine of gynecological porno. I asked him a test question: "Do you believe that Christ is the one true path to salvation?"

"I believe," he responded with a Kentucky twang, "that Jesus was not a more important teacher than Buddha, and that neither Jesus nor Buddha is more important than any individual."

He took me into his office and said, "Do you see that wall there? I can make that wall come tumbling down through sheer will power." *Oh boy*, I thought to myself, *this is gonna be some job*. "But," he added, "I don't wanna misuse my power."

Nobody ever wants to misuse their power for me. The Transcendental Meditators won't levitate for me. Uri Geller wouldn't even bend my fork. Maybe it's hopeless.

Flynt got shot a few months later, his wife

Althea took over, and she fired me. I called up family and friends so they wouldn't learn this news from the media. Ken Kesey said, "Why don't you come to Egypt with us? The Grateful Dead are gonna play the Pyramids."

I lay down in a long-dead king's sarcophagus in the middle of the Great Pyramid and started chanting. I wanted a sign so badly. But nothing happened. The only sign I got was that the tomb smelled from somebody's urine. Maybe the guides were being tested for illegal drugs.

Recently, though, it finally happened. I got my sign. I was watching a movie on cable TV, *Falling in Love* with Meryl Streep and Robert DeNiro. I wasn't sure whether I wanted to continue watching it or not. Outside there was a fantasic thunderstorm. Suddenly, a bolt of lightning struck, and my TV set went off.

Okay. I believe, I believe.

Why, just the other day I'm sure I heard a butterfly complaining about how it was really a caterpillar trapped in a butterfly's body . . . ■

The Realist and Best of the Realist

*Miracles do happen. **The Realist** is back. Professional scamp Paul Krassner has been talking about reviving the granddaddy of all underground magazines for over a decade, but it took several years of Reagan and a loan from a sympathetic foundation to finally make it happen.*

*During the late '50s and early '60s, **The Realist** was almost alone in offering wicked, anti-establishment satire and commentary to a literate audience. Its contributors included Lenny Bruce, Norman Mailer, Robert Anton Wilson, and cartoonist Dick Guindon, among others, and its influence far outweighed its circulation. During its most notorious period in the late '60s and early '70s, it indulged in political put-ons (such as the infamous "Parts Left Out of the Kennedy Book") and unleashed Mae Brussel's minutely researched conspiracy theories on an unsuspecting public.*

*The cream of the magazine's run from 1958 to 1974 is attractively anthologized in **Best of the Realist** from Running Press. Chock full of cartoons, interviews, fibs, and jabs to both the left and the right, the anthology is a bargain at $9.95.*

***The Realist** itself is back in the flesh as an 8-page newsletter. Since Krassner has been most active as a standup comic in recent years, the new incarnation has a quicker off-the-cuff pace than the old. If you liked **The Realist** before, you'll be pleased to meet it anew. If you only knew it as a rumor in the past, now's a good time to see what the talk was all about.* —Jay Kinney

• And be sure to tell 'em Groucho sent you . . .
Groucho Marx said in a recent interview: "I think the only hope this country has is Nixon's assassination."

"Uh, sorry, Mr. Marx, you're under arrest for threatening the life of the President. I can't tell you how much I enjoyed *A Night At the Opera*. Here, now if you'll just slip into these plastic handcuffs . . . ."

I wrote to the local office of the United States Department of Justice, inquiring about the status of the case against Groucho, particularly in view of the indictment of Black Panther David Hilliard for using similar rhetoric.

Here's the reply I received:

Dear Mr. Krassner:
Responding to your inquiry, the United States Supreme Court has held that Title 18 U.S.C., Section 871 prohibits only "true" threats. It is one thing to say "I (or we) will kill Richard Nixon" when you are the leader of an organization which advocates killing people and overthrowing the government; it is quite another to utter the words which are attributed to Mr. Marx, an alleged comedian. It was the opinion of both myself and the United States Attorney in Los Angeles (where Marx's words were alleged to have been uttered) that the latter utterance did not constitute a "true" threat.
Very truly yours,
James L. Browning, Jr.
United States Attorney
—*Best of The Realist*

• Trivial Censorship:
John Nason, vice president of public relations for Selchow & Righter, manufacturer of Trivial Pursuit, admits he was embarrassed by a question included only in the early editions of the game, namely:
"How many months pregnant was Nancy Reagan when she walked down the matrimonial aisle with Ronald?"
The answer was two months, although Nancy may now wish that she had gotten an abortion, so that daughter Patti's novel would never have been published. —*The Realist*

—B. Kliban
—*Best of The Realist*

The Realist
Paul Krassner, Editor
$23/(12 issues) from:
The Realist
P.O. Box 1230
Venice, CA 90294

Best of the Realist
Paul Krassner, Editor
1984; 256 pp.
$9.95
($11.20 postpaid) from:
Running Press
125 South 22nd Street
Philadelphia, PA 19103
215/567-5080

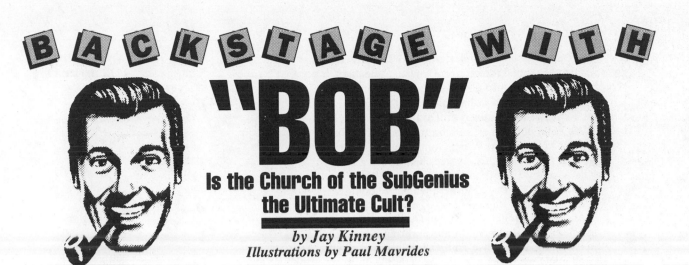

BACKSTAGE WITH "BOB"

Is the Church of the SubGenius the Ultimate Cult?

by Jay Kinney
Illustrations by Paul Mavrides

SCIENTISTS AGREE EARTH TIME IS SHORT!!!

HOW THEY DENY YOU SLACK

IT'S 9:30 OR SO, BACKSTAGE AT the Stone, a nightclub on Broadway in San Francisco. Guy Deuel, the ex-cattle rancher from Bolivia with the artificial septum, is fondling an Uzi, the Israeli automatic weapon favored by death squads in Central America. The Uzi—like the ridge between Deuel's nostrils—is plastic. Deuel, who is an imposing fortyish figure in a tan trenchcoat, looks uncannily like G. Gordon Liddy and has the air of a man who is no stranger to life-and-death situations. Deuel is a SubGenius.

Out front on stage, Janor Hypercleats is stalking back and forth across the stage delivering a hell-raising sermon to an audience of several hundred souls. Janor mows lawns for a living in Little Rock, Arkansas, and cuts an odd figure in his garish orange and green pants, looking like the penultimate hick come to the big city. It is not totally clear just what Janor is raving about in his Little Rock twang—something to do with "Launching the Head," golfing, "BOB," Heaven, and his sex life or lack thereof. But that hardly seems to matter. Janor is a SubGenius.

What has brought both Guy and Janor to San Francisco in the damp chill of November, 1985, is the chance to participate in the SubGenius Devival, a one-night-only extravaganza offered to both the general public and to devoted members of the Church of the SubGenius. There are bands from San Francisco, singers and preachers from Dallas, an intense character in shades from back East who calls himself "the Pope of All New York" and a smattering of artists, go-fers, and borderline basketcases.

IN AN ERA OF DESIGNER JEANS, designer drugs, and designer cigarettes, it was probably inevitable that someone would establish a designer cult—in this case one whose members keep redesigning its contours on an almost daily basis.

SubGenii may be brainwashed—one need only listen to an hour of drool-flecked conversation about X-ists and "BOB" and Wotan to arrive at that conclusion—but, contrary to every other cult on the horizon, the SubGenii are busily washing their own brains. If there is a "Mister Big" pulling strings from behind the scenes he stays very well hidden indeed. Of course, there *is* the nagging question of cult-founder J.R. "BOB" Dobbs—a shadowy figure in the tradition of L. Ron Hubbard and Howard Hughes—but Dobbs's death in early 1985 brought a halt to any efforts to centralize control of cult members within a rigid hierarchy.

What remains may be scary or at least nauseating —the best estimates of SubGenius membership place the cult at approximately the same size as the forces of Lyndon LaRouche—but it is a decentralized phenomenon. As police departments around the country have learned, the threat that the average SubGenius represents is the danger of the lone berserker run amok, *not* the threat of lockstep fascism.

SubGenii are not interested in selling you flowers at airports. That is not SubGenius style. They are far more likely to sidle up to you in a public lavatory and pee on your shoes. *That* is SubGenius style.

The origins of the Church of the SubGenius are hazy at best. The earliest known nationally circulated Church literature bears copyrights dating no earlier than the late 1970s. But Church old-timers like Rev. Ivan Stang of Dallas date their involvement in the cult back to the late '50s. At that time the Church was a local Dallas-based group numbering no more than a couple of dozen members. Like other obscure fringe groups of that era such as the Science of Mentalphysics group in Yucca Valley, California, or the Mark-Age saucer-contactee bunch in Florida, the SubGenius Foundation, as it was then known, was a self-perpetuating organization clustered around a charismatic leader. ☞

Jay Kinney is a former editor of and a frequent contributor to Whole Earth Review. *He's also the editor of* Gnosis: A Journal of the Western Inner Traditions *(see p. 30). Recently he adopted the role of investigative reporter in order to research the mysterious Church of the SubGenius, one of the fastest-growing religions of the twentieth century. Here he throws some light on this cult's enigmatic beliefs and history, which until now have been inaccessible to outsiders.* —T.S.

crap

POISON

GUNS

BEWARE THE
PINK BOYS

J.R. Dobbs (usually referred to as "BOB" by cult members) founded the group following a speckled career as a bit-actor in C-movies and an extended stint as an aluminum siding salesman. Dobbs's success as a salesman enabled him to build up a sizeable nest-egg and put him on sure footing for convincing others of his sincerity. When Dobbs began to hear voices in the mid-1950s—voices he identified alternately as aliens (X-ists) and as a so-called Space God (Jehovah-1)—he wasted little time in developing a small but devoted following.

According to Stang, early SubGenius emphasis was on self-development (hence the group's name) and on Dobbs's eccentric political philosophy, which shared many elements with the far right ideology of Robert Welch's John Birch Society. Things might have stayed that way—just another small fringe group in a western state—except for a few unexpec-

Cult accoutrements: meditation pyramids and over-the-counter drugs.

ted twists in the SubGenius path. The first twist was Dobbs's serious extended love affair with LSD in the late 1960s and early 1970s. During this period the Foundation evolved into a Church and Dobbs's cluster of SubGenii went through an unsavory spell where experimentation with sex and drugs was *de rigueur.* The second twist was the arrival of Dr. Philo Drummond in the late 1970s.

Drummond, who had prior experience in the public relations field and was a graduate of est, apparently saw much potential in the tiny Church and rapidly worked his way to a position of power second only to Dobbs himself. In league with Stang, who was now number three in the cult, Drummond introduced the use of "BOB"'s face on Church flyers and instituted a policy of heavy new-member recruitment. Public meetings in Dallas were advertised and began to draw sizeable crowds. Branches of the Church (called "clenches" in SubGenius parlance) spread to Little Rock and Austin. And perhaps most innovative of all, Drummond and Stang pushed for a policy of clench autonomy, both theologically and organizationally. As SubGenii proliferated, so did the gods and demons in the SubGenius pantheon. What had started as a monotheistic neo-UFO cult in the 1950s had transmogrified into a polytheistic grab-bag in the 1980s.

One indication of the new regime instituted by Drummond was the extensive use of false Church

210

...LIKE DOGS BEGGING FOR A TREAT

names in place of members' real names. Though Stang and Drummond's names were authentic enough, most post-1979 SubGenii took assumed names as part of their initiation into the cult. Janor Hypercleats and Sterno Keckhaver (both from Little Rock), Tentatively A. Convenience (of Baltimore), Pastor Buck Naked (of Dallas), Puzzling Evidence (of Oakland), Lies (of San Francisco), St. Byron Werner (of L.A.)—all sported transparently ridiculous monickers. This, in combination with the policy of making every cult member a *de facto* minister, brought a bizarre air of unreality to Church proceedings, with Popes, Saints, and Reverends all competing for positions of power over each other. It also brought the Church to the attention of the FBI and IRS, who were concerned that a new outbreak of mail-order ordinations, all claiming tax-exempt status, might lend further momentum to the growing ranks of the tax revolt.

THE SUBGENIUS DEVIVAL IS STILL GOING strong as the clock at the Stone hits midnight. Pastor Buck Naked has come and gone with his auto-harp songs about electrical devices embedded in his brain. Rev. Ivan Stang has stirred up the crowd with a ritual demonstration of Time Control consisting of sledgehammering to smithereens the wristwatch of a trusting volunteer from the audience. Janor and Sterno have "Launched the Head." The Band That Dare Not Speak Its Name, a local aggregation of anti-musicians, has gotten the faithful to their feet with stinging anti-songs about "BOB." And now the evening is reaching a frenzied climax with the arrival of Rev. Meyer, "the Pope of All New York."

As a dry-ice mist rises from the stage, Meyer, ac-

HOW TO FOOL THE AUTHORITIES

A chart depicting the complicated SubGenius cosmology and pantheon.

The Reverend Stang delivers a cable-televised rant from the Church's Dallas headquarters.

companied by two armed bodyguards, stalks out to the podium and delivers a bellowing tirade against "pinks," MTV, yuppies, personalized license plates, and "the Conspiracy." Meyer possesses an uncanny and disquieting charisma that local commentators have likened to that of the late Rev. Jim Jones. Back on his own ground in New York he has filled the trendy Danceteria to overflowing with several public SubGenius rallies. But here in San Francisco, a few doors down from Carol Doda's topless act at the Condor and across the street from the fourth generation mohawks at the Mabuhay Gardens, Meyer is just another late night act. Or so it seems to Meyer, who cuts his speech back to a mere twenty minutes and stalks off stage abruptly to a final explosion of applause, cheers, and weary table-thumping. The Devival is devolving and will shortly taper off into canned DEVO music and dancing.

Perhaps the Church of the SubGenius is merely a harmless eccentric sect sprung from the same sun-baked environment that Jack Ruby and Lyndon Johnson both called home. Texas is the home of broad gestures and the SubGenii may be one of the broadest yet.

Yet one need only watch the glint in Guy Deuel's eyes as he cocks the Uzi in the dressing room and talks about "showing those pinkboys a thing or two" to realize that one man's meat may be another man's poison. The Church of the SubGenius has long since outgrown its humble roots and is stalking bigger game. Consider it all a joke at your own risk. ∎

The Book of the SubGenius and The Stark Fist of Removal and Arise: The SubGenius Video

This book is it—the Bible of the Church of the SubGenius. The rationales, scriptures, iconic art, myths, personae, and pure unadulterated rants of this disturbed denomination can be found therein. You may be shocked or mystified if you dare to dive in, but you won't be bored.

*The **Stark Fist** is the Church's official (and more-or-less annual) newsletter. It averages 100 pages of letters, art, reports, and clippings from hundreds of Church members around the world.*
                                                    —Jay Kinney

*Or maybe you'd rather not read. Subject yourself instead to the mind-bending **Arise: The Subgenius Video: The Movie**, an "Instructional Video Barrage Tape" that employs the patented "Subliminimal Hypno-Pediatrics Trance-Inducement Tone." You'll never be the same. I'm not.*   —T.S.

• St. Janor later explained to me what had possessed him to suddenly perform an unsanctified Launching.

"After I received the Transmission I knew it was the time of the Launching. The Head had to be off the earth to be photocopied by the Xists . . . the Arnold Palmer Head is the only living being with the skill needed to defeat the Yists. With his handicap—no body—his only possible rival would be the Zists from the Backwards Time Universe, or else Trevino. Trevino's already working with the Yists . . . in fact, every golfer is working with a different race of aliens. Thus every golf tournament is a universal psychic war. The Launchings are to create enough psychic energy to push Palmer to the top. If Trevino wins . . . you may mock me now, but you won't think it's so funny when this entire planet falls into the sandtrap. But if earth is driven into the correct Black Hole, we'll all gain infinite Slack for eternity. The Yists are trying to kill Palmer but they can't because this world is stronger than the Dream World. All SubGeniuses MUST WATCH GOLF TOURNAMENTS."
                                    —The Stark Fist of Removal

• Countless personal saviors!!! The SubGenius knows, bull-dadaistically, that each SubGenius should do WOTAN's work exactly as He reveals it to him, and that He has wildly varying messages for different people in different situations.

By the same token, it is madness to accept any one "personal savior"—even Dobbs—as a permanent guide. Perhaps "Bob's" greatest invention is the concept of SHORT DURATION PERSONAL SAVIORS, or "Shordurpersavs" in Tibetan. The true Sub accepts into his heart, as his own personal savior, anyone or anything with which he happens to be impressed at the moment. Shordurpersavs change from hour to hour, from whim to whim. It could be the hero of a movie you just saw, the author of a book, a bottle of Thunderbird, a good pal, a dog, a sex object. Not professional gurus you are locked into believing, but temporary ones according to the need of The Now. They change so fast that it never gets embarrassing; you aren't inclined to 'proselytize' them off on disinterested others who will later laugh at you; you know their effects will wear off in minutes—although the very idea is unthinkable while under the Influence. One need not mention them at all—a superb Tenet, since one is sometimes deeply ashamed for having a particular, unsavory Shordurpersav: some can be Personal Saviors and False Prophets at the same time.

As said before, SLACK is a trickster.
                                    —The Book of the SubGenius

The Book of the SubGenius
Rev. Ivan Stang
1983, 1987; 194 pp.
$9.95
($11 postpaid)

The Stark Fist of Removal
Rev. Ivan Stang, Editor
$5/issue

Arise
The Subgenius Video
The Movie
$39.95 postpaid
1987; 120 minutes

All from:
The SubGenius
Foundation
P. O. Box 140306
Dallas, TX 75214

Your Pathway to
Cosmic Truth
—By Mail!!

DO YOU HAVE "different" tastes? Intrigued by the bizarre, the kooky, the outré—as long as it keeps its distance? Enjoy getting unsolicited, *unspeakably weird* things in the mail—for free? Love to snicker in superiority (perhaps largely imagined) at the incredible gullibility of others? Enjoy reading the headlines on sleazy tabloids, and ads for local psychic fortune tellers? Appreciate unexpected glimpses of the strange "realities" behind religions other than your own? Entranced by the thought processes of the mentally ill? *Painfully aware that all the great geniuses and inventors of the past appeared totally insane to everyone around them?*

Then . . . **HAVE WE GOT A HOBBY FOR YOU!!**

The Traveling Snake-Oil Medicine Show isn't dead—it just travels by mail. Simply by writing for information—*without sending money*—you can embark on a neverending tour of the zoo of beliefs, the circus of gullibility, the freak show of Faith, the arena of the utter strangeness of true genius, of that which is all-too-literally ahead of its time.

Few hobbies are simpler. Here's how it's done:

You type up a form letter, saying something ambiguous like, "I am interested in your product/services. Please send details, catalog." Xerox a few dozen copies of it. Go through

The Keys to INSTANT SUCCESS, MYSTIC KNOWLEDGE, MIRACULOUS INVENTIONS & CONTACT WITH THE SPACE BROTHERS *are Within Your Grasp— For Only a 25¢ Stamp!*

by Rev. Ivan Stang,
**Philosophur Ekstaticus
Church of the SubGenius**

this article, as well as the cheesy ads in the back of your favorite lowbrow magazines (*Soldier of Fortune*, perhaps, or the *Weekly World News*, or that great old stand-by, the *National Enquirer*) and mail off for anything that interests you. With the more fanatical groups, a simple request for information like this can net you several thick volumes of priceless *bulldada* (a collectors' term meaning "that which is great because it doesn't know how bad it is").

Your 25¢ investment will pay off geometrically as your address is sold from one mailing list to another. Soon, A MILLION CONTRADICTORY PATHS TO HAPPINESS will be vying for your *personal* attention in the mailbox, paths ranging from inadvertently hilarious delusions to the wisdom of the ages, yet—and this is the most revealing part—each one *the only TRUE Path!!*

Weirdness-by-mail is a *safe* hobby; in my ten years of collecting, I have never once had any kook, psychotic, holyman or enlightened genius appear at my door. The Secret Service, yes. But they weren't trying to sell me anything.

HELPFUL HINTS:

Spirit mediums, UFO contactees, and fly-by-night Mystery Schools are notoriously short-lived. At the time of writing, all addresses were good, but we can't guarantee how long they'll last.

When ordering magazines, Canadians should always add a dollar for extra postage; for overseas orders, add $2. Prices quoted are in U.S. dollars—use international money orders or checks drawn on U.S. banks. ☞

Ivan Stang is a co-founder of the Church of the Subgenius (see pp. 209-212). A different version of this survey of weirdness-by-mail appeared in a past issue of Whole Earth Review, *and led to an outrageously entertaining book called* High Weirdness By Mail, *which I highly recommend if you are maniacal enough to want more ($9.95; $11 postpaid from The Subgenius Foundation, P.O. Box 140306, Dallas, TX 75214).*
—T.S.

Some descriptions submitted by other Subgenii, including: Dr. Philo U. Drummond, T.J. Tellier, Dennis Cripps, Glenn Bray, Lou Minati, Remote Control, and Ted Schultz.
©1989 Rev. Ivan Stang

WEIRD SCIENCE

When writing to these outfits, It's a good idea to sound as nutty as they do. You'll get faster service and a lot more loot. But keep in mind that some may not be nearly as "nutty" as you think, lost as you are in a backwash of "conventional science" ignorance.

THE EARTH IS THE CENTER OF THE UNIVERSE!
Bible-Science Association
2911 E. 42nd St.
Minneapolis, MN 55406

Your headquarters for Creationism over Evolution. The booklet *Geocentricity* offers, for 35¢, Biblical *and scientific* proof that the Earth is standing still at the center of a revolving Cosmos. I'm with them—screw all those telescopes and astronomy stuff anyway. Humanists like Copernicus, who say this planet is nothing special, are just trying to avoid thinking about The Judgement. "It is not the Earth that is spinning, but the sky that is spinning." *Something's* spinning, that's for sure. Free catalog of books, audio cassettes, and videos (!) on the *real* history of our planet, all Biblically verified. Adam and Eve lived 6,000 years ago. Videos of the ruins of their home, and also of the Tower of Babel. Native Americans are ancient Hebrews. Photos of the Ark of the Covenant. "Giant Man Tracks" next to dinosaur footprints in Texas prove Covenant Men walked with the Great Reptiles. 50¢ for a dozen tracts, Newsletter, $12/yr.

EVOLUTION IS TRUE SCIENCE! YOUR CREATION-SCIENCE IS RELIGION IN SHEEP'S CLOTHING! SHAME ON YOU!

EVOLUTION
SECULAR HUMANISM

LAKESIDE RESORT CONDOS OF THE GODS
The Stelle Group
P.O. Box 75
Quinlan, TX 75474

"Dawn of a New Age City." An actual town where you can escape the end of the world and learn from the "ancient Brotherhood," except that it isn't really quite built yet. Based on *The Ultimate Frontier*, a techno-occult book foretelling disasters for the turn of the century. Starts off looking like a planned community built on alternate technology—fuel alcohol, wind energy, hydroponics . . . then you find out they're going to make you an "Initiate" of the White Brotherhood, and you have to kiss your capacity for critical thought bye-bye. Free info.

FINAL SCENE OF "THE LATTER DAYS"

THE ULTIMATE SUPERBRAIN HUMAN FUNCTIONING SECRETS!
Fry's Modern Humans
879 Park Avenue
Perris, CA 92370

Incredible free tabloid catalog comes in two parts—first, ads for various rare books and folios on psychotronic technology, crystal levitators, time machines, Tesla space drive inventions, pyramid power, alien aircraft on the Moon, divining rods, perpetual motion machines, etc. Second half is a giant come-on for the "Modern Humans" course in Superbrain energies, much of which is devoted to explaining why they charge so much. "Our Time Camera covers from one hour to 99 million years! Just think what you could do! You'll have a blast with this gem of a unit!" "Time Cameras"?! The damn secrets of the universe have been for sale right under our noses all this time, and nobody's paid any attention! We can only pray that this knowledge does not fall into the wrong hands! Best feature is the primitive clip-art. Send $1 for more detailed catalogs.

COMMUNIST DESCENDANTS OF THE ABOMINABLE SNOWMAN
Inner Portraits by Stanislav Szukalski
Glenn Bray
P.O. Box 4482
Sylmar, CA 91342

This large, beautifully printed book is a real treasure on two normally conflicting counts: Szukalski's artwork is astonishing, while his bizarre discoveries in his science of Zermatism, to which his art relates, are among the most compellingly weird this writer has encountered. There are two races: true Humans, and Yetinsyn half-breeds, the degenerate progeny of human women raped by Yetis (i.e., Bigfoots, Pans, Abominable Snowmen). The Yetinsyny tend to be criminals, communists, and dictators. There's far more to it than that, though, and it's nearly impossible to do justice to the *style* of this book; Szukalski is an unsung Crazed Genius whose written rants, beautiful art and tragic life story all swing between the upliftingly surreal and the psychotically paranoid. A God among kooks. $12.00 postpaid and actually well worth it! (Serious Zermatists can pursue further studies in a series of videotaped Szukalski lectures: $38.50 each.)

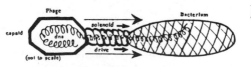

LIFE IS PHYSICS, NOT CHEMISTRY!
The Final Secret of Life
6519 40th NE
Seattle, WA 98115

Most fringe scientists aren't burdened with a lot of undo modesty, and this outfit's no exception. *The Final Secret of Life* is the name of their magazine, and it contains headlines like "The Final Breakthrough—It's Here!" But who knows? They could be right! What they're saying is that biochemists are barking up the wrong tree —enzyme chemical reactions can't explain the reactions in living cells. Instead, all of the little microfilaments and macromolecular structures that appear in electron micro-photographs are miniature electrical circuits, coil windings, superconductors, and motors! There's plenty of philosophizing, too. A gem of fringe science! Subscriptions are $25/yr.; write for info.

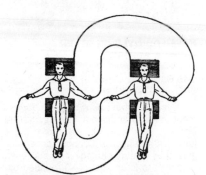

FIG. 3.—Two subjects in closed relaxation circuit. Each subject with left hand (−) to head (+) and right hand (+) to spine (−) of other subject.

ONE-STOP WEIRD SCIENCE SOURCE
Borderland Sciences Research Foundation
P.O. Box 429
Garberville, CA 95440-0429

Among the granddaddies of weird science, these guys have been around since 1945—long before New Age latecomers. They publish a backlog of papers on subjects like ether physics, radionics, dowsing, Tesla, hollow earth, UFOs, cancer cures, etc., etc. Their bi-monthly journal features nifty plans for all kinds of build-it-yourself devices like Jet Lag Neutralizers and Homo-Vibra Ray Machines, some of which they also sell already assembled. The Journal of Borderland Research is $20/yr ($3.50/sample); their "occult organ" Living Sphere is $25/year ($7.77/sample); write for free info.

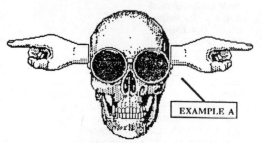

EXAMPLE A

UNIVERSE TWO:
NOT BETTER, JUST DIFFERENT
The Quarternion Journal
P.O. Box 315, Station A
Vancouver, B.C. V6C 2M7, CANADA

Devotes itself to "highly abstract possibilities in science and art." Highly abstract is right! Nuttiest damn theories on logic, reality, and the universe you could hope to find. Bizarre diagrams illustrating the

foundations of existence. This is what you might call "naive quantum physics." $2 per issue.

ORGONE BLANKETS!
MULTI-WAVE OSCILLATORS!
FOR SALE CHEAP!
Klark Kent Super Science
P.O. Box 392
Dayton, OH 45409

Klark Kent isn't kidding around. Ready for the New Age business boom, he takes Mastercard and Visa for his wacky devices, sold for "experimental purposes only," you understand. The Lakhovsky Multi Wave Oscillator comes built into its own suitcase so you can take it anywhere—think of the commotion you'll cause next time you try to carry it on the plane. It's hard to pin Kent down on what exactly this $640 device is supposed to do, but why bother him with details? (One piece of literature, sent for "information purposes only," says it cures terminal cancer, arthritis, allergies—you name it.) And what New Age date could resist the line: "Wanna join me under my orgone blanket?"

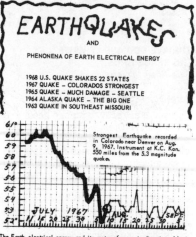

EARTHQUAKES AND PHENOMENA OF EARTH ELECTRICAL ENERGY

1968 U.S. QUAKE SHAKES 22 STATES
1967 QUAKE – COLORADOS STRONGEST
1965 QUAKE – MUCH DAMAGE – SEATTLE
1964 ALASKA QUAKE – THE BIG ONE
1963 QUAKE IN SOUTHEAST MISSOURI

Strongest Earthquake recorded in Colorado near Denver on Aug. 9, 1967. Instrument at K.C. Kan. 550 miles from the 5.3 magnitude quake.

The Earth electrical energy and its major changes in direction of horizontal flow, showing an extreme reading 2 days before the Quake.

NATURE'S MYSTERIES UNLOCKED
WITH UNIFIED NATURAL LAWS
Uni-Geo
5122 Harvard
Kansas City, MO 64133

Matter becomes lighter before tornadoes, but heavier before earthquakes! "This data cannot be refuted. . . . TIME is a great precision controlling force over a wild, erratic EARTH ELECTRICAL ENERGY which was by instruments found to have a controlling relationship with NATURE'S functions of MATTER, EVAPORATION, GROWTH and NATURAL DISASTERS." See? It all ties in. The government has "for 20 years of carnage" deliberately roadblocked the knowledge by which we could have predicted ALL natural disasters. This poor old dude has been totally and deliberately ignored by the so-called experts. How can you or I be sure he's wrong? Free info; complete data $4.

MORE ANSWERS THAN EINSTEIN
Kyklos Foundation
22143 Sherman Way
Canoga Park, CA 91303

One thing about these weird-science types: they love comparing themselves to geniuses of the past. The Kyklos Foundation's magazine, Cycles, has headlines like "The Nature of the Universe! First New Theory Since Einstein!" It seems to exist for one noble purpose: to promote the rantings of a guy named Aldo Aulicino, whose picture appeared on one cover with the headline "Does He Really Have All the Answers?" Guess what the answer was. Most of the articles aren't signed—gee, who do you think writes them?

Aldo's got this theory that in prehistoric times the earth was inhabited by intelligent creatures called protocceti. They had a big civilization, but blew it up with a nuclear explosion, wiping out the dinosaurs. That's when they decided to move into the ocean and evolve into dolphins. Nowadays, unbeknownst to us mortals, it's the superintelligent dolphins who are really running the show. They must have some sense of humor.

The kook-spotter's giveaway about Cycles is that Aldo's theories take up about five percent of the contents. The rest is a mighty rant about his lofty genius and the myopia of the ivory-tower scientists who have failed to recognize it, with some random political and social opinions thrown in for good measure. $6/yr.; ask for free info.

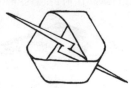

THEY WANT YOU TO THINK
IT'S "SCIENCE FICTION"
Rex Research
P.O. Box 1258,
Berkeley, CA 94701

Sells reprints of technical papers about neglected inventions of all kinds. Many old studies on bio-energetics, unusual motor designs, suppressed miracle cures, forgotten doohickies, and energy generators that may yet turn out to be the ones that save our planet. A monumental research job. Catalog $2.

UFO CONTACTEES

Of the thousands of people who receive the telepathic siren call of the space people, only a handful go public. Most aren't making any money, or even trying to, an indication of their sincerity. They heard the voices in their heads, and took them at face value.

YOU HAVE BEEN REMEMBERED BY THE SUPERIOR RATIONAL
Rational Culture
Caixa Postal 78.019-26150, Belford Roxo
Rio de Janeiro, RJ BRASIL, South America

Flying saucer cults have become so prevalent in South America that they represent a new religion; this is one of the biggest "denominations." It's also the funniest, partly because the translations from Portugese into English are so badly done as to severely amplify the already psychotic tone. "Our world is a bird that fabricates other birds, that we are and that here we are in passing." See? Not only are their newsletters and "space bible," *Universe In Disenchantment,* dictated by the space brothers, the book was actually *printed* by them! Millions of copies, imported by spaceship, imbued with healing power. Just owning a copy will cure any disease and even clear your home of poltergeists. The cosmic alien authors, collectively called the Superior Rational, offer a history of the Universe in which we didn't evolve from monkeys, but from ash-monsters formed from primordial "resin." "The primitive bodies were little monsters and afterwards monsters. Then monsters, after big monsters and after huge monsters . . . improving as the deformation progressed: they screamed-utter, made gestures to understand each other." This may sound really stupid to you, but in size this cult is gaining on the Mormons. Write for price list and info under current exchange rates; say you need lots of info because you are "with the Superior Rational." SPECIFY THAT YOU WANT IT IN ENGLISH!!

BEWARE! S-DAY APPROACHES!
A.T.A. Base
1500 N. Texas Blvd.
Weslaco, TX 78596

You wouldn't have suspected that the Armageddon Time Ark Base is located in Weslaco, Texas, where a hardy band of saucer contactees is preparing the earth for the hideous S. and X. Days when the shit's gonna hit the royal fan. But not to worry—if you've followed the instructions put out by these folks, instead of dying in the mass disasters you'll be awarded your own piece of land on the new, purged planet, you'll get a supply of 5-dimensional manna to eat, and, best of all, you'll get the keys to a 12-seater mini-starship to tool around in! Sound neat? Well, you better start packing, because the only way to join up is to "present yourself at The Base," where you'll udoubtedly be put to work doing menial labor—but think of the reward! Meanwhile, send $2 for their magazine, *S. Day Report.*

SURVIVE DOOMSDAY WITH THE SPACE BROS.!
Blue Rose Ministry
P.O. Box 332
Cornville, AZ 86325

If you are "ready," you can become one of the Chosen Ones who will be rescued by saucer from our doomed planet. These folks are the select trance mediums for space reps from dozens of worlds. Many booklets and cassette tapes offered, including guided tours of the Outer Planets by astral beings. For instance, "Ankar 22" of Jupiter describes all social and technical aspects of his home planet. This information is available telepathically, for NOTHING; yet NASA spends MILLIONS on crude rockets, and hasn't even been able to detect the huge cities on Uranus!! This one uses lots of revealing, low-brow punctuation techniques: *"You can 'learn' the 'mystic connection' between the Hopi's, the Pope's and the UFO's!"* The *Solar Space Letter* is $8/year; beg for sample.

INTERPLANETARY NEWS!
The Planetary Center
7803 Ruanne Court
Pasadena, MD 21122

Contactee Laura Mundo, a sweet little old lady, has been publishing saucer teachings in a newsletter for years. Her autobiography, *The Mundo UFO Report,* is only $2 —a steal! (Unlike many other saucerians, Mundo hasn't been doing it for the money.) In it she reveals the paths to becoming a Pre-Atomic Energy Being. (The Trinity, by the way, really means neutrons, protons, and electrons.) Classic contactee stuff.

HAVE YOU LIVED ON OTHER WORLDS BEFORE?
Unarius
145 S. Magnolia Ave.
El Cajon, CA 92020

This outfit must be a huge embarrassment to less flamboyant New Agers. Ruth Norman, aka "Uriel," by virtue of being a great Light-Bringer of Consciousness disguised as a nutty old lady, has successfully managed to keep herself surrounded by fawning teenage boys. Her husband was Jesus incarnate—but He died a few years back, durn it! He and almost every other dead holy man *and* great deceased scientist speak through Ruth, however, and the results fill more than eighty books. As vividly illustrated by photos of Ruth's garish costumes and Temple, this is one of the most patently, brazenly, ludicrously, and *inadvertently* fake saucer cults going; because of that, it's also one of the most successful. Some choice teachings: Earth is about to become the thirty-third member of the Interplanetary Confederation. Satan has learned his lesson and is now a good guy. (If he can change, so can you!) The aliens, guided by Ruth, will arrive in a huge "city" made of thirty-three saucers stacked in a pyramid. Newsletter, $8/year, or $1 for wonderful *Introduction to Unarius* booklet, well worth it for the shock you'll get when you fully comprehend that people BELIEVE this stuff.

WAR ON SKEPTICS
Secrets Newsletter
HC 80 Box 156
Marshall, AR 72650

It will be "too late for all but a handful to escape the pulverizing, the fire and deadly smoke that will come raining down from out of the strange craft we call Flying Saucers, totally obliterating cities, towns and the countryside (fear of this invasion is the real reason for Mr. Reagan's 'Star Wars' program)." $1 for sample; $8/yr.

INVASION OF THE SAUCER MEN
SST Publications/DELVE Magazine
Gene Duplantier,
17 Shetland St.
Willowdale, ONT., CANADA M2M 1X5

Great $1 catalog of UFO books; titles like *The Martian Alphabet, Secrets of the Popes, Hollow Earth at the End Time.* Many hard-to-find Hollow Earth books and contactee autobiographies here.

JESUS CONTACTEES & OTHER WEIRD RELIGIONS

The good news is, Jesus Christ has come again. The bad news is, He keeps coming and coming, again and again, under dozens of different names. It's getting hard to keep track of just how many Jesi are running around out there. For some reason, He has chosen not to contact any mainstream Christians, but works within strict New Age guidelines, speaking through mediums and Neo-Theosophists like the ghost of your dead grandma or any other common earth-bound spirit. How are Jesus contactees any different from UFO contactees? You got me.

BIG B.V.M. FLAP CONTINUES
Diamond Star Constellation
Rte. 2, Box 608
Necedah, WI 54646

Apparitions of the Blessed Virgin Mary "and other Celestials" appear to these worthies, bearing messages of peace/hate for the innocent/guilty. Newsletters, $3 each, go into great detail about Her secret warnings to mankind. Some UFO connections. In 1950 the B.V.M. appeared to Mrs. Fred Van Hoof, and has been in regular contact ever since. The Van Hoofs erected a shrine in Her honor that includes life-size sculptures of Jesus, the Apostles, St. Francis, and The Virgin Herself—all your favorite superheroes—but what about Santa Claus? Throw him in and they'd have one hell of a Christmas display. Intro booklet is $1.50.

THE SECOND CUMING
Truth Missionaries of Positive Accord
P.O. Box 42772
Evergreen Park, IL 60642-0772

It's tough to get a handle on this group; they have few precedents, and their material is thick with that hard-to-read verbosity that characterizes ambulatory schizophrenics. Offers Biblical proof of a "Goddess Eve"—part of it involves cosmic fellatio between consenting male and female "tachyon deities." The original male tachyon deity "spurted" into the mouth of the female tachyon deity, who in turn injected it into the womb of the Virgin Mary. Repetitive but highly original and complex ravings about Holy Sperm, Yahweh's ejaculation, Pure Milk Rays, etc. Where some faiths count the angels on a pinhead, this one counts the chromosomes in Jehovah's sperm and nitpicks unto infinity about other Triple-X-rated theological details. But what about God's POOP? What about the Goddess's BOOGERS?? All materials are free; I imagine it's hard to give this stuff away, unheeding Earth-fools being what they are.

(After this review first appeared in *Whole Earth Review*, Vice Bishop H. Jacobsen of Truth Missionaries wrote the following reply: "I'm not sure whether you ask [about God's poop and Goddess' boogers] because of a scatological fetish or an ecological concern. . . . Deity DO have corresponding anatomical parts, and anal parts are not merely ornamental in Them, any more than any parts. I guess the poop would be biodegradable in Heaven. Maybe they have assigned creatures to dispose of it. I don't think there are any 'Goddess's boogers'. What She breathes would not make any. Her nostrils always stay clean. Their poop might be the 'manna', called 'angels' food' in the Bible. Whatever, I'm sure they're efficient.")

NO WONDER THIS CULT IS SO SMALL
Shrine to Virginity
1569 Don Gaspar Avenue
Santa Fe, NM 87501

A lone crusader against sex, PERIOD! Some excerpts: "Sex-life breeds all sins, ALL EVILS AND ALL WARS." "The fruit of sex-life is suffering and death." "God never told man how to increase and multiply but the Devil did." "Married couples should try to live a virgin, chaste and undefiled way of life as a little child lives. Sexual marriage is pornography, and a grave sin." Boy am I in trouble. Tell her you're tired of sinning and you want—nay, NEED—ALL her writings. Asexual cloning is the way to go. Even the genitals of reptiles and amphibians must be BURNED. If God had meant us to derive PLEASURE from base reproductive organs, He would've given us penises and vaginas with erogenous zones.

E-YADA-YADA-YADA
Universal Life Church
152 Thompson Ave.
Mountain View, CA 94043

The ancient, funny-named Master Entity "E-Yada-di-Shiite" speaks through the late trance-befogged medium Mark Probert in a series of primitive, hand-lettered pamphlets and cheap tapes. "The world is an immense sleight of hand . . . Lose Your Entanglement with Matter . . . Streamline Your Mind." The tapes are amazing—"E-Yada" actually has some very sharp routines, although, like most channeled entities, he occasionally has trouble maintaining his holy-man accent. Send SASE.

ANY MINUTE NOW . . .
Tara Center
Box 6001
N. Hollywood, CA 91603

This well-funded group of New Agers keeps promising that the new God Junior is about to reveal Himself; he's a Pakistani living among the poor in London, but "cannot" reveal himself until the world press starts to give him some credence. This Mexican standoff has been going on for six years now; meanwhile, the faithful keep subscribing to the newsletter, forming "Transmission Groups" to send out good vibes, and . . . waiting . . . This "Slowpoke Jesus"—well, actually Maitreya the Christ, the New Age version of Jesus—sends out occasional antihunger messages by overpowering the mind of Benjamin Creme, a charismatic medium from the Alice Bailey school of the occult. Express solidarity, and you'll get their cliffhanger-style mailings. The latest newsletter says Maitreya is about to start miraculously effecting AIDS cures in London. Watch the newpapers! Free info.

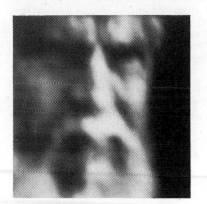

YUP, AH REMEMBERS CREATION JES LAK IT WUZ YESTERDEE
Search & Prove
Box K
St. Paul Park, MN 55071

God Almighty calls Himself "Mora" when addressing this particular cult. He definitely "talks down" for this one, sounding like a friendly old hick codger. Funny how He changes styles depending on the financial standing and social class of the potential follower.

THE ULTIMATE "DUH"
Eckankar™
P.O. Box 27300
Minneapolis, MN 55427

The Stupidest Cult. A coloring-book occult/oriental philosphy in which daydreaming and wishful thinking become "the ancient science of soul travel." Learn to project your astral body *while driving!!* Strange astral-world cosmology reminiscent of 1940s pulp science fiction. Proof that you can't go broke underestimating the intelligence of the American seeker. Ask for every free brochure they can spare, and they'll probably send you a book by the current Living Eck Master.

217

WEIRD MISCELLANEOUS

THE FILTHY BOTTOM MADE ME DO IT
Schizophrenics International
P.O. Box 50456
Ft. Worth, TX 76105

Definitely lives up to its name. Has that certain "something" that only comes with true psychosis. Ask for a copy of the free booklet *The Psychology of Purity and Chastity* by Ed Mood. "Even after we become children of the Creator we are still emotionally carnal and are in need of conversion to a human vegetable. That is what schizophrenia is all about." He says that mental illness allowed him to "purify" himself. "Sex is spiritual dirt and insanity, since it stinks worse to the tree, it is spiritual manure. . . . The emotionally carnal person eats his dirt and having eaten, proceeds to manufacture his flesh after the manner of barnyard animals by using his dirty bottom. The human vegetable converts his dirt and manure by keeping his face to the light and manufactures his flesh by using the top half of his body, as a tree, up in the air, where it is clean." Don't miss this one.

. . . AND WHEN I WOKE UP, I KNEW EVERYTHING!
Brainbeau
Box 2243,
Youngstown, OH 44504

"The World's ONLY Radical." Inexplicable. One sees Brainbeau's crazy little ads in all sorts of oddball publications. You send for information, and you get more crazy little ads—pages and pages of them. But the ads themselves each bear a different plan for a new world order—a world of Brainbeau! His name alone says a lot. Text of one ad: "What makes criticism of my solutions go in one ear and out the other is the knowledge that I'm probably the sole possessor of a mind-changing W.W.II jeep accident head injury incident that involved eradicating previously held beliefs and substituting others via a round-the-clock me-to-me talkathon. Forty-one years later I'm still talking to myself." Send SASE and he'll talk to himself to you! A true "free spirit."

ABSURD NEWS
View From The Ledge
Deadfromtheneckup, Inc.,
P.O. Box 57141,
Washington, D.C. 20037

"Man Loses 5 Fingers to Saw—Dog Eats One." "Woman Wins Award for Fall Off Toilet." Brilliantly selected clippings and news articles, all illustrating that this is, indeed, an insane universe. You'll hardly be able to disagree . . . and it's all true! You get it in return for contributions of weird clippings.

BLIVET UPON BLIVET OF BIZARRENESS
Health Research
P.O. Box 70,
Mokelumne Hill, CA 95245

Health Research sells so much bizarreness it will make your head hurt trying to figure it all out. Books on every weird theory imaginable: the occult, alternative health, UFOs, arcane science, hollow earth, orgone therapy—their mimeographed lists just go on and on. Many are old books on which the copyright has run out—esoteric in their time, impossible to find now. Over 900 warped, out-of-print SHUNNED TEXTS. So voluminous is their selection that they publish *two* catalogs—one on the occult and one on health, $2.50 each.

CATTLE MUTILATIONS
Stigmata and Crux
Project Stigma,
P.O. Box 1094, Paris, TX 75460

The only continuing report on the disturbing epidemic of mysterious livestock mutilations. Reports from all over the world, assembled with a minimum of editorializing. There's still no explanation, although earthly helicopters manned by some secret group seems much more likely now than the UFO theory. You think cattle mutilations are a joke? There have been something like 20,000 since 1960, most of them **hideously weird.** $3 each for *Stigmata* newsletter; $5 for *Crux* (yearly journal).

THE SIMPLE ANSWER TO ALL THE WORLD'S PROBLEMS
Little Free Press
Rt. 2, Box 38C,
Cushing, MN 56443

Definitely the most idealistic, and arguably the most naive set of pamphlets in our archives. The author's plan for total world utopia involves, simply, everyone working for nothing; all competition would be abolished. Work without pay—is that too much to ask? It's a pathetic halfway measure, though. We'd still be *working.* Otherwise, it might be a great idea . . . on some other planet, using some other race besides humans. Free, of course.

HIP AND KOOL HORROR TRUTH
A.M.O.K.
P.O. Box 875112,
Los Angeles, CA 90087

Secret societies. Situationists. Illuminati. UFOs. Surveillance. Satanism. Psychedelics. Magick. Surrealism. Quantum physics. Freaks. Murderers. Kitsch. Etc. The complete library of hip weirdness. $1.

MAKING WAVES
Further Connections
Waves Forrest
P.O. Box 768
Monterey, CA 93940

One of the Robin Hoods of suppressed data. Anyone who seriously wants to look into the possibility that major scientific breakthroughs ARE being hidden by THEM owe it to themselves to send for this info. Includes oxidation therapy, free energy, the Apollo "moon hoax," lots more. Send $3 for magazine *Now What,* $4 for a massive listing of over 400 sources.

MY HERO
The Amazing Colossal Mindblaster
Remote Control
P.O. Box 3108
Scottsdale, AZ 85257-0060

NOT to be MISSED! Truly hilarious "editorials," terrifying nonfiction about things you aren't supposed to know, and superb and inherently *sick* collages guaranteed to sever the optic nerves. AND KOOK LISTINGS!—the *right kind* of kook listings. MOUTH-WATERING! Some of the words in these reviews were taken direct from the pages of *Mindblaster.* $3/issue, write for info before sending money.

NOBLE . . . ALMOST TOO NOBLE
Factsheet Five
Mike Gunderloy
6 Arizona Ave.
Rensselaer, NY 12144

Every three months, almost 70 pages of reviews much like these—in fact, including some of these—appear in *Factsheet Five.* Much of the small magazines and books covered are sci-fi fanzines, punkzines, anarchist newsletters and dime-a-dozen amateur art and poetry magazines, but if you can hack your way through all that, there are plenty of great new cult and extremist listings to be found. Editor Mike Gunderloy has been faithfully cranking out this useful directory of outcasts for years . . . a regular, dependable source for sources. Only problem is, he's too fair and objective. That's no way to sell magazines! $2 each.

From here, friends, you're on your own . . . and who knows who'll be watching you once some of these people start sending you mail? . . . Heh heh heh . . .

Roadside America and Weird, Wonderful America

Vacationers, did you know that you can visit a memorial cairn at Ground Zero Numero Uno near Alamogordo, New Mexico? See conclusive proof that evolution NEVER HAPPENED at the Creation Evidences Museum in Glen Rose, Texas? Gaze upon the wonders of Liberace's closet in Las Vegas, Nevada? Blow away dinosaurs with your mini M-16 at the Prehistoric Forest in Marblehead, Ohio? Forget Disneyland! This is the **real** America!

And **Roadside America** is your guide. This book is not for tourists who insist on calling themselves "travelers" and buy their vacation wardrobes at Banana Republic. This is a travel guide of the tourists, by the tourists, and for the tourists. The only museums **Roadside America** is interested in are the kind that feature wax dummies in bloody Indian massacre scenes under ultraviolet light. If you have the right attitude, you will find that places you once thought to be unredeemably boring are actually gardens of tourist delight. (Oklahoma, for instance, boasts Oral Roberts' Prayer Tower AND Enterprise U.S.A. AND the Tri-State Spook-light!!!)

Roadside America does, however, have one humongous flaw: The authors refused to mar their sparkling narrative with such picayune details as **addresses** and **phone numbers** and **directions**. How do these guys think we're gonna find these places—by PSYCHIC AFFINITY? Granted, many of the attractions (i.e.,Wall Drug, South Dakota and House on the Rock, Wisconsin) are located on such desolate stretches of highway that you'd have to be a blind, mummified, roller-skating parrot to miss the signs leading you in. But some good sights—such as the Nut Museum in Old Lyme, Connecticut—are pretty well hidden.

This is where **Weird Wonderful America** comes in handy. It gives complete information on how to get to some of **Roadside**'s best destinations—including addresses, phone numbers, admission prices and hours of operation. **Weird Wonderful** is also better organized: attractions are listed, not by **category** (as in **Roadside**), but by **state** (which is, after all, how most people travel).

But as useful as it is, **Weird Wonderful** lacks **Roadside**'s gonzo enthusiasm for the disgustingly tacky side of American tourism. It unaccountably misses must-sees like Rock City, Georgia, while devoting untoward amounts of space to such **thrilling** destinations as the Girl Scout National Center and the Bowling Hall of Fame. If you get stuck shelling out $3 a head for someplace like **that**, you have no one but yourself to blame. So keep both guides in the glove compartment. You'll need them next vacation when you're looking for someplace cheap to dump your carload of screaming brats. 　　　　　　　　—Sarah Vandershaf

• Finally, an answer to the question frequent air travelers have been asking for years: What do the Hare Krishnas do with all that money they collect in airports? The answer is simple: Among other things they use it to build golden palaces in the middle of nowhere! . . .

The Palace of Gold has been called "The Eighth Wonder of the World" by some, and while we are hesitant to take our praise that far right now, we think these Koo-Koo Krishnas are definitely on the right track. On display at the palace are plans for a one-hundred-acre Transcendental Theme Park called Krishnaland. . . .

The designs for Krishnaland are ambitious, but even partial

Tourists take in the view from the deck of the National Freshwater Fishing Hall of Fame Museum (housed inside a giant muskie) in Hayward, Wisconsin. 　　　　　—**Weird, Wonderful America**

completion by the target year of 2000 will guarantee New Vrindaban a place of honor among tourism's elite. Trams, the Swan Skyride, and live elephants will transport the faithful throngs from the Land of Krishna Hotel to the Deity Swan Boat, the Plaza of Light, and the Trinavarta Victory Tower. 　—**Roadside America**

• Rock City's greatest achievement, Mother Goose Village, . . . sits inside a dark room the size of a small auditorium. It stretches before you into the darkness—a huge ultraviolet tableau—an alien landscape of dozens of intermingled dioramas depicting Mother Goose rhymes topped by a ten-foot-tall castle. Entire families shuffle like zombies around the village, barely illuminated by the glowing dioramas. No children cry. All are in awe. Hushed voices of parents and children mingle with the unrecognizable music echoing from above. There's Jack Spratt. And Little Bo Peep. And a dish running away with a spoon. Who needs drugs? Life doesn't get any freakier than Mother Goose Village. 　　　　　　　　　　　　　　　—**Roadside America**

Roadside America
The Modern Traveler's Guide to the Wild and Wonderful World of America's Tourist Attractions
Jack Barth, Doug Kirby, Ken Smith, and Mike Wilkins
1986; 221 pp.
$9.95
($11.45 postpaid) from:
Simon & Schuster
Mail Order Sales
200 Old Tappan Road
Old Tappan, NJ 07675
800/223-2336

Weird, Wonderful America
The Nation's Most Offbeat and Off-the-Beaten Path Tourist Attractions
Laura A. Bergheim
1988; 265 pp.
$8.95
($9.40 postpaid) from:
Macmillan Co.
Front and Brown Streets
Riverside, NJ 08075
609/461-6500

(Below, from left to right) 1) Three thousand bushels of corn and assorted grains decorate the walls of Mitchell's Corn Palace [in Mitchell, South Dakota], the agricultural showplace of the world. **2)** "Hi there! I'm the state of Nevada, and I glow in the dark. Guess why?" **3)** South of the Border signs are legendary. Miniature versions can be purchased at most of the nine S.O.B. gift stores. **4)** Claude Bell's T. Rex at The Wheel Inn, Cabazon, California. 　　　　　—**Roadside America**

INDEX

Compiled by David Burnor

Note: *Italics indicate the name of a book, periodical, film, or video. Bold-faced page numbers indicate a review.*

223

ABOUT THIS BOOK

The Fringes of Reason was born in 1964, when as a seventh-grader my mind was permanently warped by Frank Edwards's sensationalistic classic, *Stranger Than Science*. I misspent many subsequent hours transfixed by volumes of the weird lore of flying saucers, bigfoot, ghosts, and the hollow earth. My continuing love for this neglected genre of journalism is reflected by the humongous library of "strange-but-true" literature I've collected together over the years, including an entire run of *Fate* magazine, 1950s and '60s UFO magazines, five filing cabinet drawers full of weird newspaper clippings, and over a thousand respectable and not-so-respectable anomaly books. (All of this eccentric research, by the way, has finally driven me to the weirdest pursuit of all: graduate study in insect evolutionary biology at Cornell University.)

In 1986 editor Kevin Kelly invited me to guest-edit an issue of *Whole Earth Review*, where I had been working as managing editor, that would focus on my predilection for the unusual. I joined forces with my favorite graphic designer —my wife, Rebecca Wilson—to produce *Whole Earth Review* #52 (Fall 1986), subtitled "The Fringes of Reason." That issue struck a chord out there in reader-land, becoming one of the only issues of the magazine ever to sell out, and garnering unexpected reviews in newspapers and magazines across the country. Large lots were even purchased by college professors to serve as supplemental reading in critical thinking classes. The book you hold in your hands, also co-produced with Rebecca, includes most of the material from that issue, plus lots more. It's only the tip of the iceberg of what I *wanted* to include, but I chose to go for thoroughness of coverage of selected topics rather than an exhaustive but superficial approach.

Do you have comments (critical, complimentary, or otherwise) about this book? Would you like to contribute a piece of writing on some fringe topic? Are you aware of a good fringe periodical, book, or organization that you think our readers ought to know about? Do you participate in an unconventional belief system that we didn't mention? We'd love to hear from you. Send all reviews, recommendations, strange pamphlets, self-published books of unorthodox lore, bizarre products, etc., to the address listed on this page. The information collected may be used to assemble a future *Fringes* volume or in *Fringes* updates in *Whole Earth Review*. We'll pay for the writing we publish, including letters of comment.

ABOUT ORDERING BOOKS

"Access" is a *Whole Earth Catalog* tradition. In the reviews in this book, we've supplied complete information for ordering directly from publishers. This is a reliable way to track down a hard-to-find book, but we strongly recommend that you order through your local bookstore whenever possible—this will save you shipping costs and may be quicker as well. If you *do* order from publishers, keep in mind that the shipping costs quoted are for single copies. This amount usually decreases with multiple-copy orders, so it's best to inquire before sending too much money. The prices listed are for U.S. orders. Readers in other countries should inquire about additional shipping costs.

ABOUT THE
WHOLE EARTH CATALOG &
WHOLE EARTH REVIEW

Originally conceived by Stewart Brand in 1968 as a mobile truck store, the *Whole Earth Catalog* became a portable store printed on newsprint that ultimately developed into a series of remarkable volumes of concentrated generalist information (*The Last Whole Earth Catalog*, 1971; *The Whole Earth Epilog*, 1974; *The Next Whole Earth Catalog*, 1980; *The Whole Earth Software Catalog*, 1984; *The Essential Whole Earth Catalog*, 1986). Stewart started *CoEvolution Quarterly* in 1974 to

serve as an ongoing extension of the *Whole Earth Catalog*, and in 1984 its name was changed to *Whole Earth Review*. These days it's edited by Kevin Kelly, and each issue of this general-interest magazine includes 144 pages of unorthodox news, firsthand reports of personal experiments, art, cartoons, and book and product reviews. There's no advertising (except for two pages of subscriber classifieds). Subscriptions are $20/year (four issues) for U.S. surface mail; foreign subscribers add $4/year for surface delivery, and $8/year for airmail. Send checks or credit card info to the address below.

Recently Whole Earth has begun to issue *Catalogs* centered around particular themes. One of these is the book you hold in your hands, *The Fringes of Reason*, and the other is *Signal: Communication Tools for the Information Age* (also published by Harmony Books). You can order additional copies of *The Fringes of Reason* directly from us postpaid for $13, and copies of *Signal* for $15.

OUR ADDRESS:

FRINGES
Whole Earth Catalog
27 Gate Five Road
Sausalito, CA 94965
415/332-1716

HIGH FINANCE

All of Whole Earth's projects are generated under the umbrella of Point Foundation, a nonprofit organization mandated to encourage educational projects and conjure up innovation. Open accounting has always been a Point *modus operandi*, and in this spirit we present the following breakdown of how the cover price of this book gets divvied up:

$6.35 to Harmony Books
6.28 to the bookseller
1.20 to the book wholesaler
.16 to John Brockman Associates
.96 to Whole Earth
_____
14.95 Fringes cover price

—T.S.

(Facing page) A small part of the intrepid crew who worked on this book look on in amazement as the rest are abducted by ant entities from Beta Galactose. *Front row, left to right:* Ted Schultz (editor), Rebecca Wilson (designer), Don Ryan (photographer). *Middle row:* Janet Butcher (Linotronic operator), Hal Robins (illustrator), Giovanni Bacigalupi (production assistant). *Back row:* Elaine Karsevar (typist), Dixon Wragg (proofreader), Susan Erkel-Ryan (production manager). *Photo by Teena Rosen.*